ISBN 978-1-5277-6458-3
PIBN 10888704

1 MONTH OF FREE READING

at
www.ForgottenBooks.com

By purchasing this book you are eligible for one month membership to ForgottenBooks.com, giving you unlimited access to our entire collection of over 1,000,000 titles via our web site and mobile apps.

To claim your free month visit:

www.forgottenbooks.com/free888704

English
Français
Deutsche
Italiano
Español
Português

www.forgottenbooks.com

Mythology Photography **Fiction**
Fishing Christianity **Art** Cooking
Essays Buddhism Freemasonry
Medicine **Biology** Music **Ancient
Egypt** Evolution Carpentry Physics
Dance Geology **Mathematics** Fitness
Shakespeare **Folklore** Yoga Marketing
Confidence Immortality Biographies
Poetry **Psychology** Witchcraft
Electronics Chemistry History **Law**
Accounting **Philosophy** Anthropology
Alchemy Drama Quantum Mechanics
Atheism Sexual Health **Ancient History**
Entrepreneurship Languages Sport
Paleontology Needlework Islam
Metaphysics Investment Archaeology
Parenting Statistics Criminology
Motivational

THE

History and Antiquities

OF THE

PARISH OF BOTTISHAM

AND THE

PRIORY OF ANGLESEY

IN CAMBRIDGESHIRE.

no 1-1

BY

EDWARD HAILSTONE, Jun.

Cambridge:

RINTED FOR THE CAMBRIDGE ANTIQUARIAN SOCIETY.

OLD BY DEIGHTON, BELL AND CO.,

AND MACMILLAN AND CO.

1873.

CAMBRIDGE ANTIQUARIAN SOCIETY.

MAY, 1873.

President.

Rev. W. G. SEARLE, M.A., Queens' College.

Treasurer.

W. M. FAWCETT, M.A., Jesus College.

Secretary.

Rev. S. S. LEWIS, M.A., Corpus Christi College.

Council.

Rev. S. BANKS, M.A.
Rev. J. E. B. MAYOR, M.A., Professor of Latin.
Rev. J. R. LUMBY, B.D., Magdalene College.
C. C. BABINGTON, M.A., Professor of Botany.
Rev. H. J. HOTHAM, M.A., Trinity College.
Rev. W. W. SKEAT, M.A., Christ's College.
Rev. H. R. LUARD, M.A., University Registrary.
F. A. PALEY, M.A.
F. C. WACE, M.A., St John's College.
HENRY BRADSHAW, M.A., University Librarian.
W. ALDIS WRIGHT, M.A., Trinity College.

HISTORY

OF THE

PARISH OF BOTTISHAM.

𝕮𝖆𝖒𝖇𝖗𝖎𝖉𝖌𝖊:

PRINTED BY C. J. CLAY, M.A.

AT THE UNIVERSITY PRESS.

THE

History and Antiquities

OF THE

PARISH OF BOTTISHAM

AND THE

PRIORY OF ANGLESEY

IN CAMBRIDGESHIRE.

BY

EDWARD HAILSTONE, Jun.

Cambridge:

PRINTED FOR THE CAMBRIDGE ANTIQUARIAN SOCIETY,

SOLD BY DEIGHTON, BELL AND CO.,

AND MACMILLAN AND CO.

1873.

PREFACE.

THIS work, put before the public with the utmost diffidence, is intended to supply, as far as possible, materials for a history of the Parish of Bottisham, whether civil or ecclesiastical. My aim has been throughout to arrange them, with few exceptions, in chronological order, and at the same time to assist in preserving all traces and landmarks which, from the hand of time and other causes, would inevitably soon disappear. From the plan of the work it will be seen that the first part is principally devoted to manorial history, while the second part is intended to refer exclusively to that of the Priory of Anglesey, and those lands which formed a portion of the possessions of the Priory of Tonbridge in Kent. Thus the foundation only is laid for some far abler hand than mine to present to the reader a picturesque account of the parish at various stages in its history during the middle ages.

Some of the documents given in Part II. were extracted from the Public Records for my late father. Of these, some I have been enabled to verify; but, from various causes, the others are not yet available for public research.

Of the blocks for woodcuts some were cut for my late father, and with the addition of new ones have been utilized. The lithographs have been copied as faithfully as possible from drawings of my late father and my own by Mr Edward J. Tarver.

b

The two, however, which face p. 325 were originally drawn for the *Illustrated London News* when the Royal Archæological Society met at Cambridge in 1854, and sent a party to view the remains of the priory.

In conclusion, I would take this opportunity of thanking all those who have in any way contributed to my efforts; particularly the Cambridge Antiquarian Society, and my kind coadjutor in making the indices.

EDWARD HAILSTONE, Jun.

6, Porteus Road, Maida Hill,
London.

TABLE OF CONTENTS.

PART I.

CHAPTER I.—THE VILLAGE.

CHAPTER II.—THE CHURCH.

CHAPTER III.—Other Places of Worship.

CHAPTER IV.—Family of De Clare.

CHAPTER V.—Family of Tone.

CHAPTER VI.—Family of Vaus.

CHAPTER VII.—Family of Jenyns,

APPENDIX.

PART II.

ADDENDA ET CORRIGENDA.

HISTORY OF BOTTISHAM.

PART I.

CHAPTER I.

THE VILLAGE.

ᴮOTTISHAM is a large village lying about midway between the *Position.*
owns of Cambridge and Newmarket. It is bounded by the
illages of Great Wilbraham, Little Wilbraham, Stow-cum-Quy,
Iorningsea and Swaffham Bulbeck, and its extent from the
iver Cam on the north to the southern boundary of Great
Vilbraham is upwards of seven miles. It is not therefore sur-
rising that a village so large should find interesting materials
ɔr the study of the historian and the antiquary.

This parish contains besides Bottisham proper, the hamlets *Hamlets.*
f Bottisham Lode and Langmeadow, both of which hamlets are
tuated about two miles and a half from the mother village.
he Parish is situated in the hundred of Stane and the
ᵊanery of Camps[1].

It is somewhat curious that in documents of various dates *Spelling.*
ᵊ find so many differently spelt names to signify this place.
ᵊese are *Bodekesham, Bodichesssham, Bodegesham, Bottlesham,*
ɔtlesham, Bodkysham, Botkysham, Bottesham, Botesham, Bots-*
m, Botsam* and *Bottisham,* which last is the one now in use,
ɔugh pronounced *Botsam*[2].

Various derivations of more or less probability have been *Deriva-*
tion.

[1] Now North Camps.
[2] Bodekesham, Bodegesham, Bodichessham, and Botekesham is the spelling
nd from the earliest times down to the end of the fourteenth century, when
find Botlesham and Bodekesham; but in Henry VIII.'s reign we find
kysham and Botesham, and the transition is speedy to the present form.

H. B.   1

suggested for the name of this place. *Bod-ek-ham*, the village in the bottom at the corner : *Boteges* = patches is also proposed, from the fact that the hamlets lie so far apart from one another : but the most likely is *Bodeke*, the name of a Saxon lord, and *ham* a village. This name of Bodeke is still common in Germany.

omesday ook. Almost the first mention that we find of Bottisham is in the year 1086 A. D., when Domesday Book was compiled ; under the title of Cambridgeshire we find : "The land of Walter Giffard. In Stanes hundred. Walter Giffard holds Bodichessham. He pays tax for 10 hides. The land is 20 carucates. In demesne there are 5 hides and there are 6 carucates. There are 25 villeins with 12 borderers who have 14 carucates. There are 14 serfs and 4 mills of 14 shillings. The meadow is 6 carucates. From the marsh there are 3 tench and 400 eels. In the whole they are worth and were worth 20 pounds. In the time of King Edward[1] 16 pounds. Of this manor Earl Harold[2] held 8 hides and Ailric the monk had 2 hides which he could not give or sell without the licence of the Abbot of *ilric.* Ramsey whose man he was." In the *History of Ramsey*[3] (c. 89) I find the following statement as regards the land which the abbey of Ramsey held in Bottisham : "The same bishop Œthericus[4] gave to the church of Ramsey land in Bodekesham, that is to say, three hides with the remainder of his alms, which land Athelstan[5] the Abbot delivered to the charge of a certain monk named Ailric, a relation of the aforesaid bishop, to be kept

---

[1] Edward the Confessor.

[2] As Harold was a usurper he was not styled "Rex," but "Comes," in Domesday Book.

[3] Gale *Scriptores*, III. 445.

[4] Episcopus Dorcastriæ, ib. p. 438. From the book of the anniversaries to be observed by the church of Ramsey we find:—"Sexto idus Dec. obiit Ethelricus episcopus, qui dedit Shutlingdune, Thereford, Eleswurth, Ailingtun, Bernewelle, Hemington Stow, Bodekesham, Overton, Westmulne, Grethune, et in Broughton iij hydas cum omnibus appendiciis eorum:" vide Dugdale, *Mon. Angl.* II. 566. For the confirmation of this land to the abbey of Ramsey by Edward the Confessor, vide ib. II. 559.

[5] Was made Abbot of Ramsey in 1020 A.D., and continued until 1043 A.D., when he was slain in his church, on the eve of St Michael, by his servant, ib. II. 548.

as a farm. And the said Ailric[1] for many subsequent years,
that is to say, up to the arrival of the Normans into England,
gave to the church of Ramsey a regular table of accounts.
Afterwards, however, when the state of affairs was changed and
things came into the hands of new masters, came Walter
Giffard senior, and by violence seized the same land for himself,
and by default of justice, nay rather by injustice being allowed
to take its course, possessing it during his whole life without
disturbance, left it to his heirs to be enjoyed after him up to
this day." Walter Giffard was a stout follower of William the *Walter*
Conqueror, and was made Earl of Buckingham about the year *Giffard.*
1070 A.D. He was descended from Osborn de Bolebec, who
married Aveline, sister of Gunnora Duchess of Normandy and
great-grandmother of the Conqueror. As a reward for his bra-
very he was presented with many manors of the conquered
country, which afterwards passed to his two co-heirs, William
Marshall Earl of Pembroke, and Richard de Clare. The family
of this latter who became so powerful in the eastern counties, inherited the manor of Bottisham, which thus became united to
the honor of Clare—Madox tells us that the honor of Clare
consisted of 131 knights' fees. A knight's fee appears to have
comprised 300 acres of land, so that the honor of Clare
must have consisted of 39,300 acres![2] The badge of the
Clare family was a white swan, and this may account for
the sign-board of a public house in Bottisham, as well as many
in the surrounding villages bearing this representation. Besides *Ancient*
the afore-mentioned hamlets in Bottisham there originally was *hamlets.*
another named Angerhale.

The hundred rolls[3] of the reign of Edward I. contains this *Hundred*
statement of the hamlets and villages in the hundred of Stane: *Rolls.*
"These are the villages and hamlets of the hundred of Stane.
Swafham Prior, Reche, a hamlet of the same village, Swafham
Bolbek, Bodekesham, Angerhale, a hamlet of the same village,
the Lode, Longmeadow, a hamlet of the above-mentioned

---

[1] Perhaps the same Ailric who gave five hides of land in Berewik to the
church at Ramsey. *Hist. of Ramsey*, c. 91.
[2] *Archæologia*, Vol II. p. 334.
[3] A.D. 1279. *Rot. Hund.* p. 484.

Bodekesham, Great Wilbraham, Little Wilbraham, Stowe, Quy a hamlet of the same village. The hundred of Stane contains 6 villages with their hamlets." We have no mention of the position of this hamlet of "Angerhale," nor does any trace of the name now remain, unless we take the name of the Priory *Anglesey derived.* of Anglesey to be derived from it as if to mean the island of Angerhale. There must have been a collection of houses in this hamlet of some importance, because we find mention at this date[1] viz. 1279 A.D., of many men who took their surname from this place ; as for instance, Thomas de Angerhale, William the son of Matthew de Angerhale, Martin de Angerhal, Richard the son of James of Hangerhale, and Martin the son of Thomas of Angerhale. The same hundred rolls[1] give us the measurement of Bottisham : "In the marsh of Stowbridge as far as the Lode of Swafham Bolbek, and contains two 'leucas' in length and two 'leucas' in breadth : the measurement of the Heath of the fields of Little Wilbraham as far as Fukislowe, and contains in length two 'leucas' and in breadth half a 'leuca.' " We find also from these rolls that "there was in the village of Bottisham a certain old bridge beyond the pool and the holme, and the jurors say that it is now obstructed to the injury of the dignity of the king." Now the waters of Bottisham flowed down in old times along the boundary between Quy and Bottisham up towards the Lode, passing by a spot still called "the ford" at the back of Bendish Hall, and crossed further northward by a bridge on the road or lane from Anglesey to Quy, *Sax Bridge.* and which, though now reduced in size, retains the name of Sax Bridge. I am inclined to think it not without the bounds of possibility, that the hamlet of Angerhale was situated along this road, and that Angerhale's eye, or Anglesey, is the "holme" or island just mentioned which was the site of the Priory. The hamlet of Bottisham Lode takes its name from the stream which *Lode derived.* drains the adjacent lands. In Saxon, laδian = purgare, to clear ; and we find this hamlet accordingly first written Lade and Lada, afterwards corrupted into Lode. But a different meaning may be ascribed to the termination of the name Cricklade, a town in Wiltshire, and "a load" is used as a mining term to

---

[1] *Rot. Hund.* p. 484.

express a seam. In the 13th century, many took their sur-names from this hamlet, but the name is extinct unless it be found in the family of "Leeder," one of whom came from the borders of Suffolk and resided at Bottisham Lode Mill. Before the inauguration of the celebrated Bedford Level for the pur-pose of draining the fens, all the lands to the north of Bottisham Lode were a series of marshes and gave their names to Simon le la More, Wymo de la More, Martin de la Mare or More, and others, and the name of Marsh, pronounced "Mash," is still *Lode* common in the parish; so it is that these lands are now called *moors.* 'Lode moors." The term is derived from "mare," the sea, and the lakes or broads that used to exist were called Whittlesea *mere*, Soham *mere*, &c.

We not only find the surnames of John de Langmede or *Schort-* Langmeadow, but we find John de 'Schortmede.' This land *mede.* may have been contiguous to the long meadow and have con-tained a few houses built upon it. The mention of 'Shortmede' occurs in a document dated 1272 A.D., and therefore we may suppose that by 1279, when the inquisitions were taken, the few houses that stood there had been pulled down or deserted. The whole parish contains an area of 5581 acres, and upon it was spread in 1861 a population of 1508 souls. We have seen *Manors.* that the parish of Bottisham, with its manorial rights, were allotted to Walter Giffard after the Conquest. This Walter Giffard died about 1104 A. D., and was buried at Longeville[1]. He married Agnes, daughter of Gerard Flaitell and sister of William, Bishop of Evreux, and had two children. The eldest, Walter Giffard, who with his wife Ermengard founded the Abbey of Nutley in Buckinghamshire, died without issue about 1164 A. D. The second, Roesia, was married to Richard Fitz Gilbert de Clare, and had issue Gilbert de Tonnebridge, or de Clare, who married Adeliza, daughter of the Earl of Clermont. The eldest son of this Gilbert, named Gilbert Strongbow, mar-ried Elizabeth, sister of Waleran Earl of Mellent, and from this marriage is descended Wm. Mareschal Earl of Pembroke, one of the coheirs of the Giffards. Richard de Clare, Earl of Hertford, and founder of Tonbridge Priory in Kent, was brother of Gil-

---

[1] Vide Lipscombe's *Hist. of Bucks*, Vol. I. p. 200.

bert Strongbow. He married Adeliza, sister of Ranulph Earl of Chester, and was father of Gilbert Earl of Clare, who died without issue in 1151 A. D., and was buried at Clare in Suffolk. But Richard de Clare had another son, Roger Earl of Clare, who died in 1173, and married Maud, daughter of James de St Hilary. From him was descended the other coheir of the Giffards, Richard Earl of Clare, who died in 1206, and married Annie, the daughter of William Earl of Gloucester, coheir of her father and founder of Sudbury Hospital in Suffolk. Richard de Clare divided the manor of Bottisham between two religious houses, the Priories of Anglesey and Tonbridge, as the hundred rolls[1] of Edw. I. tell us. "The jury say that the Lord Gilbert de Clare, Earl of Gloucester and Hertford, holds Bottisham entire in chief of the Lord the King of the honor of Walter Giffard, who was Earl of Buckingham, which manor the Countess Matilda, mother of the said Gilbert, now holds in dowry for the term of her life. They also say that the said Earl holds a view of frankpledge in the aforesaid village once a year, and all that pertains to a view of frankpledge and whatever pertains to royalty, and has held it from the time the memory of which does not exist, but by what warrant we are ignorant. They say also that the predecessors of the aforesaid Earl gave the whole manor of Bottisham together with all the lands, and demesnes, and tenements in villenage and cottage, the meadows, pastures, grazings and mills and liberty of bull and vert. And all other the appurtenances and easements to two religious houses, namely, to the Prior and Convent of Anglesey the moiety of all the aforesaid, and to the Prior and convent of Thonebregg the other moiety, and to the aforesaid Prior and convent of Angleseye the advowson of the church of the Holy Trinity of Bottisham, which they now enjoy and hold to their own use, and the mansion where the said Priory is founded and the conventual church is situated, saving to them and their successors the free rents of the free tenants in the same town, and saving to the same suit of court from three weeks to three weeks, and saving to them the homages and reliefs of free tenants and wards and escheats and all pleas."

[1] Vol. II. p. 487.

We thus find two manors established, that of Anglesey, and *Anglesey.* Tonbridge. We shall subsequently treat in detail of the history *Tonbridge.* of these two religious houses. But there wère other manors besides these. Firstly the manor of Allingtons, so called from *Allingtons.* the celebrated family of this name, who settled at Bottisham for some years and afterwards removed to Horseheath in the same county, and secondly the manor of Vaux or Bottisham Lode, which was in 1302 A. D. possessed by Robert de Vaux *Vauxes.* and Alice his wife, and belonged to the same family up to 1364 A.D., when William Vaux was attainted of high treason and his manor given to Radulph de Hastings by the king, together with one messuage and a hundred acres of land called Horspath[1]. This manor was afterwards united to that of Allingtons, and passed into the hands of the family of Jenyns, who have resided for some generations at Bottisham Hall, a mansion built upon the latter manor. There was another mansion of importance in this parish called Bendyshe or Bendidge *Bendyshe.* Hall. Whether this originally belonged to the manor of Bottisham, or was a separate manor, I have not been able to determine.

Many of the fields still retain their names which have been in use for many centuries. For instance, all the large fields lying between the parish of Quy and the road which runs from Bottisham to Bottisham Lode are called "Braddons," *Braddons.* that is to say, *Broad Denes*, shewing that they were on the edge of the *Skirtland*, or district lying between the highlands and the fens. The same name of Denes is also applied to the sand hills on the sea shore at Yarmouth in Norfolk. The field, which is bounded on two of its sides by the roads leading from Bottisham Lode to Quy and Bottisham respectively, I find called the Northfield or 'Campus Borealis' in the 2nd year *Northfield.* of the reign of Edward III.; and the field immediately north of this, on the other side of the road, is called at the same date 'the stone field' or 'Campus Petrosus,' by the for- *Stonefield.* mer of which names it is still designated. I find mention in a document of 1305 A. D. of the marsh of 'Craneye' in Bottis- *Craneye.*

---

[1] In the parish of Barnwell.

ham, but I am not aware that the name exists now in any
Scharps. form. "Scharps" occurs in a deed dated 1403, as the name
of a piece of ground.

Green Hill. The Green Hill, a piece of ground opposite Bottisham
Church, and near the entrance to Bendish Hall, is mentioned
as such in the will of Thomas Gaytts of Bottisham, dated 20th
October, 1531 [1]. It still retains its name. In a will-dated
16 May, 1545 [2], Robert Foster of Swaffham Bulbeck, leaves, for
Allington's Lane. five loads of clunch to be laid in *Allington's Lane*, 20 pence.
This I take to be the road leading from Bottisham village to
Bottisham Hall and Swaffham, which is always spoken of
as 'Swaffham Lane,' not 'Swaffham Road,' by the villagers at
the present day. The fact that five loads of clunch were put
on this road at this date, shews that before this it was probably a green lane. From the will of Joane Lorkyn of Bot-
Lorkyns. tisham in 1521, July 9, we find her lands, called *Lorkyns* [3], to
have been situated in Bottisham, though the name is extinct.
John Wright of Bottisham, in his will dated the 21st February,
1527 [4], leaves "to the reparation of the church (of Bottisham)
3 shillings and 4 pence and a *Lede*," meaning, I suppose, a long
strip of land or Lode, but the term is very quaint; to his son
John he leaves two acres of free land, three half-acres with a
Tag hill. Hedland at *Tag-hill*, a rood on the top of *Cage-hill*, head south,
Cage hill. and abuts on the land of Mr Laurence Forster; another rode
by the land of Maister Allyngton: where these lands are is
uncertain, but Cage-hill must be another name for Green-hill,
upon which stood the parish cage within a few years. The
will of Wm. Bunte [5], of Bottisham, dated the 28th of March,
Garrards. 1517, mentions a tenement and croft named *Garrards*, and
Thurstons. another tenement and croft lately called *Thurstons:* Henry
Sterne, of Quy, in 1521 [6], leaves to Henry Crane and Margaret
Alderfeild. Crane 3 acres of Barley in *Alderfeild* of Anglesey. Possibly

---

[1] Wills from the registers at Ely.   Vide Cole MSS. Vol. LX. fol. 225.
[2] Ib. fol. 42.
[3] Ib. fol. 156.   This family of Lorkin, or Larkin, appears to have been
numerous in the XVI. and XVII. centuries.   Vide Parish Register.
[4] Cole MSS. Vol. LX. fol. 202.   [5] Ib. fol. 143.
[6] Ib. fol. 151.

his latter family may account for the name of 'Craneye marsh.'
But most curious is the name of *Vineyards*[1], still applied to a   *Vineyards.*
tract of land situated between Bottisham vicarage and Ton-
ridge hall. It is not only called so at the present day, but
we find mention of it in the year 1541, in the will of Thomas
Thompson of Bottisham, dated the 12th September. It is not
improbable that the vineyard belonged to the priory of Ton-
ridge. At least we know that many monasteries in England
had vineyards of their own cultivation. Dugdale mentions[2]
those at Rochester, Abingdon, Gloucester, Michelney, Pershore,
and other monasteries; and Wm. of Malmesbury tells us that
at Thorney Abbey the vines were either allowed to trail upon
the ground or trained to climb small stakes fixed to each plant.
Of other pieces of ground 'Frockings,' near to 'Langhams,' on   *Frockings.*
the Anglesey estate, may have taken its name from Walter
de Throkking, who owned land in its immediate vicinity, in
the second year of King Edward III., and who took his
surname from Throcking in Hertfordshire: *Cook's Hill*, on the   *Cook's*
Anglesey estate, probably took its name from one of the large   *Hill.*
family of Cooke, resident in Bottisham in the 16th and 17th
centuries; and *Gunstone's Lane*, of which I find mention in   *Gunston's*
the will of Margaret Manning[3] of Bottisham Lode, dated the   *Lane.*
5th of January, 1540, lay adjoining the Northfield, and probably took its name from John Gunston, who was alive in
A.D. 1522.

In the *Calendar of State Papers*[4] I find mention of this
John Gunston, and, as it shews the average wealth of most
of the more important parishioners at that time, I will quote
it in full:

"The Loan. An annual grant to be made by the spiritualty
for the king's personal expenses in France for the recovery
of the crown of the same.

"The *Prior of Anglesey* taxed at 100 li.

"Also the hundred of Stane, Bottisham.

---

[1] Geoffrey *de vinario* occurs in a document, c. 1272 A. D.
[2] Dugdale, *Mon. Ang.* Vol. II.
[3] Cole MSS. Vol. LX. fol. 15.
[4] Vol. III. Part 2, pp. 1047—1116.

"*Laurence Foster*, gent., in lands 40 marks, in goods 20 li.

"*John Gunston,* 50 li.

"*Rob. Sewall,* 42 li.

" *Thos. Goldsmith,* 20 li.

"*John Hasyll,* 50 li. ......56 li. ......100 marks. ...... 30 li. ..... 20 li. ......xvi li. x."

From these were the tithes calculated that they were obliged to contribute.

Richard Gunston was one of the commissioners appointed in 1552 to take an inventory of all the bells, plate, and vestments in the church of Bottisham.

The lards; the 'ommon; the ough. The pieces of land lying adjacent to the river Cam in the poor fen were called 'the Hards.' South of them was a piece called 'the Common,' and south of 'the Common' a large piece, now the poor fen, called 'the Rough.' These tracts of land I find marked as such in a pamphlet relating to the drainage of the fens, published in 1685 A.D., and I believe they still retain their respective names.

CHAPTER II.

The Church.

HE key to much local history is always to be found in the
rious traditions which are current respecting the soil, but
e great repository of parochial history is the village church. *Church.*
his I will now attempt to describe in detail. And it is
ore worthy of note, because, I believe that in most respects,
hether the extreme beauty of its architecture, or the abund-
ice of monumental history, it is one of the most interesting
the county of Cambridge, fit alike for the researches of the
chitect, herald, or antiquarian, and not beneath the notice
the passing traveller.

And first of its dedication. It is dedicated to the Holy *Dedica-*
id undivided Trinity, though from its contiguity to other *tion.*
clesiastical buildings in the same parish, it has been ascribed
roneously to other saints. It is situated in the diocese of *Diocese.*
y, in the archdeaconry of Sudbury, and the deanery of *Archdea-*
conry.
imps. The priory of Anglesey was formerly patron of the *Deanery.*
ing, having been presented with the advowson by Richard *Patronage.*
Clare, though we shall see that it was claimed by the abbey
Nutley in Buckinghamshire, which claim was decided in
our of Anglesey. After the dissolution of monasteries in
e reign of Henry VIII. the advowson was given to Trinity
llege, Cambridge, who then became the impropriators[1];
d for a long time the church was served by a non-resident
ar, till in 1837 the Rev. John Hailstone was appointed,
d a vicarage-house built. The present incumbent is the
v. John Brown McClellan, late Fellow of Trinity College.

[1] 32 Hen. VIII. Baker MSS. Vol. xxviii. fol. 161.

The living is taxed in the king's books at £16. 0s. 0d., and paid a tenth of 32 shillings. It is now worth £268. 0s. 0d. a year. Cole says that in 1339 the prior of Longeville had a pension from the church of Bottisham of £41. 13s. 4d.[1]

Plan.   The ground-plan is exceedingly symmetrical and of beautiful design, though various dates may be assigned to different portions of it. It consists of a spacious chancel, north and south aisles, separated from the nave by five arches resting upon clustered columns, north and south porches, and a tower base at the western end of the nave, fronted on the western side by a handsome porch so as to form a galilee. Admission to the building is gained by a large western entrance, doorways to the north and south porches, as well as a smaller priests' doorway leading into the chancel. The various dimensions are these :

Measure-ments.   The chancel from the first step to eastern wall, 38 feet 3 inches.

Breadth of the same, 19 feet.

Length of nave from chancel step to doorway of the tower base, 66 feet 2 inches.

Breadth from centre to centre of column, 23 feet 6 inches.

Length of aisles, 72 feet 6 inches.

Breadth in the clear, 11 feet.

Diameter of columns, 2 feet 6 inches.

N. porch, interior, exclusive of doorway, 10 feet 2 inches broad, 10 feet 4 inches long.

S. porch, interior, exclusive of doorway, 10 feet 2 inches broad, 9 feet 3 inches long.

Tower base, 16 feet 9 inches by 13 feet 3 inches.

Galilee, 12 feet 3 inches by 13 feet 3 inches.

Thickness of walls : tower, 3 feet 9 inches; galilee, 3 feet 3 inches; nave, 2 feet 6 inches; chancel, 2 feet 3 inches.

Interior Chancel.   These are the various measurements of the plan of the church. It would be well to remark, that in very many village

---

[1] Cole MSS. Vol. xxxi. fol. 216; Bacon, *Lib. Reg.* p. 231. In a deed, dated 1305 A.D., Brother William de Talaya, for the prior and convent of Longeville, procurator-general in England, acknowleges the receipt of 50s. sterling, part payment of 100s., due to them from the convent of Anglesey annually.

TOWER.

churches the chancel is not in a direct line with the nave but leans a little to the left side. This is said to arise from the fact of our Saviour's head leaning a little to the left of the cross whereon he was crucified. In the case of Bottisham church, however, the chancel runs true with the nave. As we walk round the interior of the chancel we shall first observe the windows. These consist of two on the north side, two on *Windows.* the south side, and one east window. The architecture of these windows is not remarkable for beauty: the arches are not four-centred[1] as in most Perpendicular windows; the moldings of the cusping are very scant and poor; thewe sternmost windows on the north and south sides consist each of three days or lights; the more eastern window on the south side also consists of three lights, while the one opposite to it on the north side has only two lights. These two latter windows appear to have been cut down to half their original length at some period; at least traces of longer ones are visible in the masonry on the exterior. The east window is very large and consists of three lights. Its whole breadth is about a third of the width of the chancel wall. The moldings are the same as the others. It is difficult to assign dates to these windows, for while the walls belong to the Early English period of Gothic architecture, these are of exceedingly late workmanship; perhaps about 1600, A. D., or a few years earlier, when we find in wills many bequests for the reparation of the church.

The altar table is approached by three steps; one leading *Steps.* from the nave to the chancel, another as you pass the priests' doorway, and another running all round the altar table itself. There is nothing remarkable about the table; it is covered by a handsome cloth worked in embroidery and the gift of some of the parishioners. Behind is some woodwork which originally formed part of the wooden screens; it was placed there when the church was restored in 1839, and is of Decorated workmanship. There are also neat altar rails of modern work. Cole, when he visited the church in 1770, says that he found the "altar railed in and wainscoted about it, and on one step above

---

[1] Except the East window.

the altar under the east window is I.H.S. in a glory painted on the wall[1]." This is now gone.

edilia. In the south wall are three Early English arches with rich moldings forming sedilia. One of these arches on the east side has apparently fallen into decay and been replaced by a smaller round arch with plain chamfered edges. The centre of this arch is nearer to the column than the wall on the east side, and consequently the remaining space is marked by a very rude attempt at a molding. This repair is of the date of the end of the sixteenth century, when the windows were put up. It is curious to observe how in this church, in two distinct periods of architecture, the principle of design from the equilateral triangle is carried out; the arches of this sedilia form an instance of it.

tscina. Nearer to the eastern end in the same wall is a double piscina of the same date as the sedilia, but the top of it is formed by horizontal moldings instead of two arches. The

E.S.COLE

cap and base moldings are the same as those of the sedilia, but the shaft is of Purbeck marble, while those of the sedilia

[1] Cole MSS. Vol. iv. Description of Bottisham Church.

are of clunch. Unfortunately this piscina has been so often whitewashed as not to shew much of its original beauty. Its moldings and its square head tell us that we must assign an early date to this part of the church. Probably it was built at the end of the Transition and beginning of the Early English style, and may be assigned to the commencement of the reign of King John. Underneath the sedilia runs for its whole length a richly molded stringcourse, while none, however, is found underneath the piscina.

The chancel arch is of the Early English period, and, *Chancel* though molded on the eastern side of the arch, runs to a *arch.* plain chamfer as it approaches the centre of the wall. The floor consists of stone till you approach the second step. From *Flooring.* there to the last wall decorated tiles have been laid down, relieving the aspect of the chancel, which is very barren, with a little colour. The body of the church was reseated in *Seats.* 1839, with open seats in the nave and pews in the aisles, according to the spirit of that day. They are very unsightly, and no doubt will be eventually replaced with something more ornamental. The chancel was likewise disfigured by pews, but these have been now replaced by some handsome open seats enriched by carved tracery, the work of Messrs Rattee and Kett of Cambridge. Cole tells us that the chancel, when he visited the church, was stalled round to the north and south doors; and in so influential a parish as Bottisham one cannot but imagine that there must have been much carving in the church. Where did it all disappear to? Probably taken away by some one and used for firewood! The roof of *Roof.* the chancel is not remarkable. It has been put up within the memory of the present generation, and tradition says that when it was made it was found too large across, and so slight cornices had to be constructed at the plate to receive it. It is molded and probably constructed out of the old roof. Cole, in the extract I have just given, mentions a north doorway in the chancel. He must have been mistaken, as there exists no trace in the masonry which would lead one to suppose that this doorway had been blocked up.

The south doorway is a neat specimen of the Early Eng- *Door.*

lish style. It is small but well molded both on the interior
and exterior; on the outside the archmold consists of two ribs,
marked out by plain chamfers, and protected by a simple
hoodmold. This archmold is continued through a plain abacus
to a simple base at the ground. The interior molding is also
plain, and above is a hoodmold terminating in grotesque faces.
This has been so repeatedly whitewashed that it is difficult to
say whether or no this door-case does not beneath the surface contain its original colour. Perhaps some day it may be
revealed, carefully preserved—thanks to the plasterers and
whitewashers!

Nave.   Passing through the chancel arch, we enter the nave, and
I think no one can gaze upon its general form without being
struck by its symmetry; its general effect is exceedingly pleasant
and grateful to the eye. We pass from the Early English
style to the Decorated, with all its richness and its less severity
rchmold. of treatment. That side of the arch which is nearest to the
nave, and which separates nave from chancel, is exceedingly
rich in moldings, and yet well adapted to suit its predecessor
on the other side. It descends upon corbels fastened to the
wall in the angle and containing a cap and necking, and beneath a simple finish off without ornament. Above this arch-
. win- way the walls are bare except where pierced by two windows,
ows. each containing double lights with plain chamfered moldings
ave. and overlooking the chancel roof. But underneath this arch
tone there remains what was once undoubtedly a handsome stone
creen. screen, upon which stood the rood-loft.

Three stone arches richly molded and centred upon the
principle of the equilateral triangle are intersected by two
Purbeck marble shafts, the moldings of which are carried up
so as to form spandrils. These spandrils in four instances are
pierced by quatrefoil openings; the remaining two are coated
and filled up with plaster; the Purbeck marble shafts are also
whitewashed over, and thus lose their original features. Over
the top of this screen there is now placed a molded beam of
wood also whitewashed, which I believe belonged formerly to
the woodwork in the aisles, but was placed there in order to
cover the dilapidations of a parapet, which, according to Rick-

man, once adorned the upper portion of this screen. The central arch is open, and serves as a passage from nave to chancel; and the other two are blocked up with pews and may originally have been ornamented with woodwork. One cannot but hope that this screen will one day be restored to its original design, as far as practicable, and suitable to the conveniences of modern worship. No vestige remains of a rood door, or of a rood staircase, but one would have expected to find something here, when it is remembered that this is one of the churches of which William Dowsing takes no account.

The pier arches of the nave are singularly beautiful and *Pier* are engraved in Brandon's *Analysis of Architecture*[1]. The plan *arches.* of the columns consists of four roll and fillet moldings intersected by a small bowtell between two hollows. The column thus formed is exceedingly graceful and stands upon a rich base molding forming on plan a series of quatrefoils. The members of this base molding consist principally of inverted hollows and scrolls. Above is a cap consisting of an inverted hollow and scroll molding, then a second inverted hollow, scroll, hollow, roll and fillet, and lastly a necking of an inverted hollow and scroll. These piers are not of Purbeck marble but of clunch. The arch-mold is the same on both sides, consisting of two large scroll chamfers intersected by a hollow, and is protected by a roll and fillet label with inverted hollow added. The height from the point of the arch to the ground is 24 feet 2 inches, and the breadth from arch-mold to arch-mold is 9 feet 11 inches. A line drawn from the point of the arch to the centre would form a side of an equilateral triangle. Above these arches in the nave there are no triforia, but clerestory windows of unusual ornament. These consist only of a single light, but contain unusually intricate moldings and plate tracery; externally they are constructed with nearly equal display of moldings—a thing rarely to be seen in a village church.

The flooring of the nave and aisles is of brick, except where *Flooring.* stones and matrices of brasses testify to the memory of some village worthy. Upon woodwork, however, rests the pewing, *Seats.* near the stone screen, and in the aisles and open seats towards

[1] Vol. ii. Pl. 16, Sect. i.

the bottom of the nave. The pulpit and reading-desk are situated close to the right-hand and on the south side of the screen, separating the nave from the chancel; but formerly, as we learn from Cole's description of the church, the old pulpit stood against the first column of the north side[1]. The pulpit, reading-desk, and seats were newly erected in 1839. I do not know whether the old seats contained any poppy-heads, or carving of interest, but it is probable that they would have been reconstructed if they existed, into the new sittings. On

allery. the western side of the nave a gallery was erected to support an organ, and the children of the national schools, who are seated round it. At the back of this gallery there is visible a line of the gable of a previous building, containing a small lancet window above it, and evidently contemporaneous with

V. door- the tower. Underneath this gallery is a double doorway,
way. inclosing a space formed by a segmental arch, the moldings of which are to be divided into two groups formed by single

eight. chamfers. The height from the floor to the plate in the nave is 32 feet 9 inches, while the chancel only measures 23 feet

oof. 3 inches. Above is a fine timber roof, each truss consisting of tie-beam, collar, kingpost, and principals, molded with a plain chamfer, and the common rafters supported by struts. Boarding has been placed from collar to collar, so that only a portion of this fine roof is now visible. It is of the same date as the rest of the nave, and belongs to the Decorated style of Gothic architecture[2].

orth Passing from the nave to the north aisle, we are struck by
isle the extreme decoration of the windows, as well as by the fact
vindows. that their centres are not in a line with the centres of the nave

[1] Cole MSS. Vol. IV

[2] In 16 Ed. I., mention is made of 10 acres of land lying in the common "brede" which Walter de Throkking held, and which came into the Lord's hands by reason of eschaet, which was the Lord's waste ground, and was appropriated by the community of the town of Bottisham "ad opus eccīie." In 19 Ed. III., Galfridus de Teversham was ordered to pay 10s. by instalments of 2s. a year to certain parties who, in their turn, were to pay this sum "ad fabric̄ et emendāt eccīie sc̄e Trinitatis de Bodekesham." In 36 Ed. III., Petrus de Teversham sold a tree that had been blown down by a mighty wind, and devoted the proceeds "ad opus eccīie" according to ancient usage and custom of the village. Vide Court Rolls of the Manor, Aug. office.

arches. Containing two lights these windows excel in richness of cusping, and, whether viewed from the interior or exterior, are equally striking. The upper part of the tracing consists of a quatrefoil merging at the lower corner into the two arches which form the lights. These arches contain cusping of three hollows. The plan of the mullions contains equally on its four sides a scroll, and half a roll and fillet, and is figured by F. A. Paley in his *Treatise on Gothic Moldings*[1]. The hood-molds of these windows are continued along the face of the walls so as to form a string course, and over the north and south doorways rise so as to form a portion of a panel. This has an effect of exceeding richness. The hood-mold over the doorway itself is brought down so as to run underneath the windows on a line with the present sittings. But at the eastern ends of the north and south walls are two curious windows, square-headed and with a transom so as to have double tracery. They are both of two lights, and do not come down so low as the other windows. This portion of the church is on both sides railed off by wooden screens, and contains monuments which block up the view of these as well as the eastern windows. The moldings of the square-headed windows are the same as the others, and, as the workmanship looks the same, I think they must be of the same date; either they were intentionally placed there in order to form chauntries, or because the architect had made a miscalculation in the north and south walls. Besides these windows, there are large three-light ones at the east and west end of these aisles, one of which is figured in Brandon's *Analysis of Gothic Architecture*[2]. The moldings are the same as those of the north and south windows, but they are worked into richer tracery in proportion to the size of the window. In the centre compartment above, an equilateral triangle is enriched by cusping of six points resting on an arch containing cusping of four points: on each side of this a trefoil cusping rests upon an arch filled in with cusping of two points. On the western wall there is nothing underneath these windows but the string course, which runs throughout the length of the aisles; but on the eastern wall this string course is carried

[1] Ed. Fawcett, p. 15. [2] Vol. II Pl. 27, Sect. i.

2—2

down, and forms a panel with the arch-mold which is carried down, a little below this, and rests upon a base within two feet of the floor. It is exceedingly difficult to conjecture what was the object of this ; for an altar, if erected here—and it was pretty sure to be—would obliterate all view of these rich moldings : now at the present day, they are both hid by unsightly monuments which we will look at presently.

Roof.   The roof of the north and south aisles is nothing more than a plain lean-to, resting upon interior as well as exterior cornices formed with plain moldings, and containing struts attached to the rafters. The exterior of these roofs, as well as that of the nave, is covered with lead in a good state of preservation. Both of the aisles appear to have contained *Chaun-* chauntries. That in the north aisle was founded by William *tries.* Allington, who was Speaker of the House of Commons in the reign of Edward IV. There is no vestige of an altar remaining, but on the right-hand side against the wall there stands a bracket with very elaborate Perpendicular moldings. This chapel, as well as the first archway of the nave, was completely blocked up and used as a repository for all refuse till the restoration in 1839, and contains on the south side the tomb of its founder, denuded of its brass plates and inscription. The patent rolls inform us that, whereas Elizabeth de Burgh endowed a chauntry at the priory of Anglesey, to be served by two secular chaplains, who were to say masses for her soul and for her heirs for ever, and "whereas a certain chapel has been newly built, to the praise of Almighty God, the glorious Virgin Mary his mother, and Saints Martin and Mary Magdalene at Botesham by our beloved and faithful *Dedica-* William Alyngton, in consideration of the poverty of the *tion.* convent an Indenture was made, whereby the priory should find two chaplains of the religious brethren of their priory of Anglesey," one of whom should perform divine service in the same priory at the altar aforesaid, and the other should perform divine service in the chapel aforesaid, every day, for the souls aforesaid, and for our good estate and that of our very dear consort Elizabeth Queen of England, while we live, and for our souls when we shall depart from this light, as well as for the

BOTTISHAM CHURCH.

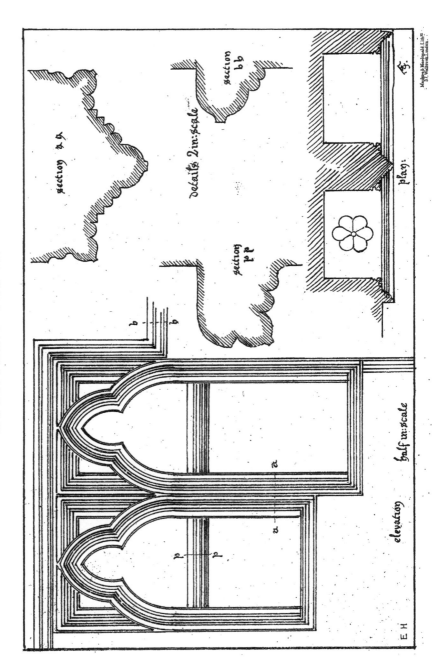

section a.a.

Details 2in:scale

section b.b

section p.p

plan:

elevation   half in:scale

E.H.

Maffyn Moore old Lith.
37 Whitcross London.

good estate of the aforesaid William, and Joan his wife while they live, and for their souls when they shall have departed from this light to be for ever celebrated, &c. This Indenture is dated on the 14 March, 1475 A.D.[1] We may suppose therefore that this chauntry was founded during the previous year, and thus we get the date of this bracket, while it was probably under the influence of this William Allington that the Perpendicular stone screen was erected.

But some years before this, a chauntry must have been *Chauntry, S. aisle.* founded in the southern aisle, for though there is no vestige of an altar beyond a raised step, there remains in the south wall an exceedingly beautiful piscina and sedilia, with shelf *Piscina. Sedilia.* of very rich decorated moldings that would seem to have been erected at the same time as the rest of the nave. This ornament consists of two arches with cusping of two points lying in a square head, the same moldings being carried all round, surmounted by the string course from beneath the windows, which is continued above as far as the eastern wall. The molding of the shaft contains in the centre a roll and fillet, and on each side two inverted hollows, a square recess and then a roll and fillet between two wave moldings. The string consists of a roll and fillet resting upon two inverted hollows, and the molding of the shelf may be described as an inverted hollow, followed by a roll and fillet, an inverted hollow and a wave. The whole series of moldings are exceedingly effective, and the arches are formed upon the principle of the equilateral triangle. We have no clue as to the founder of this chapel; possibly it may have been instituted for some of the Allingtons, or one of the family who took their surnames from the parish. It could not have been for Elizabeth de Burgh or any of the family of the Mortimers, or mention would have been made of it in the "Liber niger de Wigmore," preserved in the Harleian collection of MSS. in the British Museum.

Before we leave the aisles, it is necessary to observe the *Wood screens.* exceedingly fine pieces of woodwork which enclose the eastern ends. Tradition says that formerly this screen ran right across the church, and it is extremely probable, for the sides were

---

[1] *Rot. Pat.* Ed. IV. p. 1, m. 20.

placed in their present position in 1839, and, so to speak, "cooked up" out of the pieces found lying about at that time. They are of the Decorated style, and seem to have been built at the same period as the rest of the nave. The western front of that in the north aisle consists of three compartments, each being subdivided into four lights, headed by exceedingly intricate flamboyant tracery well preserved. The moldings of the central shaft in the middle compartment are a little bolder in form and carried up to the top, so that folding-doors are thus formed. This inner tracery is surrounded by richly-molded horizontal and perpendicular woodwork upon which is a molded ledge. Above is a rectangular panelling filled again with flamboyant tracery, and the whole is surmounted by battlements. That in the south aisle is similar in treatment, but each compartment in both screens contains variations in tracery. A spandril from one of these screens is given in Brandon's *Analysis of Architecture*[1].

F. TOWNSEND DEL

nt.   Cole[2] tells us that the font formerly stood under the last arch, on the south side of the nave. It now stands near its former position, but midway between it and the south wall of

[1] Vol. II. Pl. 14, Sect. II.   [2] Vol. IV.

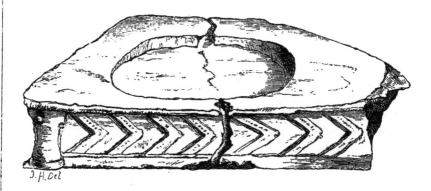

J. H. Del

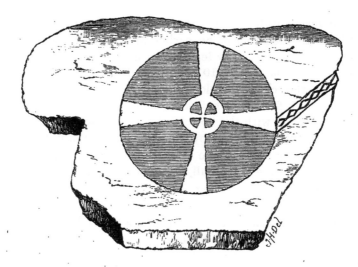

JH Del

the aisle. Its structure, though neat, is not elaborate. A hexagonal basin descends by means of broach stops on to a square base of three steps, with a protruding stone on the west side. It is of Decorated style, and contains, curiously enough, a paucity of molding in so richly decorated a church. But a few years ago some stones were found which proved, when put together, to have formed a font of Norman style, and close by was a stone containing a Maltese cross, which seemed to have been at one time the tympanum of a doorway, and is the earliest relic we have of the original church. There is no cover belonging to the present font, nor are there traces of one having ever existed.

Passing through the segmental arch at the western end of the nave, we approach the tower. This tower is rectangular in form, and consists of four stages. The thickness of the walls for the first three stages is 3 feet 9 inches, and that of the last stage 2 feet 9 inches. The ground floor contains north and south lancet windows; on the east side a segmental archway, containing three groups of simple chamfers. The western doorway leading to the galilee is formed by a pointed arch, molded with three simple chamfers, descending through a rudely-molded column to the ground. It belongs to the style of transition between Norman and Early English. The next stage contains north and south lancet windows, with deeply-splayed jambs; on the east side an archway, which is seen also on the inside wall of the nave, and was, I suppose, a window looking over the gable of an earlier building; on the west side is an archway, which now leads to an upper floor of the galilee. This opening is 5 feet 10 inches high, and 2 feet 6 inches broad in the clear. It looks as if it had been a doorway, but stands 5 feet 1 inch from the floor line of the galilee, while on a level with the floor of the tower's second stage. By this means the belfry is now entered, but could it have been intended as an entrance to a parvise used as a library? On this stage, in the east wall, is a locker, 1 foot 3 inches by 1 foot 5 inches. Mounting 18 feet 3 inches, we come to the next floor, and 11 feet 3 inches more brings us to the bell-chamber. On each wall of this floor is a pointed window of two lights, simply molded with hood-molds and quatrefoil tracery.

There are five bells, justly noted for their excellent tone. They bear the following inscriptions :—1st bell, "Thos. Newman, Henry King, churchwardens, 1829, Wm. Dobson, founder;" 2nd bell, "John Draper made me, 1606;" 3rd bell, "John Draper made me, 1626;" 4th bell, "Nicolson Ricardus fecit me" (this inscription is in old characters, and on this bell is the head of a king and queen); tenor, "John Draper made me, 1626." This John Draper was a celebrated bell-founder at Thetford, and made many of the bells hereabouts. With reference to the condition of the bells Cole says that "above the arch of the belfry was this writing: 'John Hickman and Thos. Cooke, churchwardens, new glazed the church, and

repaired the leads and the bells in the year of our Lord 1660.'"
This writing is long since obliterated. If we mount up to the
outside of the roof of the tower, we find a battlemented parapet,
in which the moldings do not return, and planted at the four
corners are pinnacles, giving an appearance of finish to the top.
The view from the tower could hardly be picturesque, looking
over a country so flat and uninteresting. The chief feature is,
of course, Ely Cathedral, and the glimpse of the collegiate
buildings of the university is not unpleasing. The height of
the tower is about 66 feet to the top of the battlements. It
has been said that most of the churches in this part of Cambridgeshire were originally intended to have been surmounted
with spires. It may have been so with Bottisham church; certainly it would add much to the beauty of its general effect.

Passing through the western doorway of the tower base, we *Galilee.*
come to the galilee, apparently of the same date. It consists
of two floors, a wooden staircase leading from the one to the
other floor, which is lighted by an arch with an iron grating at
the west end. The western doorway is peculiar. A very lofty
pointed arch, with a hood-mold and chamfered edges, forms a
large recess, the wall of which is filled in with flints. In this,
at the lower end, is formed the doorway by an arch with plain
chamfers and a hood-mold, which betokens an early period of the
Early English style. At the exterior are two shafts, with molded
bands in the centre, of neat moldings, but which have been
badly imitated in restoration in 1839. Above the grating over
this doorway is a stone, with very rudely-carved tracery, in a
recess for an image, which was found in restoring this part of
the church. The angles of this porch are chamfered on the
exterior, and the gable end is surmounted by a handsome
floriated cross of stone. The masonry of this galilee and the *Masonry.*
lower part of the tower is not coursed. The upper part of the
tower was coursed when repaired, though places have been left
uncoursed, and I have been told that before it was touched the
whole surface of the tower was uncoursed.

The north and south porches are great adjuncts to the *Porches.*
general symmetry of this church. That on the north side is in
bad repair, and is used now as a vestry; consequently, the outer
doorway has been plastered up, and a small wooden door

inserted, and the moldings of the original doorway have been much broken. They seem to be, however, two wave moldings and a roll and fillet, and are the same on each side of the doorway; each side is protected by hood-molds. The inner doorway is richly molded on the outside. It consists of three members, divided by two hollows, the two outside members containing a roll and fillet, and the central one marked by two contiguous receding portions of a circle. On the outside is a hood-mold. It is figured by Paley[1]. On the inside a segmental arch falls down upon a column, up to which the string course beneath the windows is brought, having an exceedingly good effect. This doorway also is plastered up, and a smaller door inserted. The east window of this porch was taken out in 1839, in order to make way for a fireplace, but the west window remains, and is a square-headed three-light window; the arches are filled with cusping of four points, and the whole is richly molded throughout. These are not filled with glass, but contain their old stanchions. The gable end of the roof of this porch terminates in coping, having at the top and bottom angular recesses, enriched by cusping, and the quoins of Barnack stone are chamfered off at the edges. Above the outer doorway, on the outside, is a niche with a hood-mold, richly cusped, and formerly no doubt containing a statue. The coping terminates at the top and sides with a stone fleur-de-lis. The *S. Porch.* south porch is very similar in construction to the north porch. The doorways contain exceedingly rich moldings, though varied from those in the north porch. They are drawn by Paley in his treatise[1]. This southern porch was in very bad repair till 1870, when the exterior walls of this side of the church were plastered over with cement, and imitation joints of the stonework depicted with black mortar. The effect of it is not good, and it does not preserve the character of the original. Much of the plaster in this porch was then taken away, revealing on the inside the moldings of the inner doorway in their entirety, as well as traces of a bright vermilion colour with which it was decorated. On the outside, a niche similar to that in the north porch was disclosed to view, the interior of which was decorated with chocolate-coloured crosses upon a vermilion ground. This

[1] *Gothic Moldings*, ed. Fawcett, Pl. 17.

niche is shewn in a drawing of the church made by Cole, and dated September 20th, 1743, so that it must have been covered up since his time. A sun-dial stood above this niche in Cole's drawing, and existed till 1870, when by the ignorance of the workmen both niche and sundial were coated with cement, and the colour of the former disappeared. On each side of the hood-mold, on the exterior of this wall, are two stone tablets, apparently of the Renaissance style, and their borders containing representations of an hour-glass. It is exceedingly difficult to say what these were for, but I think they must have been monumental, though no vestige of any inscription remains. The east and west windows, as well as the coping of the roof in this porch, are the same as on the north side of the church.

The buttresses on the exterior walls present features of *Buttresses* beauty and variety. The chancel is supported on each side by an Early English simple buttress of three stages; the tower wall has on each side a massive buttress of about the same date, of also three stages; originally there was also another on each of these sides, but these have merged into the interior wall, and the upper part of them only protrudes from the nave roof. The aisle buttresses, however, are the most elegant, of which a measured drawing will be found in Brandon's *Analysis*[1]. They have, as well as the remaining walls, quoins of Barnack stone, the edges of which are chamfered. The first stage of each is adorned at the top by a wave molding, and above a recess is formed terminating in a cusped gable surmounted by a fleur-de-lis. They are still further enriched by a string course running beneath the windows and round the buttresses for the whole length of the church. Beneath the rectangular windows towards the eastern ends of the aisles, these string courses run round and return so as to form rectangular panelled recesses; that on the north wall is again divided into two, while on the south there is but one; and this fact seems to shew that they were intended for no other purpose than to satisfy the whim of the architect. The stone coping at the ends of the nave is equally fanciful, for, instead of being confined to the gable ends of the roof, it is continued down the wall of the clerestory,

[1] Vol. II. Pl. 19, Sect. I.

running down the roofs of the aisles and ending in a cusped gable.

'lint ork. The masonry is of clunch stone, while the quoins are of Barnack stone, but beneath the level of the window in the nave we find beautiful examples of flint panelling so neatly cut, that it would be difficult to insert a penknife between the joints. This flint-work is found beneath the east and west windows of both aisles, beneath the rectangular windows *rcades.* and in the spandrils of the arcade on the south wall. These arches have puzzled many antiquaries and architects. They consist of segmental arches richly molded, enclosed in five square panelled recesses, formed by continuing the string course downwards, and originally were as richly molded on the interior wall. The two arches towards the western end of the aisle still retain their pristine beauty, but the moldings of

E.S.COLE. del.   UTTING.S.

the remaining three were literally chopped off, in order to bring the new sittings up close to the wall. This was in 1839, when there was not such reverence for Gothic design as there *tone* *offins.* is now. Each of these arches contains a stone coffin, and the question naturally presents itself—which came there first, the coffins or the arches? If the arches were built on the site of an earlier fabric, it could not have been much earlier, for the aisles are carried further westward than the nave, and there remains no trace of any Early English masonry in this part of the walls. At the same time, it is exceedingly unnatural that the centres of the windows should not coincide with the centres of the nave arches, and if the reason of this is the irregular position of these coffins, added to the fact of the aisles being longer than the nave, then the architect would have a space left towards the eastern end of the north and south walls, and may have indulged his fancy for decoration by inserting the rectangular windows, and the exterior panelled recesses formed by the string course. The coffins are of an earlier date than the building of this part of the church, and it is possible that the suggestions given may form a true explanation of a feature which I venture to think unique in a village church. When the flooring was taken up, and the pews in the south aisle removed, the following interesting memorandum was made by the late vicar. He says, "A singular discovery was made of stone coffins; five of them were placed partly in the wall under the drop arches, which support the windows on the south side of the church, and all were but a few inches from the surface of the floor: another, a smaller one, lay more towards the interior. A slab of stone wider at the head than at the foot can be seen outside the church in the wall under these arches, which indicates the position of each of the coffins at burial. The coffins have coped lids ornamented with a cross, tapering from head to foot, with a ledge at the shoulder. The length is 6 feet 6 inches, and the breadth 2 feet 2 inches at the top, and 1 foot 2 inches at the bottom. Upon examining one of them, it appeared as if it had never been disturbed; the bones were quite perfect and laid straight; the hair on the scalp was not decayed, and remained till touched matted in curls. There were remains of some covering to the body, which immediately dropped to pieces upon admission of air, and the salt, or whatever was used for embalming, lay in a considerable heap between where the ribs and thigh-bones rested. On the right shoulder was placed a small chalice (now in the museum of the

Camb. Ant. Soc. with fragments of the wood and hair) of pewter or some other alloyed metal very brittle, and broken. On the breast lay a piece of wood 1 foot 6 inches long, pitched on the under side. There were also some large nails in the coffin. A smaller coffin parallel to the above, nearer to the interior of the church, was opened: the bones appeared in the same fresh and undisturbed state. There were the remains of some covering to the head and bosom; and the hair being much longer and more curled, it was conjectured to have been the body of a female. The remaining stone coffins were not examined."

Royal arms.

After the Reformation was fairly established in England, one of the first things done was the erection of the Royal arms in every village church; these formerly were placed over the nave arch at the east end, and as the art of heraldry was then declining were often wrongly painted. Accordingly from a deed[1] in the Library of All Souls' College Oxford, we gather a record of the deputation from Clarencieux king-at-arms (Camden) to visit the churches in Northamptonshire, Huntingdonshire, Cambridgeshire, Norfolk, and Suffolk. For this deputation William Newman was appointed deputy-herald, and each parish was rated at ten shillings to have the Royal Arms properly proportioned in lieu of the old ones. The date of this document is February the first, in the fortieth year of the reign of Queen Elizabeth, so that we may suppose that the newly-painted arms were put up some time after 1598 A.D.

Commandments.

The Commandments were painted on two unsightly tablets of wood in the year 1749, and are now attached to the east wall of the chancel[2], but there is no Lord's Prayer or Creed.

Inventories.

The best idea of the wealth and importance of a church is gained from the inventories of its goods, taken from time to time. There is one extant of Bottisham in Caius College Library which runs thus: Ecclesia de Botekesham appropriata Priori de Anglesey et habet vicarium et taxatur ad xxx marcas et solvit pro synodi ijs. et iiij*d.* procur' xviij*d.* pro den. Beati Petri xl*d.* et sunt ejus ornamenta hec. vi paria vestimentorum (quorum duo sunt cum tunicis et dalmaticis) vii super pellicia,

---

[1] MS. No. 278.

[2] These were formerly placed with the Royal Arms over the screen. Vide Cole MSS. Vol. IV.

j rocheta, velum templi, i missale, iij antiphon. bona cum ij psalteriis et quatuor psalteria per sesta gradalia, cum troperiis, ep'
lar' martyrologium, ij manualia, una (portiforium) legenda in
duobus voluminibus, iij calices, iiij frontalia, una crux enea, pix
eburnea, crismatorium bonum (eburneum), iiij phiole i lanterna,
turibulum, fons cum serrura, quinque paria corporalium, una
casula, et una alba de novo data, ij bandekyns ex dono Dni
Andree......(modo tunica et dalmatica) cum stolis duabus......
......et Willi Mareschalli et una casula ex dono Willi le Hert,
j pannus de serico de dono Elye de Bekynham, par frontalium,
j par corporalium cum delfinis de......ex dono (Joh ?) Zouch arm.
Item una nova capa chori precio marc ex dono Willi Code defunct.

There are two other inventories of the plate and bells taken
at various periods. One of these purports to be—"Extract of all
the plate and bells remaining and belonging to every parish
church and chapel in the Hundred of Stane Staplehow and
Flendish in the county of Cambridge, made on the 24th of March, *A.D.* 1549
3 Ed. vi. taken out of such inventories and certificates as the
vicar, parson, or curate, churchwardens and parishioners of every
one of the parish churches there exhibited unto us. Sir Robt.
Peyton, Kt., Thomas Rudston, and Wm. Walpole, the king's
commissioners for the same.

Hundred of Stane.

Ecclesia de Bottsham	There is one crosse of silver pcell gilt cont' xlvi oz. item one senser of silver pcell gilt cont' xxxiiij oz. item one pix of silver and gilt with little glasse therein cont' xiij oz. Belles iij one sanctus bell."

The other runs as follows:

Bottesham. This is a treue and pfeite inuentorie, indented, *A.D.* 155
made and taken the vj day of August, anno R.R.E. VI. sexto, by
us Richard Wylk, clerke, Henry Gooderycke, Thomas Bowles,
and Thomas Rudston, esquyres, comyssion⁹s; amongest other
assigned for the surveye and ken of man⁹ of all goodes, plate,
jewells, bells, and ornam^ts, as yet be remayninge forthcomynge
& belonginge to the poche churche there as hereafter followeth.

Plate. Fyrst there is a crosse of sylver pcell gylt p. oz. .... xlvj ounces.

Item, one senser of sylver pcell gylte p. oz....... xxxiiij oz.

Item, one pyx of sylver & gylt w^t ye glasse & a stane of sylver p. oz... xiij oz.

Item, one chalyce w^t ye patent of sylv^r double gilt p. oz. .... xvij oz.

Item, one other of sylver p. oz..................... xvj oz.

Ornaments. Item, there is one cope of redd velett w^t vestement, deacon & subdeacon of the same. The arnes being decked w^t an ouche & certen stones sett in sylver. Item, one olde blacke cope of velett, vestem^t to ye same, iij copes of whyght damaske & vestement to ye same. Item, one whole sute of blewe sattyn, viz. iij copes, a vestement, deacon & subdeacon. Item, one vestement, deacon & sbdeacon & one cope of blewe brodered w^d sylver wyer, one payer of organnes, ij corporax clothes w^t their cases, one cross staffe of copper.

Bells. Item, in the steple there iij great bells, one lytle sanct^s bell. All which pcell^s aboue wrytten be delyu^{D}ed & comytted by us the saide comyssion^{D}s unto ye salve keepinge of John Hasell, John Baron, Robt. Challesse, Thomas Smyth, Thomas Bunte, and Richard Gunston, pishen^{D}s, there to be at all tymes forthcomynge to be answered except & res^{D}ud one of the said chalyc^{e}s, p. oz. xvj oz., one old black cope of velett, delyu^{D}ed to Robt. Cooke, Wyllm Wrenne & John Rolff churchwardens there for thoulie mayntenance of dywyne s^{D}uyce in ye said poche churche.

Henry Goodryk,	Ric. Wylkes,
Thomas Rudston[1],	Thomas Bowles,
	John Hesill,
Wyllm Walker Vyker,	Rycher Gunston,
Roberd Challys,	Roberd Coke.

From the will of Elizabeth de Burgh we find the following item: "A l'eglise parochiale de Bodekesham xl^s, et un drap d'or," that is, a cope. This will is dated A.D. 1355, and was proved on the 3rd of December, 1360, five years afterwards[2].

Though Blomefield says that the church was dedicated to

---

[1] He held the manor of Momplers in Swaffham Bulbeck.

[2] Royal Wills, No. 32.

the Holy Cross[1], we may conclude that he was mistaken, and that it was in reality to the Holy Trinity, may be inferred from the fact, that the wake or feast of the parish is celebrated on *Feast.* Trinity Monday at Bottisham; at Bottisham Lode the feast is held on the Tuesday, and at Langmeadow on the Wednesday and Thursday, when it was customary for the inhabitants to have wrestling-matches, and other sports, with the inhabitants of the woodlands on the borders of Suffolk[2].

One would have expected in a church so large and so light, *Stained* and so richly endowed, to have found much stained glass. At *glass.* the present day there is not a vestige remaining. Gifts, however, of memorial windows would much increase the beauty of the building, and add colour to what is now so cold and bare in its general appearance. Cole[3], however, tells us, that on his first visit to this church he found in the south window of the chancel, nearest to the screen, these arms, though gone in 1770: viz. g. a lion rampant within a bordure, engrailed, A., for Wm. Gray, bishop of Ely, from 1458—1478, A.D. In the opposite north window, though broken and set the wrong end up, in 1770 were these arms, for Clare Earl of Gloucester, which family founded Anglesey Abbey in this parish, viz. O. 3 chevronels g., and these others, gone in 1770, for Mortimer, viz. Barry of 6 O. and az.; on a chief of the 1st, 2 pallets of the 2nd with 2 esquires dexter and sinister of the 2nd. The escutcheon of pretence broken and filled up with a piece of painted glass. But Cole gives a drawing which represents, Barry of 6 O. and az. an escutcheon A. on a chief O. 2 pallets az. between as many gyrons of the last. He also observes that the colours in the arms of Mortimer are wrongly placed. This coat of arms is thus blazoned in Glover's Roll: " Barrè a chief palee a corners

---

[1] *Collect. Cantab.* Ed. 1750, p. 32.

[2] The principal sport of the inhabitants of the eastern counties was the game of ball called camping. It was much like football, and was played within the memory of the present generation. It has given its name to a field next the parish-church, where the sport was principally indulged in. It is derived from the Anglo-Saxon *campian*, to strive or contend. Clay, *Hist. of Landbeach*, p. 60, mentions an entry about 1720 A.D.: " Half-a-crown payable by custom on Shrove Tuesday for the Foot-ball men."

[3] Vol. IV.

geronè d'or et d'azur a ung escuchon d'argent[1]," and no doubt the arms stood thus in the north window of Bottisham church. Besides, in the same window, Cole mentions the figures of two saints, and underneath, Sanctum Nicholaū Sanctū Gregoriū.

Monu-ments. For so large a church there are not many monuments of great men remaining, but those that are now to be seen are not without interest. For the sake of clearness we will divide them into two classes; those in the interior, and those in the exterior of the building. The former we will again divide as follows: brasses or matrices of such, slabs with inscriptions, altar-tombs, monumental effigies, and mural tablets.

Brasses. First, as to brasses there are none to be seen, but there are not a few stones whose surface bears evidence of once having borne a brass upon them.

Elias de Beking-ham. In the centre of the nave there lies the matrix of a large brass. It consists of a large and floriated canopy with an angel at each side, and underneath the figure of a priest habited in a cope. Round the edge of the stone is the following inscription in Lombardic characters: "Hic jacet Elias de Bekingham quondam justiciarius Domini regis Anglie cuius anime propitie-tur Deus." He was appointed

Justiciarius itinerans, A.D. 1275.
Serviens ad Legem, A.D. 1276.
Justiciarius ad assisas Juratas et certificationes, A.D. 1276.
Justiciarius de Banco, A.D. 1285.
Justiciarius itinerans, A.D. 1288[2].

He was of the family of Bekingham of Bekingham, in the county of Nottingham, where they had lands from 12 Edw. I. to 18 Rich. II. Elias de Bekingham was party to a fine for lands in Stoke by Newark, in the same county, 29 Edw. I. Holin-shed, in his *Chronicle*[3], gives an account of the inquisition taken of the misdemeanors of justices, called "Traile Baston," or "draw the staff." The form of the writ is registered in the book which belonged to the abbey of Abingdon, A. D. 1304, 32 Edw. I. But in 17 Edw. I., 1289, "To conclude," he says,

---

[1] Planché's *Heraldry*, p. 124. Bowtell, do. p. 37.
[2] Dugdale, *Orig. Jurid.* pp. 25, 27, 28, 29.
[3] Ed. I. p. 840.

"there was not found any amongst all the justices and officers cleere and voyde of uniust dealing, except John de Metingham and Elias de Bekingham, who only among the rest had behaved themselves uprightly [1]." There is no record of the date of his death, but it is probable that he died soon after, as his name does not occur after 1304. He was a benefactor to the church, for we have seen, from the inventory in Caius Coll. Library, that they were indebted to him for a serecloth. It is not unreasonable to suppose that he lived at Bendish Hall, though there is no absolute proof of it [2].

At the eastern end of the nave, by the pew appropriated to Bottisham Hall, there lies a stone which formerly contained brasses of a civilian and his wife, with an inscription underneath. Under it stood also a brass plate for his sons. It is not known to whose memory this stone was laid down, but the matrix seems to indicate the costume of the early part of the XVth or the end of the XIVth century, and might thus accord with the period at which Robert or Thomas Botekesham died. These two were mayors of Lynn, and wealthy and influential inhabitants of that town at this period, and as they do not

Family o De Bote-kesham.

[1] Ib. p. 798.

[2] He was appointed, March 10, 1269, A.D., subdeacon of Norborough, in Nassaburgh hundred, Northants. Vide Whalley, *Northants*, Vol. II. p. 530. He was also subdeacon of Warmington, in the hundred of Willibrook, in 1281, A.D. May 19. Ib. II. 481. He was a landowner at Southorp, in Nassaburgh hundred, and obtained licence in 17 Edw. I. to give up to the abbot and convent of Peterborough one messuage and two carucates of arable land, with ten acres of wood, two watermills, and 60s. yearly rent in Suthorp, held by knight's service and homage of the said abbot and convent, who held them in chief of the crown. The conditions of this benefaction were, that the abbot and convent should find two monks who should daily celebrate divine service in their abbey for the soul of the late queen Eleanor, and that on the IV. Cal. Dec. (Nov. 28), the anniversary of the said queen, they should celebrate mass at Suthorp by three chaplains, and feed 200 poor persons. Ib. II. 497. In 1279, A.D. he held of the P. of Anglesey one acre of land in Bottisham by the service of 2s. of the fee of the Earl of Clare; 3 acres of the Earl rendering by the year 12d.; 8 acres, which were of Hugh Luwechild, rendering 2s. 0½d.; one messuage of the heir of William the son of William the son of Martin; a fourth part of a knight's fee of John de Deresle in Bottisham, and doing scutage to the same; two acres of John the son of Geoffrey by the service of 4d.; one messuage of William de Angerhale by the service of 2s.; and he was a party to a fine for lands in Bottisham in the years 2 Edw. I., 9 Edw. I., and 33 Edw. I.

possess any monument in any of the churches there, it is not improbable that they were buried in the place from which they took their surname. Another larger stone lies at the end of the nave, containing matrices of a man in a civilian's costume, with his wife, and an inscription; one matrix of a plate for sons and another for daughters, and at the corners matrices for shields of arms. This also may have commemorated some of the same family as the preceding, but the costume seems to point to a little later date.

At the west end of the south aisle, by the font, there lies an old coped coffin-lid. This formerly lay the other side uppermost, at the door of the screen leading to the Allington monuments, and contained a place for a brass plate. This plate probably was in memory of John Salisbury, who lived here, and died in 1639, A. D. He was a benefactor to the parish, and gave money for teaching three poor children; and as the board recording this benefaction stood on the wall above this coffin-lid, it is likely that he was buried beneath[1].

lench.   Of slabs with inscriptions there are but two that claim our notice. One lies in the nave next to the stone commemorating Elias de Bekingham, and from its inscription purports to be to the memory of Elizabeth, wife of John Clenche, who died Nov. 25, 1700, aged 30 years. From the parish register I find that she was buried on the 28th of November. She was the second wife of John Clench, who lived at Bendish Hall, and of whose *avies.*   family more will be said hereafter. The other slab is in the chancel, upon the same stone as that on which the altar-table stands. This is to the memory of the Rev. Joseph Davies, who died May the 5th, 1763, aged 61 years. He was sequestrator of Bottisham from 1758 to 1763, and was rector of Barton Mills, co. Suffolk, and vicar of Great Wilbraham in this county. He was buried here on the 9th of May, 1763, A. D.

llington.   Of altar-tombs there is but one, and the identification of that somewhat difficult. A letter in the *Cambridge Independent Press* of April 1, 1871, gives us weighty reasons for concluding that it was erected to the memory of William Allington,

---

[1] The entry in the Parish Register is quaint: "old father Salisbury was buried the 31st Dec. 1639, A.D."

who was speaker to the House of Commons in 1472[1], and who died in 1479, A. D.[2] Of this influential man more notice will be given hereafter when speaking of his family. His tomb lies under the screen on the southern side of the north aisle, near to the chancel. On its upper surface is the matrix of a brass, now gone, and around its upper edge a place for a brass inscription, now also gone. There are indications in the east wall of the remnants of a stone canopy, of which a portion, I believe, was in existence before the reseating of the church in 1839, and I have seen some stones in the vicarage garden which seem originally to have belonged to it. On the north side of the tomb, which is of Purbeck marble, are carved places for three coats of arms, upon which were nailed brass plates; but these are gone, and now no vestige remains to tell whose memory the tomb was intended to preserve. Cole gives the following description of the tomb[3]: "The flat tomb in the north aisle is, in all probability, designed for one of the family of the Allingtons, for on the south-west corner of the screen, which separates the chapel from the rest of the north aisle, are the arms of Allington and Argentein (Quarterly, 1 and 4, sa. a bend Ar. int. 6 Billets Ar.: 2 and 3, gu. 3 covered cups Ar.), and which most likely came off from one of the stones lying here about; on a wooden shield, very old, per pale, 1st quarterly of Allington and Argentein, impaling, quarterly 1 and 4, checquy gu. and O., and a canton ermine, 2 and 3, gu. 3 stirrups with buckles and straps O., by the name of Scudamore. About the 1st and 4th doubtful." He adds, "I think there is an escutcheon of pretence on this coat with a cross of four birds in the four quarters." This wooden shield was fastened to the south-west corner of the screen at the top in 1839, and was then stained over in order to make it look like the rest of the woodwork! Now the first of these two coats of arms is easily accounted for: William Allington, the father of

---

[1] Parry, *Parl. and Councils of England*, pp. 192, 193.

[2] Cat. *Inq. post mortem*, Vol. IV. p. 392. Manning, *Lives of the Speakers*, pp. 117—119, where he is confounded with his nephew, William Allington, who married 1, Elizabeth Wentworth, 2, Elizabeth Sapcoates.

[3] Vol. IV.

the founder of this chapel, married Elizabeth, daughter and
heiress of John Argentein[1]. The second shield must be explained thus: 1. quarterly of Allington and Argentein: 2.
quarterly, 1 and 4 checquy, gu. and or, and a canton ermine
for John Reyns, who married Catherine, daughter and heiress
of Peter Scudamore, and who thus brought in 2 and 4 gu.
3 stirrups with buckles and straps, or. Joan, the granddaughter of John Reyns, married John Ansty, of Holme
Hall, in the parish of Quy (now the residence of Clement
Francis, Esq.), and Mary, the issue of this marriage, married
John Allington, another son of William Allington of Bottisham, "qui stetit contra fratres." The escutcheon of pretence
is derived from Joan, daughter and heiress of John Ansty,
and wife of William Allington, whose memory this altar-tomb
preserves. It is probable, though the pedigrees of this family
do not say so, that this William Allington was the eldest son,
for in one of the windows of Horseheath Hall there was
this coat of arms painted, viz. per pale, baron and femme;
1, the arms of Allington differenced by a label of 3 points; and
2, quarterly, Reyns and Scudamore, and an escutcheon of
pretence for Ansty.[2]

*Monu-
mental
effigies.*   We now come to the class of monuments known as monumental effigies. Of these are excluded those that partake of
a mural character. In 1839, under the flooring of the base
of the tower were discovered certain stones, which when put
together, formed the effigy of a woman reclining upon a
cushion, and between two columns forming part of a canopy.
The material is a light sandstone, and the date is about 1480.
It is impossible to say whom this represents: the lady wears a
lappet head-dress, so usual at the end of the 15th century:
her left arm, bent over her breast, exhibits a glove from the
hand nearly to the elbow. Something which she is holding in
her left hand, perhaps a cross, has been broken off, and beneath
the folds of her dress are seen her feet, clad in shoes, with
buckles and straps, and resting on oak leaves bearing acorns.

---

[1] Harl. MSS. No. 6775, fol. 57.
[2] Vide visit. of Hunt. Ed. Ellis. *Camden Soc. Publ.* Vol. XLIII. p. 88.
Harl. MSS. No. 6775, fol. 57.

Some more pieces of stone of the same description were found in the same place. They cannot be made to accord with this effigy; indeed, a hand which is quite perfect shews no glove at all. In 1870, part of another monumental effigy was discovered. In that year there stood along the east and west walls of the south porch, stone ledges, so as to form benches. When these were removed, some pieces of a monumental slab were found, which when put together shewed the effigy of an ecclesiastic, in chasuble, on a coffin-lid-shaped stone; the head of the figure, resting on a cushion, was gone. This as well as the effigy of the lady has been deposited in the Allington chapel at the end of the north aisle. Besides the altar- *Pledger* tomb at the south side, this chapel contains two mural monu- *monument.* ments. One is against the north wall, and consists of a large Elizabethan tomb, representing a man in armour kneeling before a faldstool, and behind him a lady also kneeling and wearing a ruff. The lady, as the inscription beneath imports[1], was first the wife of Robert Allington, by whom she had eleven children, namely, Giles, James, George, Anne, Elizabeth, Alice, Francisca, William, John, Margaret, and Beatrice. Her second husband was Thomas Pledger, the son of Thos. Pledger of Ashden, in Essex. She died May 16, 1598, aged 78, and was buried on May 17. He died March 13, 1599, aged 70, and was buried on March 15th. His name is spelt on the monument Pledger, but in the parish register and in various MSS. it is found as Pledgerd or Pledgerde. On this monument there are three shields of arms. The first, over the top, is for Pledger and is thus: sa. a fess engrailed int. 3 Bucks trippant O. spotted of the field for Pledger. Crest—a Buck's head erased holding an oak branch with acorns O. leaves

[1] It runs thus:—"Here lyeth Margaret the daughter of William Coningesbye of King's Lynn one of the Justices of the Common Pleas at Westminster, who married with Robert Alyngton Esq. son and heir of Giles Alyngton of Horseheath, Knt. by whom he had five sons and six daughters William, John, Giles, James and George, Alice, Anne, Margaret, Elizabeth, Frances and Beatrise; and after she married with Thos. Pledger, gent. with whom she lived four years, and died 16 May 1569, æt. 78, and he died 13 March 1599 aged 70, and lieth here buried. By his last will and testament he gave £40 to be bestowed upon 8 of the poor and antient inhabitants dwelling in this parish of Bottisham for ever."

proper. This coat of arms was granted to him by Wm. Harvey, Clarencieux king at arms, in the seventh year of the reign of queen Elizabeth. He married the widow of Robert Allington, who was the daughter of Wm. Coningsby of King's Lynn, who was a judge in the time of Henry VIII.[1] Over her head is the following shield, containing 10 coats, 6 on the side of the husband and 4 on that of the wife. Beginning with the side of the husband, No. 1, sa. a bend engrailed int. 6 billets Ar. is for Allington. 2, gu. 3 covered cups Ar. for Argentein. (Wm. Allington married Eliz., heiress of John Argentein.) 3, az. 5 eagles O. displayed, one, three, and one, a canton ermine, for Fitz Tek. (Helena d. and co-h. of Vido filius Tecæ or Fitz Tek married John de Argentein, in the time of king Stephen, and brought to him the ownership of Wymondeley magna in Hertfordshire, from whom it passed in descent to the family of the Allingtons.) 4, gules on a bend Ar. three leopards' faces sa. for Burgh. (William Allington of Bottisham, who died in 1446, married Joanna, daughter of William Burgh of Borough Green.) 5, Per fess Ar. and sa. a pale counterchanged, 3 Griffins' heads erased O. for Gardner. (Sir Giles Allington, who died in 1522, married Mary d. of Thomas Gardner.) 6, Ar. fretty sa. and a canton of the last for Middleton (Sir Giles son of the last-mentioned Sir Giles, married Alice, daughter and heiress of John Middleton.) On the side of the wife 1 and 4. gu. 3 conies sejeant within a bordure engrailed Ar. and a crescent of the last for Coningsby. 2, O. a lion rampant gu. for Streche? 3, sa. a fess erm. int. 3 goats' heads erased of the 2nd for Feriby or Ferby (Sir Humfrey Coningsby Knight and Judge, married ——, d. and heiress of —— Feriby of Lincolnshire. Over the figure of Thomas Pledger are the arms of Pledger impaling the four last of Coningsby.

Allington. Next to this tomb and against the east wall is a monument of white marble, representing a curtain drawn aside from the centre, and disclosing reclining figures of a boy and girl. The inscription beneath on black marble runs as follows:—

"Stay Passengers, and wonder whom these stones
Have learned to speak: two infant *Allingtons:*

[1] Judge of Common Pleas in 1541. Vide Dugdale, *Orig. Jurid.* p. 84.

These the world's strangers came not here to dwell;
They tasted, liked it not, and bad farewell:
Nature hath granted what they begged with tears:
As soon as they begun to end their years."

"Jacemus hic Lionellus et Dorothea eximiorum Gulielmi et Elizabethæ Allington filius filiaque. Fato succubuimus anno Sal. 1638."

These were the children of William Allington, fourth son and ninth child of Sir Giles Allington by Dorothy Cecil. He was made Baron Allington of Killard, co. Cork, Ireland on the 28th July, 1642, and died in 1648. He married Elizabeth, eldest daughter of Sir Lionel Tollemache of Helmingham, Suffolk. Lionel was born on the 28 Feb. 1636-7, and was buried on the 28th of June, 1638. Dorothy was born on the 24th of May, 1638, and was buried on the 15th of August in the same year.

On the other side of the church, viz. at the end of the *Jenyns.* south aisle, there stands a large mural monument of white marble. A man and wife holding hands, are seated upon a massive base, upon which there is the following inscription :—

"In this vault lies the body of Dame Elizabeth Jenyns, wife
to Sir Roger Jenyns, who died May 1, 1728, æt. 62.
She was a lady of great virtue and piety
and through the whole course of her life of
an unblemished reputation : a constant
attender of public as well as a strict
observer of stated hours of her private
devotion. Her piety, as well as her uncommon
tenderness and compassion of nature
engaged her to daily acts of charity
as well in her life as at her death. She was
of a mild temper, a graceful and winning
presence, an easy and engaging
conversation, though her own infirmity
often interrupted the natural
cheerfulness of her disposition. She was
an affectionate wife, an indulging mother,
a sincere friend, and a good Christian. At her

death, Sir Roger Jenyns by her desire, settled the
schooling of 20 poor children : and as his
addition, the clothing of them and a school to teach
them and others in for ever."

On a tablet above the figures is this inscription : " In this
vault lies the body of Sir Roger Jenyns, Knt., lord of the manor
of Allington and Vauxes in this parish, who descended from
Sir John Jenyns, of Churchill in Somersetshire. He married
Elizabeth, daughter of Sir Peter Soame of Heydon, in Essex
Bart. by whom he had only one son, Soame Jenyns, who married
Mary Soame of Dereham Grange, in Norfolk. He died 22nd
of September, 1740, aged 77." ·

The entries in the Parish Register shew that Dame Elizabeth was buried on the 10th of May, 1728, and Sir Roger on
the 1st of October, 1740. As we shall see hereafter, he was
the first of this family to possess Bottisham Hall, having purchased it from the Allingtons. Over the monument at the
top of the pediment are these arms. Baron. Ar. on a fess gu.
3 bezants O. on a canton az. a crescent O. for Jenyns.
Femme. gu. a chevron O. int. 3 mallets O. for Soame. Above
is the crest—a demi lion rampant O. supporting a spear erect
of the 1st headed az. the motto—Ignavis nunquam. "Above
these," says Cole, "from the wall hang the same arms in
streamers and penons with helmet, gloves, mantle, and sword.
The arms of Jenyns and Soame in a shield on the corner of
the chapel in which the aforesaid monument is enclosed[1]."
These streamers &c. stood in the church till 1839, when they
were removed to Bottisham Hall. The canton az. with the
crescent O. is accounted for by the fact that Sir Roger was
the second son of Roger Jenyns of Hayes, co. Middlesex. Near
this tomb against the south wall is a plain marble tablet recording the death of Soame Jenyns, son of Sir Roger, who
died on the 18th Dec. 1787, and was buried on the 27th Dec.
aged 83 : of Mary his first wife, who died July 30, 1753 : and
Elizabeth d. of Henry Grey of Hackney, his second wife, who
died July 25, 1796, æt. 94, and was buried on the 2nd of August.

Another similar tablet records the death of the Rev. George

[1] Vol. IV. fol. 5.

Leonard Jenyns, Vicar of Swaffham Bulbeck, and Canon of Ely, who was born 19 June, 1763, and died Feb. 25, 1848, and Mary his wife, daughter of the late Wm. Heberden, M.D., who died Aug. 18, 1832, aged 69. Also of Charles their son, who died in infancy, in Ap. 1796. Cole says, that "under the first south window of the nave and above the 1st pillar hung an achievement with these arms :—Per Pale 1. Ar. on a fess gu. 3 Bezants, and a crescent in chief sa. for difference, for Jenyns, impaling O. on a chev. eng. gu. 3 trefoils slipped Ar. int. 3 Leopards' faces gu. for Harvey. Motto, "Ignavis nunquam." Roger Jenyns, the son of John Jenyns, M.P., married a Miss Harvey. He was nephew to Sir Roger Jenyns. On the south wall of the aisle are two achievements. The first bears these arms. 1. Ar. on a fess gu., 3 Bezants for Jenyns impaling Erminois a fess of 4 lozenges vert on a chief az. an annulet between two suns O. for Heberden, the wife of Rev. George Leonard Jenyns. The other bears these. 1. Jenyns as before, impaling Ermines 4 lozenges in fess vert on a chief az. a crescent purpure between two suns or. I cannot explain this latter achievement. I remember hearing something about their having been repainted and some mistake made, and I can only conjecture that, as the Jenyns-Harvey achievement has disappeared, these two achievements may have been thus, Jenyns-Heberden and Jenyns-Harvey. Cole places in the Jenyns-Harvey achievement, a crescent for difference, and rightly, for John Jenyns, the elder brother of Sir Roger, had as his grandfather, Thomas Jenyns of Hayes, who was the offspring of Sir John Jenyns, by a second marriage with Dorothy, daughter of Thomas Bulbeck, and widow of John Latch.

On the wall of the north aisle there is another tablet to the memory of Maria Jane, wife of George Jenyns, who died at Alverstoke, Hants, March 13th, 1867 æt. 68; of George Gambier, son of the above George Jenyns, who was buried in St. James' Church-yard, Dover, aged 15; of Jemima Maria Hicks Jenyns, who died at Ryde, Jan. 9, 1858, æt. 28; of Roger Leonard Gambier, who died Feb. 12, 1855, aged 13; of Soame, who died March 10, 1821, aged 11 days; Leonard, who died Aug. 28, 1823, aged 7 months; and of a son, born and died May, 1824.

ugh.   A marble tablet in the chancel on the south wall has an inscription thus : "Near this place are deposited the remains of the Rev. Wm. Pugh, M.A., a Senior Fellow of Trin. Coll. Camb. and Vicar of Bottisham, in the county of Cambridge who departed this life on the 9th day of April, 1825, aged 57 years." He was appointed vicar in 1811, and left a large benefaction to the poor.

ushing-ton.   On the other side of the church, in the nave, on the north side near to the stone screen of the chancel, a tablet is fixed with this inscription :

"To the memory of Hester Paulina Lushington, who died
July 24, 1795, aged 18.

As purity of heart will be accepted at the
day of Resurrection through the merits
of her Saviour Jesus Christ,
she has not lived in vain.

Her parents have erected this memorial as a testimony of
her virtues
and of their affliction."

She was the eldest daughter of the Rev. James Stephen Lushington of Rodmersham, Kent, Prebend of Carlisle and vicar of Newcastle-upon-Tyne, who lived for some time at Bendish Hall. She was baptized on the 17th of Oct. 1776, and was buried on the 29th of July, 1795, after dying of a decline. Her mother wore a ruff.

Exterior.
Hasell.   Leaving the church by the south porch you pass over three flat stones which contain no inscriptions. These formerly stood a little way off, but were moved here when the porch was repaired in 1870. Cole tells us[1] that the following inscriptions were copied by him when he visited the church. (1) "Here lyeth the body of Frances Hasell, the wife of John Hasell, gent., who died Sept. 2, 1689." (2) "Here lyeth the body of John Hasell, gent., who departed this life June 15, 1705, aged 49 years." (3) "Here lyeth the body of Mary Hasell, the wife of John Hasell, gent., who died May 4th, 1698." This family, though now quite extinct, was very numerous and of certain influence in Bottisham. John Hasell, or Hassill, was witness to

[1] Cole MSS. Vol. IV.

many wills about the time of Henry VIII.[1] A William Hassyll was bailiff of the town of Cambridge in company with John Jenyns in 1525[2]· In 1613 John Hasell of Bottisham and Richard Hasell, his son, under the will of Agatha Borrowdaile of Bury, were appointed trustees of certain property left for the good of the parishes of Newmarket and Woodditton, and were at every seven years' end "to have for their paynes a ring of gold value 30 shillings and expenses[3]."

"On the north side of the churchyard at the west end of the north porch" is, says Cole, "a good handsome altar monument made in the form of a coffin in freestone, and this inscription on it. "Here lieth the body of John the son of John and Mary *Lack.* Lack (lived at Langmeadow) who departed this life September 9th, 1742, aged 20 years.

> 'In youthful days death may be nigh,
> Then always be prepared to die'."

This inscription is now quite obliterated, and by the side of this tomb are two others exactly like it, which I take to be for John Lack, labourer, who was buried May 27, 1747, and the other for Mary Lack his wife, though there is no legible inscription on either. Of the remainder of the tombstones in the churchyard, it will be interesting only to mention those of extinct families as well as those of some influence in the parish. Near the south doorway of the chancel are two stones in the form of a coffin, enclosed in rails, to the memory of Thomas Free, who died Sept. 30, 1852, aged 64, and Sarah his *Free.* sister, who died March 15, 1856, aged 64. He was for some time the occupant of the house at Bendish. His father was coachman to Mr Lushington, and after his departure took the farm and was succeeded by his son. This family is now extinct.

On one flat slab this inscription to Sarah Banks, died 26 May, *Banks.* 1749, aged 31, wife of George Banks, farmer, of this parish, who died 15 Feb., 1748, aged 51 ; also to Frances Rockell, daughter of the above, who died 18 April, 1800, aged — years.

On the north side of the churchyard a plain coped stone to *Jennings.* Dinah Jennings, who died 1861, aged 92.

[1] Ib. Vol. LX. [2] Ib. Vol. XLI. p.237. [3] Tymms, *Bury Wills and Inventories*, p.160.

Hailstone.   Within railings is a flat stone with an inscription to John Hailstone, son of Rev. J. Hailstone, vicar of this parish, who died Nov. 26, 1852, aged 11 years; also Frank, born Oct. 16, 1854, died Jan. 11, 1855.

King.   At the north-west corner of the churchyard are railings enclosing altar-tombs for the family of King, recording the deaths of

Ann, wife of Henry King, died Feb. 23, 1850, aged 86.

Martha, daughter of Henry and Ann King, died Ap. 12, 1858, aged 55.

Henry King, died June 16, 1838, aged 69.

William, son of Henry and Ann King, died Dec. 22, 1824, aged 23.

And two others, who died in their infancy.

Julia Charlotte, died July 12, 1856, aged 8.

Sidney John, died March 29, 1863, aged 10.

Henry William, died June 16, 1863, in his 20th year.

These three last were the children of John and Caroline King.

John King died Aug. 26, 1820, aged 47.

Rance.   Martha Rance, relict of the late Henry Rance, died Sept. 25, 1829.

There are contiguous to these head and foot-stones to the following.

King.   Catharine King, died 1868, aged 51.

Catharine King, daughter of the above, died 1861, aged 8.

Eliz. wife of Geo. King, died 1851, aged 73.

Susan, their daughter, died 1845, aged 36.

Henry King, died 1783, aged 44.

Susan King, his wife, died 1823, aged 82.

George King, died Oct. 24, 1817, aged 41.

Coe.   On the same side of the churchyard are head and foot-stones to the memory of Capt. Thos. Coe, R.N., died in 1838, aged 59, and Martha Ann Coe, died 1840, aged 54. Also to Thomas

Haystead. Haystead, gent., died 1831, aged 62. Mary Haystead, died 1828, aged 73. There are also flat-stones to the memory of

Jennings. Sarah Jennings, died Jan. 14, 1850, aged 83, and Eleanor Jennings, died Jan. 24, 1834, aged 68 years.

On the south side are many head- and foot-stones to the *Newman.* family of Newman, who have long resided in this parish as farmers. These are for—Thomas Newman, aged 66, died 1800. Sarah, his wife, aged 83, died 1825. Eliza, their daughter, died 1784, aged 10. Sarah, died 1782, aged 13. Thomas Newman, died 1855, aged 77 ; his wife, Sarah, died 1848, aged 67. Ann, their daughter, died in 1828, aged 14 years. Amy, daughter of Edward and Charlotte Anne Newman, died an infant, 1871. William Newman, died 1833, aged 29. There are many stones to the family of Taylor. Many of this family in various genera- *Taylor.* tions seem to have borne the name of Overin. Another stone stands for Benjamin Kettle, died July 23, 1816, aged 89, seventy *Kettle.* years master of the free-school. Ann, his wife, died Nov. 18, 1768, aged 57. Thomas, his son, died Oct. 1, 1799, aged 45. Sarah, his second wife, died Ap. 28, 1845, aged 80. Giles Edwards, died Ap. 27, 1792, aged 38. Ann, his wife, died Ap. 5, *Edwards,* 1788, aged 23. Eliza, their daughter, has also an inscription to *&c.* her memory, now quite illegible.

There are also stones to the family of Todd, Folkes, Alliston, Camps, Spicer, Giffen, Aves, Stubbing, Barton, Flack, Danby, Cracknell, Saggers, Knowles, Davies, Thurston, Elsden, Willis, Brand, Pursell, Hart, Wheeler, Crofts, Ford, Alliston, Rider Casboult, as well as Tabitha Dennis, who died in 1765,. aged 35. *Dennis.* Eliza Mary, daughter of Thomas Meakin, died 1854, aged 9. *Meakin.* Frances Crisp, died 1861, aged 39. Eliza Harding, died 1851, *Crisp.* aged 34. Ann Parker, died in 1856, aged 83, Mary Ann *Harding. Parker.* Smith, daughter of Thomas Parker, died 1864, aged 55: Thomas Parker, died 1849, aged 68.

These names serve to shew the families that most constantly resided in the parish, but the names of Shipp and Webb may be added to them. On comparing the monuments in and about this church with the parish registers, I am surprised to find so few tombs. Not one records the death of any of the numerous family of Dositer, farmers, in this parish ; of Misson, of Thompson, Foster, Webbe, Clench (except Elizabeth Clench), Fowkes, Parker, Salisbury, Pamplin, Lawsell, Sewall, Manning, Jelly, Mott, Grain, Grange, Long, Vale, Burton, Wybrow, Eaton, Golding, Wilkin, Crane and others, all of whom were of some influence as having ranked as gentlemen, farmers, or trades-men.

At various spots in the churchyard may be noticed very small old wooden posts with a C marked upon them. These, 38 in number, shew where lie the bodies of those who perished in consequence of the dreadful visitaticn of the cholera, which took place in 1834.

The following is a list of the vicars of Bottisham. It is compiled from Cole's MSS., Baker's MSS., Trin. Coll. registers, and various other documents. It is unfortunately incomplete.

Hugh, the son of Augustin and Eluina his wife.

Richard de la Lade, son of Hugh de la Lade, occurs in 1222, A. D.

John, occurs April 28, 1251.

Symon, formerly perpetual vicar, occurs May 25, 1287.

Richard Freeburn, presented by the P. of Anglesey, 1324.

Subsequently vicar of Fulbourne, Hoxne, Suffolk, and Thorpe, co. of Norfolk.

Adam, canon of Longstanton, was admitted Dec. 11, 1338.

Bartholomew Peryn, 1341.

Adam, 1344.

Thomas, vicar in 1346.

William de Wykkewan, appointed June 5, 1349, presented by the Prior and convent of Anglesey, *pleno jure.*

John Curteys.

William Saleman, 1352.

William de Salmon, presbyter, March 23, 1379.

William Marshall, died 1393.

Robert Aleyn, Dec. 2, 1393, resigned in 1395.

Plac. Cant. 18 Ric. II. No. 30, Rex v. P. de Anglesey and Robt. Aleyn Clerk de present. ad vic. de Botekesham. Judic. de non pros'. p̄ defectū narrandi.

John Bertelot, May 6, 1395, resigned.

Exchanged with Nicholas Hale for the rectory of Stanway, Essex, in 1400 rector of S. Nicholas, Colchester, in 1406 vicar of Thurrock Parva, Essex, and Feltham, Middlesex, one of which he resigned.

Nicholas Hale, March 6, 1398, resigned.

Nicholas Baynard, April 30, 1399.

William Spencer, died in 1464.

Robert Knyght, appointed Sept. 18, 1464.

Bartholomew Rodswell, 1506.

William Breton, resigned 17 March, 1534.

Thomas Moodye, presented Mar. 17, 1534, admitted March 28, 1535, resigned.

William Walker, presented Nov. 17, admitted Nov. 22, 1542; presented by the master and scholars of King's Hall, now Trinity College.

In the Harleian MSS., Brit. Mus., No. 4115, p. 6, is a letter announcing his resignation, dated Sept. 17, 1552; pres. to Wilbraham Magna, July 9, 1538.

Robert Rooke, appointed 1556, died in 1557.

John Wryght, Oct. 16, 1557.

John Cooke, March 13, 1566.

—— *Eastdale.*

Baldwin Caswell, Sept. 24, 1573, resigned.

Christopher Jeniver, appointed Jan. 6, 1575, died 1611.

John Gilder.

William Barton, inst. Oct. 21, 1611, resigned.

Compounded for first fruits in Nov. 1611, by paying £16. 0s. 0d.

Thomas Kechin or *Kitchin,* 1613, resigned,

Compounded for first fruits.

Thomas Cooke, March 15, 1616.

Compounded for first fruits.

—— *Coote,* 1617.

Anthony Topham, compounded Ap. 17, 1619.

Samuel Sackvile, comp. Feb. 19, 1620.

Richard Watts, comp. March 29, 1621.

Thomas Medhope, comp. 1630.

Dr George Helton or *Henton,* comp. 1631.

Dr Gulson, 1633.

Charles Chamberlain, 26 March, 1634.

Edward Burton, app. June 13, comp. Oct. 1638.

—— *Crossland,* app. 1644.

According to the Parish Register, he was sequestered "for saying that the Party had taken up arms against the king," March 26, 1644[1].

---

[1] Walker's *Sufferings of the Clergy,* I. 118, and II. 215; Vide Carter (*Cambs.* p. 138-9), who says that he was "a time server, and one that observes bowing towards the east, standing up at 'Gloria Patri,' reading the second

Richard Britten, 1655.

William Fordham[1], 1668, buried at Bottisham, Nov. 21, 1687.

Thomas Walker, about 1690, presented by Parliament.
Vide Lansdowne MSS. No. 459.

William Rashleigh, up to 1693.

Jonathan Smith, 1693.

——— *Gostwick*, 1693.

Abraham Jordan, 1696.

Roger Parne, D.D.[2]

Edward Bathurst, 1708.

John Craister, D.D., 1716.

Thos. Paine, 1725.

Sequestra-tors. *Joseph Davies*, 1758, rector of Barton Mills, Suffolk, and vicar of Great Wilbraham, curate of Swaffham Bulbeck.

Thomas Waterworth, appointed and resigned Dec. 1763.

Michael Lort, Regius Professor of Greek, 1763, resigned in 1770.

Thomas Spencer, 1770, resigned in 1771.

Christopher Hodgson, resigned in 1773.

Robert Hilton, resigned in 1773.

John Cranke, 1775.
Afterwards Vicar of Shudy Camps.

William Lort Mansel, 1783.
Subsequently Master of Trin. Coll. and Bishop of Gloucester and Bristol.

Thomas Gilbank, 1790, resigned in 1797.
Afterwards Rector of Dickleburgh.

Harry Porter, 1796, resigned in 1801.
Professor of Hebrew and afterwards Vicar of Enfield.

Jonathan Raine, D.D., 1801.

William Pugh, 1811.

service at the Communion-table, and suchlike superstitious worship and Popish innovations in the Church," &c.

[1] In his time the vicarage was worth £30 per annum, parsonage about £150. —Baker MSS.

[2] "A person of great talents and high reputation in the University in his time, one of the College Tutors, and played rather a distinguished part in the long Bentley strife. Librarian to the University in 1735. In 1748, having betrayed symptoms of insanity, he was removed from College upon an allowance. Large materials for a history of his College collected by him are extant in the College muniment-room."—Cole.

John Brown, 1825.

Vicars.

Thomas Musgrave, 1837.

Bishop of Hereford 1837, and Archbishop of York 1847.

John Hailstone, 1837, resigned 1861, presented by the Queen. 1863 Rural Dean of North Camps.

John Brown McClellan, the present Vicar, and 1871 Rural Dean of North Camps, late Fellow of Trinity College.

The following names occur as chaplains in Bottisham in *Chaplain* various documents.

1232. John Lungpree.	1345—1371. Seman de Wytheresfield.
1334. Wm. Lenewe.	
1334. John Le Blested, died 1355.	1350. Edward de Woldherst.
1334. John Chanyn.	1350. Richard atte Slough.
1334. Phil. Smith.	1357. John Hulyne.
1334—1339. Wm. de Arderne.	1367—1406. John Curteys.
1334—1340. John Lungpree.	1371. Wm. de Lawndene.
1334—1357. Nicholas de S. Ivone.	1386. Thos. fitz Richard.
	1386. Thos. Gryllow.
1340. Rog. Bette.	1386. Robt. Aleyn.
1340. Walt. James.	1389. John Welyot.
1341. Martin Gerard.	1389. Reginald Leverington.
1341. Gilbert le Bocchere.	1406. Richard Couper.
1345. William de Arderne.	1406. John Smith.

The following occur as curates:

Curates.

Robert Brydkirke, Parish Priest or Curate, 1520.

Sir James Tennande, priest, 1521.

Sir Robert Dullingham, 1540 and 1543.

Sir Luke Taylor, 1541.

William Cutler, 1544.

Sir Robert Hogge, 1546.

Christopher Spendlove, 1619.

Henry Yates, 1621.

William Noble, 1632.

Nicholas Gill, 1633.

Robert Cademan, 1635.

John Wiseman, 1636.
Andrew Whiskin, 1641.
Rowland Williams, Feb. 6, 1667.
John Cooper, minister, 1694.
Abraham Jordan, Oct. 1695.
John Whitfield, 1707 to Aug. 22, 1714.
Charles Chester, 1798.
——— *Henshaw,* 1805.
——— *Buckland,* 1811.
——— *Henshaw,* 1825.
C. W. Ord, 1852.
Samuel Charlton, 1854.
John Batteridge Pearson, Fellow of Emmanuel College.
James Hunnybun.
Charles W. Crosse.

arish
lerks.

These are the names of the parish clerks as taken from the Parish Registers.

—— Mott, succeeded by
—— Mott, succeeded by
William Mott, succeeded by
Thomas Pamplin, made clerk in 1726, died in 1744, succeeded by
Stephen Osbourn, died in Feb. 1788, succeeded by
Stephen Osbourn, his grandson, succeeded by
Samuel Stubbing, July 16, 1791, succeeded by
Thomas Flack, May 1829, succeeded by
Edmund Wells, the present parish clerk.

But Alexander Burrell appears to have been clerk about 1713 from the following entry :—

"Mrs. Elizabeth Burrell the wife of Alexander Burrell (clerke) was buried on the 4th of July, 1713."

And Roger Gunstone appears to have been clerk about 1610, for there is in the register the following entry :—

"Roger Gunstone, clerke, married Susan Long, 3 December, 1610."

In the same registers we find these as churchwardens :

1561.	Thomas Noble.
	John Whitinge.
1563.	Do.
1569.	Do.
1599.	Oct.19, John Banyoll.
	John Whitinge.
1600.	Andrew Bette.
	John Barnarde.
1602.	Thomas Ventris.
	John Hasell.
1605.	Thomas Tompson.
	John Wilkins.
1606.	William Brown.
	William Culpie.
1607.	John Duffield.
	Thomas Tompson.
1608.	William Brown.
	William Caber.
1609.	John Keate.
	Peter Scott.
1610.	Do.
1611.	John Keate.
	Peter Scott.
1612.	John Wilkins.
	Edward Brand.
1613.	Do.
1614.	Do.
1615.	Robert Cooke.
1616.	William Fowkes.
	Thomas Bridges.
1617.	Do.
1618.	Do.
1619.	Edmund Duffield.
	William Pursell.
1620.	Do.

1621.	Edmund Duffield.
1623.	Robert Cooke.
1624.	Edmund Duffield.
	Robert Bridges.
1625.	William Duffield.
	Edmund Duffield.
1626.	John Howlett.
	Robert Cooke.
1630.	Robert Cooke.
	William Burton.
1631.	Robert Cooke.
1632.	Lawrence Sewell.
1632.	Robert Cooke.
	Lawrence Keate.
1633.	Robert Cooke.
	William Hockley.
1634.	Edmund Duffield.
	William Hockley.
1635.	Edmund Duffield.
	William Hockley.
1636.	Robert Bridges.
	William Larkin.
1637	John Tilbrooke } sidesmen.
	John Cooke }
1639.	Richard Scott.
	Joseph Hurrey.
1641.	Francis Stone.
	Edward Salisbury.
No churchwardens found till
1664.	Almot Clenche.
	Henry Wallis.
	Robert Smythe.
1669.	Francis Garrow.
	John Salisbury.
1673.	Do.

CHAPTER III

OTHER PLACES OF WORSHIP.

Bottisham Lode Church. HAVING noticed at length the features of the Parish Church, there remains something to be said of another Church at Bottisham Lode. During the incumbency of the late Vicar, the Rev. J. Hailstone, it was strongly felt that this hamlet, as well as that of Langmeadow, from their great distance from the mother church, were greatly in need of closer spiritual *Its origin.* ministrations. Accordingly, in 1852, by the exertions of the Vicar, a subscription was set on foot; and solicitations having been liberally responded to on all sides, the foundation-stone was laid on a site given by Trinity College, adjoining the main street of Bottisham Lode. Rohde Hawkins, Esq. furnished the plans and the building was completed in 1853, when it was consecrated by the Lord Bishop of the Diocese. Though a fund was opened for a permanent endowment of a clergyman, this church was served by curates till the incumbency of the present vicar. It was then resolved to separate ecclesiastically this portion of the parish from Bottisham proper, and in 1863 *Incumbents.* it was made into a consolidated Chapelry, of which the Rev. Charles Harris was the first Incumbent. He was succeeded by the Rev. Herbert Gardner; then came the Rev. James Edmonds, who in his turn resigned it into the hands of the Rev. Austin Willett, who was succeeded by the present Incumbent, *arsonage.* bent, the Rev. James Bonser. There is a neat Parsonage adjoining the churchyard, and the present stipend of the *alue. hurch- ardens.* Incumbent amounts to about £70. The first Churchwardens elected were Mr William King and Mr Benjamin Leader, and these continued to serve till the death of the latter, when Mr Charles Parker was elected in his place. The office of

Sexton was formerly filled by William Ayres, and is now Sexton.
occupied by William Peers.

The church consists of a chancel, on the north side of Church,
which is a vestry, a nave, and a wooden open porch on the descrip-
tion.
south side. The font is at the end of the nave. One step
separates the nave from the chancel, and there is one step at
the rails, as well as a raised stone on which the altar-table
is placed. The altar-frontals were the gift of Mr Willett, as
well as other portions of the church furniture. A neat little
organ stands in the chancel. The churchyard as yet is Monu-
ments.
marked by few tombstones or signs of graves. One, however,
records the death of Mr Benjamin Leader, who tenanted the
mill at Anglesey for some years; two are erected for the family
of Tottman; while opposite to the south porch is buried the
Rev. John Hailstone, for some time Vicar of the united parish,
and possessor of Anglesey Abbey. A little open turret rising
above the west end of the church contains two bells, and Bells.
underneath is a serviceable clock. On the opposite side of the
street a large and useful school-room has been erected detached Schools,
from the master's house which stands next to it. Of this Lode.
building, as well as the parsonage, J. Clarke, Esq., of Newmarket, was the architect. But, while noticing the parsonage
and schools at Bottisham Lode, those at Bottisham must not
be omitted. The school-room built in 1847, and adjoining Schools,
the master's house, is a neat building of brick, and the Vicarage Bottisham-
Vicarage.
on the Newmarket road is a very picturesque house constructed
by the Rev. John Hailstone, from designs prepared by the late
John Walter, Esq., Architect, of Cambridge.

The Church of England is not, however, accepted by all
the parishioners of Bottisham. For some years a congregation Indepen-
of Independents have formed themselves at Bottisham proper dent
Chapel.
under the auspices of Mr John Bradford Paul. Their chapel
formerly stood on the Cambridge road at the end of the
village, but in 1868 a new building was erected not far off in
the main street near the rectory farm. The present minister
is the Rev. A. H. Richardson. At Bottisham Lode also is a con- Baptist
gregation of Particular Baptists. Their chapel was opened for Chapel.
the first time on Aug. 9, 1810, and, as the *Cambridge Journal*

of that date specifies, "This infant cause owes its origin to
Mr Thomas Reynolds, resident in that place." The building
stands a little off the main street nearly opposite to the church,
and the present minister is the Rev. A. Woodrow, late of
Saxmundham.

*Parish
Registers.*   The registers at Bottisham go back as far as 1561 A.D.
On the 16th of November is the first Baptismal entry. From
1651 to 1658 A.D. there are no entries of Baptisms, shewing
thereby the confusion into which revolution had placed the
country. The first Marriage entry is in 1563. Amongst the
marriage entries I find the following memorandum : "Mem :
that upon the 16 day of March being Whitsunday Anno 1624
there came an old woman and her son to the church of Bottisham as two strangers and intreated Mr Watts Vicar that they
might receive the Communion at that time with him, which
he granted them, because he would not discourage any from
coming to their church. The parties inhabit in a place called
Nuns Hoult[1]—as strangers they were admitted and no otherwise
—witnesses all the communicants—By me curate there, Henry
Yates." Another memorandum records the appointment of
William Mott as parish registrar thus : "Mem:—These are
to certify that Wm. Mott, being chosen Parish register (*sic*)
within the Parish of Bottisham by such of the inhabitants and
Householders as are chargeable to the relief of the poor of
the said Parish of Bottisham, was this day being the 12th day
December 1653, sworn by me Sir Thomas Willys, Barronett,
one of the justices of the peace for this county and also approved
by me Roger Rant Esqre. one of the justices of the said county
as able and fit to put in operation all and every the powers and
authorities to him the said William Mott as Parish register
limited by an Act of Parliament touching marriages and regis-
tering thereof as also touching Births and Burials. Witness my
hand this day 12 Dec. 1653.

R. O. Rant."

The register of marriages is missing from 1687 to 1693,
and in 1710 they began to be solemnized at Trinity College

---

[1] This was an osier bed in the parish of Swaffham Bulbeck, formerly part of
the possessions of Swaffham Nunnery.—Vide Min. acc. temp. Hen. VIII.

Chapel. Burials began to be registered in 1569. John Bunt who was buried on 1st of January occasions the first entry. In 1570 occurs a quaint name, viz: Celesticola Knocke, wife of Robert, who was buried on the 25th of August. From 1585—1596 no burials are to be found. Those for the year 1631 are also missing, while those for the years 1632—1652 have been re-copied from the Diocesan register. In 1662 occurs the following entry. "Mrs Ceaster Citchenman, the wife of Bryan Citchinman, gent. of Cambridge was buried the 20th day of November." Also "John Bottesham, a towne child was buried the 31st day of December, 1665;" from which it would seem to have been the practice to name base children from the parish of their birth. In 1787, on the 27th of December, is the burial entry of Soame Jenyns, the author, with the following comment:—"What his literary character was, the world hath already judged for itself; but it remains for his Parish Minister to do his duty, by declaring, that while he registers the burial of *Soame Jenyns*, he regrets the loss of one of *the most amiable of men*, and one of the *truest Christians*. To the parish of Bottisham he is an irreparable loss. He was buried in this church, Dec. 27, near midnight, by William Lort Mansell, sequestrator; who thus transgresses the common forms of a register, merely because he thinks it to be the most solemn and lasting method of recording to posterity that the *finest understanding* has been united to the best heart."

Blomefield, in his Collections for Cambridgeshire, as well as Cole[1], mention that "in 1393 John Demoke, or Dymoke, died, and gave 6s. 8d. to Anglesey Priory, and 6s. 8d. towards maintaining the lights or torches in Lode Street, Longmeadow, and Bottisham streets, to which lights most that died here gave legacies, they being of great use to direct strangers and others by night." *Torches in the streets.*

The position or character of these torches we have little means of determining. One of the following list of benefactions would seem to shew that they were of wax:— *Benefactors to them.*

Isabel Foster, widow, in 1515 bequeathed 20d. to the torches

---

[1] Blomefield, *Coll. Cant.* p. 183. Cole MSS. Vol. IV. p. 14.

in Bottisham Street, and the same sum to the torches in Lode
and Longmeadow Street[1].

William Bunte, in 1517, left two bushels of barley for those
in Lode Street, while one bushel each for those in Bottisham
and Longmeadow[2].

Joane Lorkyn, in 1521, left 3s. 4d. to those in Bottisham,
20d. each to those in Lode and Longmeadow[3].

Richard Newton, in 1521, left 8d. to those in each of the
three streets[4].

John Wright, in 1527, left 12d. to the repair of the bells
and the torches in Lode Street, and 8d. to those in Bottisham
and Longmeadow[5].

Simon Shereman, in 1527, left 12d. to those in Lode, and
8d. to each of the two remaining streets[6].

Thomas Sewall, in 1528, left 2d. to each of the three
streets[7].

Robert Rande left a coomb of barley to those in Longmeadow
Street, and a bushel to Bottisham and Bottisham Lode
Streets[8].

Thomas Gaytts, in 1581, left a quarter of barley to Longmeadow torches, and two bushels to each of the two remaining
streets[9].

William Bunte, in 1545, left a pound of wax for those in
Lode Street[10].

When these torches were demolished, or what became of
the money, is quite unknown, but shortly after this century

ottisham eacon. Bottisham contained but one single beacon. Dugdale, in his
map (dated 1662, A.D.) of the great level, representing it as it
lay drowned[11], marks a mound with a beacon erected on it at
the side of the highway leading from Newmarket to Cambridge.
This map is drawn to scale, and the position of this beacon
corresponds to the end nearest Bottisham of Newmarket race-

eacon ourse. course, and the name of the Beacon course is still given to that

1 Cole MSS. Vol. LX. p. 119.   2 Cole, Vol. LX. p. 143.
3 ib. p. 156.   4 ib. p. 164.
5 ib. p. 196.   6 ib. p. 200.
7 ib. p. 210.   8 ib. p. 223.
9 ib. p. 225.   10 ib. p. 78.
11 *Hist. of Embankment,* Ed. 2, p. 375. London, 1680, fol.

part of the heath which terminates at the point where "the four mile stables" stand now, four miles, that is to say, from Newmarket. This beacon probably stood in Fuller's time, for while speaking of three illustrious men born in Bottisham, and called from their native place, he adds: "Let Bottisham hereafter be no more famed for its single becon, but for these three lights it afforded[1]." The mounds upon which these beacons were erected were early British "tumuli," or places of sepulture. "On the 11th of May, 1815, the Rev. Thomas Kerrich exhibited to the Archæological Society an urn found in a barrow on the Beacon hills, Newmarket heath. The drain of barrow measured thirty yards. The perpendicular height was eight or nine feet. There are more of these tumuli remaining; some of them very near to the place at which this, out of which the urn came, lately stood. They command an extensive view over the town of Cambridge, Gogmagog hills, &c.[2]" As there are now no tumuli within some little distance of the four mile stables, it is probable that the tumulus alluded to was that whereon Bottisham beacon rested. Some tumuli exist still nearer to Newmarket, on the Stetchworth estate, bearing the title of "The Links," and thus shewing that they also had beacons erected upon them, but they could hardly be said to command a view of Cambridge and the Gogmagog hills, even before the country was enclosed. While the country was open, half cultivated as it was in the middle ages, and containing large tracts lying under water, or but imperfectly drained, it must have been singularly bleak and desolate, and travelling a matter of no great safety. Bottisham, from the straggling character of its population, was singularly exposed, and highway robberies must have been not unfrequent there. Cole[3] mentions "the absolution of John Kendall, of Newmarket, in the church of Bottisham, 1458, who swore that he had been unjustly "accused of attacking, at a place in Bottisham called Orewelhede, John Porter and Thomas Grene, servants of Richard Horne, of Bottisham and stealing a horse of a grey color, value 10s., and

---

[1] Fuller's *Worthies of Cambs.* Ed. 1840, Vol. I. p. 230.
[2] *Archæologia*, Vol. XVIII. p. 436.
[3] Cole MSS. Vol. XXV. fol. 121.

another red sorrel, price 12s., two pakkes with linen cloth and
other merchandise, to the value of 24li. Before magister Robert
Ayscough, L. D., and Edmund Conyngesburgh, Dec. D., John
Ansty, sen., and Robert Ansty, Esqres., &c., six Presbiteri, seven
clerici officiated." Orewelhead is by the Newmarket road, at
the top of what is called Whiteland springs. Nothing further
is known of this Richard Horne; whether he was a relation of
the Horne of Cambs., who was Lord Mayor of London in 1487,
and bore arms gu. on a chev. int. 3 talbots pass. Ar., a
bugle horn sa., it is impossible to say; but a John Horne is
found as a witness to the will of Thomas Gaytts, of Bottisham,
which was proved on the 27th of January, 1532[1]. This highway from Cambridge to Newmarket was probably a good road
at an early period, but most of the other roads of the parish
were but little more than green lanes, or what are called in the
fen, droveways. Hence the population of the various hamlets
were little inclined to mix with one another till the year
1837.

Bottisham Lode, and the town of Bottisham, as it was called,
were separated by a green lane, and it was hard work for a
carriage to get from Bottisham to "the city," as Bottisham Lode
was called, and I believe is sometimes called now. This appella-
tion of "the city" probably owes its origin to the existence of
the Priory of Anglesey in the immediate vicinity, just as
cathedral towns are always denominated cities throughout
England. In the sixteenth century we find various benefactions
for the repair of the highways. For instance, in 1530, Robert
Rande left 3s. 4d.[2] In 1531 Thomas Gaytts left 3s. 4d.[3] In
1543 John Hasyll, of Swaffham Bulbeck, left 16d., or a cart
with a day's work[4]. In 1545 Robert Forster, also of Swaffham
Bulbeck, left five loads of clunch to be placed in Allington's lane,
by which I suppose is meant the road between Swaffham and
Bottisham[5]; and in 1541 Thomas Tompson, of Bottisham, left
6s. 8d. for the highways[6].

harities.   But in various times Bottisham has been richly endowed

[1] Cole MSS. vol. LX. p. 225.   [2] ib. p. 223.
[3] ib. p. 225.   [4] ib. p. 33.
[5] ib. p. 42.   [6] ib. p. 64.

with charities for the poor. First, Thomas Pledger, who died in 1599, left 21 acres 2 roods 19 perches for 8 poor people, and in 1621 Giles Breame left almshouses for 3 poor men. This latter benefaction is recorded on a board which formerly stood on the south side of the great screen in the church, but now is affixed to the north wall. Its inscription runs thus:—"Giles Breame Esq. son of Arthur Breame of East Ham in the county of Essex and Ann Allington daughter of Robert Allington of Horseheath in the county of Cambridge, Esqre; who married the daughter of Thomas Edwards of Swaffham in the said county: which Giles Breame disposed of the greater part of his estate to the building of almshouses, did build 6 almshouses in East Ham and endued them with £40 a year for 6 poor men, 3 in Bottisham in Cambridgeshire and 3 in East Ham in Essex by the payment of 20 nobles a year to each of them: the said Giles Breame died March 31, 1621, and made Sir Giles Allington of Horseheath aforesaid and others his executors to perform this trust. The estate which was first settled is sold and another settled for the same use at Braintree in Essex and now in the occupation of Edward Horton. This put up.

Churchwardens 1728. { Gilbert Misson. Matthias Dositer "

Giles Breame was buried at East Ham. His monument there bears the following coat of arms: Quarterly 1 & 4. az. on a chev. Ar. int. 3 talbots' heads erased O. as many mullets sa. 2 & 3. az. & O. a cross fleury counterchanged, impaling, sa. a lion rampant O. a canton of the 2nd for Edwards[1]. The next charity is that of John Salisbury. A small board now hangs over the inner doorway of the north porch of the church, having been removed from its former position near the tomb of Thomas Pledger. Its inscription runs thus:—"John Salisbury of Bottisham, who dyed in the year of our Lord God 1639, did sometime before his death give £10 to the town of Bottisham for ever, the use whereof quarterly to be disposed of by the minister and churchwardens of the said Parish for the teaching

---

[1] Lysons, *Environs of London*, Vol. IV. p. 144.

of 3 poor children of the said parish"—seven acres of land
were purchased with this sum and the annual value is about
£7. 0s. 0d. In the parish register I find John Childe 1675 in
the list of benefactors, but what he gave is unknown. In 1711
Mary Clench left a rent-charge for apprenticing poor children,
this charity now produces £5. 0s. 0d. This Mary Clench was
the wife of John Clench the elder, and mother of John Clench
who married Elizabeth, buried at Bottisham, and afterwards
Joanna Ward and removed to Wilbraham. In 1728 Sir Roger
and Lady Elizabeth Jenyns settled the schooling of 20 poor
children and clothing for the same. The annual value of this
bequest is £25. 0s. 0d. The dress of the boys is a green coat
with a green cap and red tassel; that of the girls a green dress
with a white cape and white bonnet. The school-house devoted to this charity stands in the main street of Bottisham
not far from the church. Above the doorway is the representation
of a 'green coat boy' and the arms of the Jenyns family.
Daniel Woolard seems to have been the first schoolmaster. He
was buried Nov. 12, 1746, and succeeded by Benjamin Kettle
who died July the 23rd, 1816, after having been 70 years schoolmaster. He was succeeded by John Dilliston, when by agreement the free school was incorporated into the national school
of the parish. In 1739 Samuel Shepheard, M.P., who lived
at Bendish and Anglesey and afterwards removed to Exning
in Suffolk, left a rent-charge for the poor, of which the annual
value is about £26. 0s. 0d.: but 3 years before in 1736 Dr. John
Craister the vicar gave £47. 10s. for which a house was purchased and the charity now yields about £14. 0s. 0d. Alderman
William Mott of Cambridge, who was brought up as a brick-
layer in this parish, settled in 1762 by deed of gift £5 out of
the land in Great and Little Eversden after a sermon by the
priest on that occasion preached here the last Sunday in March:
to the minister for preaching 10s., to the churchwardens and
overseers each for distributing 5s., to the clerk 2s. 6d., the
rest to poor settled inhabitants not receiving collections in such
proportion as the minister, churchwardens and overseers think
proper[1]. This charity used to be doled out in sixpences to

[1] Vide also *Gent. Mag.* Vol. LIX. p. 572.

such as came to hear the sermon, but now the distribution
of this charity is amalgamated with others. Alderman Mott
died September 28, 1772, aged 79 and was buried at Trinity
Church, Cambridge. In 1796 Elizabeth the wife of Soame
Jenyns left £200 3 per cent. consols for the poor, producing
an annual rental of £6. 0s. 0d.; but in 1825 the Rev. Wm. Pugh
vicar left the large sum of £3945. 16s. 8d. invested in 3 per
cents. and producing £118. 7s. 6d. yearly. This large charity is
devoted to various objects so as to promote the welfare of the
population. Thus, for benefactions Bottisham has been a
favoured village. The time however is now almost past when
large bequests of money are made to the poor, and the principle
of modern charitably disposed persons seems rather to be that
of helping those who help themselves.

"Chi si ajuta, Dio ajuta."

The poor had however misfortunes to contend with, for *Fires.*
twice during the last century was the village afflicted by that
most grievous scourge, fire. Amongst some loose papers of
Thomas Watson Ward, of Wilbraham, Cole found the following petition:—

"Cambridgeshire. Whereas on Sunday the 16th instant
a most dreadful fire broke out in the Parish of Bottisham
in the county aforesaid at 10 of the clock in the night of
the same day which in about the space of two hours consumed
the houses, outhouses, barns, household stuff, corn, and other
stock of above 20 families within the said Parish to the value
of £3000 and upwards to their utter ruin, so that they must
inevitably perish without the timely relief of such as are
charitably disposed. We therefore the minister and some of
the principal inhabitants of the said parish do hereby humbly
request and desire on the behalf of the said poor sufferers
your charitable aid and assistance towards the support of them
and of their families in this their distressed and afflicted condition. Witness our hands this 19th of November, 1712.

"Pray be pleased to gather from house to house"

| J. Whitfield, *Curate.* | J. Clenche. |
| Alex. Parker, | Rd. Dositer. |

Tho. Pamplin.   William Golding.
William Jelly.   Francis Newman.
Joseph Lawsell.   Thomas Maile.

Cole says the paper was torn and so no list of subscribers was seen. It was dated May 6, 1729, and subscribed J. L. and endorsed "Mr Clenche's illness prevents his writing himself." An extract from a newspaper of about the year 1795 gives an account of another large fire. It says:—"Friday, the village of Bottisham between Cambridge and Newmarket was in the greatest distress owing to a fire breaking out in the center of the place, which entirely consumed 6 houses and a malting. No lives were lost or corn burnt. It began about 11 o'clock in the morning, and was not extinguished till late at night, there being no engine at hand."—This fire was at the rectory farm not far from the church.

The next large fire broke out in Bottisham on the night of Friday, the 13th of February, 1846, whereby no less than 18 cottages were consumed and 70 poor people rendered houseless and destitute. It was caused by an incendiary, by name John Webb, who, as he afterwards confessed, put a handful of lucifer matches into some outbuildings belonging to the farm tenanted by Mr. Free, when they blazed out so fiercely that there was scarcely time to run away and avoid detection. The night was very tempestuous, and the wind kindled up the flames with great fury. It was with great difficulty that the occupants of the neighbouring cottages could be awakened from their slumbers, and the aged and infirm dragged forth into the street. The scene soon became one of extreme terror, infant children running through the churchyard in a state of nudity, and mothers semi-clad wandering in a distracted state in search of their helpless offspring. At this juncture the kindness of the poor people to one another was peculiarly striking, some assisting to move furniture and effects from the spot where the fire was raging, others making tea from their scanty stock for the benefit of those who were shivering in the cold. Meanwhile the fiery element still gained ground, and fears were entertained that nearly the whole village would be consumed.

At length, by the exertions of some labourers, a house was pulled down, and the gap thus caused impeded the flames.

Next morning the scene was one of confusion and disaster; the sufferers seeking refuge for the ensuing night, the vicar and churchwardens doing all they could to comfort and provide for the outcasts, and groups of parties hastening over from the neighbouring places to view the scene of desolation. The National School, hastily divided by wooden partitions, provided accommodation for four families: the Infant School served for another: and the Free School founded by Sir Roger Jenyns was allotted to the sixth family. The remainder of the sufferers were billeted from house to house, amongst their relations and friends. Nor was sympathy wanting amongst the inhabitants of neighbouring parishes. In three days after the event £200 was contributed unsolicited by any of the inhabitants of the parish.. Gifts of clothing soon followed, and at length the vicar was compelled to refuse any further donations. All the sufferers were liberally provided for.

Shortly after this, another fire took place, by which all the farm-buildings tenanted by Mr. Newman were destroyed as well as six calves, twenty pigs, some favourite greyhounds, and some ducks. Three cottages were also consumed. This fire broke out about three in the morning, and was supposed to have been the work of an incendiary.

CHAPTER IV.

FAMILY OF DE CLARE.

AMONGST the families of note that have been connected with
Bottisham, the great and powerful De Clares claim our first
attention. They took their names from the town of Clare in
Suffolk, and though at first they were only styled De Clare from
their manors in and about that town, they afterwards assumed
the title of Earl de Clare. Their connection with Bottisham
has the following origin. We have seen that at the period when
Domesday book was compiled Walter Giffard held Bottisham in chief from the king. His wife Agnes bore him a son
also named Walter, who married Ermengard, and who, in conjunction with his wife, founded the abbey of Nutley, in
Buckinghamshire[1]. His sister Roesia married Richard Fitz
Gilbert de Clare, who was buried at St. Neots, in the county of
Huntingdon. The offspring of this marriage was five in
number, the eldest of which, Gilbert de Tonnebridge (in Kent) or
de Clare married Adeliza, daughter of the Earl of Clermont, and
had two sons, Gilbert and Richard. Gilbert, surnamed Strongbow, played an important part in the history of England. He
died in 1148 A.D. and was buried at Tintern abbey. His wife
Elizabeth, sister of Waleran, Earl of Mellent, bore him a son,
named Richard, who was Earl of Strigul in Ireland. This

---

[1] In 1179 A.D. 26 Hen. II. William Fitz-Ralph and William le Chaplein for
the wife of Geoffrey Fitzwilliam account to the King for the Honor of Earl
Giffard. They account for the farm of the Honor, the increment of Wichinton,
the aid to marry the Lady Maud, the King's daughter, the escuage of Ireland,
the increment of Bodekesham, xviiis., &c.—*Mag. Rot.* 26 Hen. II., quoted by
Madox, *Bar. Ang.* p. 71.

Richard married Eva, daughter of Dermot, King of Dublin, and before his death, in 1176, had a daughter named Isabel, who married William Mareschall, Earl of Pembroke, and who was made coheir of the Giffard family. To go back to Richard, the brother of Gilbert Strongbow, brings us to Richard de Clare, Earl of Hertford, the founder of the Priory of Tonbridge in Kent. He married Adeliza, sister of Ranulph, Earl of Chester, and had issue Gilbert, Earl of Clare, who died without issue in 1151 A.D., and was buried at Clare, and Roger, who succeeded his brother in the Earldom of Clare, and died in 1173 A.D. He married Maud, the daughter of James de St Hilary, and had a son, Richard, Earl of Clare, who, with Isabel Mareschall, became coheir of the Giffards. On the division of the property, Bottisham fell to the lot of Richard de Clare, so that it is unnecessary to enter further into the descent of the Earls of Pembroke. Richard de Clare married Annie, the daughter and coheir of William, Earl of Gloucester; she was the foundress of Sudbury Hospital in Suffolk, and brought the Earldom of Gloucester into the family of the De Clares.

This Richard died in 1206 A.D., and is stated by some authors to have founded a religious house at Anglesey. We shall however have occasion hereafter to consider more in detail the earliest records of the foundation of that house. Richard de Clare had a son and a daughter: the daughter, named Roesia, married Roger de Mowbray, and the son, Gilbert, succeeded his father in the Earldoms of Clare and Gloucester, and became also Earl of Hertford. He died in 1229 A.D., and lies buried at Tewkesbury. His wife Isabel, the daughter of William Mareschall, Earl of Pembroke, bore two sons and died ten years afterwards. The eldest of these, Richard, Earl of Clare, Gloucester and Hertford, first married Margaret, the daughter of Hubert de Burgh, from whom he was subsequently divorced. He then married Maud, the daughter of John de Lacy, Earl of Lincoln, in 9 Hen. III., who bore issue Gilbert the Red and Thomas de Clare.

Richard de Clare died on the 18th of June, 1262, A.D., and was buried at Tewkesbury. From the inquisition taken in the following year we find the extent of the tenements and fees possessed by him in the County of Cambridge. The jury then declared "That William, the son of Martin, and John de Darlee, held one fee in Botekesham. And they said that the Earl held in Botekesham of rent of assize twelve pounds five pence farthing. And they said that the Earl was patron of the priory of Anglesey; and that the pleas and perquisites of the Courts of Bodekesham and Croyroys (=Royston—Crux Roesiæ) amounted to forty pounds: and he had no demesne in the County of Cambridge, so that he had in Bottisham of rent of assize £12. 0s. 5¼d., the patronage of the Priory of Anglesey, and a share of £40 for the perquisites of the Courts of Bottisham and Royston[1]." From the remembrance of the muniments of Philippa, wife of Edmund Mortimer, Earl of March, we find that King Henry gave him rights to fairs and markets in the town of Bottisham, all which rights were enjoyed by his descendants[2]. Gilbert, surnamed the Red, succeeded his father as Earl of Clare, Gloucester and Hertford. He married first Alice de March, from whom he was divorced before the thirteenth year of the reign of Edward the First, and he then married Joanna de Acres, the king's daughter, and became the most powerful noble in the realm. He died in 1295 A.D., and his widow then married Ralph Monthermer, to the great anger of the King. In this reign was taken the inquisition of the several hundreds in the County of Cambridge. From this document we find that Gilbert de Clare held Bottisham entire in chief of the King of the honor of Walter Giffard, Earl of Buckingham, and that his mother, the Countess Matilda, held it in dower for the term of her life. He also held in the same place view of frank-pledge once a year, and all things pertaining to it, and whatever pertained to royalty. The Priors of Anglesey and Tonbridge held the manor of Bottisham, but a certain portion seems to have been reserved to the De Clares, which was held by the aforesaid priors, as well as various tenants, and free tenants of the heirs of William, the son of William the son of Martin, John de Deresle, John the

---

[1] Inq. post mortem, 47 Hen. III. Whether John de Darlee is not a mistake for John de Deresly, vide Hundred Rolls, temp. Ed. I.

[2] Brit. Mus. Add. MSS. 6041, fol. 92 b.

son of Geoffrey, Sir Symon de Mora, William de Robercot, William de Angerhale and Geoffrey Marshall. Gilbert de Clare died in 1295 A.D., and his son Gilbert being then under age, the title of Gloucester and Hertford fell to Ralph Monthermer, together with view of frank-pledge, and other rights, during the lifetime of his wife Joanna[1]. The inquisition taken after her death in 1305 states that she held in conjunction with her husband Gilbert, in Bottisham, one acre of land, and a rental of £12. 3s. 1d., together with view of frank-pledge. Her son Gilbert, who had succeeded to the honours enjoyed by his father, did not live long, for he was slain at the battle of Bannockburn, in 1314 A.D. His only son died in infancy, so that his estates devolved upon two of his sisters, Margaret and Elizabeth. The earldom of Clare then became extinct, but that of Hertford passed to Elizabeth, while that of Gloucester passed to Margaret, and thence into the hands of the family of Stafford.

The eldest son of John de Burgh was William, who suc- *Family of* ceeded his father in the title of Earl of Ulster, while from his *De Burgh.* mother he gained the right to be styled Earl of Hertford. He married Maud Plantagenet, and died in 1333, leaving his sole daughter Elizabeth as his heiress, married to Lionel, Duke of Clarence. At his death, in 1369, Philippa was left sole daughter and heiress, who was the wife of Edmund de Mortimer, Earl of *Family of* March, and in right of his wife Earl of Ulster. Thus the great *De Morti-* house of Clare had become extinct, and its fortunes, after pass- *mer.* ing through the house of Burgh, had merged into those of the Earls of March. Thus we find that at the death of Edmund Mortimer, on the 27th of December, 1381, he was possessed of £14. 3s. 9d. rent in the parishes of Bottisham, Swaffham Prior, Swaffham Bulbeck, and Horningsey, as well as the view of frank-pledge in the parish of Bottisham[2]. At the death of Edmund, Roger de Mortimer (or de Mortuo Mari) succeeded as Earl of March and Ulster. He was born on the 11th of April, 1374, and was buried at Wigmore after his death, which took place on the 20th of July, 1398. He married

---

[1] Plac. de quo war. 27 Ed. I.

[2] Inq. post mortem 5 Ric. II. He was a benefactor to the House of Anglesey.

Alianore, daughter of Thomas de Holland, and sister and coheir of Edmund de Holland, Earl of Kent. She was married a second time to Lord Powys, and died on the 23rd of December, 1405 A.D. On the 6th of November, 1391, a son was born to the first marriage, and named Edmund. Consequently, he succeeded as Earl of March and Ulster, and before his death, on the 19th of Jan., 1424, married Anne, the daughter of Edmund, Earl of Stafford, sister of Humphrey, Duke of Buckingham. There was no issue of this marriage, and Anne espoused, for the second time, John de Holland, Earl of Huntingdon. Edmund de Mortimer had, however, a sister who, after marriage with Richard Plantagenet, Earl of Cambridge, and brother of Edward, Duke of York, had a son Richard, who became heir to Edmund, Earl of March, and was the father of King Edward the Fourth. Thus the property of the Earls of March fell into the hands of the King. The inquisition taken after the death of the last Earl of March declared that he held a tenement in Bottisham called "Vauses Rent," as well as a court-leet in the same parish, together with £14. 10s. 0d. rent of assize, in that place and Litlington, Abington, Harlton and Morden, as parcel of the feod of Gloucester[1].

amily of tafford.   Mention has been made before of the marriage of Margaret de Clare with Hugh, Baron Audley, Earl of Gloucester. As coheiress of Gilbert de Clare she inherited certain lands in Bottisham. These passed through her daughter and heiress, Margaret, to the husband of the latter, viz. Ralph, second Baron, and Earl of Stafford by creation on the 5th of March, 1351; of his sons, Ralph, the eldest, though married to Maud, daughter of the Earl of Derby, died without issue in the lifetime of his father, and Hugh, the second son, succeeded as Earl of Stafford. He married Lady Philippa Beauchamp, daughter of Thomas, Earl of Warwick, and before his death, in 1386, had four sons, Ralph, Thomas, William and Edmund. Ralph was murdered in 1385, so that the title came to the next son, Thomas: he married Anne, sister and heiress of Humphrey Plantagenet, Earl of Buckingham, but firstly Anne, daughter of Thomas of Woodstock. At his death, without issue, in 1392

---

[1] Inq. p. mortem, 2 Hen. VI.

A.D. the next brother, William, was the heir. This William was born in 1378, so that he was a minor when the estates devolved upon him. He died on the 6th of April, 1395, and his next brother, Edmund, succeeded. An inquisition was made in the 22nd year of Richard the Second's reign, and it was then stated that, by reason of the minority of William, Earl of Stafford, "there came into the hands of the king, at the death of his brother Thomas, amongst other lands, one knight's fee in Bodekesham, which the Prior of Anglesey, William Wolf, Maurice Tone, Robert Passelewe, William Magot, Geoffrey Portere, John Jemys, and William Myttelweye held, and it was worth, when it should happen, one hundred shillings. And the jurors said that Thomas, Duke of Gloucester, received all the issues and profits of the aforesaid knight's fee from the time of the death of Thomas, late Earl of Stafford, till the time of his death; and that Edward, Duke of Albemarle, received all the issues and profits of the aforesaid knight's fee from the time of the death of the aforesaid Thomas, Duke of Gloucester, and still receives them; and they said that the aforesaid fee is holden of the Lord the King in chief, as of the honor of Gloucester by knight's service[1]." Upon attaining his majority, Edmund succeeded to the title and estates, and married, by special license from the king, Anne, the widow of his eldest brother, Thomas. He died on the 22nd of July, 1402, and had one son and two daughters. Of the daughters, Philippa died young, and Anne, we have seen, was married first to Edmund Mortimer, Earl of March, and secondly to John Holland, Earl of Huntingdon. Humphrey, the son, who succeeded his father to the Earldom of Stafford, was created, on the 14th of September, 1444, Duke of Buckingham, and was slain at the battle of Northampton, in 1459. He married Anne, daughter of the Earl of Westmoreland, who, after his death, was united to Sir Walter Blount, knight, and died in the 20th year of the reign of Edward the Fourth. By her first husband she had a son Humphrey, who married Margaret, daughter and coheiress of Edmund, Duke of Somerset, and died in 1455, at the battle of St Albans. His son Henry, who succeeded him, married Catherine, daughter

Family of Buckingham.

---

[1] Inq. p. mortem, 22 Ric. II.

of Richard Widville, Earl Rivers, and was beheaded at Salisbury in 1485. His son Edward married Alianore, daughter of the Earl of Northumberland, but he was beheaded in 1521, and his estates forfeited to the Crown, though his son Henry partially regained them, while the earldom of Buckingham became extinct. The descent of these three families of 'De Clare, Mortimer and Stafford, will be better seen by the annexed pedigree[1].

De Bottisham.   At the period when the family of De Clare were most influential in Bottisham are found the names of many who were tenants of the various Earls, and took their names from their native place. These men appear in three different characteristics, that of simple landowners, that of merchants, and that of priests.

Aug. de B.   First, we find the name of Augustin de Bodekesham and Eluina his wife, who, with Hugh his son on behalf of William the son of Lambert, pleaded against Richard of Dullingham concerning certain land in Dullingham in 1199 A.D.[2]. They appear to have gained their cause, and the property seems to

Hugh de B.   have descended from Augustin the father to Hugh the son in regular course. Consequently, in a 'fine' or final concord, dated July, 1202 A.D., and made between Hugh de Bodekesham plaintiff and Richard the son of Walter deforciant, we find that the aforesaid Richard acknowledged two acres of land with the appurtenances to be right and hereditament of the said Hugh, and Hugh on his part for this agreement conceded to the aforesaid Richard and his heirs the moiety of the aforesaid land with its appurtenances, to be held by him and his heirs for ever by the free service of four pence for all service, except foreign service, to be paid in two payments by the year[3]. Two years after this, however, another 'fine' was made between Hugh de Bodekesham and William the son of Lambert plain-

---

[1] But Humphrey, Duke of Buckingham, was the last of this house who possessed a fee in Bottisham; for the King, Ed. IV:, granted in the first year of his reign to Cecilia, his mother, lands, &c., to the value of 5000 marks, amongst which mention is made of £12 rent, with the appurtenances and court-leets of the honor of Gloucester in Bottisham, Royston, Morden, Meldreth, Tadlow, Abington, Harlton, and Toft, and fees and parts of fees belonging to his father. Vide Rot. Pat. 1 Ed. IV. p. 4, m. 1, quoted in Add. MS. 6693, fo. 49.

[2] Palgrave, Rot. Cur. Reg. II. 114, Nov. 8, 1199 A.D.

[3] Hunter, *Fines,* I. 302.

De .
ham

Aug

Hug
de B

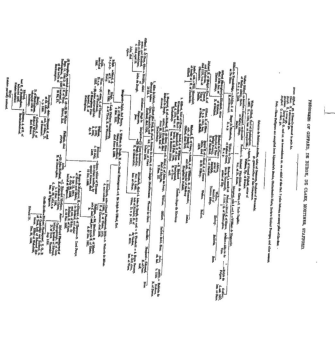

PEDIGREES OF GIFFARD, DE RIDDEL, DE CLARE, MORTIMER, STAFFORD.

De
hai

Au,

Hu,
de ₁

tiffs, and William Malet deforciant, concerning two acres of land in Dullingham. And a certain Gerard, the son of Wido, called the same William Malet, and guaranteed to him and quit-claimed him of all right to certain of his lands; and for this quitclaim, William Malet gave and conceded to the aforesaid Hugh three acres of land with the appurtenances in Dulling-ham, and certain land lying before the door of Robert the son of Richard, that is to say, at the head of the croft of Roger the Palmer one rod and a half near the land of Walter[1] * * * Rad-strete, and one rod and a half near the land of Geoffrey Stugit at Hartibege, and one rod which abuts upon Green Strete, near the land of the aforesaid Geoffrey, rendering thereby at Easter threepence, and at Michaelmas threepence, and[1] * * * and to William the son of Lambert forty shillings[2]. Another 'fine' is extant, dated September, 1200 A.D., between Reginald the clerk plaintiff and Hugh de Bodekesham deforciant, con-cerning five acres of land with the appurtenances in Dulling-ham, whereby the said Reginald conceded all rights to the aforesaid land to Hugh and his heirs, and the said Hugh for this quitclaim gave to Reginald half-a-mark of silver[3]. Another 'fine' was made in 1202, between Hugh de Bodekesham plain-tiff and a certain Gerard deforciant, of two acres of land with the appurtenances in Bottisham. By this agreement Hugh's title to the land was maintained, and a certain piece of land given to the aforesaid Gerard by the service of 31 pence, of which $15\frac{1}{2}d.$ were to be paid at Michaelmas, and $15\frac{1}{2}d.$ to be paid at Easter[4]. This Hugh is in various documents styled Parson and Clerk of Bodekesham, and possessed land in Stan-don, co. Herts[5].

A contemporary of his was Geoffrey de Bodekesham, as we *Geoffrey* find by a plea made in 1199, between Eustace de Eie and Geoffrey *de B.* de Bodekesham and Reginald de Ditton[6]. In the next year a plea was made between Alan the chaplain and Geoffrey de Bodekesham concerning one virgate of land with the appurte-

---

[1] Blank in the original.

[2] Hunter, *Fines*, I. 312.   [3] Ib. I. 287.   [4] Ib. I. 306.

[5] Vide, New Record office, Chap. Ho. department, *Dom. Deeds*, Nos. 101, 102, 116.

[6] Palgrave, Rot. Cur. Regis, I. 281.

nances in Ditton[1]. Two years after, in 1202 A.D., a 'fine' was
made between Geoffrey de Bodegesham and * * * concerning
half a virgate of land and nine acres in Dittone, whereby the
said Geoffrey remitted and quitclaimed the right he had in the
said land in favour of Eustace, and the said Eustace conceded
to Geoffrey and his heirs three[2] (acres?) at Staniland, and half
an acre at the road of Hinton, and half[2] (an acre?) at 'Bissanal,'
and one acre at Walhill, by certain service, of which four-pence
halfpenny was to be paid at Easter, and Eustace took homage[3].

artin
B.

The next name mentioned in documents as a landholder is
that of Martin de Bodegesham and Agatha his wife, who caused
a fine to be made between them and Robert de Katestun of six
shillings rent in Caston in 1218[4]. This Martin appears to have
had a son named William, and a grandson also named William,
whose wife's name was Alice. We now come to the period of
the Hundred Rolls of the time of Edward the First. There we
find that Alice de Bodegesham and Catherine de Frating held
in Teversham parish seven acres of land of William Warbilton,
and John Arnet held of Alice de Bodegisham three acres and a
half by the service of three shillings a year. In Bercham, a hamlet of Linton, Alured Mantein held free forty acres of land with
a messuage, two acres and one rood of meadow of the heirs of

ill. fil.
artin.

er. Will.
. Will.
. M.

William the son of Martin de Bodekesham by the service of
five shillings, and the said heirs held them of the bishop of
Ely, and the said bishop of the Lord King in chief. The heirs
of William, the son of William the son of Martin, must have
been very influential in Bottisham at this period, for besides
holding certain lands from the Earl of Clare in chief, they had
no less than twenty-five free tenants in the parish. John, the
son of Geoffrey, was also influential. He is sometimes styled
John de Longo Prato or Langmeadow, as also is Geoffrey. His
free tenants numbered fourteen. William, the son of William,
and Alice his wife, appear to have had two daughters: their
names were Semele and Matilda. Of the latter, Milicent de
Leycester held two acres in Teversham parish by the service of

---

[1] Palgrave, Rot. Cur. Regis, I. 225.   [2] Blank in original.
[3] Hunter, Fines, I. 306.
[4] Blomefield, Hist. of Norfolk, Vol. II. p. 257.

twopence yearly. Semele appears to have had some property in Ditton Valence or Wood Ditton, which, by a document dated 1282 A.D., she made over to her sister Matilda and her husband, Henry the son of Odo of Swaffham Bulbeck, together with her house and lands in Bottisham[1].

Joseph de Botekesham and Cecilia his wife were also living *Joseph de B.* at this period. They probably resided at Wicken, for they had large possessions there; and in 1272 A.D. a fine was made, whereby they gave all right over a messuage and twenty acres of land in Wicken to the Prior of Anglesey and Convent of the same place. In the Hundred Rolls of 1279 occur the names of two of his sons, Richard the son of Joseph at Bottisham, and Henry the son of Joseph at Quy. It is not improbable that Cecilia was the daughter of Henry de Hupwere, and widow of Torold de Burgo, and the owner of Thornhall in the parish of Wicken.

Passing now to a different period of history, we find various merchants of note who took their surnames from their native place.

Firstly, we find Thomas de Botesham, mayor of Lynn, in *Thos. de B.* 1356, 1362, and 1368[2]. Thomas Botehesham was also mayor in 1433[2]; but it must have been another Thomas, for a Thomas Botekysham was alderman of one guild in Lynn, while another Thomas was alderman of another. In 1380 we find that John de Brunham, John de Perteneye, and Adam Skert, burgesses of Lynn, grant to Jeffrey Talboth, Thomas Botekysham, John de Dockyn, &c. two shillings, which they used to receive of the heirs of John de Syssewell of West Lenne, for the liberty of a ferry of a passage boat over the water. Dated at Lenne Bishop on Sunday after the feast of the purification of the Blessed Virgin Mary, 3 Rich. II. "This guild," says Richards[3], "which was that of Corpus Christi, must therefore have been in possession of a ferryboat, &c., and must have been a fraternity of some consequence." There was another large merchants' guild dedicated to the Holy Trinity, which was said to have its rise

---

[1] Cole MSS. Vol. xviii. fol. 46.
[2] Mackarell, *Hist. of Lynn*, p. 274.
[3] *Hist. of Lynn*, Vol. i. p. 443.

and beginning before the reign of King John, as appears from
the answer of Thomas Botesham, alderman of it, and his brethren in the time of Richard II.[1] Thomas Botesham appears
also as alderman of this guild in 1370 A.D., and in 1379 A.D.[2]
These two names could not represent one individual, as appears
from a transcript of the original statutes and foundation of the
guild of S. Clement, Pope and Martyr, founded in the parish
church of S. Clement in Cambridge, from Trinity College Library MSS. marked O. 7. 15[3]. These statutes are dated A.D.
1431; and under the title of 'exequiæ observandæ non hic
expressæ' we find "obitus Thome Botsham, Rob'ti Garlond, and
Joh'ne ux'is eor'd'," which proves that he was dead before 1431,
whereas a Thomas Botekesham was mayor in 1433, so that the
two persons would probably be son and father. Thomas Botkes-
ham of Lynn gave (though when is not stated) to the nuns of
Swaffham Bolebec a good iron chest to keep the books in[4].

Rob. de B.　　　Robert Botehesham was also a merchant at Lynn. He
was mayor three times: first in 1395, secondly in 1403, and
thirdly in 1410[5]; but during this year I find him with eight
other merchants of Bishop's Lynn praying for a safe-conduct
across the sea[6], and his name does not appear afterwards.

John de B.　　　John Bottysham was treasurer of the town and corporation
of Cambridge in the year 1425 and bailiff in the year 1432[7].
This may be the same John that was a goldsmith of London, as
appears from the Issue Rolls, dated July 5th, 1385: "To my
lord the king in his chamber, by the hands of John Bottesham of London, goldsmith, for a knife to be used in the woods,
and a horn ornamented with gold, weighing 16 ounces less one
drachm of gold, made by him for the lord the king for his
hunting horn in the summer season, this ninth year, together
with the making thereof and tassels of green silk for the same,
£25. 17s. 4d.[8]"

[1] *Hist. of Lynn*, Vol. I. pp. 450, 451, 452.　　[2] Ib. p. 462, p. 467 note.
[3] Cole MSS. Vol. XLV. fol. 12.　　　　　　　[4] Blomefield, *Coll. Cant.* p. 183.
[5] Mackarell, *Hist. and Ant. of Lynn*, p. 274.
[6] Nicholas, *Acts of the Privy Council*, Vol. I. p. 317.
[7] Cole MSS. Vol. XLV. fol. 12; Vol. XXXII. fol. 136. Cooper, *Annals*, I. 173.
[8] Devon, *Iss. of the Exchequer*, p. 231.

Though this parish bred many men who took their surnames from it, alike famous by reason of the lands they held or the commerce that they promoted, there were many who dedicated themselves to the priestly office, of whom some became illustrious in the middle ages. Robert de Botysham held the vicarage of Folsham in Norfolk, in 1307, to which benefice he was preferred by its patron, Robert de Say[1]. Andrew de Botekesham had the king's letters of presentation to the rectory of St Margaret's, Lothbury, succeeding John de Haslingfeld on Feb. 16, 1317[2]. Francis Bottisham was vicar of Clacton Parva, in the archdeaconry of Colchester, and the deanery and hundred of Tendring, from which benefice he was preferred on the 21st of July, 1367, to the vicarage of Steple, with the chapelry of Stanesgate, in the archdeaconry of Essex and the deanery and hundred of Denge[3]. Thomas de Bottlesham was archdeacon of Rochester in 1397[4]. Bartholomew de Bodekysham appears to have been a benefactor to the University of Cambridge from the following item in the account of the mass for the benefactors: "item pro anima M'ri Bartholomæi de Bodekysham[5]." Richard Botysham was ordained by William Gray, Bishop of Ely, accolite of Over in the same diocese in 1455. On the 3rd of November, 1458, he was instituted to the rectory of Wycham in the Isle of Ely, which he resigned on the 6th of January, 1461. He appears to have been ordained to the title of his benefice of Holton in the diocese of Norwich[6]. But most famous of all were the triumvirate of learned men, as Fuller calls them, viz. William of Botlesham, John of Botlesham, and Nicholas of Botlesham. William and John have been confounded with one another by various writers, as well as with their contemporaries, William and John, who were also priests of eminence, but not bishops as were the former. For the sake of perspicuity, we will first take those who did not attain to the episcopal throne. William

[1] Blomefield, *Hist. of Norfolk*, Vol. VIII. p. 208.
[2] Rot. Pat. 2 Ed. II. Newcourt, *Rep. Eccl. Lond.* I. 301.
[3] Ib. II. 154, 559.
[4] Le Neve, *Fast. Eccl. Angl.* II. 580.
[5] Cole MSS. Vol. XXI. fol. 130.
[6] Cole MSS. Vol. XXV. fols. 50, 65, 74, 187, 188.

Botelesham was incumbent of Wilby in the hundred of Hamford in Northamptonshire: he succeeded Peter Mouvrelee, priest, on the 5th of August, 1373, and on the 24th of April, 1403, was preferred to Thornhaugh in the hundred of Nassaburgh[1]. John Bottesham was appointed archdeacon of Leicester in the diocese of Lincoln, by the king, on the 7th of February, 1389—90[2]: but the Pope gave this preferment to Poncellinus de Ursinis, a cardinal priest, by the title of S. Clement; upon which arose a lawsuit betwixt the contending parties, which remained a long time undecided, but at length John (rather than offend the see apostolic) renounced his pretensions. The king confirmed the cardinal's appointment on the 18th of December[3]. Then one John Elvet procured a grant of the same from the king on the 30th of May[4]; but the king soon after varying from that grant made another to Richard Holland on the 17th of July[5]. At length, the suit being determined in favour of the king's right of presentation, he revoked the grant made to Richard Holland and settled it on John Elvet[6]. After this he was made prebend of London for the stall of Ealdland, Ealdeland, Ealdlond, or Ealdelond, succeeding John Dysseford, who resigned on the 21st of May, 1412[7]. Whether this is the same as the preceding is doubtful, but we find M'gr John Botelesham, presbyter, made rector of Brampton Magna on the 6th of March, 1394[8]. We find also a John Botissham, rector of Hanslope in 1406, as appears from the following extract from the Issue Rolls of the Exchequer: "To Richard, earl of Warwick, sent as the king's ambassador to the duke of Burgundy, to treat with him upon certain secret affairs concerning our lord the king and good of his whole realm.' In money paid to him by the

---

[1] Whalley, *Northants.* Vol. II. pp. 155, 597, from Reg. Hen. Beaufort, Bp. Lincoln.

[2] Le Neve, *Fast. Eccl.* II. 60. Pat. 13 Ric. II. p. 2. m. 11.

[3] Pat. 14. Ric. II. p. 2. m. 39.

[4] Pat. 15. Ric. II. p. 2. m. 7.

[5] Pat. 16. Ric. II. p. 1. m. 20, 26.

[6] Le Neve, *Fast. Eccl.* Vol. II. p. 360 note.

[7] Ib. Vol. II. p. 383. Reg. Dec. et Cap. fol. 26. Newcourt, *Rep. Eccl. Lond.* Vol. I. p. 146.

[8] Whalley, *Northants.* Vol. I. p. 490.

hands of John Botissham, rector of Hanslope, his receiver, &c., for his wages and passage by sea in the embassy aforesaid. By writ, &c. £40. 0s. 0d.[1]."

We now come to Nicholas of Bottlesham, of whom Cole gives us a short notice. "He was born (says he), as his name imports, in this parish (Bottisham), from whence he was sent to Cambridge, and placed in the convent of the Carmelites, of which fraternity he afterwards became a monk: this convent stood between King's and Queens' Colleges, in the very place where our Provost's (King's) garden is, the walls of which are still standing, and make the division between the said gardens and those belonging to the master of Queens' College; nay, to this day, our gate which goes out of the chapel yard to Saint Catherine's Hall and Queens' College, is always called the Fryer's gate. These fryers were very near, but by what appears of them, very bad neighbours; for there was such an animosity between them and the fellows of King's College, that there was an order made that whenever the last had occasion to go out towards their convent, they might do so armed to defend themselves: what gave rise to this dissension I never heard. However, this by the bye, for friar Nicholas de Bottesham was quite out of the scrape, and never bore our college any grudge, being dead before it was founded. He studied philosophy and divinity at Cambridge, and made great proficiency therein; but transplanting himself from thence he went to Paris, where for his singular talents he was created doctor of the Sorbonne: from whence returning afterwards to Cambridge he was elected prior of his convent, and was famous for his great learning and knowledge, and here published many books of good estimation: a catalogue of which you have in Pits and Bale. But dying at last in his convent at Cambridge, about 1435[2], he was buried in the chapel belonging to the same. Nicholas de Bottisham was official to the archdeacon of Ely in 1374[3]." Fuller gives the same account of him[4], though in a succinter form. Subjoined

---

[1] Devon, *Iss.* p. 347.
[2] 1439 A.D. Carter's *Cambs.* p. 133.
[3] Cole MSS. Vol. XLI. fols. 6, 16.
[4] *Worthies*, Vol. I. p. 192.

is the list of his works from Bale's catalogue, in which is the following preface[1]:

"Hæc enim sunt quæ Lelandus de Botleshamo tradit."
"Commentarios sententiarum.
"Quæstiones theologiæ.
"Tabulare studentium.
"In cantica Ridevallis.
"Conciones et Lecturas.
"Lib. IV. circa primum patrem prologi.
"Lib. I. circa primam dubitationem.
"Lib. I. ad utilitatem studentium hæc.
"Lib. I. De commendatione Aaron, aliqua."
"Præter hæc nihil opusculorum ejus in bibliothecis hucusque vidi."

The second of Fuller's triumvirate of learned men was William de Bodekesham. Cole says[2] that "he was prior of Anglesey in 1397. He was born in this parish, from whence, as was customary in those times, he took his name. I find he was subprior of Anglesey in 1388, and was by the bishop of Ely appointed to be confessor to the prioress and nuns of Swaffham, just by[3]. He was prior of Anglesey, according to Willis, an. 1397, which seems to be a mistake, for he was long before that a bishop in partibus, by the title of bishop of Bethlehem; and from the visionary see was translated to the then rich one of Llandaff, the temporalities of which were restored to him on the 25th of August, 1386. He was a Dominican friar and a doctor of divinity of the University, and for his learning and eloquence much esteemed by king Richard the Second, who translated him from Llandaff to the see of Rochester, notwithstanding the monks had lawfully elected one John Barnet to that bishopric: but he was also favoured by pope Urban the Sixth, who also encouraged this translation,

---

[1] Bale, *Scrip. Ill. Cat.* p. 577.
[2] Cole MSS. Vol. IV. fol. 12.
[3] There seems to be some confusion here between two persons of the same name. The nuns of Swaffham certainly elected the Sub-prior of Anglesey, Wm. de B., as their Confessor in 1389, vide Ely registers and Leland, *Collect.* Vol. V. p. 402.

and to whom he was very dear, by reason of his abiding with him in his persecutions; the temporalities were restored to him by the king on the 12th of February, 1389. I must not forget to mention that he was a fellow of Pembroke Hall. Walsingham, Bale, and others call him John, but falsely. Wharton says that he received his temporalities and spiritualities at Lambeth from the archbishop, having taken the oath of obedience before on the 14th or 15th of December, 1389. He died about the beginning of February, 1399, and notice thereof having been sent to the archbishop on the 26th of the same month, he was buried in the church of the brothers of his order in London. In another account of him, Cole says, "that the bull for his translation from Landaff is dated 17 Cal. Nov. 1385. The temporalities were restored on the 21st of August, 1386. His will is in register Arundel, fol. 266, and appoints to be buried in the cemetery of the friars Preachers in London. It is dated Feb. 16, 1399, in which month and year he died, viz. about Feb. 20; notice of his death to the archbishop is dated Feb. 25. A sure token of the poverty of Landaff bishopric by being exchanged for Rochester. This I should guess," Cole adds, "is remarked in contradiction to Dr Rawlinson, who in his list of bishops of Rochester, p. 89, in *The History and Antiquities of Rochester Cathedral*, published by him in 8vo., 1723, says, that William de Bottlesham, bishop of Landaff, was translated from that then opulent see hither [1]." Thus far Cole's account of him, which does not seem to be free from error, for I find that he was preferred by papal authority in 1386 to the see of Llandaff, the temporalities of which were restored to him on the 21st of August in that year[2]. In 1389 he was appointed by bull of provision, under Urban VI., dated 27th of August, Bishop of Rochester[3], and on the 14th of December following made his profession of obedience to the archbishop[4], and received the spiritualities and temporalities

---

[1] Cole MSS. Vol. xxviii. fol. 19.

[2] Le Neve, *Fast. Eccl. Angl.* Vol. ii. p. 247; Pat. 10 Ric. II. p. 1, m. 31, p. 2, m. 20.

[3] Reg. Courtn. fol. 328; vide Hasted, *Kent*, ii. 39; Wharton, *Angl. Sacra*, Vol. i. p. 379.

[4] Ib.

from the archbishop on the same day[1], and having done fealty
to the king, he obtained the restitution of his temporalities
from him also on the 12th of Feb. 1389—90[2]. After his death
the archbishop, by virtue of his prerogative, issued his license
for the election of a bishop in the room of William de Bottlesham on the 26th of Feb. 1399—1400, and granted the custody
of the spiritualities to Robert Hallum on the 15th of the following March[3]. His will, though dated 16th Feb. 1399—1400,
was not proved until the 23rd of May, 1402[4]. Upon the coronation of Richard the Second, Walsingham informs us he made
a speech to the people, in which he laboured to allay the
prevailing discontents, and exhorted his auditors to forsake
their fornications and adulteries, and imitate the purity and
innocence of the young king[5]. The following list of his works
is from Tanner's *Bibl. Britt. Hib.* p. 109:

In Cantica Salomonis, Lib. I.

In Threnos Hieremiæ, Lib. I.

In Epistolam ad Romanos, Lib. I.

Of the third of the triumvirate, John de Bottlesham, Cole
gives the following account[6]: "He was born at Bottisham and
was Licentiate of Law, and about 1398 was vicar general to
the archbishop of York, Richard Scrope[7], and after domestic
chaplain to Thomas Arundel, archbishop of Canterbury, which
may account, perhaps, for the lion ramp. A. in a field G. and a
bordure: a part of the arms of the archbishop in the chancel of
this church (Bottisham)." (He adds this note: "These arms
are in the south window of the chancel, near the screen, perhaps for William Gray, bishop of Ely, vide Vol. IV. p. 1.")

"About 1380 he was prebendary of the stall of Osbaldwic,
in the metropolitan church of York[8], and in 1385 he was made
archdeacon of Leicester; but in the mean time the pope con-

---

[1] Ib.   [2] Pat. 13 Ric. II. p. 2, m. 11.

[3] *Fast. Eccl.* II. 565.

[4] Ib. note; Reg. Arundel, p. 2, fol. 167; Reg. Courtn. fol. 168 a.

[5] Vide Ackermann, *Hist. Univ. Cant.* Vol. I. p. 61.

[6] Cole MSS. Vol. IV. fols. 13, 14.

[7] In another place, viz. Vol. XXXII. fol. 78, he says in 1380 A.D., and was
appointed chancellor about 1390 A.D. and 1396 A.D.

[8] Vide also Cole MSS. Vol. XXXII. fol. 105.

ferring it upon one Ponceline de Ursinis, he quitted his claim to the dignity, and after having passed two or three stalls in the cathedral of Lincoln, fixed to that of Brampton, to which he was installed on the 15th of January, 1393. Afterwards, on August 27, 1397, he was made master of St Peter's College, in Cambridge, where he had received his education, and to which he was a considerable benefactor, as he was also to our University. At last, upon the death of his namesake and townsman, William de Bottisham, bishop of Rochester, he was provided of that see, to which he was consecrated in the cathedral of Canterbury by the archbishop on the 4th of July, 1400, where he did not sit many years, but more than Godwin and all after him make him, who says that he died immediately after consecration, and before he saw his cathedral church; whereas he did not die till near four years after, viz. on the 17th of April, 1404, and lies buried in his own cathedral[1]." Here again Cole's account is not accurate, for he was made prebend of the stall of Crackpole St Mary, diocese of Lincoln, in 1386, Oct. 4th, succeeding therein Thomas Brandon[2]. He then was promoted to the stall of Milton Ecclesia, and was installed on the 18th of January, 1389—90[3], in the place of one Barret, who resigned. On the 7th of May, 1391, he was collated to the prebend of Brampton, and installed on the 15th of January following, vice Lincoln, deceased[4]. His appointment was ratified on the 3rd of November, 1393[5]. He was soon after appointed to the prebendal stall of Osbaldwick, in the diocese of York, and his appointment was ratified on the 2nd of October, 1397[6]. On the 27th of August, 1397, he had succeeded William Cavendish as master of Peterhouse, Cambridge[7]. This office he appears to have held till 1400, when on July 4 of that year he, who was mentioned also as chaplain to the archbishop of Canterbury, was consecrated bishop of Rochester[8]. His will is dated 15th of April, 1404, and was

---

[1] Reg. Bottlesham, fol. 186 b; vide Hasted, *Kent*, Vol. II. p. 39.
[2] Le Neve, *Fast. Eccl.* Vol. II. p. 137.   [3] Ib. p. 187.   [4] Ib. p. 117.
[5] Pat. 17 Ric. II. p. 1, m. 11, p. 3, m. 24.
[6] *Fast. Eccl.* III. 207; Pat. 21 Ric. II. p. 1, m. 16.
[7] *Fast. Eccl.* Vol. III. p. 668.
[8] Wharton, *Angl. Sacr.* Vol. I. p. 379; *Fast. Eccl.* Vol. II. p. 565.

proved on the 24th of the same month[1]. Cole has confounded him with another John de Bottisham, who was appointed archdeacon of Leicester. Bale gives the following list of his works[2]:

"Sermones ante Regem Factos, Lib. I.

"Disputationes Scholasticæ, Lib. I.

"Et alia quæ Ipse non Vidi."

Tanner ascribes the works of John de Bottisham to William de Bottisham, and adds, "Opus quoddam Tabulare pro Utilitate Studentium, Lib. I.[3]"

This bishop does not seem to have been much resident at his see, for though he is mentioned as giving sentence upon Sir William Sautre, the Lollard priest, in 1401, he was on the 1st of July, 1402, appointed ambassador in company with John, Earl of Somerset, captain of Calais, Richard, Lord de Gray, his lieutenant, William Heron, Lord de Say, Thomas Rameston, John Norbury, captain of Guienne, Richard Holm, canon of York, and John Arald, Esq., in order to demand payment of certain sums due for the redemption of John, formerly king of the French[4]. At this time English commerce with the Low Countries was rapidly increasing, but, owing to the hostilities between England and France, constant capture was made by either side of merchant vessels, and numerous complaints were made. John of Bottlesham appears to have proceeded to Calais in July, for on the 18th of the same month, in company with William Heron, Richard de Holm, and John Urban, he writes a long letter addressed to the Privy Council respecting the capture of a certain Flemish vessel by John Hawle, and his accomplices, Edmund Arnald and John Willyham. The ship belonged to a young man of Abbeville, named John De la Chapelle, and the whole of its freight, consisting of corn and flour and hemp, was appropriated by the English merchants. The letter also alludes to a capture of certain vessels by Henry de Fowy, and the seizure of a ship by Richard Spicer and his brother[5]. In consequence of the

---

[1] Reg. Courtnay, fol. 204 b and 217 a.

[2] Bale, *Scrip. Ill. Cat.* p. 49.   [3] Tanner, *Bibl. Britt. Hib.* p. 114.

[4] Rymer, *Fœd.* Vol. IV. Part I. p. 31.

[5] Exstat in Brit. Mus. Cott. MSS. Galba I. fol. 134.

repeated complaints of the injustice done to merchants, a treaty was concluded at Lenlinghen on the 14th of August, 1402, by the ambassadors, John, Bishop of Rochester, William Heron, Richard de Holm, and John Urban, lieutenant of the admirals of England. The articles were as follows:

1. That all merchantmen, sailors and fishermen, taken by either side should be released, except those who had already escaped by fraud.

2. That if any should be captured by sea that they should go free for the first time.

3. That appeal should be made to either country in case of future capture.

4. That all captured goods should be restored to their owners, and that commissioners should be appointed to effect this and try causes consequent thereupon. But that justice should take its course upon attemptates of the truce.

5. That freedom of passage to merchants should be publicly proclaimed in both countries.

6. That infractors of the truce should be punished.

7. That banished individuals should not be received, nor food nor aid given to them.

8. That reprisals should not have effect, but that goods should be restored to their rightful owners.

9. That new safe conduct should not be necessary to pass from one country to another, and that safe conduct if asked for be not refused[1].

There were constant attemptates made against this truce; for next year, in 1403, John, Earl of Somerset, Hugo Litterell, knt., John Urban and William de Pylton were commissioned to go and see after it[2], which resulted in another treaty being concluded at Lenlinghen in 1403, on the 27th June[3]. In the same year another commission was appointed to get the money for the redemption of King John[4].

Whether from the fact that his fellow-townsmen and namesakes were, at this time, flourishing merchants at Lynn, or whether the duties of his see were more urgent, John Bottles-

[1] Rymer, *Fœd.* Vol. IV. p. I. p. 34.
[2] Ib. p. 44.　　　[3] Ib. p. 46.　　　[4] Ib. p. 44.

ham does not figure again as an ambassador. He probably went back to Rochester, where he died next year. In the list of Benefactors of Cambridge University, direction is given to "pray for the soul of Master Joannin de Bodkysham, Bishop of Rochester, who gave to the common chest of the University twenty pounds. He gave besides to each college of that University twenty pounds, and besides this he bestowed on the college of Saint Peter's all his own books of canonical and civil law, and many other good works he did to the same University and caused to be done[1]."

Both William de Bottisham and John de Bottisham bore the same arms, viz., Az. 3 birdbolts two and one, points in base, Ar.[2]. Blomefield says that at Riddlesworth Hall are the arms of Botesham, thus: gu. 3 birdbolts in fess reverted Ar. Motto— "Nec ab oriente nec ab occidente[3]." Burke's *Armoury* gives Bottesham or Boltesham (Northumberland), gu. 3 birdbolts in pale Ar. and Boltsdam, Devonshire, Ar. 3 bolts in pale gu.; but he also gives Botesham or Boltesham, gu. 3 plates.

From the scant notices of the illustrious men who bore this surname these arms are worth tracing to their origin. We find subsequent to the period of the learned triumvirate few who bore the name. William Bodesham in 33 Hen. VI. appears to have had lands in Somersetshire[4]. John Bottesham lived at Over, as husbandman, as appears by his will, dated 20th May, 1521. He left legacies to young Thomas Botesham and Richard his son, and a certain sum for the works in the nave of Over church[5]. Thomas Botysham of Over dates his will 20th October, 1548, and had a wife named Agnes[6]. The surname does not occur again except in the case of John Bottesham (a town child), who, as the parish register states, was buried at Bottisham on the 31st of December, 1665.

[1] Cole MSS. Vol. xxi. fol. 129; *Hist. Univ. Camb.* Vol. i. p. 5.

[2] Vide Brit. Mus. Add. MSS. No. 12,443; Bedford, *Blazon of Episcopacy*, p. 90.

[3] Blomefield, *Norfolk*, Vol. i. p. 281. It is worthy of note that a document, dated 1372 A.D., quoted by Cole (MSS. Vol. iv.), bears a seal of green wax, upon which is a very diminutive shield with a fess, and this legend, S' Nichol' d' Botish'm +.

[4] Dugdale, *Hist. of Embanking*, p. 100.

[5] Cole MSS. Vol. lx. fol. 153.   [6] Ib. fol. 66.

CHAPTER V.

TONE.

ANOTHER family, now quite extinct in Bottisham, possessed *Tone.* of considerable influence in the 13th and 14th centuries, was that of Tone, Thone, or Towne. Wymer Tone, and Alan his brother, appear as witnesses to various documents which, though undated, were probably drawn up before 1235. At the same period we find William Tone the son of Alan, and Symon the son of Tone. Symon appears to have had two sons, Nicholas and John Tone, both of whose names are found in the documents of the general Inquisition, taken in Edward the First's reign. It is there stated that John Tone held of the heirs of William the son of William the son of Martin 4 acres of land of the fee of the Earl, by the yearly service of 4 shillings. He also held 5 acres and the moiety of a fold of the heirs of John de Deresle by the service of one penny. The heirs of Nicholas Tone held of the Earl one croft by the service of $12\frac{1}{2}d$. They held of the heirs of John de Deresle 1 messuage by the service of 7 pence to be paid at the four terms of the year. They held one acre of Martin de Lada, rendering service thereby, and of the Prior of Anglesey they held one messuage and 2 acres by the service of 23 pence. Simon Thone de Lada de Botekesham occurs in a deed of the age of Edward the First[1], and in another dated "die veneris in f'o ap'lorū Simonis et Iude anno r' r' Ed'i fil. Ed'i xi," that is 1317, we find mention of Nicholas Tone and Alice his wife, and their children Nicholas and Isabella[1].

Of Isabella nothing further is known, but Nicholas appears to have married a certain Matilda, mention of whom is made in a document dated 1351[1]. Nicholas Tone the younger was a witness to many documents, but his name does not appear after 1382.

[1] Cole MSS. Vol. IV. fol. 8.

We then find the name of Maurice Tone, probably his son, who was married to a lady named Joan. In 1390, a license had been granted to Maurice Tone to have divine service in his oratory at Bottisham Lode, and this license seems to have been renewed to Joan, relict of Maurice Tone in 1396, when John Bertelot was vicar of Bottisham[1]. Maurice Tone therefore would seem to have died before 1396, but his name appears as a witness in 1399 in a document, therefore I suppose he must have had a son named Maurice. This family soon after became extinct, for in 1400 A.D. Wm. Tone, clerk, sold the property of Maurice his brother in Bottisham and elsewhere to Sir Wm. Thyrning, knt[2]. Cole infers, though I know not upon what authority, that the oratory of Maurice Tone was a chapel which existed in old Bottisham Hall before the present mansion was erected. He says of it: "This chapel is very neat—it has a stone altar railed in one step: in the windows several small figures and heads of the twelve apostles, very elegantly painted; in one pane a shackbolt: in the woodwork, under the windows of the chamber which looks into the chapel and which comes over above half of it, the same device with a cup chained to it, part of the arms of Argentines, and belonging to the Allingtons." What Cole calls a shackbolt or shackle was probably a stirrup with buckles and straps, the arms of Scudamore, as has been before pointed out. This chapel was standing within the memory of the present generation.

PEDIGREE OF TONE.

Simon Tone =

Nicholas, = Alice. ob. c. 1363 A.D.[3]		John, ob. post 1332 A.D.
Nicholas, = Matilda. ob. post 1382.	Isabella.	
Maurice, = Joan. vixit 1372—1396.		
Maurice, 1399 A.D. William, a priest.		

[1] Cole MSS. Vol. IV.; Blomefield, *Collect. Cantab.* p. 34.

[2] Vide Rot. Claus. 2 Hen. IV.

[3] For John Gray and Matilda his wife acted that year as his executors; vide Court Rolls of the Manor.

Many men about this time took their names from Bottisham *Lada.* Lode. Amongst the earliest names mentioned in Bottisham we find Hugh de Lada, Richard his son, Jerome de Lade, and Thomas de la Lade, canon of Richard, Prior of Anglesey. Alan de Lada, Martin de Lada, and John the son of Leuric de Lada, all were living about the time of the Inquisition of Edward the First. We then find Martin the son of Eustace de Lada held of the Earl of Clare in Bottisham 2 virgates of land and paid by the year two shillings and did suit to the county and hundred for the whole village. He had under him also seven free tenants, so that he must have been a person of some importance. This Eustace de Lada had other sons, viz. Ralph and Richard; to a deed of the former of which is affixed the seal of his brother, which represents a dog sinister passant. It contains an inscription: Sigill' Ricardi Filii Eustach' + [1]. William de Lade was canon of the house of Anglesey in 1378 and became prior in 1402; and after this date the name completely disappears.

More important, however, is it to notice the various and *Bendish.* distinguished families who tenanted the estate of Bendish and lived at Bendish Hall. This house and the land belonging to it took its name from its former possessors. Of these Thomas de Bendish held the estate, as part of the honor of Clare in 1288 A.D., when his name first occurs—up to the year 1339, he and his wife Isabel are constantly mentioned in contemporary documents. But in this year the land appears to have passed into the hands of John de Bendish, who in 1346 sold a messuage and 20 acres of land to Edmund de Overton and Matilda his wife. From 1349 to 1390 the name of John de Bendish is not found, but as his name occurs in the latter year and not afterwards it is probable that he died about that time.

Meanwhile in 1355 John de Bendish enfeoffed Robert de Royly and Roger Baillot in one messuage and a hundred acres of land in Bottisham, who again alienated them to Edmund de Bendish, son of John, who possessed them up to the year 1390, and was succeeded by Thos. de Bendish in 1392 [2].

[1] Cole MSS. Vol. IV. fol. 14 b.
[2] Vide Court Rolls of the Manor.

By a comparison of dates, it seems that this family is no other than that which possessed the manor of Bendishes in Radwinter, and lands in Steeple Bumstead co. Essex. Peter de Westley, according to Wright[1], first assumed the name of Bendish in the reign of King John, and Thomas, who died in 1342, was the first who styled himself De Bendish only. He was succeeded by John, who, by his wife Alice, had a son Edmund, who, at his father's death in 1392, obtained possession of the estates. This latter was present at the siege of Calais, and died in 1401. Then came Thomas his brother, from whose son Edmund the Bendishes of Barrington are descended, his mother having been Margaret, daughter and heiress of Thomas Bradfield of that place.

But to return to Bendish Hall in Bottisham, the site of which is marked by a moat situated on the low ground to the west of the Green hill, not far removed from the church. Within the memory of some of the oldest inhabitants there stood within the space enclosed by this moat a fine large house built of red brick, with a fine bay window at one end of it and a chapel in an attic at the other end of it. Cole says that it was a very good old house and stood in a charming garden, with fish-ponds and all other conveniencies about it, and was let to Mr Shepheard at the annual rent of £40, which he was to lay out on the house and gardens. The chapel at the top of the house he says was very neat[2]. After the time of John and Thomas de Bendish there is no mention of the estate till the year 1527, when John Wright appears to have been the possessor of it, and according to the terms of his will dated on the 21st of February of that year, he leaves to Elizabeth his wife the house that he dwelt in till his daughter Margaret should marry, when she was to have it as well as three acres of land and 13s. 4d. To his wife Elizabeth he also left his house at the Green Hill (by which name the triangular piece of ground abutting on the

---

[1] *Hist. of Essex*, Vol. I. p. 627 and II. p. 93.

[2] In a collection of drawings belonging to the Camb. Ant. Soc. there is a rude representation of this old house, signed R. R. 1801, and entitled *Bottisham Parsonage and Church*; a line of elms to the left of the picture seem to indicate an avenue or entrance-drive leading to the house from the Cambridge road.

road and opposite to the church is still designated and on which formerly stood the cage), and then to his son William, and to her two acres of land for life, and then to his daughter Margery, of which two acres in roods lie in a croft beside Coks and a rood and a half above Bendyshe sometime Scott's. This John Wright appears to have had two sons and one daughter. John the eldest married Margaret * * * * and died in the year 1527, as his will, dated June 28, was proved on the 18th of December following. He had a son named also John, who married and whose descendants lived for some time in the parish as farmers, and who also served as churchwardens. Now the will of William Barnard of Swaffham Bulbeck, dated the 9th of November, 1545, stipulates that Robert his son was to have his house in Bottisham called "Bennys," with a crofte and 5 horses, the best in the stabyll, &c. To his daughter Alice he leaves his house in the Lode-street, or £20. To Catharine his daughter £10. To Margaret his daughter £10. Margaret his wife and John his son he appoints executors and residuary legatees. This will was proved on the 28th of November following. Hence it it is not improbable that the Margaret alluded to as his wife was the Margaret Wright before mentioned, and that through her he became the owner of Bendish. Robert Barnard thus became the owner in 1545, but he probably never lived at Bottisham; while his younger brother John settled here, married, and had three sons and two daughters, the last child being baptized in Dec. 1599.

A year before this, Robert Clenche, described in the pedigrees of his family as a gentleman of the isle of Ely, married Joan Webbe, the daughter of Thomas Webbe of Tunbridge Hall. He probably bought the estate of Bendish, as his family continued to reside in Bottisham and his great-grandson is described as owner of the estate. This family of Clenche is of great antiquity and was possessed of considerable influence. John Clenche appears to have been a gentleman living at Wethersfield in Essex, married to Joan the daughter of John Annis, sen. of the same county. He had two sons; John the eldest married and was succeeded by Richard Clenche of Sudbury, his son and heir; the second son, John also, married

Family of Clenche.

Catharine the daughter and heiress of Thomas Almott of Creeting All Saints in Suffolk, and consequently settled at Creeting.
He was on the 27th of November, 1581, constituted third baron
of the exchequer, and was so much in favour with the queen,
that she called him ' her good judge.' There is a portrait given
of him in Dugdale's *Origines Juridiciales*[1], and a full-length
picture of him, hung at Wilbraham Temple during the possession
of that estate by John Clenche his descendant[2]. It is worthy of
note, in passing, that the surname of this family is written
Clenche, Clinch, Clench, and Clynche. Judge Clench seems to
have removed from Creeting to Holbrooke in the same county,
where he died in the year 1609 A.D., aged 72. To his memory
is a fine monument in Holbrooke church[3]. After the death of
Judge Clenche the estates devolved upon his eldest son Thomas,
who served the office of High Sheriff for the county of Suffolk in
1616. He married first the daughter of John Barker of Ipswich,
and by her had three sons and two daughters. John the eldest
of these was High Sheriff of Suffolk in 1639; Thomas and
Edward died in infancy; Catharine married Henry Byng of
Grantchester in the county of Cambridgeshire and Thomasin
died unmarried. Secondly, Thomas Clenche married Elizabeth,
daughter and coheiress of the family of Risby and relict of. one
of the family of Wingfield of Crowfelde. Thirdly, he married
Ann, daughter of William Berde of Coston, relict of Sir Anthony
Wingfeld of Howegoden in Suffolk, knight. John Clenche, the
second son of Judge Clenche, is described as of Belings in
Suffolk. He married Joanne, daughter and sole heiress of Robt.
Homes of Wiverston in Suffolk, the relict of John Prettyman of
Bacton in the same county, and had issue four sons, George,
John, Almott and Edmund: Of these sons Almott married
Susanna Webbe of Bottisham. This Susanna was baptized on
the 13th of January, 1598-9, while Joan, who is described in the
pedigree of this family as her sister, was married on the 23rd of

---

[1] p. 96.

[2] Probably the same portrait as that which hung in the house of the Spar-
rowe family, in the Butter-market, Ipswich; vide Wodderspoon, *Mems. of Ipswich*, p. 32.

[3] Page, *Suffolk Traveller*, p. 23.

December, 1598. It is possible therefore that she may have been really the sister of Thomas Webbe the elder, who is described as her father, and consequently aunt to Susanna; for Almott Clenche was not the brother of Robert before mentioned, but nephew, being the son of his brother John. The issue of Almott and Susanna was amongst others a son, Almott, who was buried at Bottisham on the 8th of May, 1685, and Susan, who was buried in the same churchyard on the 30th of September, 1700. Either Almott Clenche the elder, or Almott Clenche the younger, was churchwarden of the parish in 1665, but as the name does not occur in the registers with the exception of those instances before mentioned they most probably did not reside in the parish, but fought on the Royalist side as did their cousin, Captain Robert Clenche. The next son of Judge Clenche was Thomas and after him came Robert Clenche of Bottisham, to whose marriage reference will again be made. The next son, John, is described as of Thiselden Hall at Burgh in Suffolk. He married Mary the daughter and coheiress of William Herbert of Hollesley in Suffolk, and had issue John, Daniel, Catharine, Thomas, Benjamin, and Isaac. Judge Clenche had eight daughters; Margery the wife of Edmund Dameron of Henley in Suffolk; Joanne, married first to John Waker of Brunden in Essex, and secondly to Walter Mercer of Oxfordshire; Love, the third daughter, the wife of Thomas Bacon of Bramford in Suffolk; Catharine the wife of John Freeland of Harksted; Ann the wife of John Jeffrey of Cheriton in Suffolk; Priscilla died a virgin; Thomasin married to Thomas Randolfe of Kent; and Elizabeth the wife of Thomas Hall of Clopton in Suffolk.

We must now go back to the marriage of Robert Clenche to Joan Webbe of Bottisham. Seven children resulted from this marriage, all of whom appear to have been born at Bottisham. The first, Susanne, was baptized Mar. 23rd, 1599—1600; Priscilla, Mar. 22, 1600—1; Robert, Feb. 28, 1601—2; Edward, Sept. 22, 1603; Francis, July 5, 1607; Thomazine, Oct. 6, 1608; and Catharine, Jan. 4, 1610—11. Of these, Robert, the eldest son, married a lady, whose Christian name was Mary. She died a widow, and was buried at Bottisham, July 26, 1702.

Of her husband we hear nothing further, except that Cole tells us[1], that on the death of John, the grandson of Judge Clench, without issue, the estate of Creeting came to Captain Clenche, who was a gallant officer, and served his king and country faithfully; but suffered with his king and country, and was forced to compound with rebels and usurpers for his own estate, which was £1200 a year, temp. Car. I. In these troublous times parish registers were not well kept, and for some years we find no entries. It is impossible to say, therefore, for certain, whether Captain Clenche was killed in battle, or returned to Bottisham. His wife bore him two sons; Robert was baptized at Bottisham, March 14, 1643—4, and John appears to have been born elsewhere. Of this latter we hear but little, save that he received possession of the estate in Bottisham from his uncle Edward in 1658, and was Mayor of Cambridge in 1663; his wife, Mary, was buried at Bottisham on the 13th of October, 1711. From her was descended the last owner of Bendish, viz., John Clenche. An elder son, Thomas, died, and was buried, February the 25th, 1663—4; while a daughter, Catharine, who was born on the 24th of January, and baptized on the 26th of January, 1704—5, was buried an infant on the 7th of February in the same year. John Clenche, the second son, was born on the 23rd of April, and baptized on the 3rd of May, 1665, at Bottisham, whither it would seem that his father had removed after the king's restoration. He was married three times; who the first wife was is uncertain; the second was Elizabeth Cropley, who was buried at Bottisham on the 28th of November, 1700, and to whom there is a memorial stone in the nave of Bottisham church. She had two children, Mary, the eldest, born March the 23rd, 1696, and christened on the 1st of April in the same year. She married Watson Powell, Esq. of Hilton, in the county of Huntingdon, and had issue two sons and two daughters. Elizabeth Clenche had also a son, John, who was born on the 15th of November, and baptized on the 20th of the same month, in 1698; but he did not live long, as he was buried on the 31st of March, 1711, at Bottisham.

[1] Cole MSS. Vol. xxviii. fol. 113; vide also Vol. iv. fols. 2 and 16, and Vol. xx. fol. 42.

Watson Powell was the son of a lady who was niece to Thomas Watson, Bishop of St David's from 1687 to 1699 A.D. He succeeded to the estate at Bendish in right of his wife; but he afterwards sold it to the present possessor, St Peter's College, in Cambridge; and after the death of his first wife, remarried and settled at Warwick. Twenty years after the death of his second wife, John Clenche fell in love with Madam Joanna Ward, the relict of Mr Ward of Wilbraham Temple, and mother of Thomas Watson Ward, Esq. by her first husband. She was another of the nieces of Bishop Watson of St David's, the third being Mrs Mary Watson, who lived single. Cole says[1] that "Mrs Clenche was a very fine woman, of very masculine sense and understanding; but died of grief at Cambridge, where she removed for her health, on her darling son's foolish marriage, at about 18, to a barber's daughter at Cambridge, a young woman of great beauty, and as small share of understanding, on whom, though Mr Ward doated to excess to the very last, yet so strange a complexion was he of, that he had very frequent amours with other women, which as frequently embroiled them together; and at last, when he died of a consumption, he left her a jointure of about £300 per annum on condition that she married not again, which has driven the poor woman, of a warm complexion, to live wholly with a fellow of Trinity College, whose name I have forgot, but son to a tradesman of Bury, and of a poor, pale, and miserable appearance. It is supposed she has children by him. His eldest son is married very happily into a gentile (*sic*) though numerous family; one of the daughters of Mr Pemberton of Girton, and eldest son to Mr Pemberton of Trumpington." Mr Clenche appears to have removed to Wilbraham Temple, where he died in 1729, and was buried in Great Wilbraham church. Thus, at his death, the family became extinct in Cambridgeshire.

In the church of Great Wilbraham, side by side with the achievements of the family of Ward, hangs one for Mrs Clenche, the relict of Mr Ward. It contains the following coats: 1. gu. 6 annulets braced in pale 2 and 1, and a chief O. for Clenche impaling, 2. A. on a chev. az. int. 3 martlets sa. 3 crescents O.

[1] Cole MSS. Vol. XL. fol. 11.

for Watson, with the crest of Clenche, viz. a dexter arm ppr. clothed gu. holding a club ragulée at one end ppr., and armed and spiked O. issuing from a radiated crown O., and on the circle of which is written, "Tien le droit." Underneath this escutcheon is the motto, "Mors iter ad vitam." Above this achievement hangs another for Mr Clenche's former wives, and contains 9 coats, thus—

Baron.
1.　as before for Clenche.
2.　A. on a bend cotised sa. three escallops A.
3.　A. a chev. int. 3 mullets gu.
4.　O. 2 bars az. on a canton A. a chaplet gu.
5.　Quarterly gu. and O. a fess nebulée int. 3 lions' heads erased, all counterchanged.
6.　gu. a chev. A. int. 3 owls O.
7.　gu. a chev. Or int. 3 lions rampant A. impaling.

Femme.
1.　A. on a bend cotised gu. 3 lions passant O.
2.　Erm. on a chief gu. 3 owls A.

There is much difficulty in identifying these coats, as the colours are already much worn. However,

1.　is certainly for Clench.
2.　is for Almott, Judge Clench having married the heiress of Thomas Almott of Creeting, though Page[1] gives the arms without the cotises; it is difficult to be sure, however, of the cotise in the original, the colours are so indistinct, and the dust so accumulated upon the rumpled surface of the achievement.
3.　is for Catharine, the wife of John Freelove or Freeland, the daughter of Judge Clench.
4.　is for Holmes; Joanne, daughter and sole heiress of Robert Homes or Holmes, relicta Prettyman, having married John the second son of Judge Clenche.
5.　very much worn, is for Barker, though Page[2] gives the arms thus: party per fess nebulée vert, and sa. 3 martlets O. a canton ermine.

[1] *Suffolk Traveller*, p. 593.
[2] Ib. p. 70.

6. is for Fleming ?

7. is for Good ?

Femme. 1. Lem is the only family that bears these arms, but without the cotises; therefore I am inclined to think that the arms are wrongly transcribed, owing to the dust and worn state of the achievement.

2. is for the family of Cropley, some of whom settled at Soham in 1730, and came from Middlesex, and are a branch of the family of that name at Ely.

After John Clenche married Madam Joanna Ward of Wilbraham Temple, he resided in that parish till his death in 1729, and consequently the house at Bendish was left vacant till it was let to Samuel Shepheard, Esq. M.P. This gentleman had, *Shepheard.* previous to this, some influence in the neighbourhood, for he sat for Cambridge town in the Parliament of 1708—10. Against this election a petition was lodged, and the election was declared void; but, on a new election taking place, Shepheard regained his seat. He continued to sit in the Parliaments of 1710—13, 1713—15, 1715—22, to which last, Thomas Sclater Bacon, Esq. had been elected; but, on being petitioned against, he lost his seat, and Shepheard was elected in his place. About this time he appears to have settled at Bottisham, and was put up for the county in 1722, which election he seems to have won, and sat in that parliament till 1724. At the next election, though warmly backed by the interest of his friend, Mr James Jennings of Ely, he seems to have lost, but was re-elected for the Parliament of 1727—1734, and sat again from 1734—1741, and 1741—1747, when he died in the month of August, and a new writ was ordered to supply his place. In 1739 Mr Shepheard bought the site of Anglesey Abbey from the family of Parker, who were then seated there.

Whether he ever resided there is doubtful. Cole says that he gave it to Mr Joseph Pyke, son of Mr Pyke, formerly Town-Clerk of Cambridge, who lived in the house with him as a sort of secretary, as a portion with his wife. His granddaughter, who married Viscount Irvin, certainly possessed it, and sold it in 1793 to the widow of Soame Jenyns, Esq., of Bottisham Hall. Samuel Shepheard removed from Bendish Hall to the

H. B.   7

magnificent red-brick house at Exning, which he built, and offered Cole the remainder of his lease, which offer was graciously
declined. Before his death, which took place at Exning, he
did not omit to benefit the poor of that parish, as well as of
Bottisham, by a handsome sum to be distributed in charity.
After the sale of Bendish to Peterhouse College, in Cambridge,
there seems to have been no resident there till it was tenanted
for a short time by the Rev. Joseph Davies, the minister of
the parish, and when he left it was inhabited by the Rev.
James Stephen Lushington, about the year 1774.

ushing-
n.

This gentleman, the progenitor of an illustrious race, was
of Rodmersham in Kent, Prebend of Carlisle, Vicar of Newcastle-upon-Tyne, and of Latton in Essex. He was first
married to a daughter of Bishop Law, and by her had one
son. After her death, he espoused Mary, the daughter of
the Rev. Humphrey Christian, of Docking, in Norfolk, and
during their residence at Bendish they had three sons and one
daughter born to them. The eldest, John William, was baptized in Bottisham Church, on the 20th of January, 1774.
The second, the Right Hon. Stephen Rumbold Lushington,
was baptized on the 10th of June, 1775. Hester Paulina was
christened on the 17th of October, 1776, and was buried on
the 29th of July, 1795, after falling victim to a decline; and
the third son, James Law Lushington, Esq., was baptized on the
24th of July, 1780. The Right Hon. Stephen Lushington
died on the 5th of August, 1868. He was a member of the
Privy Council, a Justice of the Peace, Doctor of Civil Law,
and Member of Parliament for Rye from 1807—1812, and for
Canterbury from 1812—1830. For some years he held the
post of Chairman of Committee of Ways and Means, and was
joint secretary to the Treasury from 1814—1827. He then
filled the post of Governor of Madras till 1832, and in 1839
took the degree of D.C.L. of Oxford. He was the author of the
Life and Services of Lord Harris. He was twice married, first to
Anne Elizabeth, second daughter of George, first Lord Harris,
by whom he had issue six sons and two daughters. She died
March 25th, 1856, and in 1858 he married Marianne, daughter
of the late James Hearne, Esq., which lady died in 1864.

After the Rev. Mr Lushington left Bendish Hall, the old house was pulled down, and a neat farm-house built upon its site. This and the farm was then tenanted by Mr Free, who had formerly been coachman to Mr Lushington. At the death of Mr Free he was succeeded by his son, Thomas Free, who died in 1852, and the farm was then occupied by the present tenant, Mr John King, jun.

On the plot of land near the present vicarage stood a large "*Vineyards.*" farm-house entered by long stone steps, not far from the present blacksmith's shop and the police-station. There is but little mention of this house to determine its date, but it may have been built by Thomas Webbe, a London attorney, who came from Clifford's Inn, and settled here[1]. In one of the Harleian MSS.[2] he is stated to have been descended from the Webbes of Staffordshire. He married Susanna, daughter of Edward Smyth, of Wilbraham, and had a numerous offspring[3]. Thomas, the eldest, was born here, and baptized at Bottisham on the 25th of May, 1594. On the 10th of April, 1617, he married Elizabeth, daughter of Daniel Goodrick of Ely. She was buried at Bottisham in 1646. Her husband is stated in the various pedigrees to have been living in 1619, but his name does not appear in the register of burials, so he probably changed his residence. Another son of Thomas Webbe the elder, named Edward, died almost in infancy, and was buried Ap. 1st, 1609. The second daughter, Susanna, was baptized at Bottisham, January 13th, 1598, and married Almott Clenche, the nephew of Robert Clenche, the son of the Judge. Of this marriage there arose the following issue:—A son, Almott, who was buried May the 8th, 1685, and Susan, buried September 30th, 1700. Joan Webbe, sister of Susanna Webbe, as has been already stated, married Robert Clenche, of the Isle of Ely, and one pedigree states that Thomas Webbe, senior, had one more child married to a person named Smyth, and secondly to a person unknown, of Halstead in Essex. Subjoined is the pedigree of the families of Webbe and Clenche :—

---

[1] ? if this is not the original site of Tunbridge Hall.   [2] No. 6830.
[3] Harl. MSS. No. 6770, fol. 134, No. 1043, fol. 51; Cole MSS. Vol. xi. fol. 112.

PEDIGREE OF THE FAMILIES OF WEBBE AND CLENCHE.

ARMS: *Webbe.* az. on a chief O. 3 martlets gu. Crest—a griffin's head erm. O. gorged with a ducal coronet A.
Clenche. gu. six annulets, braced in pale, two and one, and a chief O. Crest—a dexter arm ppr. clothed gu. holding a club ragulée at one end ppr. and armed and spiked O. issuing from a radiated crown O. on the circle of which is written *Tien le Droit.*

Thomas Webbe = Susanna, d. of Edw. Smyth, = (2) John Fowkes, of Anglesey Abbey,
of Wilbraham. 15 Dec. 1608,
bur. 23 June, 1621. bur. 25 Dec. 1617.

Joan = Robert Clenche, gent., of the Isle of Ely, 23 Dec. 1598.

Thomas, = Eliz. d. of Daniel Goodrick of Ely, bap. May 25, 1594 ar., 10 Ap. 1617, bur. 1646.

Edward, bur. Ap. 1, 1609.

Susanna = Almott Clenche, of Suffolk. bap. 13 Jan. 1598.

* * * * * = * * * * * Smyth.
= (2) * * * * * de Halstead, Essex.

Almott, bur. May 8, 1685.

Susan, bur. 30 Sept. 1700.

John.
Benjamin.
Margaret.
Honora.

Susanne, bap. 23 Mar. 1599-1600.

Priscilla, bap. 22 Mar. 1600-1.

Robert = Mary * * * * bap. 28 Feb. bur. 26 July, 1601-2. 1702.

Edward, bap. Sep. 22, 1603.

Francis, bap. 5 July, 1607.

Thomazine, bap. Oct. 6, 1608.

Catharine, bap. Jan. 4, 1610-11.

PEDIGREE OF THE FAMILY OF CLENCHE BEFORE THEY SETTLED IN BOTTISHAM.

John Clenche, of Wethersfield, Essex = Joan, d. of John Annis, Essex.

John = * * * *

Richard Clenche, of Sudbury, s. and h.

John, of Creeting All Saints, Judge of the Exchequer. = Catharine, d. and h. of Thomas Allmott, of Creeting All Saints.

John C. = Ann, d. of Wm. Berde, relicta Sir Anthony Wingfield. | Joanne, d. and h. of Robt. Homes, relicta John Prettyman.

Thomas, *Robert* = (1) Joan, d. of Thos. Webbe, 1598. Vide A. issue, vide antea. | (1) Mary, d. and coh. of W. Herbert. (2) Dorothy, d. of Geo. Humerston of Suffolk, widow.

Margery = Edm. Dameron, of Henley, co. Suffolk. | Joanne = (1) John Waker, of Brunden, co. Essex = (2) Walter Mercer, of Oxfordshire. | Love = Thos. Bacon, of Branford, co. Suffolk. | Catharine = Thos. Freeland, of Harksted, co. Suffolk. | Ann = Joh. Jefferit Cherit co. Suffolk.

Thomas C. of Holbrooke, High Sheriff of Suffolk, 1616. = (1) Margery, d. of John Barker, of Ipswich. = (2) Eliz. d. and coh. of Risby, relicta Wingfield. = (3) Ann, d. of Wm. Berde, relicta Sir Anthony Wingfield.

Allmott = Susanna Webbe. | Edmund, = Dorcas, d. of Robt. Sparrowe, of Ipswich.

Catharine = Henry Byng, of Grantchester, co. Camb. | Thomasin, d. virgo. | (1) George, = d. and h. of Dan. Godfreye. (2) John.

John, Sheriff, 1639, ob. s. p. | Thomas, Edward, ob. inf. | Thomas, Benjamin, Isaac.

Catharine, b. 1610. | Daniel, b. 1608. | John, b. 1606.

Almott. | Susan. | John. | Benjamin. | Margaret. | Honora.

A. = (2) Eliz. d. of Sir Thos. Holland, of Quidenham, Kent, d. Feb. 25, 1629, æt. 48. Hence connected with the family of Lestrange. Vide Blomefield, *Norfolk*, I. 344.
= (3) Mary, d. of John Mott, of Essex.

CHAPTER VI.

VAUS.

ANOTHER family, whose name has nearly passed away, was that of De Vallibus, Vaux, or more commonly Vaus. The manor which bears the name of Alington and Vauxes, alone suggests the inquiry, when and how much influence some branch of this family may have acquired in the parish.

In the years 1302, 1303, 1304, and 1305 we find Robert de Vaus and Alice his wife were witnesses to certain documents, and they are therein described as of Bottisham; and in the pedigree given by Nicholls of the family of that name at Shankton in Leicestershire, Robert de Vaux of Bodeskam, co. Cambridge, is stated to be the son of John de Vaus[1]. Going backwards, we find Harold de Vaux the ancestor of this family had three sons,—Herbert the ancestor of Vaus of Gillesland, according to Burke, Ranulph the progenitor of Vaus of Tryermayne, according to the same authority, and Robert the third son[2]. Blomefield states that this last was the founder of the Priory of Pentney, in Norfolk. He therefore flourished before 1087 A.D.[3] He had three sons, William, Oliver, and Henry, of whom William had three sons, Robert his heir, Adam, and William. Robert appears in 1220 as connected with state affairs[4], and about 1275 a Sir Robert de Vaus married Clementia relict of Robert de Scales, whose marriage belonged to the king[5]. This Robert de Vaus had seven sons, Robert, who died when young,

---

[1] Nicholls' *Leicestershire*, Vol. III. p. 1129.
[2] Burke's *Peerage*—Vaux of Harrowden.
[3] Blomefield's *Norfolk*, IX. 38, IV. 388; Godwin, *English Arch. Handbook*, p. 167.
[4] Rym. *Fœd.* Vol. I. p. I. p. 81.
[5] Blomefield's *Norfolk*, IX. 21.

William, Oliver, John, Philip, Roger and Hugh. William appears to have been the eldest of these, and to have died without issue. The estates, therefore, devolved upon his brother, Sir Oliver de Vaus, who married Petronilla de la Mare. The issue of this marriage was Robert, who died young, without issue, William, who married Alianora de Ferrers, but also died without issue, and Sir John de Vaus, who married Maud, Lady of Surlingham, and who died in 1288 A.D. This Sir John is therefore the ancestor of the family given in the pedigree by Nicholls. He was a landholder in the county of Cambridge during the reigns of Henry III. and Edward I.[1] and was appointed Itinerant Justice for the counties of Cumberland, Westmorland and Northumberland in 1278, for the county of Nottingham in 1280, Lincoln 1281, Leicester 1284, Northampton 1285, and for Cambridgeshire and Huntingdonshire in 1286[2].

Robert de Vaus, his son, and the first of the family whose name occurs with reference to Bottisham, married a lady named Alice, but who she was does not appear. It appears subsequently that the land belonging to this family lay in Bottisham Lode as their manor was so called, but Robert is stated in 1302 to have possessed a piece of ground in Whitelands, near the land of Elias de Bekyngham, and the Priors of Tonbridge and Anglesey. This piece of land would be therefore adjacent to "the Vineyards[3]."

Robert de Vaus had two sisters, Petronilla the wife of Sir William de Norford, and Maud who married Sir William de Roos[4]. Of the issue of Robert de Vaus it is difficult to speak with certainty. Nicholls makes his son to be Elias de Vaux[5], who was Itinerant Justice for Norfolk[6] while Burke on the other hand makes Elias to be the great-grandson of Roger de Vaus, who he says was the fourth son of Oliver de Vaus in the time of King John. However, although we find mention of John de Vallibus, miles, as a witness to a document dated

---

[1] *Testa de Nevill*, p. 357.   [2] Cole MSS. Vol. IV. fol. 7 b.
[3] Nicholls' *Leicestershire*, Vol. III. p. 1129.
[4] Blomefield's *Norfolk*, Vol. III. p. 344.
[5] Dugdale, *Or. Jur.* p. 27.   [6] Blomefield's *Norfolk*, Vol. IV. p. 388.

1317 A.D., Elias, presumably son of Robert de Vaus, held land
in Bottisham in 1327, when Henry atte Pond was arrested to
answer concerning an agreement respecting his house and the
keeping of a "dies amoris[1]." Elias de Vaus gained £10 damages,
and was then staying in Bottisham on this "dies amoris," and
for 15 days afterwards "quo tempore perdidit terras per assisam
apud Chelmesford[2]." He married Elizabeth, daughter of Robert
de Hastings, and must have died before 1336, for in that year
Alice the wife of Gilbert the tailor is stated to have given a piece
of land to Thomas son of Robert de Vaux de Bodekesham, parson
of the church of Adyngburgh. Cole states that when he saw this
document it had appended to it a neat seal of brown wax with
these arms—a cross inter four martlets and a bordure engrailed
—round the arms is written av. m. gr. (ave maria gratia). This
seal he wrongly attributes to Thomas de Vaus, for though in the
visitation for Worcester the arms of Sir John de Vaus give
martlets, Cole himself gives from another document a pen-and-
ink sketch of a seal[3], upon which was a cross not in a shield,
and in the corners of it a fleur-de-lis and the superscription
'Sigillum Thome de Vaus.' Adyngborough or Attenborough,
as it is more usually spelt, is in the hundred of Broxtow in the
county of Nottingham; and John de Grey of Cudnoure by
a fine dated 13 Ed. III. passed one acre of land in Toneton and
the advowson of the church of Adyngburgh, which Thomas de
Vaus then held for life, by virtue of a fine levied at York the
day after All Souls, 11 Ed. III., to the prior and convent of
Felley and their successors, to which monastery it was appropriated by William, Archbishop of York, about the year 1343[4].
But the name of Thomas de Vaus continues to be described as
of Bottisham in various documents up to the time of his death
in Jan. 1352[5]. He was succeeded by Edmund de Vaus, or 'le
Vaus as he is styled. From 1350 to 1362 his name constantly
appears and he therefore probably resided at Bottisham Lode.

---

[1] ? =wedding-day.　　　[2] Vide Court Rolls of the Manor.
[3] Cole MSS. Vol. IV. fol. 14 b.　　　[4] Vide Thoroton, Notts. Vol. II. p. 178.
[5] In 1345 he had license from the Bishop to have mass performed in his
oratory at Bottisham Lode, as had also John de Vaus in 1401. Vide Cole MSS.
Vol. XXIII. fol. 59 and Vol. XXIV. fol. 233.

After the death of Edmund le Vaus the property seems to have passed into the hands of John Vaux, who is described as of Bottisham Lode in 1401, and then to William de Vaux. Nicholls' pedigree states William to have been the son of Elias de Vaus before-mentioned, who, according to Burke, had in right of his marriage obtained the manor of Harrowden in Northampton-shire. He was taken prisoner in Scotland in company with Andrew Cambel in 1347[1], and appears to have spent most of his life fighting in the wars with that country. He married, 17 Ric. II., Johanna daughter of Anachoret wife of John Russell of Bedfordshire and by that marriage gained possession of the manor of Shankton in Leicestershire. His son William Vaus married Elianora daughter of Sir Thomas Draketon of Welby, and had a son Sir William Vaus, who married Maud daughter of Sir William Lucy. The son of this marriage, Sir William Vaus, knt., was a strong adherent of Henry the Sixth, and is stated to have married the daughter of Gregory Peniston of Courtsells in Piedmont, by whom he had a son and heir, Sir Nicholas Vaus. In the fourth year of Edward the Fourth he was attainted of high treason and his estates forfeited. The king "gave to Sir Ralph Hastings, knt., in fee one messuage in Northtone, called Le Kay and other messuages there, the manor of Shanketon in Leicestershire, one close called "Hardwyke close" in Shanketon aforesaid, containing three hundred acres, the manor of Napton in Warwickshire, and one messuage and thirty-five acres of land in Napton aforesaid, the manor of Grendonse alias Valens in Shelford Magna in Cambridgeshire, the manor of Bottisham Lode, one messuage and a hundred acres of land called Horspath, &c., lately the property of William Vaus, knight attainted[2]." During the battle of Tewkesbury in 1471, this adherent of Henry the Sixth was slain, but after his death his son and heir Sir Nicholas was partially restored to his estates, and was eventually created Lord Vaux of Harrowden, whose descendant still holds the title. He married, firstly, Eliza-

[1] Rym. *Fœd.* Vol. III. Part I. pp. 19, 25, 151, 154, 155, 156, 157.

[2] Rot. Pat. Cal. p. 308. This is the earliest mention of the *manor* of Bottisham Lode. Up to the time of Edmund de Vaus suit was paid to the Lords of the manor of Bottisham, as of the Honor of Clare.

beth daughter of Henry, Lord Fitzhugh, by whom he had issue, and secondly, Anne, daughter and heiress of Thomas Greene of Greens Norton in Northamptonshire. It is curious that as early as 1424 Edmund Mortimer, Earl of March, is stated at his death to have possessed a tenement in Bottisham called "Vauses Rent." The name of Ralph de Hastings does not again occur with reference to this property, for Sir Nicholas Vaux on regaining some of his lands won back also this manor in Bottisham, and although Lord Vaux is mentioned as a tenant of the convent of Anglesey in the ministers' accounts after the suppression, he passed this manor with that of Grendons to William Peniston in 25 Hen. VIII. Subsequently however this manor was united to that of Alingtons.

Before giving some notice of the family of Allington, the pedigree of that of Vaux is subjoined:—

Harold de Vaux of Vaux = * * *
in Normandy.

Hubert = | Vaux of Gillesland. Ranulph = | Vaux of Tryermayne. Robert, founder of Pentney = Abbey.

William = Oliver. Henry.

Robert = * * * Adam. William.

Robert ob. inf. William. ob. s. p. Sir Oliver = Petronilla de la Mare. John. Philip. Roger. Hugh.

Robert, ob. s. p. William = Alianora de Ferrers = (2) Roger de Quency, in 1252. Sir John = Maud, lady ob. 1288. | of Surlingham.

Petronilla = Sir Will. de Norford. Maud = Sir Will. de Roos. Robert of = Alice * * * John de Bottisham. | Vallibus, miles?

Elias = Elizabeth, d. of | Robt. de Hastings. Thomas, parson of Attenborough. Edmund = Emma * * * Johanna John of Bottisham Lode.

William = Johanna, d. of Anachoret, w. of John Russell, of Beds.

William = Helen, d. of Sir Thos. Draketon, of Welby.

William = Maud, d. of Sir Will. Lucy.

Sir William, = d. of Gregory Peniston, of Coursells, Piedmont. ob. 1471. |

Eliz. d. of Henry, Ld. Fitzhugh, = Sir Nicholas, = (2) Anne, d. of Thos. Greene, | 1st Lord Vaux, | of Greenes Norton. of Harrowden. |

issue. issue.

The family of Allington, which was very powerful in the *Allington.* county of Cambridge and neighbouring counties, has at various times changed their principal place of residence. Though located for some time at Bottisham it does not there date further back than the fifteenth century; and though the present representatives of the various branches of this family do not belong to the titled nobility, still they may fairly claim to belong to a race as aristocratic as any in the land.

Their ancestor was Sir Hildebrand de Alyngton, who was under marshall to William the Conqueror at the battle of Hastings. An old pedigree states that after the resistance of the men of Kent to the Norman invasion had been overcome, "Medwaycester castle was given to Sir Hildebrand Alyngton, knight. The former proprietor, Sir John, had however a fair daughter named Emlyn who, as she sued earnestly for the life of her father, even so Sir Hildebrand was as earnest a suitor to her for marriage, which taking effect, the inheritance was conferred again to the right heir."

Sir Alan de Alyngton or Alleyne, as it is sometimes written, was a descendant of the above-mentioned Sir Hildebrand. According to the same pedigree, "He was a great favourite with William Rufus, and a great devisor of building, and was thought to be the chief doer for the building of Westminster Hall, which was the Palatium Regium, and by king Henry the First converted to the use it now is, and much beautified by Edward the Third[1]."

His son, Sir Solomon de Alington, knt., is stated to have built the castle of Allington, but other pedigrees make Hugh to be the descendant of Alan, then Solomon, then Rainulph, and then Hildebert who married the daughter of Thomas Apledorfield. His son named Hugh married and had issue Thomas, of whom the son William Allington is described by all the pedigrees as of Bottisham and the husband of Dionysia or Dennis, daughter of William Malet[2]. He is also represented to be "Lord of

[1] Vide Burke, *Dormant and Extinct Peerage,* quoting an old pedigree in the possession of Mr Allington of Swinhope.

[2] Harl. MSS. No. 6769, fol. 7, No. 6770, fol. 20; Add. MSS. No. 12,471, fol. 88. In 1409 he became possessed of 2 messuages, 1 water-mill, 300 acres of

Bottisham Hall, whose ancestors were great benefactors to
Anglesey Abbey in the same town, where many of them lie
buried.".

There is no further notice of this William Allington, but it
seems that a William Alyngton, priest, was presented by Thomas
Aylesbury of Fen Ditton, knt., to Blatherwick rectory in the
hundred of Corby in the county of Northampton on the 20th
of September, 1409 [1]. As the pedigrees give another William
Alyngton about this period, it seems possible that William
Alyngton of Bottisham may have taken orders after the death
of his wife. But be that as it may, this priest became rector of
West Briggs in Norfolk by exchange in 1411, and on the 23rd
of August, 1420, he was preferred by the king to the vacant
canonry and prebendal stall in the cathedral of Bayonne formerly held by master John Stokes [2].

William Allington of Bottisham was succeeded by his son
William, who in 1405 was appointed Treasurer of the Exchequer
in Ireland under Henry the Fourth, succeeding in that office Sir
Thomas de Burgh, a priest [3]. He was executor in 1417 to the
will of the Duke of Clarence in company with Margaret the
dowager Duchess, Dominus John Pelham, Dominus Henricus
Merston, clericus, and Dominus John Colville, miles [4]; and after
serving in various embassies sent to France in the years 1418
and 1419, was appointed Treasurer of Normandy. He continued
to be ambassador to France during the years 1420 and 1421 [5],
but soon after seems to have returned to England, and in 1430
was executor to the will of Sir John de Ingoldesthorp [6], whose
ancestor had married the heiress of the house of Burgh of
Borough Green [7], to which family Sir Thomas de Burgh, William
Allington's predecessor in Ireland, belonged [8]. But William

land, 30 of meadow, and 100 of pasture, together with 100s. rent in Bottisham
and Swaffham Bulbeck lately held by John Wolf. Vide *Close Rolls* 11 Hen. IV.
n. 17 and *Fines*, 12 Hen. IV.

[1] Whalley, *Northants.* Vol. II. p. 279.   [2] Rym. *Fœd.* Vol. III. p. III. p. 188.
[3] Rot. Pat. Cal. 7 Hen. IV.; Beatson, *Parl. Ind.* pp. 319, 320.
[4] Rym. *Fœd.* Vol. IV. p. III. p. 4.
[5] Ib. IV. III. pp. 67, 68, 75, 85, 91, 96, 181, 196, IV. 5, 6, 18, 41.
[6] Blomefield, *Norfolk*, Vol. III. p. 126.   [7] Lysons' *Cambs.* p. 96.
[8] Harl. MSS. No. 6769, fol. 7, No. 6770, fol. 20.

Allington was also a relation of the house of Burgh, for he had married Joanna, the daughter of William Burgh and of Joanna the daughter of John Berners of West Horsley in the county of Surrey, and of Berners Rooding in the county of Essex. Some pedigrees state that on the 19th of October, 1446, William Allington of Bottisham died, while others place his death at the year 1448, in which year he had obtained the king's licence to make a park at Horseheath [1]. Messrs Lysons however attribute the death of William Allington, the father of the Treasurer, to 1446 [2], but the pedigrees of the family at this period of their history are in such hopeless confusion, that it becomes impossible to speak with certainty on this point. What is most probable, however, is, that the Treasurer died in 1446, and that his son was the maker of the park at Horseheath, as a note in one of the pedigrees states [3]. About this period too occurs the name of Robert Allington as a theologian and a writer of note, who in 1394 was chancellor of Oxford [4].

But passing on to the next generation, we find that the Treasurer had three sons, William the eldest, Robert the second and John the third. Of these John the youngest is described as "qui a familia Eboracensi stetit contra fratres: filius erat Willielmi," which may be taken to mean that he sided with the Yorkists against the Lancastrians. He succeeded to certain property in right of his wife. For John Reyns, who married Catharine the daughter and heiress of Peter Escudamore, had a daughter Cecilia, who, by her husband Henry Streete, had Johanna the wife of John Ansty of Holme Hall in Quy, whose daughter and coheiress [5] Mary Ansty became the wife of John Allington. The arms of this last in one pedigree are thus tricked: Allington, sa. on a bend engrailed A. between six billets A. a mullet sable, impaling Ansty, O. a cross engrailed between four martlets gu. The mullet in the first coat would, as a mark of cadency, imply that John Allington was the third son, but in a list of the arms that stood in the old hall at Horseheath there is the following coat of arms ;—Allington as before without the

[1] Lysons' *Cambs.* p. 216.　　　　[2] Ib. p. 91.
[3] Harl. MSS. No. 6775, fol. 1*.　　[4] Vide Tanner, *Bibl. Brit. Hib.* p. 38.
[5] Vide antea, p. 38 and refs.

mullet, and instead, a label of three points ; impaling, 1 and 4
for Reyns, checky O. and gu. a canton ermine, and 2 and 3 for
Scudamore gu. three stirrups with buckles and straps O.; over
all an escutcheon of pretence for Ansty, O. a cross engrailed between four martlets gu.[1]. This coat would therefore be for
William Allington of Bottisham, nephew of John and husband
of Joan, daughter and coheiress of John Ansty. Whether John
lived at Bottisham there is no means of knowing, but, in the
pedigree given by Burke, the younger brother Robert is described as of Bottisham. He married firstly Joanna daughter
and heiress of John Argentein, who, in right of descent from the
family of Fitztec, possessed the manor of Wymondeley Magna
in Hertfordshire[2]. She died on the 15th of May, 1429, and
shortly after Robert Allington married Maria daughter of
Robert Brews or Bruose of the county of Norfolk. William
Allington the brother of Robert last mentioned was the maker
of the park at Horseheath, where he appears to have resided.
He married Elizabeth the elder sister of Joan Argentein, who
was also a coheiress to the Argentein estates. She was 18 years
of age when her sister Joan died[3], and through her, her husband
became at length sole heir to the property of the Argenteins.
During his life he attained a very high political position, for besides serving the office of Knight of the Shire for the county of
Cambridge in 1429, 1437 and 1440[4], he was chosen Speaker of
the House of Commons in 1429. The Commons announced to
the king's Lords " that they had chosen one William Alington,
Esq. to be their speaker, but desired a respite of two days
before they presented him, which being granted, the said
William Alington on the fourth day of the session made the
usual protestation and was allowed." He was also one of the
council of guardians appointed by Parliament for the government of the kingdom during the king's minority under Humphrey
Duke of Gloucester the Lord Protector[5]. He died in 1459,

[1] Vide Harl. MSS. No. 6775, fol. 57.
[2] Add. MSS. No. 12,471, fol. 88; Clutterbuck, *Herts.* Vol. II. p. 542.
[3] Esch. 7 Hen. VI. No. 8.
[4] Lipscombe's *Bucks.* Vol. I. p. 14.
[5] Manning, *Lives of the Speakers*, pp. 80—82.

eized of the manor of Wymondeley Magna which he held of the
ing, and of the manor of Wymondeley Parva which he held of
he king in chief, by the service of 6s. 8d. yearly, to be paid to
he wardship of the castle of Craven, He also held Bottisham,
nd the manor of Stapleford in the county of Hertford[1], which
e received from William Alington of Bottisham, his father, the
ord Treasurer, besides other property in Norfolk and elsewhere.
Y right of his inheritance to the Argentein estates, he obtained
ne office of cupbearer at the coronation of a sovereign, an office
hich continued to be hereditary in his family[2]. He and his
ife were buried in the church of Horseheath.

It is impossible here to pass over without some notice the *John Ar-*
areer of John Argentein. Cooper, I suppose on the authority *gentein.*
f Tanner, says that he was born at Bottisham, though Tanner
uotes Cott. MS. Julius F. vii. fol. 165, in which it is stated
1 a note by William Botoner that he was born at Kyrkeby
ear Norwich[3]. Anyhow, in 1457 he was elected from Eton to
Ling's, and became Proctor in 1472. He was M.D., Physi-
ian, and Dean of the Chapel, to Arthur, Prince of Wales: Rec-
or of Harlton cum Boxted in Suffolk, in 1487, and Glemsford
1 1488; of Cavendish in Suffolk in 1490; Prebend of Dernford
1 the church of Lichfield in 1494, which he exchanged for the
rebend of Bubbenhall in 1497, and for that of Pipa Parva in
501; Prebend of Holcomb in the church of Wells in 1498;
[aster of the Hospital of Saint John the Baptist at Dorchester
1 1499; and Provost of King's College in 1501. He proceeded
) the degree of Doctor in Divinity in 1504, and died on the
nd of Feb. 1507—8, and lies buried in his chantry on the
)uth side of his college chapel.

But to return to the Allington family. William Allington *Allington.*
ft two sons and a daughter, Margaret the wife of John Colville,
night, John, and William. Of these two sons, William was the
dest, and lived at Bottisham. His tomb in Bottisham church
1s been before described. The first notice that we have of him

---

[1] Clutterbuck's *Herts.* Vol. II. p. 215; Chauncy, *Herts.* p. 270.
[2] Burke, *Dormant and Extinct Peerage—Allington of England.*
[3] Cooper, *Ath. Cant.* Vol. I. p. 12; Tanner, *Bibl. Brit. Hib.* p. 48.

is in the register of William Gray, Bishop of Ely. It is there stated that on the 9th of January 1457, "Dominus concessit Joh. Ansty Senr. Licenciam faciendi matrimonium solempnizari in capella infra manerium suum de Holme Hall in parochiâ de Stowe-cum-Quy inter Willielmum Alyngton et Johannam filiam ejusdem Johannis." The foundation of this chapel bears date May 1450, in the year of John Ansty's age 72. It was to be served by one chaplain to pray for the King and Queen, the founder John Ansty and Joan his wife, John Ansty the second, son and heir, and Joan his wife, John Ansty the 3rd, son of John Ansty the 2nd, and Sibilla his wife, John Ansty the fourth, and John Moris Arm. and Elizabeth his wife, daughter of John Ansty the founder, &c.; for the souls of Edmund Earl of March, Richard Earl of Salisbury, Richard Lestraunge, Robert Anstye and Joan his wife, parents of the founder, Margaret late wife of the aforesaid John Ansty, Thomas Bernard and Margaret his wife, parents of Joan wife of the founder, John Bernard, clerk, licentiate in law, John Somerset, late chancellor of the most holy lord the king; Hugo Funcey and Alice his wife; and Robert Offewode, and all benefactors of the founder, &c., Cecilia daughter of John Ansty the third and Sibilla &c., Joan Ansty daughter of John Ansty the second &c., and Elizabeth her sister and Mary their sister. This was approved by Bishop Gray on the 18th of September, 1455. Cole adds the name of the chaplains who served this chantry up to the time of the dissolution[1].

William Allington was according to Cole appointed to be a justice in company with John Ansty and others[2], and in 1461 he was witness to a deed whereby John Daniell resigned the office of Prior of Anglesey, and had a pension accorded to him[3], while next year he obtained a license from Bishop Gray to hold mass in his chapels and oratories anywhere in the diocese, at the bishop's pleasure[4]. Ten years after this, viz. in 1472, a parliament was summoned on Tuesday, Oct. 6th, when the commons as usual presented their speaker William Alyng-

---

[1] Cole MSS. Vol. xxv. fol. 164.　　　[2] Ib. fol. 69.　　　[3] Ib. fol. 128.
[4] Ib. fol. 74; Reg. Gray, III. 49 a.

ton[1]. They then through their speaker, William Alyngton, besought the king to shew some mark of favour to Lewes de Bruges, a noble Burgundian, Lord of Gruthuse and Prince of Steinhuse, who had shewn Edward much kindness when he was forced to fly the kingdom in the 10th year of his reign. He thereupon, in Oct. 1472, created him Earl of Winchester, with £200 per annum, to uphold the dignity[2]. In 1475 we find mention of the chapel newly built to the praise of Almighty God and the glorious Virgin Mary, his mother, and Saint Martin and Mary Magdalene, at Bottisham, by our beloved and faithful William Alyngton, for his soul, and Joan his wife[3]. In the next year he was elected knight of the shire, and in 1478, January the 19th, the commons having elected their speaker presented William Alyngton to the King[4]. On the first of September, 1477, Bishop Gray dedit Willielmo Alyngton Sen. officium Ballivi Libertatis omnium dominiorum suorum in comitatu Cantabrigiæ et Huntingdoniæ extra insulam Eliensem ad terminum vitæ suæ prout Johannes Ansty nuper exercebat idem officium[5]. In the next year he served on the commission for the repair of the Great Bridge at Cambridge[6], and seems to have taken some part in schemes then on foot for draining the fens. In 1479, according to Messrs Lysons, he was appointed a member of the Privy Council with a handsome salary[7], but death seems to have cut short his career in that year. It is then in the inquisition post mortem that we find the first mention of the manor of Alyngtons, where it is described as a member of the honor of Clare, so that it seems that this manor was created for William Alyngton in 1478, a year before his death[8]. He died without issue, as all the pedigrees state, so his lands passed to the line of his brother John. It is singular that in no pedigree is his wife Joan Ansty mentioned. There

---

[1] Parry, *Parl. and Councils of England*, p. 192.

[2] Manning, *Lives of the Speakers*, pp. 117—119.

[3] Rot. Pat. 15 Ed. IV.

[4] Lipscombe, *Bucks.* Vol. i. p. 14; Parry, *Parl. and Councils of England*, p. 193.

[5] Cole MSS. Vol. xxv. fol. 128.   [6] *Ib.* Vol. xi.

[7] Lysons' *Cambs.* p. 216.

[8] Inq. post mortem, 19 Ed. IV. Cal. Vol. iv. p. 392.

is no tomb to her memory at Bottisham Church; but as her
family were seated at the neighbouring parish of Quy, it is not
improbable that she was buried there.   But little need be said
of John Allington, the brother of William.   He served the
office of sheriff in 1461, and was married to Maria, daughter
of Lawrence Cheyney.   She died in 1473, and he in 1479,
and they both were buried at Horseheath.   Bottisham now
seems to have been deserted by the Allington family, as the
William Allington, who succeeded to the estate, succeeded also
to his father's property at Horseheath, and resided there.   He
was twice married ; first, to Elizabeth, daughter of Henry
Wentworth, and secondly, to Elizabeth, daughter of Richard
Sapcoats, but in 1485 was slain at the battle of Bosworth,
where also his royal patron fell.   He had a sister, Maria,
married to John Newport, and a brother, Edward Allington,
who married the daughter of a gentleman named Gillott.   He
had, however, a son by his first wife to succeed him, Sir Giles
Allington, who married Mary, the daughter of Thomas Gardner,
who in his turn was succeeded, at his death in 1522, by his son,
Sir Giles Allington, Knt.   In 1511 and 1519, Sir Giles Allington, sen. served the office of sheriff for the counties of Cambridge and Huntingdon, and in 1530, 1545, and 1552, his son
held the same honour.   This Sir Giles was thrice married; firstly,
to Ursula, daughter of Robert Drury, who died in 1522 ; secondly,
to Alice, daughter and heiress of John Middleton, who was
buried at Horseheath, on the twentieth of September, 1563 ;
and, thirdly, to Margaret, daughter of John Talkarne, the widow
of Thomas Argell.   Sir Giles died on the 22nd of August, 1586,
aged 86.   His first wife, Ursula Drury, bore him a son, named
Robert, who however died in the lifetime of his father, May
23rd, 1552, aged 31, and lies buried at Horseheath.   Over his
tomb is a brass in a civilian's gown (the head gone as well as the
inscription), and the arms of Allington bearing 12 billets, and
a label for difference, and the arms of Coningsby for his wife
Margaret, who after his death married Thomas Pledger,
the son of Thomas Pledger, of Ashden, in Essex, by Joan,
daughter of John Higham, of Shudy-camps, his wife.   It is
possible that Robert Allington lived for some time at Bottisham,

as during his life his father resided at Horseheath, and as Margaret Allington his wife resided afterwards with Thomas Pledger at Bottisham. But some time before this the Allington family had some ideas of selling the property, for Cole mentions an indenture tripartite between Sir Robert Drury, Sir Giles Allington, and Robert Fenrother, citizen and alderman of the city of London, whereby, with the consent of Sir Robert, Sir Giles sells to Fenrother his manor of Bottisham, with the watermill, and all the members and appurtenances in Swaffham Bulbeck, Anglesey, and Wilbraham. This document is dated the 3rd of May, 8 Hen. VIII., but the sale could hardly have been effected, for in the minister's account of 32—33 Hen. VIII., Sir Giles Allington is stated to hold certain land in Bottisham, and it is certain that James Allington, the son of Robert, re- sided there. Margaret Allington, as her monument records, had a numerous progeny. Three of these were in some way connected with the parish. George Allington entered the University of Cambridge, as a member of Trinity Hall. His will is dated Oct. 1. 1584, and was proved on the 16th of October in the same year. He directs his body to be buried at Bottisham, which was accordingly done on the 7th of Oct. 1584, and he appoints his brother James Allington, gent. of Bottisham com. Cant. his executor, and he leaves legacies to Margaret Allington, daughter of his brother Giles Allington, and Margaret Soame, daughter of his sister Elizabeth[1]. James Allington then resided at Bottisham, but he afterwards seems to have gained possession of the Lordship of Milding or. Melding, in the hundred of Babergh, and county of Suffolk: it was soon after sold to the family of Canham. James Allington was never married, and died on the 16th of Sep- tember, 1626. Anne his sister seems also to have been con- nected with Bottisham: for she married Arthur Breame, and had by him a son named Giles Breame, who was the donor of a charity to the poor of Bottisham and East Ham in Essex, and who died on the 31st of March, 1621[2]. Sir Giles Allington

[1] Vide Baker MSS., Harl. MSS. No. 7030, fol. 318.
[2] There seems to have been some mismanagement in the administration of this charity. Vide the following paper, copied by Cole (MSS. Vol. IV. fol. 7 b):

married Mary, daughter of Sir John Spencer, and was succeeded
by Sir Giles Allington, knt. of Horseheath, his son, who was
sheriff for the two counties in 1599, and who died in 1638.
By his wife Dorothy, the daughter of Thomas Cecil, Earl of
Exeter, who died on the 10th of November, 1613, he had many
children, of whom William Allington, the 4th son and 9th child,
was created on the 28th of July, 1642, Baron Allington of
Killard, co. of Cork, Ireland. He probably resided at Bottisham,
at least during the years of 1637 and 1638, when his children
Lionel and Dorothea were born and died. He married Elizabeth, eldest daughter of Sir Lionel Tollemache, of Helmingham,
who died April 14th, 1673, and was buried at Horseheath
by the side of her husband, who died in 1648. He was
succeeded by his son William, the 2nd Lord Allington, who on
the 5th of December, 1683, was also created Baron Allington
of Wymondeley, but died on the 1st of February, in the
next year. He married Catharine, daughter of Henry Lord
Stanhope, who died without issue in 1662. He then married Juliana Noel, daughter of Baptist Viscount Camden,
and thirdly Diana, daughter of William Russel, first Duke
of Bedford, and widow of Sir Greville Verney, knt. He had
the following issue. Giles, third Lord Allington, baptized
Oct. 20, 1680, died Sept. 18, 1691; Hildebrand, died without issue in 1682; Argentine, who died in the same year;
Catherine, sister and co-heiress of Giles, niece and co-heiress
of Hildebrand, Lord Allington, of Ireland, who married, on
the 28th of Aug. 1694, Sir Nathaniel Napier, knt. and bart.,
and died April 13, 1724; Diana, sister and co-heiress, born
in 1676, and married, June 18, 1700, to Sir George Warburton,
bart., died June 17, 1705, and lies buried at Lilley in the co.
of Herts. Thus the title and direct representative of this

"For Mr Allington to appear, &c. Wednesday, May 5, 1641. By virtue of an
order and a warrant from the grand committee for grievances under the hand of
Mr Glyn, who setteth in the chair, you are there to appear and make answer to
all such matters as shall be objected against you touching the poor almsmen of
East Ham in Essex, and to bring with you all such papers and writings as
concern the same, especially the indenture produced in evidence at Stratford
Langton to the Jury there, and all such conveyances whereby Mr Breame conveyed the said lands to your father."

BOTTISHA
NA HERT

PEDIGREE OF ALINGTON, ALKINGTON, OR ALKINGTON, OF HORSEHEATH AND WYMONDLEY MAGNA, HERTFORDSHIRE AND WYMONDLEY MAGNA, HERTFORDSHIRE, COUNTY OF CAMBRIDGE

M AND HORSEHEATH, COUNTY OF CAMBRI
FORDSHIRE

family became extinct, and only members of a
ch of the family now survive.

is a pedigree of the family omitting many who
rect line, and have no connection with the history

CHAPTER VII.

FAMILY OF JENYNS.

FROM the hands of the Allingtons, the manor called by their name, as well as that of Vaux, passed into the hands of the family of Jenyns, who now hold it, and whose seat is Bottisham Hall. This family, which has contained many illustrious members, takes its origin from Ralph Jenyns, who is described as of Islington. This Ralph Jenyns is stated, in a deed dated April 29th, 1563, to have become possessor by purchase of the manor of Churchill in Somersetshire. He married Jane, the daughter of Ralph Rowlett[1], Esq., and died in the year 1572 A.D. He was succeeded by his son, Richard Jenyns, who was born in 1550 A.D., but of whom little is known, except that he is probably the same personage as Richard Jenyns of Essex, who, in 1588 A.D., is found as a subscriber of £25 for the defence of the county against the Spanish invasion[2]. To whom, however, he was married does not appear in the pedigrees; but he was succeeded by John Jenyns of Churchill, born in the year 1580 A.D., and knighted in the year 1603 A.D. This Sir John Jenyns was twice married, and by each wife became the ancestor of illustrious families. His first wife was Anne, daughter of Sir William Bouchier, and his eldest son by her is described as Sir John Jenyns, knt., of Saint Albans, in the county of Hertford, chosen M.P. for that borough in the Parliament of 3 and 15 Car. I.[3] He likewise served the office of sheriff for the same county in the year 1626 A.D. The wife of this last Sir John Jenyns was Alice, daughter of Sir Richard Spenser, whose issue consisted of one son and two daughters, Anne

---

[1] Of Caldecote and Radwell, co. of Herts. Vide Clutterbuck, *Hist. of Herts*, III. 497, 550.

[2] Vide the list of contributors, printed for Leigh and Sotheby. London. 4to. square, 1798.

[3] Willis, *Not. Parl.* pp. 221, 232, Vol. III.

and Dorothy; the daughters died within a year of each other, namely, in 1656 A.D., and 1657 A.D. Richard the son became united in marriage to Frances, the daughter of Sir Gifford Thornhurst, and it seems that during his lifetime the manor of Churchill, in the county of Somerset, was disposed of[1]. For, on the 10th of June, 1652 A.D., an agreement was entered into between Richard Jenyns and Francis his wife, and Dame Alice Jenyns, widow, on the one part, and John Churchill, Esq. on the other part, being the conveyance of the manor of Churchill to Sir John Churchill and his heirs. But though in the pedigrees no mention is found of John Jenyns of Churchill as brother to Richard, it does not seem certain that he had no brothers, for a tombstone in the church of Churchill records the memory of John Jenyns, born in 1646 A.D., died in 1697 A.D., and his son also named John, born in 1685 A.D., and died in 1731 A.D. But anyhow, the family of Richard Jenyns consisted of two sons and three daughters. Of these, Ralph and John the sons died young, and the daughters, Frances, Barbara and Sarah, were endowed with nature's fairest gifts. The eldest of these, Frances, from her great beauty, obtained the sobriquet of "La Belle Jennings," and was at length the wife of Richard, Duke of Tyrconnel, and attained to a ripe age; for though born in the year 1648 A.D., she did not die till the year 1730 A.D.[2] Her sister, Barbara, though born three years later, died in the year 1678 A.D., leaving one daughter, Barbara, by her husband, Edward Griffith, Esq. Sarah, however, the third daughter, became the wife of John, Duke of Marlborough, and was born in 1660 A.D., and died in 1744 A.D. She was a favourite attendant of Queen Anne[3].

But as from this, the elder branch of the family of Jenyns,

[1] He was M.P. for S. Albans in the Parl. of 16 Car. I. Vide Willis, *Not. Parl.* Vol. III. p. 245.

[2] Her portrait is said to be given in Harding's *Memoirs of Count Grammont*, but I have not been able to verify the reference.

[3] When she offered a considerable reward for the best epitaph on the great Duke, Dr Evans of Oxford sent her the following lines:—

"Here lies John, Duke of Marlborough
Who ran the French thorough and thorough.
He married Sarah Jennings, spinster,
Died at St James, buried at Westminster.'

there was no direct issue, so the succession was kept up by the second wife of Sir John Jenyns the elder, of Churchill. This second wife was Dorothy, the daughter of Thomas Bulbeck, and afterwards the wife of John Latch, whom she survived, as her death took place in 1649 A.D. Of this marriage there were two children; the second, Elizabeth, died unmarried, but, according to one pedigree, "had £80 per annum during her life for £1000 :" what this alludes to is not known. The eldest son was Thomas Jenyns, who was born in 1609 A.D., and became possessed of the manor of Hayes in the county of Middlesex. This he continued to enjoy till the year 1656 A.D., when, at his death, he was survived by his wife, Veare, the daughter of Sir Thomas Palmer. By her he had issue four sons and two daughters, of whom the eldest was Thomas, who was drowned at Bristol in 1679 A.D. Though married to Mary, the daughter of John Knight, Esq., this last had no children, and the manor of Hayes devolved upon his next brother, Roger, who was born in 1636 A.D., and died in 1693 A.D. This Roger Jenyns of Hayes married Sarah the daughter of Joseph Latch, and became the progenitor of the family of Jenyns of Bottisham Hall.

The family of Roger Jenyns of Hayes consisted of five children, three sons and two daughters; one of these sons named Thomas, and one daughter Sarah, died unmarried; Dorothy, the youngest, became the wife of Thomas Biggs, Esq., but the other sons, John and Roger, both achieved for themselves an important position in the county of Cambridge. John, the eldest, is described as of Hayes, but afterwards of Doddington in the isle of Ely. What brought the family into Cambridgeshire is quite uncertain; but at this time many schemes were afloat for the drainage of the fens, in which the two brothers, John and Roger, took an important part, and thereby made a considerable fortune. Roger Jenyns, who was then settled at March, filled the office of conservator in the year 1666 A.D., and in 1684 A.D. was bailiff, while his elder brother was conservator[1]. The influence of both was on the increase, and in the Parliament of 1710 A.D., John Jenyns was chosen, in company with John Bromley,

---

[1] *Hist. of the Bedford Level*, 1685, pp. 64, 65.

to represent the interests of the county of Cambridge. This honour he continued to enjoy up to the time of his death in 1715 A.D.[1] Roger Jenyns married Martha, the widow of John Mingay; and about the time of the death of his father purchased the estate at Bottisham, to which parish he removed his residence. His services procured him the honour of knighthood, at Kensington, on January the 9th of the same year, and he then became Sir Roger Jenyns of Bottisham Hall[2]. He seems to have been a warm Tory in politics; and, though he never sat in Parliament, he filled the office of High Sheriff for the county in 1701, and took a keen interest in elections. By his first wife he had one son and two daughters, who died in infancy; and on the death of their mother in 1701 A.D., Sir Roger fell in love with Elizabeth the daughter of Sir Peter Soame of Heydon, and married her in 1702 A.D.

By this second marriage he had one son, Soame Jenyns, the celebrated Poet and Divine. This accomplished author was born in Great Ormond Street, London. Curiously enough, he saw the light exactly at twelve o'clock at night on the 31st of December, 1703, or the 1st of January, 1704, and he preferred to celebrate his birthday on the latter date[3]. During his youth there seem to have been no incidents in his life worthy of record. He studied first under a tutor named the Rev. W. Hill, and next under the Rev. Stephen White[4], and at his 19th year was sent to the University of Cambridge. He was then located at St John's College, as a fellow-commoner, under Dr Edmondson, one of the principal tutors. But he did not long reside there, for at the end of about three years he left Cambridge, and during the summer-time stayed with his father at Bottisham, while in winter he took up his quarters in London. In 1727 A.D. he published his "Art of Dancing," inscribed to Lady Fanny Fielding. During his residence in London he is said to have been of gay habits, to which his great powers of conversation probably disposed him. According to one authority he was much given to nocturnal frolics, as most young men were at that day, and attended in disguise every execution at Ty-

---

[1] *Brit. Parl. Register.*
[2] *Gent. Mag.* Vol. LX. p. 596.
[3] *Gent. Mag.* Vol. XXIV. p. 142.
[4] Vicar of Swaffham Bulbeck.

burn[1]; and though he afterwards was so firm an upholder of
Christianity, in early life was reckoned amongst the number of
unbelievers[2].   Be that as it may, he was early in life, at the
instigation of Sir Roger, married to his kinswoman, Mary, the
sole daughter and heiress of Col. Soame, of Dereham Grange,
in the county of Norfolk.   By this marriage Soame Jenyns received a great accession of fortune, and though for some time
all went well, the union was not a happy one.   In the year
1740 A.D. Sir Roger Jenyns died, and was buried at Bottisham
church, in which was erected a handsome monument stated to
have cost £150.   Soame Jenyns then took up his residence at
the hall, and, according to tradition, kept up a state of great
magnificence.   Stories are handed down of his handsome coach
and four, which he used to drive into Cambridge, of the grand
state room at Bottisham Hall with the velvet hangings, of the
quantity of plate, and of the great stone lions which guarded
the entrance to the mansion.   A shield of arms, which was formerly in the house, perpetuated the memory of his ancestors.
There were six coats as follows: Baron. A. on a fess gu. 3 bezants O. on a canton az. a crescent O. for difference (for he was
descended from the second marriage of Sir John Jenyns of
Churchill); impaling, 5 coats, viz. 1. A. a cross engrailed gu.
int. 4 water bougets sa. for Bourchier, 1st wife of Sir John
Jenyns of Churchill.   2. A. 3 bars wavy az., over them a lion
rampant A. for Bulbeck (granted April 24, 1559), the 2nd wife
of Sir John Jenyns of Churchill.   3. O. 2 bars gu. int. 6 trefoils slipped O. on a chief O. a greyhound courant sa. for Palmer,
wife of Thomas Jenyns of Hayes.   4. A. on a fess wavy az.,
3 lozenges O. int. 3 escutcheons gu. for Latch, wife of Roger
Jenyns of Hayes.   5. Gu. a chevron int. 3 mallets O. for
Soame, the lady of Sir Roger Jenyns of Bottisham Hall.

   But after the death of Sir Roger, Mrs Jenyns, the lady of
Soame Jenyns, did not continue to reciprocate the affection
of her husband, for, upon a pretence of a journey to Bath, she
made an elopement, and never returned to Bottisham after-

---

[1] Vide *European Magazine*, 1782, March, p. 192.
[2] *Life of Soame Jenyns*, by Davenport.   Vide *British Poets*.   Whittingham,
Chiswick, Vol. LXXI. p. 18.

wards; and it was commonly reported that she had long been
in secret alliance with her husband's friend, a Leicestershire
gentleman[1]. However, after this a separation took place by
mutual consent, and Soame Jenyns allowed her an annuity up
to the time of her death, which took place in 1753 A.D. on
the 30th of July. She had no child by her husband, but she
had a son born on the 21st of June 1750 A.D., of which nothing
further is known, and who probably died in infancy[2]. During
his first wife's time it seems that there was living in the same
house with Soame Jenyns his first cousin, a Miss Grey, daughter
of Henry Grey of Hackney, who had married another of Sir
Peter Soame's daughters and had failed in his business, which
was that of a merchant[3]; this had probably occasioned some
uneasiness in the mind of Soame Jenyns' first wife: but anyhow, within a year of her death, he married this lady in the
old chapel of Somerset House, she being then 52 years of age[4];
and though he lived with her for more than 30 years, he had
no child by her. While she lived to the ripe age of 94, Soame
Jenyns died in the year 1787, on the 18th of December, in
Sydney Street, London. He was buried at Bottisham, on Monday the 31st of December, by William Lort Mansell, the sequestrator, who wrote in the parish register that eulogy of his
virtues and disposition, which has already been described[5]. There
is a fine portrait of him by Sir Joshua Reynolds in Bottisham
Hall; and a mezzo-tinto after this picture was executed by
Dickinson in 1776 A.D., which bears out Cole's description of
him, as a man "of a very finical appearance." But he was a
man whose intellectual powers were of the very highest order.
His life was active and diversified. He had read much and
seen more. He was noted for the sprightliness of his remarks
and for the versatility of his conversational powers; and he was
said by Mr Burke to have been one of those who wrote the
purest English: that is, the simplest and most aboriginal

---

[1] Cole MSS. Vol. xxviii. fol. 161.
[2] *Gent. Mag.* Vol. xx. p. 283.
[3] Cole MSS. Vol. xxviii. fol. 161.
[4] Malcolm, *Lond. Red.* Vol. iv. p. 296.
[5] Vide supra, p. 57.

language, the least qualified with foreign impregnation. "On his death-bed he reviewed his life; and with a visible gleam of joy, he gloried in the belief that his little book on Christianity had been useful. It was received perhaps where greater works could not make their way, and so might have added the ardour of virtue to the confidence of truth. He spoke of his death as one prepared to die. He did not shrink from it as an evil, nor as a punishment: but met it with decent firmness as his original destiny ; the kind release from what was worse, the more kind summons to all that is better[1]."

In politics he was at first a Tory, though afterwards he veered round and became a Whig. In the year 1742 A.D. he was first elected to represent the interests of the county of Cambridge in the general election of that year, and soon after, by the interest of Lord Hardwicke, he was made a commissioner of the Board of Trade and Plantations, which office he held until the dissolution of that board ; it was commonly quoted as a saying of his, " that the East and West Indies were two great wings that would fly away with little Britain." For 31 years he held his seat in Parliament, representing, first the county, and afterwards the borough of Cambridge ; but in the year 1754 he was returned for the borough of Dunwich, in the county of Suffolk, but on Lord Dupplin's going up to a seat in the House of Lords he vacated his seat, and succeeded him as the member for the borough of Cambridge.

The works of Soame Jenyns that attained to the greatest celebrity besides his poetical pieces were, an essay called "The inquiry into the origin of evil" and "The Internal Evidence of the Christian Religion."—In the first of these he was much opposed by Johnson, who, according to Boswell, in a critical essay in the Literary Magazine shewed how he ventured far beyond his depth, and exposed him by acute argument and brilliant wit. The same author, Boswell, mentions how he remembers, when the late Mr Bicknell's humorous performance entitled "The Musical Travels of Joel Collyer," in which a slight attempt was made to ridicule Johnson, was ascribed to Soame Jenyns, "Ha," said Johnson, "I thought I had given

[1] Vide Biog. Notice in *Gent. Mag.* Vol. LVII. p. 1192.

him enough of it." He also quotes Mr Courtenay's description
of Johnson's triumph over Jenyns :—

> "When specious sophists with presumption scan
> The source of evil, hidden still from man;
> Revise Arabian tales, and vainly hope
> To rival St. John, and his scholar Pope;
> Though metaphysics spread the gloom of night,
> By reason's star he guides our aching sight;
> The bounds of knowledge marks, and points the way
> To pathless wastes where wildered sages stray;
> Where, like a farthing link-boy, Jenyns stands,
> And the dim torch drops from his feeble hands."

Though for some time no answer appeared to the attack
thus made upon Soame Jenyns, after the death of Johnson, the
following lines were published, signed with his name, and
intended as an epitaph :—

> "Here lies poor Johnson. Reader have a care
> Tread lightly, lest you rouse a sleeping bear;
> Religious, moral, generous and humane
> He was—but self-sufficient, rude and vain;
> Ill-bred, and overbearing in dispute,
> A scholar and a Christian—yet a brute.
> Would you know all his wisdom and his folly,
> His actions, sayings, mirth and melancholy,
> Boswell and Thrale retailers of his wit,
> Will tell you how he wrote and coughed and spit[1]."

The great flatterer of Johnson, of course, would hardly let
such an epitaph go without a reply on behalf of his patron,
so he rejoined with the following :—

> "Epitaph prepared for a creature not quite dead yet."

> "Here lies a little ugly nauseous elf,
> Who judging only from his wretched self,
> Feebly attempted, petulant and vain,
> The origin of evil to explain.
> A mighty genius at this elf displeased,
> With critic grasp the urchin squeezed.
> For thirty years its coward spleen it kept,
> Till in the dust the mighty genius slept;
> Then stunk and fretted in expiring snuff,
> And blinked at Johnson with its last poor puff[2]."

This effusion hardly enhances the reputation of Boswell's

---

[1] *Gent. Mag.* for the year 1786.

[2] Boswell's *Life of Johnson*, ed. Croker, p. 106.

style or poetical talents. He had already spoken of Soame
Jenyns with a sneer as "a sincere Christian," for in 1774
appeared "The Internal Evidence of the Christian Religion," a
work of which at first the seriousness and sincerity were much
questioned, but which afterwards achieved a remarkable success,
and became a text-book in the studies of the University of
Cambridge.

Although twice married Soame Jenyns left no son to succeed him in his property, and consequently the estates devolved
upon the descendant of an elder branch of the family. John
Jenyns of Hayes, and Doddington in the Isle of Ely, by his
marriage with Jane the daughter of James Clitheroe had born
to him three sons, of whom John the eldest, was twice married,
and died in 1723 A.D. The next son was James Jenyns, who
is, we presume, the same personage as James Jenyns of Ely, who
took a strong interest in politics : but he was unfortunate in his
marriage with Rachel Estwick, for they could not agree together, and serious doubts were entertained of her fidelity.
It is this which is alluded to in a verse of a satirical poem that
was written upon Dr Gooch afterwards Bishop of Ely ;—

"The affairs on the road they'd a great deal of talk on,
Till Shepheard's coach carried them safe to the Falcon;
There was Shepheard and Lightfoot[1] and Kettle[2] and Gooch.
But I think Mrs. Jenyns was not in the coach.
　　　　　　　　　　　　　　　Derry down, &c."[3]

It was popularly supposed that Mrs Jenyns had been too
intimate with Mr Shepheard, and in 1729 A.D. Mr Jenyns sued
for a divorce "to enable him to marry again, and to illegiti-
mate the spurious child that was born to her since the separation, or any other child that should be born." Mr Shepheard
was then a member of the Lower House, and on March the 9th,
1729—30 A.D., a message was sent from the Lords to intimate
that the attendance of Samuel Shepheard, Esq. as a witness upon

[1] Justice of the Peace at Ely.

[2] Joseph Kettle, Chairman of the Quarter Sessions, and J.P. for the town of
Cambridge, where he kept a pack of hounds. In 1736 he erected a playhouse at
Cambridge, whereupon the University got an Act of Parliament rendering illegal
dramatic performances in or near the town. He was buried at Cottenham.

[3] Vide Cole MSS. Vol. xxxi. fol. 142.

the bill was not required [1]. The bill was therefore rejected. In the year 1733 A.D., James Jenyns died, and his property went to his younger brother Roger Jenyns, of New Windsor, in the county of Bucks. A tablet to his memory in the church of Clewer hard by informs us that he was a Justice of the Peace for the counties of Berkshire and Buckinghamshire, and for near thirty years Clerk of the Assizes to the Norfolk circuit. He was twice married; first, to Dorothy the daughter of John Harvey, and secondly, to Elizabeth the daughter of Benjamin Ewen, Esq., who survived him 26 years. A son of his by his first wife was John Harvey Jenyns of Ely, who had by his wife Elizabeth, the daughter of the Rev. Edward Chappelow, besides John who died in infancy, a son, who succeeded to the property left by Soame Jenyns, as well as to the House and Manor of Anglesey Abbey, from Elizabeth the wife of Soame Jenyns. Born on the 19th of June, 1763, he in due course entered at Cambridge, and after taking his degree became a clergyman, and, in November 1787, was preferred to the incumbency of the two Swaffhams. In 1802 A.D., however, he was chosen to fill the 8th prebendal stall in the Cathedral Church of Ely, which he continued to hold until his death in 1848 A.D., when Anglesey Abbey was sold, and his son George Jenyns, Esq. took up his residence at Bottisham Hall, as the heir of his father. During Canon Jenyns' time, viz. in the year 1797 A.D., the present mansion was erected, the material for the bricks proceeding from a field on the Anglesey estate, which still retains the name of the Brickkiln field. George Jenyns, Esq., the present proprietor, has two brothers, Charles Jenyns, Esq., and the Rev. Leonard Jenyns, F.R.S. and F.L.S., distinguished for his works on Natural History, and who, in right of property to which he has succeeded, has exchanged the name of Jenyns for that of Blomefield, and is now the Rev. Leonard Blomefield. Of the sons of George Jenyns, Esq., the eldest, Col. Soame Gambier Jenyns, C.B., upon whom Bottisham Hall will devolve, is justly celebrated for his gallant services rendered to his country in the Crimean war and upon other occasions.

Subjoined is a pedigree of this distinguished family :—

[1] Cole MSS. Vol. xxxi. fol. 149. Lords' *Journals*, Vol. xxiii. p. 487.

(A).

Sir John Jenyns, of Churchill, = Anne Bourchier.

Sir John, of St. Albans, = Alice, d. of Sir Richard Spencer.

Richard = Frances, d. of Sir Gifford Thornhurst.

Anne, died 1656.

Dorothy, died 1657.

Sarah, = John, Duke of Marlborough. born 1660, died 1744.

Ralph, ob. inf.

John, ob. inf.

Barbara, = Edward Griffith. born 1651, died 1678.

Barbara.

Frances, born 1648, = Richard, Duke of Tyrconnel. died 1730. (La belle J.).

(B).

Mr. Blomefield.

Mr. Blomefield, author of History of Norfolk.

Elizabeth, = Rev. Edward Chappelow. died 1783.

Rev. Leonard, born 1744, died 1820.

Frank, married and left no issue: left his property to Mr. Mason.

Mr. Mason = a daughter.

The youngest son took the name of Blomefield.

Elizabeth = John Harvey Jenyns, born 1737, died 1769.

PEDIGREE OF JESTER

[To face p. 163]

(C). Richard Vachell = Miss Younghusband.

Richard, born 1672, = Miss Long. One son.

Rev. John, = Charlotte, d. of John Jenyns, born 1764, died 1827. 1796.

Maria, = C. Brackenbury. died 1831. One son, 2 daughters.

Samuel, = Miss Milward. born 1766.

Mary Anne = Charles Jenyns. born 1802, died 1837.

Tanfield, Lt. Col. Cambs. Militia, born 1774, died 1854.

Rev. George, = 1834, Catherine, d. of Rev. J. Lawson. born 1798, died 1839.

Henry, Louisa.

Mary Anne, = 1838, Major Boyd. born 1801. George. Alexander.

Charlotte, = 1822, Rev. B. Philpot born 1803. 4 sons, 8 daughters.

Rev. Harvey, = Eleanor, d. of Christopher Pemberton, M.D. born 1805. 5 sons, 2 daughters.

(D). John Prentis Henslow, = Miss Stevens. died 1854.

Rev. John Stevens, Prof. = Harriet, d. of Rev. George Leonard Jenyns. of Botany in the University of Cambridge.

Ann. Charlotte. Ellen. Louisa.

Frances Harriet, = 1851, Joseph Hooker, M.D. born 1825.

Louisa Mary, born 1826.

Leonard Ramsay, born 1831.

Anne, born 1833.

George, born 1835.

William, born 1853.

Harriet Ann, born 1854.

ychard.

Many other families of position were resident at various times in the parish of Bottisham, but whose place of abode is unknown. Of these was the family of Pychard which held land in 3 Hen. III. and was numerous in the thirteenth and fourteenth centuries. Some of their land seems to have lain by the road leading from Anglesey to Quy, and to have been situated in both the parishes of Bottisham and Quy. Cole gives some deeds relating to John and Richard Pychard in connection with this land in the middle of the fourteenth century. It is exceedingly probable that they were the ancestors of that family of the same name, who afterwards resided at Trumpington, one of whom, Thomas Pychard, Esq., served the office of High Sheriff in 1639 A.D. At all events the Pychards of Trumpington probably had lands in Bottisham, for Richard Pychard of Trumpington by his will, dated 14 Aug., 34 Hen. VIII., left his house and other lands to John Austen and Alice his wife and their heirs[1]; and in 1679 A.D., William Austin of Trumpington who may be presumed to be the descendant of John Austen gave fourteen acres of land in Bottisham for the education of four poor children of that parish[2].

nglish.

Of other families we find the names of Tristram, Pycot, and Engleys or English. William L'Engleys[3], who resided at Bottisham, must have been some relation of Sir Henry English and Margaret his wife, who lie buried in the church of Wood Ditton where they lived, and on whose tombstone is a handsome brass of a knight in armour with a lady at his side. He died in 1393 A.D. In 15—16 Ric. II. we find the name of John

Foster.

Foster, while just before the dissolution of monasteries we find the name of Lawrence Foster, gent., possibly the father of George Foster, gent., of Bottisham. This latter gentleman the only person in Bottisham found in the list of subscribers to the defence of the country against the Spanish invasion in 158

---

[1] Vide Cole MSS. Vol. lx. fol. 25.

[2] Vide Lyson's *Cambs.* p. 171.

[3] He was bailiff for the Honor of Gloucester, 7—8 Edw. III., for the counties of Essex, Hertford, Cambridge, and Huntingdon. William de L'Engleys, jun., was bailiff 12—15 Edw. III. Attached to his account is a small schedule, entitled "no'i'a illor' qui superoner' mariscu' de Bodekesham, anno xiiij." Vide *m*. *acc.* Honor of Clare.

A.D. According to the parish registers he had three sisters, Ann, Mary, and Elizabeth. They were all married; Ann on the 11th of June, 1579, to John Browne of Linton, Mary to John Amys on Feb. 5th, 1581—2, and Elizabeth to Thomas Rogers on Oct. 10th, 1586. George Foster, who was buried at Bottisham on the 10th of May, 1610 A.D., had eight children, viz., Annes born in 1581—2, George in 1585—6, Richard in 1587—8, Susanne in 1589—90, Thomas in 1591, Lawrence in 1594, Blanch in 1596—7, George in 1598 A.D. After 1662 the name disappears.

The family of Tompson seem to have possessed influence in *Tompson.* the parish. The first of these that occurs is Thomas Tompson, who died in 1541 A.D., and had by his wife Joane three sons, William, Robert, and Thomas: of these, William, who died in 1600, had two sons and a daughter; Robert, who died in the same year, had two sons; and Thomas, who was buried in 1616—7, had one son, John.

But while mentioning various families of influence, we must *Jeniver.* not omit that of the vicar of Bottisham, Christopher Jeniver. He married Eliz. Richardson on Dec. 12, 1575, and by her had three sons and three daughters, all born in this parish. His son John seems to have resided here after the death of his father; for by his wife Margaret, who was buried at Bottisham in Ap. 12, 1629, he had two sons and four daughters, and he then espoused for the second time Blanch Embrie, who was buried May 10, 1632 A.D.

Some of the family of Ventris also seem to have settled *Ventris.* here. Daniel Ventris was married, and had one daughter, Mary, born here in 1583. He, however, was succeeded by Thomas Ventris (? the son of Thomas Ventris, mayor of Cambridge in 1559 A.D.), who by his wife Bridget had three daughters, Bridget, Mary, and Jane, born in Bottisham. About 1613 A.D. he seems to have removed to Whittlesford, where he was buried, Feb. 9, 1636. His wife Bridget, daughter of Wm. Sterne, of Quy, was interred in the same churchyard two months afterwards. His daughter Martha married Thos. Dodd, of Whittlesford, and Jane became Mrs. Nightingale.

The family of Wolf also claim some attention, though little *Wolf.*

notice of them is to be found. William Wolf, who came to
reside at Bottisham Hall about the year 1371, obtained licence
on the 10th of April, 1389, to hear mass in his oratory, at
his house in Bottisham, for two years. This was renewed on
the 2nd of June, 1390, and on the 8th of January, 1397.

On the 26th of March, 1394, the same licence was granted
to John Wolf and Catharine his wife; on the 26th of October,
1403, to John Wolf and Alice his wife; and on Jan. 26, 1407,
to John Wolf alone.

Margaret, relict of William Wolf, had the same licence
granted on June 25, 1404. But, on Jan. 29, in the same year,
was issued a commission to the clergy to excommunicate the
diffâmers of Margaret the relict of William Wolf of Bottisham,
in that they said she had poisoned her husband, and also his
daughter Alicia Dunton now surviving: at the request of the
said Margaret: and to cite the diffamers to the chapel at
Downham within twenty days of the citation, to shew cause
why they should not be excommunicated.

APPENDIX I.

EXTRACTS FROM THE HUNDRED ROLLS TEMP. EDW. I. 1279 A.D. RELATING TO BOTTISHAM.

ITEM, the heir of John de Deresle and the heirs of William, the son of William, hold one knight's fee[1] in the same town, of the same Earl, and do scutage when it shall happen according to a knight's fee, and the same hold socage of the same Earl in the same town.

The aforesaid heirs of William, the son of William, hold in chief of the aforesaid Earl, in the aforesaid town, a mill, and render by the year 8s.

Also the same hold a certain place of ground of the same Earl and render by the year $\frac{1}{2}d$.

Also they hold an acre of land of the fee of Hugh of the Holme, and render by the year 1d.

Also the heirs of John de Deresle hold of the same Earl one virgate of land, and render by the year 9s.

Also Sir Elias de Beckingham holds three acres of land and renders by the year 12d.

Also Martin, the son of Eustace de Lada, holds of the said Earl, in the same town, two virgates of land, and renders by the year 2s., and does suit to the county and hundred for the whole town.

Also the same holds three roods of land of the fee of Hugh of the Holme, and renders by the year 2d.

Sir Simon de Mora holds one virgate of land of the same Earl, and does suit to the county and hundred for the Earl and for the whole town, and renders by the year 18d.

William de Robecot holds in the same town one virgate of land, and six acres of land of the fee of Hugh of the Holme, and renders by the year 15s. 8d., and in pasture six several acres of the lord Earl.

---

[1] At this period a knight's fee comprised 300 acres.

John, the son of Geoffrey, of the Long meadow, holds two virgates of land, and a fourth part of the same Earl in chief, and renders by the year 21*s.*

Also the same holds two acres of land of the fee of Thomas de Angerhale, and renders by the year 2*s.* 6*d.*

Also the same holds half an acre of land of the fee of Thomas the Abbat, and renders by the year 3*d.*

William, the son of Richard, the clerk, holds of the same Earl one virgate of land, and renders by the year 10*s.* 2*d.*

And the same holds four acres of land of the fee of Hugh of the Holme, and renders by the year 12*d.*

And the same holds one acre of land of the fee of Thomas the Abbat, and renders by the year 8½*d.*

Also the same holds six acres of land of the same at the heath, and renders by the year 12*d.*

Roger de Feltewell holds of the same Earl in chief, one messuage, and one acre of land, which is called Holme, in the same town, and renders by the year 8*s.* 2*d.*

Hugh Blunds holds in the same town, of the same Earl, one virgate and a half of land and one quarter, and renders by the year 10*s.*

Also the same holds of the fee of Thomas the Abbat, one acre one rood and a half of land, and renders by the year 7*d.*

William, the son of Matthew, of Angerhale, holds of the said Earl, one virgate of land and one croft, and renders by the year 9*s.*

Also the same holds the moiety of one messuage in the marsh, and renders by the year 2*s.*

John Picot holds twelve acres of land of the said Earl, and renders by the year 7*s.*

Also the same holds one half acre of land of the fee of Thomas de Angerhale, and renders by the year 2½*d.*

Peter Picot holds twelve acres of land of the said Earl, and renders by the year 7*s.*

The heirs of Bartholomew, the tailor, hold of the said Earl one croft, and render by the year 2*s.* ½*d.*

Also the same hold one half acre of land of the fee of Thomas the Abbat, and render by the year 12*s.*

Sir Elias de Bekingham holds eight acres of land which were Hugh Luwechild's, and renders by the year 2*s.* ½*d.*

Robert Gugun and his wife hold one messuage of the said Earl, and render by the year 3*d.*

Martin de Angerhal, the son of Matthew, holds nine acres of land of the said Earl, and renders by the year 6s. 3d.

Also William, the son of Matthew, of Angerale, holds one croft of the said Earl, and renders by the year 3s.

Richard, the son of Martin, the smith, holds one croft of the said Earl, and renders by the year 3s. ½d.

Alice Cole holds one croft of the said Earl, and renders by the year 3s. ½d.

Richard Cole holds one croft of the aforesaid Earl, and renders by the year 3s. ½d.

James Scrisps holds one croft of the aforesaid Earl, and renders by the year 3s. ½d.

William, the son of Thomas, holds one messuage of the said Earl, and renders by the year 9½d.

Geoffrey Pichard holds one croft of the said Earl, and renders by the year 12¼d.

Richard Pichard holds one croft of the said Earl, and renders by the year 12d.

The heirs of Nicholas, the ploughman, hold one croft of the said Earl, and render by the year 2s. ½d.

Richard Pichard and Nicholas Pichard hold one croft of the said Earl, and render by the year 2s. ½d.

Hugh Hostiarius holds one croft of the said Earl, and renders by the year 2s. ½d.

Also the same Hugh holds one acre of land of the said Earl, and renders by the year 12d.

Alan Scrips holds one messuage of the said Earl, and renders by the year 12d.

William, the son of Osbert, the merchant, holds one messuage and one croft of the said Earl, and renders by the year 12d.

Richard over the road and his partner hold nine acres of land and one croft of the said Earl, and render by the year 8s.

Benedict, the hewer, holds one messuage and one croft of the said Earl, and renders by the year 20d.

Also Richard over the road holds half a virgate of land of the said Earl, and renders by the year 2s. 2d.

Richard Spuer and his wife hold one messuage and one croft of the said Earl, and render by the year 3s. ½d.

The heir of Nicholas Tone holds one croft of the said Earl, and renders by the year 12½d.

William, the son of Osbert, the merchant, holds half a croft and one rood of ground of the said Earl, and renders by the year 18¼d.

Also the same holds three roods of land of the fee of Thomas the Abbat, and renders by the year 4d.

Richard, the son of Joseph, holds half a croft of the said Earl, and renders by the year 20d.

Also the same holds one acre and three roods of land of the fee of Thomas the Abbat, and renders by the year 12d.

Alan of the Holme holds six acres of land of the said Earl, and renders by the year 5s. 11d.

Richard of the Millway holds three acres of land, and renders by the year 3s. 6d.

Richard Pichard holds one croft of the said Earl, and renders by the year 16d.

Also Geoffrey Pichard holds the moiety of one croft and one rood of the said Earl, and renders by the year 12d.

The heir of Martin, the son of Gerard, holds half a croft of William, the son of the clerk, and renders by the year 20d.

Martin, the son of John Attegrene, holds a place of the said Earl, and renders by the year 20d.

The heirs of William, the son of William, the son of Martin, hold in chief of the said Earl a piece of meadow, and render by the year 12d.

William, the son of Richard, the clerk, holds a moiety of that meadow of the said Earl, and renders by the year 12d.

Martin de Lada, the son of Eustace, holds one piece of meadow of the said Earl, and renders by the year 12d.

Free tenants of the heirs of William, the son of William, the son of Martin.

Richard Pichard holds one messuage and one acre of land of the aforesaid heirs of the fee of the Earl, and renders by the year 2s.

Richard le Newe holds one messuage of the aforesaid heirs of the same fee, and renders by the year 12d.

John Thone holds four acres of land of the aforesaid heirs of the said fee, and renders by the year 4s.

William, the son of Juliana, holds one messuage of the same of the said fee, and renders by the year 8d.

The heir of Nicholas Albin holds one croft of the same of the said fee, and renders by the year 2s.

Robert Fane holds one messuage of the same of the said fee, and renders by the year 2s.

Peter Picot holds one piece of land of the same of the said fee, and renders by the year 8d.

Henry, the son of Walter Atefene, holds three roods of land, and renders by the year 3d.

Matilda, the daughter of Bartholomew, holds one piece of land, and renders by the year 8d.

The heirs of John, the miller, hold one messuage, and render by the year 8d.

Roger Livene holds one messuage and one croft, and renders by the year 18d.

Also Sir Elias de Bekingham holds one messuage of the aforesaid of the fee of the Earl, and renders by the year...

Richard, the miller, holds one messuage of the same of the said fee, and renders by the year 8d.

Thomas, the clerk, holds of the same of the said fee two crofts, and renders by the year 18d.

The heir of Hugh Cane holds one messuage and a certain portion of land, and renders by the year 18d.

Andrew, the smith, holds a piece of land of the aforesaid of the said fee, and renders by the year 2d.

Also Hugh Blunds holds a piece of land of the same, and renders by the year 2d.

Henry, the son of Otto, holds a piece of land of the same of the aforesaid fee, and renders by the year 1d.

Also William, the son of Osbert, holds one messuage and six acres of land of the same, and renders by the year 4s. 2d.

Also Sir Simon de Mora holds eight acres of land of the aforesaid of the fee of the Earl, and renders by the year 8d.

Walter Cotemere holds one messuage and one croft of the aforesaid of the said fee, and renders by the year 2s.

Richard, called Pas, holds one messuage of the aforesaid of the same fee, and renders by the year 10d.

Adam, the son of Peter, the carpenter, holds one messuage and two acres of land, and renders by the year 10d.

Richard, the son of James, of Hangerhale, formerly held a tenement, nine acres of land, and rendered 6s. to the Earl of Gloucester.

The heir of William Fuller holds one croft of the said Earl, and renders by the year 18½d.

Free tenants of John de Deresle.

Sir Elias de Bekingham holds the fourth part of a knight's fee of John de Deresle in Botekesham, by means of the fee of the said Earl, and does scutage to the said John when it shall happen for the portion of the fourth part of one fee.

The same holds from the said John one virgate of land of the fee of the said Earl of socage by the service of four shillings at the four terms of the year.

Richard, the son of Joseph, holds of the same John of the fee of the Earl to the reckoning of twenty acres by the service of $40\frac{1}{2}d$.

The heirs of William, the son of Martin, hold of the same John one piece of land of the same fee, and render by the year $5d$.

William, the son of Richard, the clerk, holds one croft by the service of one clove gilliflower of the fee of the Earl.

Henry, the son of Adam, holds one messuage of the same of the fee of the Earl by the service of $12d$.

Roger, the son of Henry, holds one messuage and one croft of the said John, and renders by the year $10d$. at the four terms.

Alan, the cooper, holds one messuage and one croft of the same of the same fee, and renders by the year at the four terms $2s$.

William Broly holds one messuage of the same by the service at the four terms of $6d$.

William, the son of Osbert, holds one acre of land and a half of the same by the service at two terms of the year of $6d$.

Annotarica holds one acre of heath land of the fee of the Earl by the service of $6d$,

The heir of Nicholas Tone holds one messuage of the same of the same fee by the service at four terms of $6d$.

Richard Pychard holds one messuage and one croft, and five acres of land, and the moiety of one fold of the same by the service of $4d$.

John Tone holds five acres of land with the moiety of a fold of the same of the fee of the Earl by the service at the feast of Saint Michael of $1d$.

William Prat, of Swaffham, holds one acre of land of the same of the fee of the said Earl by the service at two terms of $4d$.

William Robertot holds a certain tenement of the same John, but what or how much is not known, of the fee of the Earl by the service of $1d$.

Free tenants of John the son of Geoffrey.

William, the son of Richard, the clerk, holds thirty acres of land of John, the son of Geoffrey, by the service of 11s. 6d., and for a certain piece of land pays to the same John 3d.

The heirs of William, the son of William, the son of Martin, hold one half acre of land of the fee of the Earl by the service of 2d.

Sir Elias de Bekingham holds two acres of land of the same John by the service of 4d.

Alice Albin holds one piece of land, to wit, one messuage and one croft of land of the same of the same fee by the service of 26d.

Peter Pycot holds one piece of land of the same of the fee of the Earl, and renders by the year 3d.

John Pycot holds five acres of land of the same, and renders by the year 18d.

In the same manner he holds one half rood by the same service.

Geoffrey the Marshall holds one acre of land of the same fee of the Earl, and renders by the year to the same 8d.

The heir of Martin Gerard holds one acre and a half of the same of the fee of the Earl, and renders by the year 7d.

The heir of Richard Phancred holds one half acre of land, and renders by the year 2d.

Hugh, at the Lane, holds one messuage and two acres of land of the same of the fee of the Earl, and renders by the year 22d.

Richard Galien holds one acre of land of the same of the fee of the Earl, and renders by the year 2d.

William, the son of Matthew and his wife, holds two acres of the same of the fee of the Earl, and renders by the year to the same John 14d.

Richard de Attleborough holds one rood of the same John, and renders by the year ½d.

Richard, the son of Joseph, holds nine acres of the same, and renders by the year 4s.

Tenants of Sir Simon de Mora.

Walter de Balham holds one messuage of Sir Simon de Mora by the service of 12d.

William, the son of Matthew, holds one acre of land of the same Simon by the service of 6d.

Geoffrey Scrisp holds one small messuage of the same. Simon by the service of 6d.

William Berman holds one messuage of the said Simon by the service of 6d.

Martin, the son of Thomas de Angerhale, holds one messuage of the same Simon by the service of 3s.

William Munnote holds one messuage of the same Simon by the service of 18d.

Roger le Newe holds one rood of land of the same Simon by the service of 1d.

Margaret Botild holds one messuage of the same Simon by the service of 6d.

John, the son of Arnulph, holds one rood of land and a half of the same Simon by the service of 1d.

Tenants of William de Robercot.

Hugh, the chaplain, holds one messuage of William Robercot by the service of 2d.

John Pycot holds one messuage and six acres of land of the same William by the service of 6s.

Henry Berman holds one messuage of the same William by the service of 3s.

John, the miller, holds one messuage of the same William by the service of 18d.

The heir of Adam Berkin holds one messuage and one croft of the same William by the service of 13d.

The heirs of William, the son of William, hold one portion of land of the same William by the service of 32d.

Geoffrey Pychard holds one portion of land of the same William by the service of 13d.

Huwelina holds one messuage of Martin de Lada by the service of 16d.

Richard Pychard holds one acre and a half of land of the same Martin by the service of 2½d.

Geoffrey, the Marshall, holds one messuage and one croft of the same Martin by the service of 16d.

The heir of Nicholas Tone holds one acre of land of the same Martin by the service of...

The heir of Martin Gerard holds one half acre of land and one croft with one rood of the same Martin by service...

Amice at the Cross holds one rood of land of the same Martin by the service of 1d.

John le Hert holds two acres of land of the same Martin by the service of one rose crown.

John le Hert holds one croft of William de Angerhal by the service of 18d.

Sir Elias de Bekingham holds one messuage of the same William by the service of 2s.

Martin Poketin and Alice Poketin hold one croft of the same by the service of 2s.

Walter de Dalham holds one half acre of land of the same William by the service of 15½d.

William, the son of Juliana, holds one half acre of land of the same William by the service of 4d.

William, the son of Richard, the clerk, holds one half acre of land of the same William by the service of ½d.

John Pycot holds one half acre of land of the same by the service of ½d.

Richard, the son of Joseph, holds one croft of the same William by the service of 6d.

Robert Seman holds one small messuage of the same by the service of 4d.

Robert, the chaplain, holds one messuage of the same William by the service of 4d.

Sir Simon, the chaplain, holds one half acre of land of the same by the service of one clove gilliflower.

Hugh Hostiarius holds one acre of land of Geoffrey the Marshall by the service of 4d.

Peter Wymer holds one half acre of the same by the service of 2d.

Agnes, the daughter of William, holds one half acre of land of the same by the service of 6d.

Richard over the road holds three roods of land of the same Geoffrey by the service of 3d.

Simon Cappe holds one messuage of the same Geoffrey by the service of 8d.

APPENDIX II.

The following extracts were made by Cole from various Will[
preserved in the registers of Ely diocese.

Isabel Foster de Botesham, vidua, 22 Oct., 1515. Body to th[
church-yard of the Holy Trinity of Botesham. high altar 6*s.* 8*d.*[
to the torches in the town strete 20*d.*, and to each of the other strete[
20*d.* Residue to my executors Master John Cowalyus my brother[
and Master John Foster, my son, witn. Tho. Ronde, Joh. Mannyng[
Fine 10*s.*, Pro. 17 Ap., 1516.

Wm. Bunte de Botesham, 28 March, 1517, Botesham Lode. Bod[
cimeterio Sc'e Trinitatis de Botesham, high altar 12*d.*; bells 12*d.*, a[
Rep'ac'o'em le Torches de Lodestrete 2 modios ordei, ad Rep. le Torche[
de Botesham unum modium ordei, et ad Langmeadow torches id'[
To Tho. my son, my ten't and croft adjoining in quo p'maneo, vocat[
Garrards, with 20 acres of arable land. To Wm., my son, a tene[
ment cum quadam grovetta, with five acres of land in Stow Quy[
To John, my son, a tenement in crofto adjacent' nup' Thurston's, with[
5 acres in Botesham fields. To Agnes, Eliz., and Marg., his dau'rs[
2 acres and 40*s.* respectively; Joane, my wife, to occupy all thes[
lands and tent's for life with grain, cattel, &c. Executors, wife, so[
Thomas, and Edward Berneys de Soham. Witness, Thos. Taylo[
de Wilburgham. Pro. 12 April, 1521.

John Cooke of Bottesham, 6 June, 1519. High awter, to be praye[
for, and for Tithes forgotten 2*s.* That a Broder of the Fryers Prech[
ers of Cambridge, sing a Trental[1] of masses in Bottesham church a[
good Tymes whereby the service of God may be the better maintained[

Brit. Mus.
Add. MSS.
No. 5861.
Cole, Vol.
LX. fol.
119.

fol. 143.

fol. 130.

---

[1] Trental (Trigintalia), or month's mind: so called because masses were sun[
on 30 days within the year; sometimes called a trental of St Gregory as th[
custom was instituted by him. It was the usual form of benefaction among th[
poorer classes.

To Isabel, my wife, all the utensils of my house. To John Roger
my brother, my horse. That Richard, my father, have all my working
geer in my shop to the use of John my son, till he is of age, the
which cometh to 40*s.* Rest to my father and my wife. Witn. Joh.
Grene, of Swafham Bulbeck, Joh' Wood, Tho. Taylor, Tho. Plow-
right, Ric. Bruester. Pro. Die et anno antedictis, "viz., I suppose
(Cole adds) 8 July."

William Garnet de Botekisham, 26 Oct., 1520. High altar 2*s.*; fol. 136.
Rep' of the church 5*s.*; Esselyn, my wife, to have my House and
Croft till John, Laurence, and Eliz., my children, are of age, and then
sold and divided. Esselyn, my wife, to sell my lands in Swafham to
pay any debts, and to have Canham's croft in Botesham for herself.
I pray Sir Robt. Bridekirke of his charity to be sup'visor and to have
6*s.* 8*d.* Teste meipso, Dn'o Roberto Bridekirke, Joh. Vauncy, Wm·
Chalys. Pro. 17 Dec.

Henry Sterne of Stow Quye, 8 Ap., 1521, &c., &c. To Henry fol. 151.
Crane and Margaret Crane, 3 acres of barley in Alderfield of Anglesey
Land; witn., Fr. Anthonius Nyxon, Margaret Crane.

Robert Forge de Botekesham, 3 Apr., 1521. Bur. in the ch.-yard fol. 152.
of Holy Trinity of Botesha'. To Isabell, my wife, all my copy lands
and houses for life and then to John, my son, and Alice, my da'. To
Lucy, my da', 12 yards of cloth; to Elyn, my da', 6*s.* 8*d*, &c.; resid'
to my executor, Tho. Gaytts; witn. Sir Rob. Bridekirke, curate,
Tho. Byngham. Pro. 11 May.

Joane Lorkyn de Bodekysham, 9 July, 1521. High altar 3*s.* 4*d.* fol. 156.
Rep' of the church 20*s.*; to rep' of the bells 6*s.* 8*d.* I will have an
honest priest to sing for my soule satisfactione for half-a-year, 4 marks;
to the four orders of Friars in Cambridge 10*s.* each; to the House of
Anglesey 10*s.*; to the torches in the Town Strete 3*s.* 4*d.*; to those in
Lode Street 20*d.*; to those in Longmedow Strete 20*d.*; my lands called
Lorkyns to be put into Feoffee's hands to kepe a yearday[1] here for
ever for myne, Joh. Lorkyn's, and Wm. Hervy's souls yearly, with
dirige and masse of Requiem; my house and lands sometimes Wm.
Hervy's to be sold, and disposed in good deeds according to the will
of Wm. Hervy sometime my husband, and if Robt. Sewell will buy
them, he to have them better cheap by 40*s.* than another. Executors
Tho. Thomson, Rob. Sewell. Sup'visor Sir Rob. Bridekirke,
witn. Sir James Tenande, Tho. Taylor, Wm. Lorkyn. Pro. 3 Aug.

---

[1] Or obit, the anniversary of the funeral.

ol. 160.   *Thomas Froge* de Botesham, 1 Oct., 1521. Body to the churchyard of the B. Trin. ib'm; to the rep' of the church 20s.; to have
two trentals sung for my soul in that church; to my mother 20s.;
to John Froge, my brother, my best cart; to Sir Rob. Bridekirke
6s. 8d.; to Sneth, a jackett sleeveless of orrege colour. To Reve, a
blonkett jackett. Resid' to Annes Necks, my mother. Witn. Sir
Rob. Brydekyrke, Sir James Tennande, Joh' Webbe. Prov. 5 Nov.

ol. 161.   *Joh. Ballarde de Botesham Lode*, 19 Nov., 1521. Body to the
ch.-yard of the B. Trinity ib'm. High altar 3s. 4d.; to buy a vestment of black velvet for the church with all things belonging thereto,
for a priest to sing mass, in price £3. 6s. 8d.; for a new chalice 20s.;
rep' of the church 20s.; a priest to have 10s. to sing for me the
Trental of S. Gregory in the church; to the House of Anglesey
6s. 8d.; to Ellen my da' 20s., 8 combe of barley and an heckford[1],
and if she dies before 15 to be disposed in good deeds for her and my
soul; to Annes Byrdews an heckford and a qr. of barley. John, my
son, to have 20s. when 15, and Johan, my da', an heckford and 20s.
at the same age: and if they both die as above one part to Johan
my wife and the other to Rep'c'ion of the church. I will have kept
an obit for 7 years with dirige and mass for my soul, soul of Isabéll,
and soul of Tho. Sorrell, to be expended yearly 7s. The Priest to
have 4d., clerk 2d., and residue in bread and drink among the people
and the same 7s. to be levied of all my Saffron grounds[2]. Both my
ten'ts and my lands to wife for life, and then to son John; and if
he dies to be sold for celebrating masses and other deeds of charity.
To my wife all my household stuff and the rest of my goods, my
executrice. Sir Robt. Brydekyrke sup'visor and counsellor who has
6s. 8d. Witn. Sir James Tennande, Priest, Joh' Bunt, Wm. Flax-
man. Pro. 5 Dec.

ol. 164.   *Ric. Newton* de Botesham Lode. Last of Feb. 1521. Body to the
ch.-yard of the B. Trinity. High altar 20d.; torches of Botesham
Street 8d.; to the torches of Botesham Lode 8d.; to the torches of
Langmedowe 8d.; my house to be sold for the use of my children:

---

[1] Heckford or Heckforthe = a heifer, common throughout the Eastern counties. Vide Wright's *Prov. Dict.* sub. voc.

[2] Saffron was commonly cultivated in all the villages hereabouts. It sold
usually from 24s. to 30s. a pound. At the beginning of the xviiith century its
cultivation diminished and became confined to the villages on the borders of
Essex. Vide Salmon, *Traveller's Companion to the Universities of Cambridge
and Oxford and 5 adjacent Counties*, 1748, 12mo. p. 11.

and if they die, to the celebration of masses and other good deeds of charity. Resid'. to Wm. Rance executor. Witn. Sir Rob. Bridekyrk, John Hygdon, Tho. Sewall. Pro. 15 Mar.

Emma Martyn de Botesham Lode, 12 June, 1526, widow. High fol. 187. altar 12*d.*; to my da' Alys Calkin my gown, &c. Witness Sir Rob. Bridekirke, Joh'. Jassell[1]. Pro. 27 Oct.

John Wright de Botesham, 28 June, 1527. High altar 20*d.*; fol. 196. rep'acion of the bells and torches in the Lode Strete 12*d.*; I give to the torches of the town strete 8*d.*; to those of Langmedowe Strete 8*d.*; to every god-child 8*d.*; to Elene Saks, a stick of Saffron ground, &c.; to my wife Margaret, my house for life and resid'. to her. Witn. Sir Rob. Bridekyrke, Joh. Snet, Joh. Wright. Joh'. Jassell. Pro. 18 Dec.

Simon Shereman de Bottisham, 20 March, 1527. Lode. High fol. 200. altar 20*d.*; rep'. of church 12*d.*; torches in the Lode Strete 12*d.*; torches in the Town Strete 8*d.*; torches in Langmedow Strete 8*d.*; to the gyld of All Hallows 12*d.*; to the Trinity gylde 10*d.*; to our Ladys gylde 10*d.*[2]; to the Prior of Anglesey to help to hallow the churchyard 6*s.* 8*d.*[3]; to the said Prior 40*d.*; to the convent of Anglesey 10*s.*; to Wm. Lays, a matress, pair of shetes, coverlet, a bullock, and a colt. Resid'. to Johan, my wife. Witn. Sir Rob. Bridkirk, Joh' Parishe, Ric. Bentley. Pro. 4 May.

John Wright de Bottisham, 21 Feb., 1527. High altar 3*s.* 4*d.*; fol. 202. to the rep'acion of the church 3*s.* 4*d.*, and a Lede. To Mr Prior of Anglesey 3*s.* 4*d.*; to Sir Boner 12*d.*; to every chanon being priest in Anglesey 8*d.*, and to every novice 4*d.* to pray for my soul. That an honest priest syng a trental for my soul in Botesham church 10*s.*; to the Friers Austin in Cambridge a combe of barley; to the Grey Friars ib'm id'. To Joh', my son, 2 acres of free land, 3 half acres with a headland at Taghill, a rode on the top of cage-hill, head south, and abuts on the land of Mr Lawrence Forster; another rode by the land of Maister Allyngton on the east, and abuts on Newmarket way, and to Joh' 13*s.* 4*d.*; to William, my son, 2 acres of land and 13*s.* 4*d.* That Eliz., my wife, dwell in my house I dwell in till Margy, my da' marries, and then to Margy, with 3 acres to Margy and 13*s.* 4*d.*; to Eliz. my wife, my house at the Grene Hill[4] for life,

---

[1] ? =Hassell.

[2] Guilds of all sorts were commonly established throughout these villages. There is, however, no other reference to these mentioned at Bottisham.

[3] It does not appear why it became necessary to hallow the churchyard.

[4] This appears to be the ground by the highway near the church where formerly was the village green.

and then to my son Wm., and to her 2 acres of land for life, and then to da' Margy, of which 2 acres in roods lie in a croft beside Coks, and a rood and a half above Bendyshe sometyme Scotts; to Margaret Thurlow 6s. 8d.; to Joh' Robynson 6s. 8d. Resid' to wife and John Hasill the elder, my executors. Witn., Sir Rob. Bridkirke, Tho. Taylor. Pro. 26 June.

. 208.   *Rob. Baron* de Botesham, 11 Sept., 1528. High altar 12d. I will that Sir Simon Hullock do sing in the church of Anglesey half a trental for my soul and Agnes my wife; to Sir Thomas Hokeley half a trental to be sung in Botesham church for my and Annes my wives soul. My house to be sold, and 40s. to Marg'et my da' when 21. Exe' John Smith. Witn. Sir Rob. Brekirke, Rob. Reynold, John Hancok. Pro. 24 Oct.

. 208.   *Wm. Egle* de Bodkesham, 8 Nov. 1528, Load. High altar 20d.; To Dorothy my da' 26s. 8d., and 20 shepe; to the prior and convent of Anglesey to pray for my soul 3s. 4d.; to Eliz. my sister-in-law, if living, 10 shepe, if not, to Dorothy my da'; to Margaret, my wife, such household stuff as was her own, and all the saffron set at our marriage. Exec. Tho. Lawsill and Wm. Rane. Witn. John Swayne, Mawde Lowen, Joh. Canham. Pro. 18 Nov.

. 210.   *Thos. Sewall* de Botesham Lode, 25 Jan., 1528. H. altar 12d.; to the torches of every strete there 2d.; rep' of the church 12d.; to Joh. my son 13s. 4d., and to be kept by Rob'. Sewall my bro., till of age; my house and land to be sold. Witn. Sir Rob. Birdekirk, Joh. Horner, Annes Hydon. Pro. 22 Ap., 1529.

. 223.   *Robt. Rande* de Botesham, 7 Dec., 1530. Body in the ch.-yard of the Blessed Trinity ib'm. High altar 3s. 4d.; rep'. of the church 6s. 8d.; to the torches in Longmeadow Street a comb of barley; in the Town Strete a bush.; in the Lode id'.; rep. of high-ways 3s. 4d.; to my son Joh'. a young Howed[1] cow, and 6 shepe; to my da' Marg'et a gardyd' heckforde and 6 shepe; to my son Rob., a calf and my house in the Lode Strete; to my son Tho. a cotage in Longmeadow Street and a sticke of land joyning to it; to Isabel, my wife, the house I dwell in for life, and then to son Joh', &c.; to Ric., my son, 6s. 8d.; a calf and a qr. of barley; Isabel, my wife, to keep my obit in December yearly, with dirige and mass for my soul, and then to distribute to poor people as much bread and drink as will come to 3 bushels of wheat and 3 of malt. Wife and John Mannyng, exe-

----

[1] ? = Housed.

cutors. Witn. Sir Rob. Birdkirk, parish priest, Ric. Mannyng, Joh. Horne. Pro. 4 March.

John Birdowes of Botesham, 25 Dec., 1530. Body to the ch.- fol. 224. yard of the Blessed Trinity ib'm; to Andrew Byrdows 13s. 4d.; to his wife id'; to Tho., Wm., and Rob., their sons, furniture; to my bro. Wm. 2 drawing Hamorys (Hammers?), and two pair of tongs. Witn. Sir Rob. Birdkirk, Wm. Last, and Joh. Horner. Pro. last of March, 1531.

Thomas Gaytts de Bottesham, 20 Oct., 1531. Body to the ch.- fol. 225. yard of the Blessed Trinity ib'm. High altar 3s. 4d.; rep'. of the church 6s. 8d.; to the torches in Longmedow Strete, a qr. of barley; to those in the Town Strete 2 bush.; and those in the Brode Strete id'.; to Tho., my son, 30s., furniture, cattle, corn, when 17, &c.; high ways 3s. 4d.; a trental to be sung for my soul; to the prior and convent of Anglesey to pray for my soul 3s. 4d.; to the making of the cross at the Green Hill 6s. 8d.; my goods to be divided into 2 parts, one to Esabel my wife, the other to my executors to fulfil my will; Wm. a lofte, and with the advice of Sir Rob. Brydkirke my sup'visor to whom I give 13s. 4d. Witn. Rob. Sewall, drap', Tho. Goldsmith, Joh. Horne. Pro. 27 Jan.

Rob. Browne de Botkysham, 2 Nov., 1534. To Eliz., my wife, fol. 43. my house. Witn. Rob. Jackson, Stephen Wyttates. Proved 10 Oct., 1545.

L'e administrac'o'is Bonor' Ric'i Bentley de Botkysham, ab intes- fol. 3. tato decedente. Value £10. 13s. 10d.; debts of deceased £4. 14s. 6d.

John Jeakys of Botkysham, 29 May, 1540. Administration committed, dying intestate, to Alice his relict, &c., value £10. 15s. 2d.

Nicholas Deye of Botkysham, intestate, committed to Catharine his relict.

Ric. Pyerson of Botkysham, 25 Sept., 1540. Magister Galfridus fol. 4. Glynne, deputatus an'dictus com'isit administracionem, dying intestate to Joane his relict.

Wm. Bentley, of Bottysham Lode, 5 Nov., 1546, cora' magr'o, Thoma' Smyth[1] L. D., comparuit; Joh'es Bunt, executor, who renounced the executorship, and Joane Bentley, his relict, admitted, who was to pay £10 to Wm. Bentley the son.

John Mannyng in the p'isshyng of Botkysham, 29 March, 1540. Soul to God, our Lady, and all Saints. Body to the churchyard of

---

[1] Of Wilbraham Temple.

the Holy Trinity in Botkysham; high altar 20*d.*; rep'acion of the church 6*s.* 8*d.*; to Laurence my son, my meese and house I dwell in when he comes to 21 yrs.; a quarter of gweate[1], a bullock of 10*s.* price, and a rood of saffron ground in the close next to the Lode Street; a horse teeme being at Wm. Greenys of Swafham, and a cowlter lent to Wm. Lorkyn. Wm. Butt and Eliz. my wife, to be executors. Legacies of corn, &c., to his other children. Witnesses, Sir Robt. Dullingham, Tho. Wyllsby, Rob. Tebolde, Ric. Greene. Proved 17 April, 1540.

l. 9.   *Tho. Webbe* of Botkysham, 14 Ap., 1540. Soul to God, our Lady, and all Sts., and to be buried in the ch.-yard of B. To high altar 3*s.* 4*d*; to my father 20*s.*; to my mother 20*s.*; to Ric., son of John Lorde, 6*s.* 8*d.*; Rose his wife, executrix, who was to have his house in Longmeadow if she was not with child, if she was, the child to have it when of age, and if not his godson, John, son of John Bryge, when he came of age. Witn. Sir Luke Taylor, Tho. Wylsby, Tho. Sorell. Probat. 3 Jul., 1540.

ol. 15.   *Margaret Mannyng* of Botkysham Lode, 15 Jan., 1540, late wife of Ric. Mannyng. Soul to God, our Lady, and all Sts., and body to the ch.-yard; tythes forgotten 12*d.*; to Tho. Wylson and Jone my daughter my 3 roods of arable land in the Northfield next the land of John Hynde, serjeant at law, on both sides. To Alice Jekes, widow, my other 3 roods in the same field abutting on Gustons Lane. To Jone and Alice, my said dau'rs, a rood of saffron ground. Witn. Joh'. Trunp, Joh' Rand, Tho. Sorell, and Wm. Nicholas; Robt. Chapman, notary public and registrar of the bp. attends the intestineation[2]. Prov. 11 Feb., 1540.

ol. 17.   *Tho. Ballard* of Botesham, 3 Jan., 1540. Soul to God, our Lady, and all Saints, and body to the church-yard; Sybilla, his wife, all his goods. Witn. Syr Luke Taylor, John Gunston, and John Hassyll. Proved Ap. 9, a° p'd'c'o.

ol. 21.   *Agnes Eve* de Botkysham, 4 Nov., 1541. Soul to God, &c.; body to the church-yard; high altar, a tablecloth. Rob. Sewell, exec. Witnesses, Syr Luke Taylor, John Wood, and Tho. Turke. Proved 12 Dec., 1541.

ol. 49.   *John Hancok* de Botysham, 8 Ap., 1547. To have a dirige and mass of Requiem sung for me at my burial, and at my months day, with a qr. of wheat and barley, and a qr. of malt to be made into bread and drink for the poor, and at my yearly obit a qr. of wheat

---

[1] = wheat.   [2] ? = attestation.

and a qr. of malt to pray for me, and every year a solemn dirige
with mass of requiem; to Elizabeth, my wife, my house for life, and
then to John my son. Rep'ac'on of the church 6s. 8d.; execu., his
wife and bro., Wm. Bolter; witn., Rob. Lucas. Prov. June 5, —47.

John Swanne de Botesham, 14 Dec., 1546, Botesham Lode. Soul fol. 57.
to God and our Lady; my house to Alice my wife for life, and then
to my godson Ric., son of Tho. Lane of Botesham. Resid. to my
wife my exec.; witn. Syr Rob. Hogge, curate, John Rollffe, and Rob.
Brand. Proved 17 Dec., 46.

John Bounte de Botesham, 4 Ap., 1547. High altar 12d., at my fol. 59.
burial day to be bestowed 13s. 4d., and at my month's day a combe
of wheat and malte, and a heykeforthe amongst the poor. To John,
the son of Wm. Bounte £10, with all my tenements and lands; to
Jone his sister £5, and to Jane, my daughter, 36s. 8d., &c.; all my
moveables to my son Wm., his 2 children, &c.; my bro., John Wodde,
and George Rogier, executors. Witn. Syr Robert, Parish Priest,
John Rolfe. Pro. 2 May, 47.

Thomes Thomson de Botesham, 12 Sept., 1541. My lands, houses fol. 64.
and ten'ts in Botesham, to Joane, my wife, for life, then the house I
dwell in with the backside to Tho. and Wm. my eldest sons; to Rob.
my son, my house called Webb's house and backside, with an acre of
arable land lying in Vineyards called Peter Edwards', with a rood of
saffron ground; to 4 daughters, money and cattle. Rep'acion of the
church 6s. 8d., and highways 6s. 8d., Barthol'. Bangolfe to be overseer
and have 6s. 8d.; to Agnes Jorden a bush' of barley; my son Thomas
to have the house I dwell in, and to pay to his bro. Wm. 6 Li' 13s. 4d.,
Wm. to have the house I hold of my Lord Hynde[1]. Residue to my
wife executrix. Witn. Tho. Modye, vicar there, Edward Johnson.
Proved 11 May, 1548.

Wm. Bunte of Botesham Lode, 12 Jan., 1545. Husbandman. fol. 78.
Soul to God, our Lady, and all Saints. To the vicar for my tenths
and oblations negligently forgotten or witholden 12d.; to the torch-
light in Lodestre, a pound of wax; to Jone, my daughter, 4 marks,
and Maud, my wife, the residue. Witn. John Aves, Robt. Tebolde.
Pro. 26 Mar., 1546.

John Sorrell de Bottesham, 6 Jul., 1558. To Ellen, my wife, the fol. 81.
house I dwell in with the land for 21 years, and then to John my
son, under guardianship of Tho. Tomsone; to Wm., my bro., an acre
of barley; to Tho. Wren, my godson, 3s. 4d. Pro. 4 Mar., 58.

---

[1] Serjeant Hynde of Maddingley and Anglesey Abbey, &c.

Elizabeth Forghe of Bottesham, widow, 1 Feb., 1559. Body to Trinity ch.-yard of Bottesham; to the church steple 20*d.*; to Rob. Sewell, my son, a qr. of barley, &c. Resid'. to Joh' Sywell, my son. Witn. Laurence Manning, Ric. Wolson, Anth. Bucke. Prov. 30 March, 1550 (*sic*).

APPENDIX III.

Taken from the fly-leaf of Bottisham parish register, marked No. 2.

An account of the bounds of Bottisham, in the County of Cambridge, taken in possession the seventh and eighth day of May, 1719.

Imprimis. Carlick piece al next the King's highway, Little Saxbridge and Great Saxbridge, parting Quoi field and others, made crosses in all the said places. Boughs between Little and Great Saxbridge taking in half the Wash.

Hoe-fen corner by Henry Mitchell's ground, a cross, turning from the said Mitchell's ground on the left to the turning on the right-hand of Mr Parker's ground, called Hoe-fen, next Quoi, and made a cross, going on still in the said ground to the turning on the right by Carter's rails, next Quoi, by the milldam, and made there a cross. Still going along by the said dam till against Quoy stakes there, went over the aforesaid milldam toward the north, made a cross, and sung a psalm, &c. Fenhead, made a cross there by a sallow-bush, which said bush and cross is the parting of the ground called Load Moor, and the aforesaid Fenhead, at which said parting aforesaid Quoy beginneth to enter common with us right straight from the ash trees on Adams' ground to Mr Graves' ground-corner by the ditch, called the Ride, at the west corner of Fenhead, there made a cross.

Turning from the afore-mentioned corner on the right-hand to the north corner of Fenhead by the ditch called the Ride, aforesaid, by the Ringditch by Clarke's ground, there made a cross. Thus far Quoy enter common with us. This ground of Clarke's, aforesaid, separates Hornsey and Quoy, and here we are in our own ground. At the end of one of Clarke's hundred-acres over against Hornsey at the end of Charpit Load, by North-end-ditch-side, there made a cross and sung a psalm, and so forward into the north. Over New-cut-ditch into Queen's ground and made a cross, and there Hornsey, and Ditton, and we, enter common, and so along by Queen's-ditch-side towards the court, and upon Barbank made a cross (Hornsey keeps the Bush fence next the Barbank), and round the court-yard over the court ditch in the Dam-root by the Load-side made a cross. Bottisham sluce, there we sung Psalm 43.

In the Bouts against High-span-noe-ram against Swafham Bulbeck old-Load hard by the sluce, there we made a cross; from thence toward Swafham Bulbeck aforesaid.

High-span-noe-ram both sides of Skirington's-court made crosses.

High-span-noe-ram al next the hundred-acres, John Reeve hath in use, by White fen lake, made a cross, and so forth to Lye Lake next Swafham hundred-acres, there made another cross, and turn on the right hand to Dockin drove-way, the north end, next Swafham hundred-acres, and there made a cross and sung Psalm 100.

Turning on the left-hand at the west corner of Mr Pychard's ground we made a cross, &c.

To the east end of John Rolph's ground we there made a cross, &c.

To Longmeadow Moor, at the parting of Swafham droveway ditch; others there made a cross.

Longmeadow-moor right against Cowbridge and parting off Swafham moor and ours, made a cross, &c. Turn on the right hand toward Longmeadow by our ditch-side, and at the end of the ditch, parting off Swafham moor and ours, made a cross; and then turn on the left hand to Killingbeck's sheep-walk, parting of Swafham bounds and ours, there made a cross, &c.: toward Longmeadow houses till we came to the road that leadeth to Swafham town by Killingbeck's sheepwalk, there made a cross, &c.; to the first turning in Barrow meadows of the right hand, made a cross.

Barrow meadows right against little Swafham church at the sharp corner, there made a cross. William Mott, Clarke, stood therein, &c., to the Hall-sluce at the parting of the Hogpasture and Emblets, there made a cross, &c.; to the watermill on to the middle of the bridge, made there a cross on the post; likewise went as far as the water-wheel parting Swafham bounds and ours in the said mill.

Memorandum. The twenty acres by Swafham Load not taken in possession this time because it rained, but deferred till another opportunity.

Fielding.

May 8th, 1719, imprimis.   Over the King's highway, by Garlick piece, at the furlong that is called Fox-hole (which said hole is in Quoy field), at the parting of the above said Quoy field and ours, made a cross.

Hawkpath that leadeth to Hawkmill that parts Quoy and us, then Little Wilbraham field beginneth that parts Little Wilbraham bounds and ours, then we made a cross, &c.; to Wilbraham way, and made a cross.

Bridge path we went over, parting Wilbraham and our bounds, and forgot to make a cross &c.; both sandpits parting Wilbraham-field and ours, and there made crosses on both sides the pits, &c.; to Wratten way against Hogpit hole, made a cross south west, &c.; to the parting of Westly, Wilbraham, and Bottisham-heaths, there made a cross, Overin Eagle put therein, then sung the 1st and 2nd commandment, &c.; to the parting of Borough Green-heath and our heath, &c.; made a cross eastward at the parting of Borough Green and our heath aforesaid, made a cross, and so turn northward, and there standeth a thornbush by the way on the right hand as we go along, &c.; to the north corner of Borough Green-heath, at the parting of that heath and ours, we made a cross, John Winch put therein, and so toward the east at the parting of Borough Green heath, and Little Swafham, and ours, there made a cross, and sung one stave of the 84th Psalm, &c.; northwest at the parting of Little Swafham-heath and ours against Mr Appleyard's Lay Land, and made a cross; turning from thence on the left southward.   To the parting of Little Swafham and our heath at the corner of our field, and made a cross; and so forward into the north at the lower of Little Swaffham follis furlong, parting of our field and theirs, made a cross, Abraham Cutchey put therein.

At the upper end of the ditch called Swafham follis, parting of that field and ours, made a cross, &c.; toward the west.

At the road called the White way, turning from Newmarket, made a cross, parting of Swafham field and ours.

At Clark's path parting of Swafham field and ours, made a cross.

Turning on the right hand of Esqre. Clenche's headlong upon White Land-hill, there made a cross.

At the parting of Swafham field and ours by Charcroft, made a cross.

Postremo.   In Charcroft against the milldam made a cross, &c., from thence to the mill.

No opposal made by any man all the circuit.

17

J.H. 1948

PART II.

CHAPTER I.

Of Religious Houses, and their connection with Bottisham.

Priory of Tonbridge.

/o religious houses had from early times a large influence in ttisham, owing to their possessions. These were the Priory Tunbridge, in Kent, and the Priory of Anglesey, in the rish itself.

Foundation.

The Priory of Tunbridge was founded by Richard de Clare fore the year 1135[1], the end of Henry the First's reign, but it not till the year 1279 that we find its connection with Botham[2]. The establishment consisted of a prior and seven ıons, and their house was located at Tonebridge, in Kent, m which town Richard de Clare, its founder, took the appelion of *De Tunbridge*[3]. The name is written Thornebregg' ıonebregg', Tunebrug, and Tonebriggs. The order to which priory belonged is first described as that of the Premonstrasians or White Canons, but in the inquisition of Edw. I. the nks were found to be Austin Canons.

Priors.

There does not appear to be any complete list of priors own, but the following names occur as holding that office:

David, 21 Edw. I.

John Osprengge, temp. Edw. I., and 20 Edw. II.

Peter.

William Frendesbery.

William Mallyng, 25 Edw. III.

John Prynne, 1518.

Richard Tomlyn, the last prior, 1522[4].

Manor of Bottisham.

I have mentioned before, that by the inquisition of 1279 was found that the predecessors of Gilbert, Earl of Clare,

---

[1] Dugdale, *Mon.* vi. 393.

[2] Rot. Hund. temp. Edw. I. p. 487.

[3] Cardinals' bundles.

[4] Ib. Dugdale, *Mor* .. 393.

divided the manor of Bottisham between the two religious houses of Tonebridge and Anglesey, with all the lands and demesnes, and tenements in villenage and cottage, the meadows, pastures, grazings and mills, and liberty of ball and vert, and all other the appurtenances and easements; certain rights, however, were reserved to the family of the donor. From the same account we find a further statement of the possessions of the priory, viz.:

Prior de Thornebregg' holds of the said earl, in the same town of Bodekam, one messuage and 200 acres of land, which he holds in pure and perpetual alms, with the several meadows and pastures; the same holds in villenage 6 villeins, and each holds 15 acres of land, and the servile work of each is worth by the year 6s. 8d.

The same holds 5 cottages of the said earl, and the servile work of each is worth by the year 12d.

The same holds of the same earl one mill, which indeed was the property of Hugo del Bolein, and renders by the year 16s.

The same holds of the said earl one messuage in the same town, and 3 acres of land, and renders by the year 3s.

Dominus, Prior de Thonebregg', holds a croft, which Alicia le Paumer was accustomed to hold of the said earl, and renders by the year 12d.

Free Tenants of the Prior de Tunebrug'.

William Brok holds in the same town of Botekesham of the Prior de Tunebrug', one messuage and 15 acres of land, of the fee of the Earl of Gloucester, by the service of 6s.

James Scrisp holds one messuage of the same, by the service of 2s., of the fee of the lord earl.

Peter, the son of Hamon, holds one messuage and one croft of the same by the service of 2s., of the fee of the earl, which he redeemed......

Domina Cecilia[1] holds one messuage and one croft, and renders by the year 2s., of the fee of the lord earl.

[1] Qu. whether this Lady Cecilia was not the widow of Joseph de Bodekesham? For Thorold de Burgo, brother of William, Prior of Anglesey, is stated to have

The next notice of the temporals of the Priory of Tunbridge, in Bottisham, is to be found in the record of Pope Nicholas' taxation. After the first-fruits and tenths of all ecclesiastical benefices had long been paid to the see of Rome, they were granted by Pope Innocent XXII. to Henry III., in 1253, for 3 years, and the year following a taxation took place, called the Norwich taxation or Pope Innocent's valor. Subsequent to this Pope Nicholas V. granted the tenths for six years to Edw. I., to defray the expenses of the expedition to the Holy Land, which produced another taxation in 1288. Accordingly, in the account of the xxth of ecclesiastical revenues, granted to Edw. I. by the pope, assessed by Walter, Bp. of Norwich, and collected by the Prior of Barnwell, we find,

	Value.	Vicesima.
Botekesam	30 marcs	20s.
Prior de Longavilla..	100s.	5s.
Prior de Tonebrig ...	5£.	5s.

But by the taxation of Pope Nicholas in 1291, all the taxes of the king, as well the pope, were regulated until the survey in the 26th year of Hen. VIII., and in the record of this taxation we find, Bona Prioris de Tunnebrege, in Bockesham, £20. 3s. 4d.[1]

The division of Bottisham between the priories of Tonbridge and Anglesey sowed naturally the seeds of dissension between the two religious houses. The Prior of Tonbridge is never mentioned in any document relating to Anglesey, except one, bearing the date of 27 Edw. I., 1300. This is a record of pleadings in assize. It states that "the Prior of Tonbridge demands against Roger, Prior of Anglesey, the moiety of 9 acres of land, with the appurtenances, in Bod'ekesham, as the right of his church of St Mary Magdalene, of Tonbridge, and in which the

married Cecilia, daughter of Henry de Hupware (Upware near Wicken), and shortly after Joseph de Bodekisham and Cecilia his wife are described as of Wicken. They bequeathed a messuage and 20 acres of land, with the appurtenances in Wicken, to the Priory of Anglesey, and they are afterwards styled as of Bodekisham. The name of Joseph de Bodekisham disappears before 1279. Lady Cecilia therefore, his widow, may be the one here mentioned.

[1] Vide Bentham's *Ely*, App. to Supplement, p. 24*. *Bibl. Top. Brit.* Vol. v. p. 62. Cole MSS., Vol. iv. Article *Bottisham*.

same Prior of Anglesey has no entry, except by John, formerly Prior of Anglesey, who thereof unjustly, &c. disseised the afore-said Prior of Tonbridge since the first," &c.

And the Prior of Anglesey comes and defends his right, "when," &c. And he says that "the aforesaid John, formerly Prior of Anglesey, did not disseise the aforesaid Prior of Ton-brige thereof; and of this he puts himself upon the country, and the Prior of Tonbrige does the like. Therefore let there be a jurat thereof. And the jury chosen by the consent of the parties say upon their oath, that the aforesaid John, formerly Prior of Anglesey, did not disseize the aforesaid Prior of Ton-brige thereof. Therefore it was considered that the aforesaid Prior of Anglesey should be without day thereof. And the aforesaid Prior of Tonebridge should take nothing by his writ, but be in mercy for his false claim," &c.

Although mention is made of the Prior of Tonebridge in various documents relating to Bottisham in 1302 and 1318, still the convent seems never to have been much mixed up in the affairs of the parish. Elizabeth de Burgh, who succeeded to the fortunes of her ancestors the De Clares, did not desert the reli-gious house founded by her predecessor; for by her will she be-queathed "à la Meson de Tonebriggs cs. et ij draps door," or vestments for celebration. She died in the year 1360, and her will, dated 1355, was proved on the 3rd of December in the year of her decease. At this time the convent must have been very poor, for in 1351 a great fire consumed all the buildings of the monastery at Tunbridge, buildings which were described as "splendida et nobilia." The advowson of the church of Leghe in Kent was granted to the convent after this disaster, in order to aid them in rebuilding the monastery. But they never seem to have attained to any great wealth, so they were destined to be suppressed in company with 17 others in 1525 A.D.

issolu-
on.
A special bull from pope Clement VII. was obtained, in 1524 A.D., by Cardinal Wolsey for suppressing with the king's leave as many small monasteries as were needful to raise a revenue not exceeding 3000 ducats per annum. This was for the purpose of founding the two Colleges, one at Ipswich, and one to be called Cardinal's College at Oxford, which now goes

by the name of Christ Church. This bull is dated September 1524.—On Jan. 20, in the following year, this priory then with 17 others was dissolved, and the king by letters patent dated Feb. 8, 17 Hen. VIII., granted all to Cardinal Wolsey. The spiritualities of Tunbridge were then valued at £48. 11s. 4d., and the temporalities at £120. 16s. 11d., which revenues lay in the counties of Kent, Cambridge, Suffolk, Norfolk, and Surrey. The Inquisition on that portion of the property which lay in the county of Cambridge was taken on the 10th of March, 18 Hen. VIII., by the escheator Antonius Hasildene for the county aforesaid, before the jurats William Rogers, John Botoler, John Curtes, Gilbert Amys, Robert Amys, John Elye, Henry Algood, Richard Goodgame, John Godfray, John Harvy, Warenne Assbe, Thomas Bradwey, and Robert Calcote. The record specifies the bull of Pope Clement for the suppression, and the name of the late prior, Richard Tomlyn; and further, that while the prior and convent agreed voluntarily to resign all their possessions, an offer was made to them to transfer them to another religious house of the same order, an offer which was accepted and carried into effect. The record then proceeds;—" and further the aforesaid jurats declare, that the aforesaid late prior and convent now and at the time of the suppression, extinction, and dissolution of the aforesaid late monastery or priory, were seised in their demesne or of a fee in right of their aforesaid late said monastery and manor of Bodesham called 'the Pryory Hall of Tonbridge' with all and each its appurtenances in the county of Cambridge aforesaid, and of court-leet and view of frankpledge, and all and whatever pertains to court-leet and view of frankpledge, within the manor of Bodesham aforesaid. Also of and in ten messuages, five hundred acres of land, fifty acres of pasture, a hundred acres of meadow, twenty acres of wood, and a hundred shillings rent with the appurtenances in Bodesham aforesaid, and other appointments, advantages and emoluments pertaining or touching the same manor and the other the premises, and that the aforesaid manor, land, meadow, pasture, and the other the premises with all and each their appurtenances are worth by the year in all issues besides reprisals twenty pounds thirteen shillings and four pence. And the aforesaid jurats say that the aforesaid late prior and convent now and at the time of the suppression, extinction and dissolution of the aforesaid late monastery held the aforesaid manor and the other the premises, with all and each their appurtenances, of the aforesaid lord the King at this time in pure and perpetual alms, and the aforesaid church of foundation, land, site, circuit and precinct of the aforesaid late monastery, whereas the manor, land, meadow, pasture, and the other the premises with all and each their appurtenances will now revert and fall into the hands of the aforesaid lord the King, and ought to have so reverted and fallen into his hands by reason of their escheat of blood and by virtue of the suppression, extinction and dissolution of the aforesaid late monastery or priory. And that the aforesaid late prior and convent did not hold any other or more lands or tenements of the aforesaid lord the King at this time in demesne or service in chief or in any other manner of any other person in the said county of Cambridge at the time of the suppression, extinction, and dissolution of the aforesaid late monastery or priory. In testimony of which the aforesaid escheator as well as the jurats aforesaid of this inquisition have alternately affixed their seals. Given on the day and year above mentioned[1]." Another document in the same collection as the one just quoted is rendered hopelessly illegible by mould, but mention may be detected of the Priory Hall of Tonebridge in Bodesham in the county of Cambridge as well as the names of Henry Fouston, Thomas Boteler, Robert Sewall, John Bunt, ... Hitchcock, John Simpcin, Geoffrey Baron, Richard Norman, John Newman, John Pamplin and ... Benys. This may be the Inquisition taken at Oxford, 29 March, 19 Hen. VIII., alluded to by Fiddes in his life of Cardinal Wolsey, where he adds in a note; "Libat' 30 April, 19 Hen. viij, per manus Thome Cromwel[2]."

Thus then this property fell into the hands of Cardinal Wolsey, but upon his being cast in a præmunire the whole again escheated to the king. The site of Tunbridge Priory and all its possessions in the county of Kent, as part of the

---

[1] Cardinals' bundles. New Record Office.
[2] Appendix, p. 173.

revenue of the crown, were granted by letters patent 4 Edw. VI.[1] to John Dudley, Earl of Warwick, who afterwards, as Duke of Northumberland, reconveyed them to the Crown in exchange. Queen Mary granted this Priory and its possessions in the county of Kent to Cardinal Pole for the term of his natural life and one year after, upon whose death without a devise the site of the priory again escheated to the crown. Queen Elizabeth granted them to Sir Henry Sidney, and they then passed through the families of Dame Ursula Walsingham, Viscountess Purbeck, to the family of Poley, George Weller and his son George Weller Poley, Esq., of Boxted Hall in the county of Suffolk[2]. But the manor of Tunbridge Hall, in Bottisham, was not held by any of these families. No record of any special grant is now in existence, but we soon find the family of Cutts possessed of it. Now Sergeant Hynde obtained a grant of the manor of Bottisham after the general dissolution of monasteries, and as his daughter Sibilla became the wife of Sir John Cutts, of Childerley, it is not improbable that this estate formed a portion of her dowry. Anyhow, in 1574, Sir John Cutts passed certain tenements into the hands of John Pepys, of Cottenham, and in 1584 alienated this manor and certain tenements to Thos. Cooke. In 1592 William Cooke, and others, alienated the manor to Thomas Webbe, a lawyer, of Clifford's Inn, whose interest in Bottisham has been before mentioned, and who about that year came to reside at Tunbridge Hall. In 1617, John Cutts, and others, alienated the manor to Elizabeth Carrowe, widow, but the lands seem, in 1647, to have passed into the hands of George Fowkes. In 1669, a fine for this manor, together with certain lands, was concluded between Sir Thomas Marsh, Knt., and Ed. Hampden, but in 1682 the whole became the property of Sir George Downing, Bart., who, by his will in 1717, left all his estates for the purpose of founding the college in Cambridge which bears his name. Thus the college are the present owners, and their tenant is Mr John King.

[1] Rot. Escheat. 4 Edw. VI. Part 4.
[2] Vide Hasted, *Hist. of co. of Kent*, Vol. II. p. 345. Dugdale, *Mon. Angl.* Vol. VI. p. 393.

riory of nglesey. ALTHOUGH information is scarce relating to the Priory of Tunbridge and its relations with the parish of Bottisham, it is not so with the Priory of Anglesey. Possessing, as it did, the advowson of the church of Bottisham, as well as the moiety of the manor of the same, under the gift of the powerful family of De Clare, and the conventual establishment situated in the parish itself, it naturally presents features of considerable interest to any one who follows the course of its history throughout the middle ages, whether during the period of its prosperity, its poverty, or its dissolution.

ources of nformation. First, let us consider what are the sources from which we are to derive our information. These sources may be considered as twofold; manuscripts and printed books. The first of these again may be subdivided into parchments and papers. From the first of these subdivisions we glean scraps of information from various 'fines' or final agreements, which were duly enrolled at the time that they were made, pleas of assize, pleas 'de quo warranto,' inquisitions 'post mortem,' 'ad quod damnum,' and escheat rolls, charters, releases, agreements, confirmations by the bishop of the diocese, the Hundred Rolls, temp. Edw. I., and Royal Letters Patent. Subsequent to the dissolution we look to the 'originalia' Rolls and the various ministers' accounts. All of these various sources of information are to be found in the New Record Office in Fetter Lane, London. But none the less valuable are the MSS. on paper left by eminent antiquaries; such, for instance, are the Baker MSS., the Layer MSS., and other records, preserved in the Harleian collection in the British Museum, the Cotton MSS., and the valuable MSS. of the late Rev. William Cole of Milton, also in the British Museum. Added to these are certain documents preserved at Cambridge, in the Libraries of Trinity, Caius, and Corpus Colleges. The number of printed books referred to is of course large, being varied in proportion to the fact desired to be illustrated or verified. But though there as yet exists no published history of the convent of Anglesey, there are short accounts of it in various topographical works. These are:

The Architectural Topography of England (Cambs.), published by the Archæological Institute.

Blomefield's Collectanea Cantabrigiensia, published at Norwich in 1750, 4to.

Camden's Magna Britannia.

Carter's History of Cambridge, 1753.

Carter's Ancient Architecture (engraving).

Dugdale's Monasticon Anglicanum.

Grose's Antiquities of England and Wales.

Index Villaris, Adams.

Illustrated London News, 1854 (engraving).

Lyson's Magna Britannia (Cambs.).

Magna Britannia, collected and arranged by an impartial hand.

Stevens' Monasticon Anglicanum.

Tanner's Notitia Monastica, ed. Nasmyth.

Cox's Cambridgeshire.

Russell's Cambridgeshire.

Gardner's Gazetteer, Cambridgeshire, pub. at Peterborough.

Gough's Cambridgeshire.

These various accounts are all short, and give, for the most part, the extent of the present remains of the priory, its founder and dedication, the value of its revenues, and the present owner of the site.

Before looking at the time when the monastery was first *Present* established, it will be well to state its present remains, which *remains.* were restored in 1861 by the Rev. John Hailstone, sometime vicar of Bottisham, then owner of the estate, and now form the residence of his widow. The house stands in a beautifully

H. B. 11

situated piece of grass-land, adjoining the road leading from Cambridge and Quy to Swaffham Bulbeck. This grass-land is planted with fine trees dotted all over it, many of them bending over the hollows which once were watercourses and fish-ponds. Here, in front of the house, says tradition, stood a small wood of alders, which gave the name of Alderfield to the ground adjacent. One or two alder-trees are still left, but within the memory of man there stood, at what is now the lodge-gate, a very fine ash, which served as a landmark to travellers when roads were but little thought of, and when the present road was only a green lane. As the visitor makes for the spot where the house stands, he will be almost insensibly occupied in reflecting on what may have been the condition in earlier times of this historical spot; he will remember, with gratitude, that monasteries in their day contributed most to the education of the country, and the preservation of history and art, as well as afforded hospitality and relief to the neighbouring poor; he will reflect upon the causes of their dissolution, which it would be unnecessary to mention here, and he will consider that, while something better than monastic life has been adopted by the feeling of the nation, still many good and salutary lessons are to be learnt from its life and manners, and he will aid in preserving as far as possible every relic which may conduce to the elucidation of its history. All past history is worthy of admiration, not so much for the good deeds contained therein, as for the principle from which they resulted, which if applied to our present circumstances must conduce to our future greatness and goodness.

But we imagine the visitor to have approached the inner gate. There he will have approached a large flower-garden, tastefully laid out, and containing rare and costly shrubs. Further on, at the back, he will reach the orchard, called by the monks the Paradise garden ($\pi\alpha\rho\alpha\delta\epsilon\iota\sigma\sigma\varsigma$, Gr. = a garden). He will then pass on to the farm-buildings which serve for the adjacent land, constructed of the clunch-stone peculiar to the district, and lying close to the little bridge that spans Bottisham Lode, which is gently and silently wending its way to feed Anglesey mill in the distance, and then hastens to join the

ANGLESEY PRIORY.

E.H. 1860

waters of the Cam. Turning back to the farm-buildings, he will find leisure to observe the roof which covers the barn. It is of the Decorated period of architecture, and covered the old abbey barn, a long building of wood and clunch, surmounted by a thatched roof. This was standing in 1848, shortly after which the present farm-buildings were erected. Near to the bridge is a somewhat curious phenomenon amongst trees. A fine ash-tree may be seen growing upon the head of a pollard willow. The seed must have been blown by the wind on to it, or perchance brought there by some bird, struck, and the young sapling nourished itself upon the willow, till twining its roots around it to the ground, it obtained a firm footing in the soil beneath. Close by the farm-buildings stand the stables for the house itself, the clunch of which more than six hundred years ago built part of the abbey, which stood in the adjacent court-yard, and was supposed to have been the refectory. These remains were pulled down in 1861 to make way for offices and stabling. They consisted of three sides of a large chamber having two door-ways and three windows, all of simple Early English masonry. Two Early English buttresses supported the north wall of this building, and a small wooden lean-to roof converted part of the space into a shed for implements of various kinds. On the other side of the wall, which encloses one side of the present court-yard, are various remains of stone coffin-lids and stone coffins. The smallest (of which two cuts are given) was first discovered, and seems to have contained the body of a female. It was found imbedded in the foundation of the old dovecot in July, 1849, near to where now stands a clump of walnut-trees. The lid of this coffin contains on the upper surface a cross, at the head of which is a quatrefoil lying in a circle. There is one like it in the church of Horningsey, and it seems to be earlier in date than the rest. The following are some of the measurements of the coffin: 6ft. 1in. length of the inside, 8 inches depth inside, 9 inches outside, 2ft. 1in. width at head outside, 10½ in. at feet, 18 in. width of inside at the shoulder, wherein is cut a round aperture for the head to fit in. Who the lady buried here was it is impossible to say for certain, but doubtless she would be a person of some consideration, and not improba-

11—2

bly a relation of one of the patrons of the house. Now Gough
in his *History of Sepulchral Monuments*, tells us that Sir John

de Burgh was great grandson of Sir Philip
de Burgh, knt., lord of the manor of Burgh,
alias Burrough-green.   He gave the advowson of Swaffham St Cyriac to the convent
at Ely.   Sir John de Burgh, chevaler, in his
will made 1384 (7 Ric. II.), mentions Mary,
his first wife, buried at Anglesey Abbey in
Cambs.   Catharine, his second wife, in her
will made in 1409, bequeaths her body to
be buried in Burgh church[1].   Turning to
the pedigrees of the Burgh family, we find
John Boroughe married Maud, by whom he
had a son, John Burgh, miles, who married,
in 36 Edw. III., Catharine, daughter of Sir
John de Engayne and Joanna his wife, but
nothing is said in any pedigree of Mary
his first wife[2].   Gough, for his information,

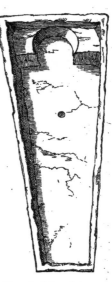

refers to a scarce work, called Philipot's *Cambridgeshire*, a
copy of which is said to be in the College of Arms, and if he is
correct, this stone coffin may have belonged to that lady.
Another coffin, a larger one, and apparently of later date, was
found in the flooring of what is now the dining-room of the
house, in 1861, and probably contained the remains of one
of the priors.

   We now come to examine the house itself.   The south

---

   [1] Gough, *Sep. Mon.* Vol. i. Part ii. p. 220. Vide also MSS. of the late Dr
Webb, Cambs. p. 141, transcribed from Baker MSS. Vol. xxviii. fol. 164.
   [2] Vide Add. MSS. No. 4962, fol. 15.

front facing the garden is of simple and neat appearance. It took its present form when the manor-house was constructed out of the ruins of the monastery. Portions of the earlier masonry are detected at the angles at the east end, where are seen four Early English buttresses of regular coursed masonry, the later work being less carefully laid. There are nine windows with plain chamfered clunch mullions, protected by a plain label above, and originally in the roof stood five gables containing stone windows, like two that look towards the north [1]. By the side of one bay-window on the south is a small porch of stone. The outer doorway of it is arched, and though much dilapidated, reveals traces of a Perpendicular archmold. The inner doorway is very perfect and of the same style. The spandrils of the arch are beautifully carved in imitation of a vine and oak branch, inserted in which are the letters P. W. R. and a shield bearing the arms of Clare impaling those of Burgh; viz. *Clare,* Or, 3 chevronels gu. and *Burgh,* Or, a cross gu. This

doorcase was no doubt erected during the time of Prior William Reche, who succeeded to that office in 1515. It formerly contained a handsome wooden door, studded with iron knobs at the corner of each panel, and containing a plain but solid

[1] In a book of drawings belonging to the Cambridge Ant. Soc. is one of the S. Front, shewing these five gable-windows. The drawing is not signed, but two others representing the sloping arches in the wall, and the remains of the cloister are marked R. R. (the late R. Relhan), 27 June, 1801. As all these drawings seem to be done by the same hand, we must conclude that the windows alluded to were to be seen in 1801, or else the drawing was made from memory or description. Tradition states that these gables, and the parapet which adjoined them, were removed when Canon Jenyns put on the present roof; they must have added much to the architectural effect of the building, and probably lighted in earlier times the dorter or dormitory of the monks.

iron knocker. This door is now inserted in an archway leading
to the offices. There is no reliable record to state what position the monastic buildings occupied, but it is probable that
this portion of the house formed originally the Chapter House,
while the chapel with its bell-tower[1] stood towards the west.
Passing then round by this side, we see the two gables in the
roof before mentioned, above a vestibule of modern erection built
of clunch and Barnack stone, originally employed at Landwade
Hall. We now come to the earlier part of the building. That
part of the plan which extends towards the north is Early

English in character, and was built in 1236 A.D. The porch
is modern ; the arched windows near it also belong to the

---

[1] Vide grant of site to John Hynde, 30 Hen. VIII. Originalia Rolls. In
what is now the kitchen-garden was found a concrete bed, about 15 feet square,
which seems to have been the base of a tower, and near it was a capital forming
the top of 6 clustered columns, 3 round and 3 pointed at one side. Near the
coffins are 9 small stones forming the base and cap of similar columns and
running in pairs, thereby indicating an arcade.

manorial period, the change from square-headed to arched
being necessitated by the stone groining of the interior. The
lean-to to the north exhibits some traces of the earliest existing
works. In a wall are some stones of decidedly transitional
character, the form of which seems to point to the supposition
that they formed the lowest stones of a large archway and
rested above the jamb of a doorway; a large ditch originally
came up to this spot, and it has been conjectured that this
portion of the building was used for the same purpose as it is
at the present day. Near this is a spot where all the bits of
stained glass known to belong to the monastery have been

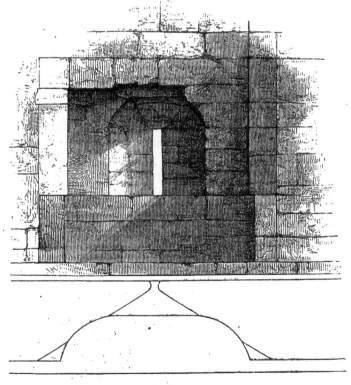

discovered, and hence there may have been in this vicinity
something of a glazier's shop. Over the porch is an arched
window of late Decorated character, and over a small square-

headed window in the vicinity is a label bearing a Decorated molding. The buttress is of course Early English. At the N. E. corner of the building, close to the two Early English buttresses, while repairing in 1856, was discovered a curious hole. There were previously some indications of a passage of some . sort, which had given rise to amusing stories amongst the labourers in the vicinity. One tradition affirmed that it was the opening to an underground passage to Swaffham Bulbeck nunnery close by. According to another story, a man went down with a light and got to some distance, when the devil put it out! When examined, there was found to be a square-headed archway, with a small aperture for light cut out of the stone, and it probably served as a well or a cellar.

On passing through the porch, we find a modern stone doorway inserted in an Early English archway discovered at the time of restoration in 1860. Through this, we enter what is now the entrance-hall, and formerly was the cloister of the monastery. This portion of the building is the most perfect remnant that we have to shew the kind of buildings that were then erected by the monastery. Two Purbeck marble octagonal shafts with richly molded capitals, and bases of Barnack stone, support the stone groining ribs, which descend upon them. These are left to us in all the more perfect state, as they were covered with plaster and concealed from view during the time that this portion of the building formed a home for ducks and geese. At the side of the walls are corbels variously molded to support the ribs of the roof. The windows, as I have said, are arched, and the tracery shews a feeble attempt to imitate earlier Perpendicular work. There are four doorways in this hall. The entrance doorway stands near to another well proportioned square-headed and arched doorway leading to the adjacent portion of the building, which contains Early English archways, and a handsome, though small, two-light Early English window. A third doorway is plain, and leads up some steps to the front portion of the building, and a fourth doorway is small, and of the Perpendicular period. It is molded and carved in the same way as the doorway before described in the south front, but it contains, on the shield of arms, the coat of Clare only. This doorway was re-

noved from the floor above, where it formed the entrance to the
prior's apartments. These apartments were approached by stairs
near this doorway, where are now some sloping arches in a wall,
of Early English character, and beautifully molded. This was,
previous to 1860, the exterior wall of this side of the house.
Close to these arches may be seen a piece of a groining rib,
which would lead one to suppose that there was originally
another side to this cloister, and in the floor above is an Early
English exterior doorway, which led to the prior's lodging.
Passing to the front, we find rooms containing but little of
antiquarian interest. The panelling in the dining-room, taken
from an old oak screen, which formerly ran across the room,
and two carved pieces of wood representing musicians, supporting on their heads a piece of modern furniture, are however
worthy of notice. There are more of these musicians in a loft
above. They originally came from the church at Little Wilbraham, where they formed hammer beams. The loft where these
images now stand exhibits the whole length of roof of this
portion of the building, containing very fine old timbers. The
old flooring is unrestored, and a set of rooms might be with ease

constructed here. There were originally within the author's memory many little compartments made out of reeds and plaster, probably of the same date as the manor-house.

These are the principal features of the building itself, but there are some features of antiquity preserved which have been found on the estate or in the neighbouring fields. These consist of celts, bronze implements, and arrow-heads of flint or bronze of the early British period, some shackles, and a piece of a monumental brass inscription, shewing only "iit" and "iiij," some keys of various periods, found here, or at Bottisham, and some glass beads. There are also some broken bits of stained glass, ranging from the Early English period down to the Perpendicular, and many coins of the period of Queen Elizabeth, Charles, James, and Edward the Third. Besides, are many counters, which are variously called Jetons, Nuremberg tokens, and Abbey pieces. They were merely used in order to assist in making calculations at a time when accounts were written with Roman numerals[1]. They are of great variety of size and design. There are also some seals which have been discovered. Two of them were found in the fields of Langmeadow, on January the 22nd, 1862. One is of bronze, and is of exceedingly rude workmanship. At the top is a quatrefoil. The impression reveals a coat of arms, those of Clare impaling Burgh, very rudely carved, inserted in a square placed angle-wise over another. This was possibly a seal of the prior, as the seal of the abbey was of a different character. The other seal, also rude, is of clay, the impression of which reveals an inscription round a sunflower, viz. s' MATIL' + TOPE +. From the rudeness with which this seal is constructed, it may be conjectured to have been intended for Matilda Tone, whose family has been before described. Another seal, also of bronze, was found here, containing a representation of St Lawrence, holding a gridiron. The inscription shewed "Saincte Lawrencii," and may have had some connection with Wicken, the church of which was dedicated to Saint Lawrence.

ounda-
on.   Having seen what are the present remains of this convent,

---

[1] Vide Snelling's *Jetons, Abbey Pieces,* &c., 1769, London, 4to. for a full account of these tokens, with drawings of their designs.

we must now go back and trace the course of its history; and first, we must inquire into its foundation and origin. The earliest notice that we can find is in one edition of the History of England by the monk Bartholomew Cotton [1]. This history was compiled before the year 1298, that is, when the historian died. We find mention in it of certain monasteries founded during the year A.D. 964. He says :—"Item ecclesia de Swaneseye, ecclesia sancti Egidii de Bernewelle super Grantam fluvium Cantabrigiæ, prioratus de Angleseye, et ecclesia de Spineto et ecclesia sancti Trinitatis de Tefordia et prioratus de Modmeney et prioratus de Miremande et cæteræ ecclesiæ in locis pluribus circa prædictam paludem ;" viz. the marsh which ends at the abbey of Thorney and Peterborough. This extract is as it stands in Henry of Huntingdon's chronicle, but in Forester's translation of the same, there is no abbey mentioned between Barnwell and Holy Trinity, Thetford [2], &c. This extract is quoted to shew that there may be a mistake of some copyist at a very early period, and consequently some difficulty in finding out who was the actual founder.

Henry the First is said by Henry de Knighton, in his " Compilatio de eventibus Angliæ [3]," to have founded this monastery : ' Iste Henricus clericus [4] regnavit xxxvj annis, et devenit probus homo, benignus et verus erga Deum et homines. Iste fundavit Abbathiam de Wellaw juxta Grymmisby et domos de Creke in Northfolke, et de Angleseye in comitatu Cantabrigiæ." This statement is accepted by Tanner [5], and Messrs Lysons [6], and Carter [7]. But many other writers affirm that Richard de Clare . was the founder. The authorities for this statement are Cox [8], Camden [9], Blomefield [10], Dugdale [11] following Leland, and Speed. We have seen that Richard de Clare bestowed a moiety of the manor of Bottisham upon the house of Anglesey, and therefore in one sense he became a second founder, if the house existed

---

[1] *Historia Anglicana*, ed. Luard, p. 28. [2] Ed. Bohn, p. 175.
[3] Vide *Decem Scriptores*, Henry de Knighton, lib. II. cap. ix.
[4] Called Beauclerk on account of his learning.
[5] *Not. Mon.* p. 42. [6] *Cambs.* p 91.
[7] *Hist. of Cambridge*, p. 138. [8] *Cambs.* p. 262.
[9] Vol. II. p. 235. He says also " or Hen. I." [10] *Coll. Cant.* p. 183.
[11] Ed. *Caley, Ellis*, and *Bandinel*, Vol. VI. p. 394.

before his time, and undoubtedly the patronage of the monastery became vested in his family. We must also remember that patrons are often designated by the name of founders. For instance, Catharine queen of Henry VIII. is thus called both patron and founder, as well as Edmund Mortimer, Earl of March, Elizabeth de Burgh, and others. Now the priory of Tunbridge, in Kent, was founded by Richard de Clare before 1135 A. D., at which time the manor of Bottisham was in the hands of Walter Giffard and Ermengarde his wife, who founded the abbey of Nutley in Buckinghamshire. That Richard de Clare therefore who divided the manor of Bottisham between the two religious houses of Anglesey and Tunbridge, must have been the grandson of Richard the founder of Tunbridge, for he was the coheir of the Giffards, and succeeded to the lordship of Bottisham. Documents at this period are generally undated, and from a careful consideration of the names and events mentioned in the earliest relating to Anglesey, we should come to the conclusion that none of them are clearly and unmistakeably previous to the year 1206 A. D. But, on the other hand, it is far more probable that Richard de Clare on succeeding to the honour of Giffard should divide the manor of Bottisham between a religious house already existing in the parish, and therefore possessing some claim upon his patronage, and one which, though more distant, was bound to his family by the relationship of its founder, than that he should found a new house in Bottisham and yet give half the manor to one far distant and already established. On the whole the evidence preponderates in favour of the opinion that Henry the First is to be regarded as the founder, and this view will be strengthened when we consider somewhat in detail the litigation which subsequently ensued concerning the advowson of Bottisham church.

edica-
ion.   The monastery of Anglesey then, presumedly founded before the end of Henry the First's reign in 1135, began its existence upon the site of the present remains. All writers agree in asserting that it was dedicated to the honour of the Blessed Virgin onstitu-
on.   and St Nicholas. Its constitution is stated by some writers to have consisted of a prior and 8 canons, but Tanner [1], quoting

---

[1] p. 42.

as his authority a MS. in the library of Corpus Christi Coll. Cambridge, marked G. 319, says there were 11 canons, and in this statement he is followed by Russell[1]: and certainly in 1515 there do appear to have been 11 canons, besides a subprior and prior. But there is only one year in which so many canons appear to have been living under the protection of the same roof. Probably therefore there were ordinarily 8 canons under a prior and a subprior ; and they were what were called Regular Austin Canons. The rule under which they lived was that of Saint Austin, bishop of Hippo in Italy, A.D. 395. There was this difference between regular and secular canons,—secular canons were so called as being conversant with the world, performing spiritual offices to the laity, and taking upon them the cure of souls. Regular canons, on the other hand, were those who were bound by some rule, and while less strict than the monks, lived together under one common roof, had a common dormitory and refectory, and were obliged to observe the statutes of their order. This rule of St Augustine was but little known till the tenth or eleventh century. They were not brought into England till after the Conquest, and they seem not to have obtained the name of Austin canons till some years afterwards. It is worthy of observation, that, during the period antecedent to 1236, when Anglesey was greatly benefited by the goods of Master Lawrence de St Nicholas, the inmates of the monastery are styled 'fratres,' and it is not till afterwards that they lose the name of 'fratres' and are styled 'canonici,' in the various documents relating to the convent. Their habit was a long black cassock, with a white rochet over it, and over that a black cloak and hood. Monks were always shaven, but the canons wore beards and caps upon their heads. It is not known which is the first house of this order that was founded in England, but undoubtedly Anglesey was one of the earlier ones. The reign of Henry the First was most prolific in monastic institutions, many new orders having arisen in England during his reign. The number of houses professing the rule of St Augustine alone, instituted between 1100 A.D. and 1135 A.D., amounts to no less than 56. Anglesey and Barnwell Priory, which are

---

[1] *Cambs.* p. 348.

both included in this calculation, seem to have been, up to the era of the dissolution, the most influential, with the exception of Thorney abbey, in the county of Cambridge.

Priors and Canons.   It has been a work of great difficulty to collect the names of the inmates of this monastery. The scarcity of documents relating to the house, and the infrequency with which the priors and canons are mentioned by name in those documents, renders the task almost a hopeless one. Occasionally the prior's name is mentioned in connection with legal proceedings, but the canons' names are derived almost exclusively from the accounts of ordinations extracted by Cole from the registers of various bishops of Ely. From these sources, then, the following scanty list is derived:—

Priors.

RICHARD is the first prior that occurs by name, in 1222.

William de Fordham, occurs in 1231.

Henry, occurs in the time of Hugh de Balsham, bishop of Ely, after the year 1257.

Hugh, in 1263.

John de Girnthorn alias Tyrrington, occurs from 1272—1275.

Henry, occurs 1278.

John de Bodesham, resigned in 1298.

Roger de Weston, elected 8 January, 1298, occurs in 1307.

Walter de Withersfield, elected Oct. 3, 1316, died in 1338.

Walter de Yelvedon, elected Sept. 22, 1338.

Richard de Wrattinge or Wrottinge, elected July 5, 1352; and occurs in 1362.

William de Quy, occurs 1371 to 1391.

William de Bodekesham, occurs in 1397.

William Lede or Lode, 1402.

Hervy, 1404.

John Huy, was elected in 1408.

John Daniel, elected in 1444; and resigned in 1461.

John Wellys, elected 12 January, 1461, occurs 1471.

John Leverington, occurs in 1489.

Thomas Burwell, occurs in 1498.

George Holland, prior of Stoneleigh, Hunts., el. 1508.

John Barton, elected Feb. 19, 1515, and resigned the same year, with a pension of £10, by the bp. of Ely.

William Reche, elected March 28, 1515.

William Seggewicke, 1515, and was prior in 1523, probably the same as William Reche.

John Fordeham, in 1532, probably the same as

John Bonar, 1533, last prior.

The following are the names of some of the canons of the house:—

Thomas de la Lade, canon, 1222.

Hugh de Tyrrington, canon, 1254.

John de Bodekesham, }
William de Anglesey, } fratres, 1300.

Henry de Berri (Bury). }
John de Aswelle (Ashwell), vicar of } fratres, 1317—27.
Waterbeach in 1338 A.D. }

John de Bodekesham,
The subprior,
E. de Ely,
Richard Pichard, } canonici, 1314.
Henry Muchet,
Walter de Yilevilden,
Richard de Queye,
Walter de Wyth,

William de Quye, }
William de Abyngton, } ordained priests, Aug. 20, 1349.

Fr. John de Stowe, to be accolitus, }
Fr. Richard de Stowe, to be subdiaconus, } June 11, 1351.

Fr. John de Beche, to be subdiaconus, }
Fr. John de Stowe, to be diaconus, } March 23, 1351.

William de Wilburgham, canon, 1352.

John de Wyggenhale, canon, 1352.

John de Beche, diaconus, Sept. 21, 1352.

[1]*Fr. Semannus Harper*, capellanus, 1374.

John Myntemoor de Trumpiton, canon, 1377.

[1] William, vicar of Bottisham, cited him before the bishop of Ely. Neither party appeared, and the cause was postponed. No charge is mentioned. Dated Wednesday after the Feast of Saint Matthew Apostle and Evangelist, 1374. Vide Reg. Arundel in Cole MSS. Vol. XLI. p. 17.

[1] *Galfridus de Burton*, capellanus, died 1376.

William de Bodekesham, subprior.

John de Bodekesham,
William de Lode,
Richard Wollepyt,   } canonici, 1378.
William Tiryngton,
John de Cambridge,

Fr. Thomas de Cambrigge, priest, 1444—5.

William Myles, accolite.

John Wellys,
John Balsham,   } exorcists, 1455.
Laurence Bottysham,

John Myntemoor de Trumpington[2], ordained deacon, July 16, 1375; priest, June 7, 1376.

William Botylsham, accolite and subdeacon, 14 Cal. Jan. 1377; deacon, 13 March, 1377; priest, 3 April, 1378.

John Hervey, accolite and subdeacon, 7 Ap. 1386; priest, 6 Ap. 1387.

Thomas Lynne, accolite and subdeacon, 7 Ap. 1386; deacon, 6 Ap. 1387; priest, 23 Sept. 1391.

John Botelsham, deacon, 10 Kal. Oct. 1386.

---

[1] Cf. the following document. Whereas Dominus Galfridus de Burton, chaplain, abiding in the Priory of Anglesey, within the said priory has closed his last day, we Thomas de Gloucester, clerk, commissary of the venerable father in Christ and Lord Bishop of Ely, seeing that the said priory with all the canons, brethren, converts, corrodans, servants, dependants and inhabitants there and others departing in it, are solely and incontestably and immediately subject to the said venerable father and his servants and lie under his jurisdiction, lest the goods of the defunct be unduly scattered &c. 4 Kal. Sept. 1376, sequestrate and appoint Walter Mitelwey and Thomas Gerard of the parish of Bodekesham executors of the will of the said Galfridus. On Saturday next after the feast of St Matthew the apostle and evangelist in the church of St Michael the will is exhibited. Vide Reg. Arundel, 1376, fol. 53 b. quoted by Cole, MSS. Vol. XLI. fols. 44, 56.

The executors confess that the deceased bequeathed to the said Agnes Peçok 40s. of which are owed to them 20s. Vide fol. 150 a. 1381 A.D. Cole, XLI. fols. 93, 94.

[2] On Jan. 9, 1376, he was brought before the bishop of Ely at the rectory of Balsham on the charge of continual absence from the monastery, and sentenced to imprisonment at the pleasure of the prior of the house. (Vide Cole, XXIV. fol. 25, from Reg. Arundel, fol. 21 b.)   •

William Yelden, deacon, 10 Kal. Oct. 1386; priest, 6 Ap. 1387.

William Leverington, Thomas Whaplode, and *John Beketon,* subdeacons, to be ordained to all sacred orders, 20 Ap. 1406; accolites, 14 March, 1404; subdeacons, 10 Ap. 1406.

John Rede de Bodkysham, ad primam tonsuram, 14 Kal. June, 1380.

William Tiryngton, accolite and subdeacon, 14 Kal. June, 1380; deacon, 10 Kal. Oct. 1380; priest, 8 June, 1381.

John de Cambridge, accolite and subdeacon, 14 Kal. June, 1380; deacon, 10 Kal. Oct. 1380; priest, Feast of S. Matthew, Ap. 1381.

Thomas Ely, subdeacon, 21 Sept. 1392; deacon, 21 Dec. 1392; priest, 1 March, 1393.

John Wykes, accolite, 16 June, 1397; subdeacon, 22 Dec. 1397; deacon, 23 March, 1398; priest, 24 May, 1399.

John Freckenham, subdeacon, 24 May, 1399; deacon, 20 Dec. 1399; priest, 28 May, 1401.

John Brinkley, deacon, 1 June, 1409; ordained priest of the order of the preachers at Cambridge, 28 March, 1411.

John Haslyngfield, subdeacon, 23 Sept. 1413; deacon, 3 March, 1414; priest, 22 Dec. 1414.

John Burgh, accolite, 19 Sept. 1416; subdeacon, 6 Mar. 1416; deacon, 21 May, 1418.

William Mylys,
John Wellys, } subdiaconi, 1456.

William Mylys,
John Wellys, } diaconi, 1457.

William Mylys,
John Wellys, } presbiteri.

John Balsham,
Laurence Bottysham, } subdiaconi, 1459.

John Balsham,
Laurence Bottysham, } diaconi,

Thomas Cambrigge, subprior,
John Wellys, seneschallus domus ac sacrista, } 1461.
William Mylys, presbiterus,
John Wrottynge,
Laurence Rede, } diaconi,

Alexander Boyden,
John Sturgeon, } subdiaconi, 1462—3.
Alexander Sample,

Richard Norman, accolitus, subdiaconus, 1466—7.

Richard Norman, presbiterus, 1467.

Alexander Boyden,
John Sturgeon, } diaconi, 1466—7.
Alexander Sample,

Alexander Sample, presbiterus, 1467.

John Bokenham, } accoliti, 1467.
Thomas Preston,

Fr. Robert Tybbot, } subdiaconi, 1486.
Fr. William Swyfte,

Fr. Thomas Reyner, } diaconi.
Fr. William Freman,

Robert Tybbot, diaconus, 1486.

Fr. William Freman, presbiterus, 1486.

William Swyfte, diaconus ad primam tonsuram, 1491—2.

John Grene, } accoliti ad primam tonsuram, 1491—2.
Richard Hore,

William Swyfte, presbiterus, 1493—4.

John Grene, } diaconi, 1494.
Richard Hore,

John Falne, } accoliti, 1495.
Richard Sporle (? a mistake for Roger),

John Grene, presbiterus, 1495.

Richard Hore, presbiterus, 1495—6.

Roger Sporle, subdiaconus, 1497—8.

Fr. Robert Dullyngham, } ad primam tonsuram, 1499—15
Fr. John Ludlom,

Roger Sporle, presbiterus.

William Swyfte, subprior,
Richard Hoore,
Roger Sporle, seneschallus, } canonici regulares, 1515,
Robert Dullyngham, sacrista,
Simon Hullocke, coquinarius,
John Bonar,

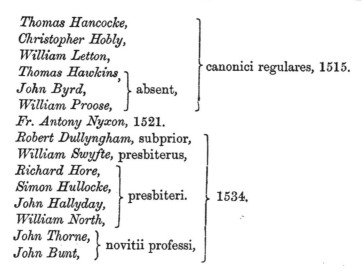

Thomas Hancocke,
Christopher Hobly,
William Letton,
Thomas Hawkins,
John Byrd, } absent,
William Proose,
Fr. Antony Nyxon, 1521.
} canonici regulares, 1515.

Robert Dullyngham, subprior,
William Swyfte, presbiterus,
Richard Hore,
Simon Hullocke,
John Hallyday, } presbiteri.
William North,
John Thorne, } novitii professi,
John Bunt,
} 1534.

These last seem to have been the canons who, under their prior, John Bonar or Bonyard, surrendered the monastery at the dissolution. None of them received a pension except the prior, John Bonar, and he appears in 1552 to have been in receipt of a pension of £20 per annum.

CHAPTER III.

PECULIARITY OF EARLIER DOCUMENTS.

THE earliest documents still existing that contain mention of the monastery of Anglesey are, as was the custom of the time, without date: and thus it is extremely difficult to place them in any order of time; but, on the other hand, a few chronological indications are given to us, if we carefully consider the names of benefactors to the house that occur in various charters, as well as the witnesses to those documents, and the various forms in which the bequests are expressed.

It may be well to mention some peculiarities of diction in the earlier deeds. And first, it is to be observed that the inmates of the convent are styled "fratres" in contradistinction to "canonici," by which name they are afterwards designated. This term "fratres" seems to have been used at a prior date to 1236 A.D., when by the liberality of the rector of Tyrrington, Master Lawrence de Saint Nicholas, the major portion of the conventual buildings were erected, and when the monastery began to be possessed of considerable property in Cambridgeshire. Secondly, the earlier bequests were made, "in usus pauperum infirmorum," "for the benefit of the poor sick," a style of bequest that does not appear in the later charters. This expression would appear to indicate that the documents in which it is found belong to a period anterior to 1206 A.D., when the convent possessed a moiety of the manor of Bottisham. If this be so, they support the statement of Henry de Knighton, that the monastery was founded by Henry I. and not Richard de Clare as later writers affirm. The phrase is only to be found in three charters. Subsequent to this the phrase employed is only "moved by piety for the salvation of my own soul and those of my ancestors and successors." Men thought with this world's goods to purchase security in the next world; and this abuse increased to such an extent as to interfere seriously with the government of the country, and caused the introduction of those acts known by the name of the "Mortmain Acts." Thirdly, a comparison of the names of witnesses, and a calculation as to the time in which they could have lived, assists in deciding on a possible date. These witnesses, it will be remembered, were persons resident in or near the place from which the document is dated. Fourthly, and lastly, the names of certain tracts of ground, and the roadways adjacent to them, together with the names of their owners, deserve full attention.

Under these calculations, then, the earliest charter would be that of Baldwin de Scalariis, "who granted to God and the Blessed Mary of Anglesey and the brethren serving God there, three acres of his land in the town of Dullingham, that is to say, *the Longelond,* in free, pure, and perpetual alms." *Charter of Baldwin de Scalariis,*

Not long after this comes the charter of Juliana, daughter of Baldwin de Scalariis, who "for the salvation of her soul and of those of her ancestors, gave, granted, and confirmed to God and the Blessed Mary of Anglesey, and the brethren serving God there, for the use of the poor sick, half an acre of her land in the town of Dullingham, which lay in the middle field, near the land of Hugh, the son of Augustin de Bodekesham, in free, pure, and perpetual alms [1]." *of Juliana, daughter of Baldwin.*

The family of De Scalers, or De Scalariis, was one of great name at this period. Hardwin de Scalers came over with the Conqueror, and obtained from him various grants of land in Cambridgeshire and Hertfordshire. He had two sons, Richard and Hugh [2]. From the former of these was descended Stephen, whose wife, Juliana, was a benefactress to the Priory of St Rhadegund in Cambridge, now Jesus College, and whose descendants, William and Richard, continued the benefactions of their ancestor. Lucia, the daughter and heiress of the last-mentioned Richard, married Baldwin Freville, and became the progenitor of that family. Hardwin's other son, Hugh, held property in various counties, and detained lands from the *Family of De Scalers.*

---

[1] This and the preceding charter are in the New Record Office.

[2] Vide Clutterbuck, *Hertfordshire,* Vol. II. p. 398. *Abbrev. Placit.* p. 99.

monks of Ely, as did his nephew Stephen. Like his brother
Richard, he was a benefactor to the monks of Lewes, which
benefactions were confirmed by his descendants. His son
Geoffrey was the grandfather of Thomas De Scalers or Deschallers, who was lord of the manor of Whaddon in Cambridgeshire.
Cole says that the families of De Scalers and Deschallers are
quite distinct, though confounded by Salmon in his *History of*
Hertfordshire, and he argues that the two families are different;
for Hardwin de Scalers bore gu. six escallops ar. 3, 2, and 1,
whereas Thomas Deschallers of Whaddon bore ar. a fesse between 3 annulets gu.[1]; but in the *Abbreviatio Placitorum,*
Thomas de Scalers, the son of Geoffrey, the son of Geoffrey de
Scalers, is expressly mentioned as owner of the manor of Whaddon, co. Camb.; so that it would seem that the family of Geoffrey
de Scalers bore these arms for difference. It does not appear
from any account of the family who Baldwin de Scalers was,
but he was probably another son of Hugh, who held lands in
Dullingham, and these came by succession into the possession
of Baldwin. His charter above mentioned must be placed
somewhere about the early part of the thirteenth century.
Geoffrey de Scalers was also connected with the house of Anglesey; for it appears that in the time of Henry III. and Edward I.
the Prior Angles', "P'tus de Abington, Samson le Blund, et
Eborardus de Orewell," held in Stepel Morden and in Orewelle
the fourth part of a knight's fee of the barony of Geoffrey de
Scalers[2].

harter of
lice, wi-
ow of
hilip.

The next benefaction received by the prior and canons was
that of Alice the widow of Philip. She appears to have granted
a *selion* of land in the town of Wilbraham, which lay in Westfield, and abutted upon the meadow at Svameles. It is almost
impossible to identify this piece of land in any way. It proba-

---

[1] Cole MSS. Vol. xviii. fol. 5.

[2] *Testa de Nevill,* p. 354. I can find only one other document in which the
name of Baldwin de Scalers occurs. This is the confirmation of Theobald de
Scalers of the church of Dullingham to the Priory of Thetford, granted to it by his
father Robert. To this deed Baldwin was witness, in company with William,
Archdeacon of Ely, Henry de Scalers, Thomas de Dullingham, Geoffrey de
Scalers and Robert de Valoignes. Vide Dugdale, *Mon. Angl.* ed. 1682, Vol. i.
p. 666.

bly lay in the parish of Great Wilbraham, where Philip seems
to have resided. A selion of land, a phrase which is often to
be met with in documents of this date, is, properly speaking, a
piece of land between two furrows, that is to say a ridge, and
included according to some an acre, according to others half an
acre[1]. Each village seems to have had its northfield, middle-
field, westfield, &c., and the expression merely denotes on which
side of the village the land in question lay. The expression
Svameles is not to be identified with any modern name. This
document is also remarkable for being the earliest which contains a seal. Nearly half of it remains, that is, of a round seal
of white wax about an inch and a half in diameter. In the
centre of it was a floriated fleur-de-lys of early style, but
nothing remained of the legend except "s' ALVEVE.+......"

The next charter to the convent is that of Richard Le Brun *Charter of*
of Dullingham, who was a witness to the charter of Baldwin de *Richard*
Scalariis. He grants, for the safety of his soul and those of his *Le Brun*
ancestors and successors, one half acre of his land in the field of
Dullingham, which is called middlefield, with the appurtenances
lying between the land of Hugh, the clerk of Bodekesham, and
the land of Roger, the son of Seleda, and which abuts upon
Holway on one side, and on the headland of Adam the shepherd on the other. Here we have the position of the land
marked out with greater precision. Hugh, the clerk of Bodekesham, was, as has been already noticed, the son of Augustin,
and a person of some influence as a proprietor. The word
"forrera" or headland that often occurs indicates the head of the
field where the furrows cross (= terra capitalis seu transversalis).
Who Roger the son of Seleda was it is impossible to say, or
where Holway may have been[2]. Neither of these names occur
again, nor are they of any particular importance.

About the same date as the last charter is one of Robert, the *Charter of*
son of Hugh. He granted to the church of Anglesey in frank- *Robert,*
almoigne all the tenement with homage, service, and all appur- *son of*
tenances, which Thomas Perteix held of him in the town of *Hugh.*
Clare, save two pence to be rendered in two equal payments at

---

[1] Vide Spelman, Gloss. sub voce.
[2] ? the road leading past the Hall of Little Wilbraham.

Easter and Michaelmas, to the Earl of Clare. To this document Elias de Ashwell and Hugo de Bodekesham were witnesses. The former of these two was owner of some considerable property at Haslingfield, of which, according to Lysons[1], 120 acres were purchased by the convent, probably out of the goods of Sir Richard, the rector of Melbourn. Two documents remain of Beatrice, the widow of Elias de Ashwell. One of these, to which no date is attached, records the sale of all her land, which she received in dowry in the parish of Haslingfield, for the sum of 100s. The second, which, though nearly illegible, bears the date of 1257, is a receipt for two..., owed to her by reason of a certain composition made between her and the Priory of Anglesey, and paid at their court holden in Haslingfield.

In Guilden Morden, too, the convent received a bequest of Henry Freman, who gave them in frank-almoigne all the land he had of the gift of Mabel, daughter of Walter Paddoe, subject, however, to a rent-charge of 2d. yearly, of which for 20 years the priory was absolved.

About the same date Walter de Westley bestowed in alms 3 acres of land in Westley, "which lay in Farelond, near the court-house," and abutted upon the land of John Waleyl. Amongst the names of witnesses occurs that of Richard de Howebridge de Lada, Richard the son of Simon de Botekesham, and Ralph Matefrey. This last appears to have held some property in Dullingham as well as Teversham, in which latter parish he granted 8d. rent, in which John the son of Roger de Queye was bound to him from 6 acres of land, which he received in marriage with Isabel the daughter of Ralph Matefrey. If she died without issue (which appears to have been the case), this rent was to go to the brethren at Anglesey. It was confirmed to the "canons and brethren" of the convent at a later date by Master Henry de Hinton, into whose possession the land seems to have come.

But Ralph, the son of Matilda, also granted for the use of the poor sick a rood and a half of land in the same parish in frank-almoigne, and in 21 Edw. III. we find a confirmation by

nd at slingd pursed.

arter of nry eman.

Walter Westley.

Ralph atefrey.

f Ralph, n of atilda.

---

[1] *Cambs.* p. 208.

Vm. de Clatton of 6*d.* annual rent, which appeared due from
n inspection of the monastic deeds during the priorate of
Valter de Yelvedon.

Hervey, the son of Seleda, gave in alms a shop in the *Charter of*
1arket-place of Cambridge, between the shop of Martin Aluard *Hervey, son of Seleda.*
nd that of Geoffrey the son of Alice. From the names of the
itnesses, this charter was made in the time of Richard, parson
f Bodekesham, John de Ry, Hugh de Bodekesham, and Henry
he clerk of the same parish.

Another document of about the same date gives us some *Purchase*
lea of the flourishing state of the convent. For the brethren *of tenement from*
hen purchased for the sum of 70 marks of silver all the tene- *Walter,*
1ent which Walter, the son of William, the clerk of Little *son of William,*
Vilbraham, held of the tenement which belonged to Hillary of *the clerk of Little Wil-*
Vilbraham and Stephen his brother, subject to the yearly pay- *braham.*
1ent of a pair of gloves of the price of one penny, or one penny
n actual coin.

During the priorate of Hervey the convent quit-claimed *Quit claim*
'homas, a servant of the University of Cambridge, and Matilda *of Thomas, servant to*
is wife, of all right in two messuages with two acres and one *the Uni-*
ood of arable land in Mill Street in the town of Cambridge, *versity of Cam-*
ying between the land of William Seman and Simon de Brad- *bridge.*
ey, and formerly held by Robert, the son of Robert Hubert;
eceiving in exchange one messuage in Trumpington Street,
etween the land of Richard Tunpan and Henry Pippe, and
0*s.* of silver. Amongst the witnesses occurs the name of
ohn Bich, then mayor of Cambridge. We now hear of Wal- *Charter of*
er Nepos, Walter Nephew, or Walter Le Newe of Wil- *Walter Le Newe.*
raham, who gave to the convent of Anglesey one acre of his
nd in the town of Wilbraham for the use of the poor sick.
Ialf an acre of this is said to abut upon the fields of Bodeke-
1am, near the land of Roger, the son of Geoffrey, and half an
cre abutting upon the fields of Quy, near the land of Roger,
he son of Richard. The witnesses of this deed are nearly all
he same as to the following charter of Roger, the son of Gerold,
ho gave one acre of his land in the town of Wilbraham Regis,
hich lay in Cambedene. The name of Wilburham Regis, or
ings Wilbraham, is very curious. There is no distinct account

of three separate parishes in Wilbraham, but the name of Wilburham Regis occurs in various documents; and in one deed,
viz. the charter of Eustace, the son of Roger of Little Wilburham, we find as a witness Sir Richard, parson of Wilburham
Regis, which would seem to indicate that there was a church
founded there.   But from a reference to Domesday book we
find that the manor of Great Wilbraham was always in the
hands of the king, and the church of Wilbraham Regis is that
now belonging to Great Wilbraham.   In 1279, we find that the
king retained half of this manor in his own hands, and subsequently, while the Knights Templars held one portion, the
other moiety fell into the possession of the family of Lisle.
Where then was Cambedene?   If it has any relation to Camegate and Cambelfield, mentioned in the charters of a subsequent
date, then it must be near a spot called in the documents Depegrave, and adjacent to what is described as Dedcherlfield.   It is
also mentioned as being situated between two roads of the
breadth of fourteen feet.   These names Depegrave and Dedcherlfield indicate a Saxon burying-place, and may therefore be
the spot where so many early British remains were discovered in
1851 A.D.   Whether this spot was the site of a battle-field or
not, it seems to have been situated, as nearly as may be conjectured, in Wilbraham Regis, and it may be that the king gave
his name to that part of Wilburham at the time of the supposed battle.   The latest date, however, that Wilbraham Regis
is mentioned is in 1291, at Pope Nicholas' taxation.

`But in Little Wilbraham, Roger, the son of Richard, ex-
pressly grants and confirms by charter, "three pence, which his
father gave to the Blessed Mary of Anglesey, and the brethren
serving God there, for one rood of land which Roger held of
them, to be received by the aforesaid brethren for ever, from
him and his heirs, on the day of the Conception of the Blessed
Virgin Mary, before the birth of Christ, in free, pure and perpetual alms."   The charter then goes on to state:—"And if
by chance I the said Roger or my heirs shall make default in
the payment of the said money within the octaves of the aforesaid feast, it shall be lawful to the aforesaid prior and brethren
to distrain me and my heirs on the common of the aforesaid

town of Wilburham until we shall have paid them the aforesaid rent."

But far more important than these small bequests was the *Advowson of Botti-sham.* possession of the advowson of Bottisham, which was given to Anglesey Priory by Richard De Clare. The right to its possession did not pass unchallenged. Walter Giffard, and Ermengarde his wife, who held Bottisham before the family of De Clare, had founded an Abbey of Austin canons at Nutley, or Creendon, in Buckinghamshire. As will be seen in the following plea made in the 15th year of the reign of King John, the Abbot of Nutley claimed the advowson :—" Richard, Earl of Clare[1], was summoned to shew why he did not permit the Abbot of Nutley to present a fit person to the church of Bodegesham &c., whereupon the said abbot produces a charter under the name of Walter Giffard, and Ermengarde his wife, ancestors of the same earl, in which is contained that they gave and granted to God and the church of Saint Mary de Creendone, and to the abbot and canons there, &c. a great many lands and all the churches and tithes which were in their gift, and which mentions churches, amongst which the church of Bodegesham is named. He produces also a charter of King Henry, his father, confirming that gift, and the church of Bodegesham is mentioned amongst others. He produces also the charter of King John, confirming the same in the same manner. He produces also the confirmation of the blessed Thomas the martyr, formerly Archbishop of Canterbury, who confirmed to those canons all the possessions which were bestowed on them by Walter Giffard, and Ermengarde his wife, and all the churches of his land, and mentions many, amongst which the church of Bodekesham is named, &c. A day is appointed," &c. Nothing further seems to transpire as to the decision of this cause till 1222 A.D., when a final concord was made, "in the court of the Lord the King at Westminster, in the sixth year of the reign of King Henry, the son of King John, in one month from the day of Saint Michael, before Stephen de Segrave, Ralph Hareng, Thomas de Heydon, justices, and other faithful men of the Lord

---

[1] Must be a mistake for Gilbert de Clare, for Richard died in 1206.

the King, then and there present. Between John Abbot of
Nutley, claimant by Martin his canon, who was put in the place
of the same abbot, to gain or lose, and Richard, Prior of
Anglesey, deforciant, by Thomas de la Lade, his canon, who
was also put in the place of the same prior to gain or to lose,
concerning the advowson of the church of Bodekesham. Whereupon a plea was made between them in the aforesaid court,
to wit, that the aforesaid abbot acknowledged the advowson
of the aforesaid church of Bodekesham with the appurtenances
to be the right of the same prior and church of Saint Mary
of Anglesey, and has remised and quit-claimed the same from
him and his successors to the same prior and his successors
for ever. And for this acknowledgment and quit claim, fine
and agreement, the aforesaid prior and his successors will
render yearly to the same abbot and his successors and to
the church of Saint Mary of Nutley half a mark of silver
at Easter during the whole life of Richard de la Lade, at
that time parson of the aforesaid church of Bodekesham.
And after the decease of the same Richard, or if he shall
assume a habit of religion, the aforesaid Prior of Anglesea
and his successors shall render by the year to the aforesaid
abbot and his successors, seven marks of silver annually at
the four terms of the year, to wit, at the birth of the Lord
23s. 4d., and at Easter 23s. 4d., and at the feast of Saint John
the Baptist 23s. 4d., and at the feast of Saint Michael 23s. 4d.
And if the aforesaid prior or his successors shall not render
the aforesaid money at the terms aforesaid to the aforesaid
abbot and his successors, it shall be lawful to the same abbot
and his successors, to distrain the aforesaid prior and his successors upon that moiety of land in Bodekesham which Richard,
Earl of Clare, gave to God and the church of the Holy Mary
of Anglesey in pure and perpetual alms, until the aforesaid
money shall be paid to the said abbot and his successors.
Cambridge." Thus the Priory of Anglesey secured to themselves the advowson, no doubt a desirable piece of patronage,
even though burdened with the annual pension of seven marks
of silver = £4. 13s. 4d. This pension seems to have been regularly continued down to the time of the dissolution, as fully

appears in the *Valor Ecclesiasticus*[1] and the ministers' accounts
of 27—28 Henry VIII. Here also it will be observed is the
earliest mention of the benefaction of Richard de Clare. The
next mention of this gift is in the Hundred Rolls made in 1279.
The Richard then who is alluded to must be not Richard
de Clare founder of Tonbridge priory, for he had not succeeded
to the barony of the Giffards, but his grandson, who married
Amice, daughter of William, Earl of Gloucester, and who died
in 1206. It seems strange that the convent of Anglesey
should have succeeded in obtaining the advowson of Bottisham,
if the charters which the Abbot of Nutley produced were
genuine; the convent of Anglesey being already in possession,
it was found impossible to dislodge them. Roger Brigham,
who was Prior of Ely sometime before 1215, and died in 1229,
issued a charter confirming "to our most dear friends in Christ
and the maintainers of a worthy religion, the prior and convent
of Anglesey, the church of Bodekesham with all its appurtenances which our venerable father John, Bishop of Ely (i.e.
John de Fontibus, 1220—1225), granted to, and conferred upon
them and converted to their own proper uses, as is contained
in his charter. Saving in all things the rights of the church
of Ely, and saving those of the vicarage which our aforesaid
venerable father John, Bishop of Ely, taxed for the vicar for
the time being, residing in the same church, saving the episcopal rights which the same vicar for the time residing there
shall sustain. This confirmation is alluded to and strengthened
by letters from Stephen Langton, Archbishop of Canterbury,
Primate of England, and Cardinal of Rome, dated 1225 A D.,
in the month of October. No further litigation with regard to
this benefice seems to have ensued, and no more documents are
extant concerning it till the year 1495, when we find the collation of Bishop Alcock couched in these terms :—

"To all the faithful of Christ to whom this present writing
shall come, John, by the grace of God, Bishop of Ely, greeting
in the Lord. The favour of religion and the direction of equity
demands that those who are sprinkled with the fragrance of
good character, we should nevertheless think worthy of richer

[1] Vide Vol. iv. p. 233.

favour and foster with stricter charity. Know all of you, that we, regarding the honesty and poverty of our beloved sons in Christ, the prior and canons of Anglesey, and the good conversation of their lives and manners, which commend them to the Lord, the church of Bodekesham, with all its appurtenances, the patronage of which is known to belong to the same monks, we have, with the assent and will of our prior and monks of Ely, and for the safety of our souls, and those of our ancestors and successors, and being moved by the intuition of divine piety, granted and conferred to their proper uses, and for the support of the poor and those entertained there. To have and possess the same for ever, we transfer and canonically institute the said persons therein. Saving a competent vicar, who as vicar shall act and reside for the time in the aforesaid church and sustain the severall burdens thereof, and saving in all things the right of our church of Ely. And lest any contention should chance to arise in times to come touching the said vicarage, we have charged the same in this manner ; to wit, that the vicar, whoever he may be for the time, shall have all the altarage with its appurtenances, except the small tithes of the aforesaid canons in the same parish, and except the oblations of those persons living with them, and the burials of those staying there, together with a fit residence and twelve acres of land in three parts of the territory of the same town from the land of the church assigned to the use of the vicarage. And that this our grant and collation may obtain strength and firmness of endurance, we have corroborated this present charter by putting thereto our seal and............ These being witnesses : Master John de Foxton, Master Robert de Eywart, Master Stephen de Manicester, John de Neketun, Master Stephen de Hedun, Master Roger de Capell, Master Laurence de Lincoln, and many others[1]."

Valter de ilbra- am. But in Wilbraham the convent of Anglesey at this period obtained the most grants of land. In 1232 a fine was made between William, prior of Anglesey, plaintiff, and Walter de

[1] From a Roll headed "Registrat' fuerunt tempore Nichi . . . . — Anno Dn̄i ccccccxxxiij et aᵒ. çons' sue xviijᵒ." now in the New Record Office. Vide also the same document, with some slight differences, in Cole MSS. Vol. xxvi. fol. 72, from Bp. Alcock's *Register*, fol. 221.

Wilbraham, defendant, concerning twenty acres of land, with the appurtenances, in Wilbraham. By this agreement the prior of Anglesey granted the land to the same Walter to be held during his lifetime from the convent of Anglesey, rendering annually three shillings and one penny at two terms of the year, to wit, eighteen pence at the feast of Saint Michael and nineteen pence at Easter for all service. After the death of Walter the land was to revert to the same prior and his successors, and the church aforesaid, quit from the heirs of the same Walter for ever. It does not seem clear whether this Walter de Wilbraham is the same as the person of the same name who was elected Prior of Ely in 1241, but he probably was distinct from Walter Nepos or Walter Le Newe, as he was called.

Distinct again is the person styled Walter, the son of *Charter of* *Walter, the* Philip of Wilbraham, who was also probably the son of Alice, *son of Phi-* whose charter has been mentioned. In his charter, dated *lip.* 1234, the position of his land is marked out with the greatest accuracy. His gift comprised six acres of land in the fields of Wilbraham, "which," says the charter, "I held of Walter Le Newu for twelve pence annually, in the same town; of which half-an-acre lies between the land of the aforesaid Walter and the land of Robert, and abuts at one end upon the field of Bodekesham, and at the other end upon the land of Martin the Chamberlain, and in the same field, one selion near the land of Geoffrey Newman, abutting at one end upon the field of Bodekesham, and at the other end upon the land of William Thurkili, and in Middle-field, one acre lies near the land of Hugh, the son of Walter, and abuts upon Strete; and in Kambesfield[1] one acre lies near the land of William, the son of Emma, and abuts upon Strete-brede, and in the aforesaid land, as it lies, and is considered more or less; and again in Kambesfield, half-an-acre near the land of Walter Bruere, and abuts at one end upon the land of Richard Alward and the land of Roger, his son, and at the other end upon Stretebrede, the land of William Talemasche; and one rood and a-half in the same furlong lay between the land of Alan Mulere and the land of Osbert, the son of Florence,

---

[1] ? = Cambedene.

and abuts upon Stretebrede; and in Middlefield one selion lies
near the land of Alan de Deresle, and abuts upon Brinkelway[1],
and one selion near the land of the said Alan, and abuts upon
Brinkelway in the same furlong; and one selion near the land
of the said Alan, and abuts upon Strateway[2]; and in Windmill-
field one rood, near the land of Hilary the chaplain and the
land of Robert Derebocht, and abuts upon Monksway; and in
the same field three roods lie near the land of the aforesaid
Alan, and abut upon Bodekeshamfield; and in the same field
one selion, for one rood lies near the land of the said Alan, and
abuts upon Bodekeshamfield. To have and to hold, &c., quit
from me and from my heirs for ever, and entirely free and discharged from all secular service, custom, and demand. And I
and my heirs will warrant, &c. And for this gift and grant the
aforesaid canons have given me eighteen marks of silver as a
consideration," &c. This charter is endorsed, "The charter of
Walter, the son of Philip. Feofment of the house of Anglesey.
Six acres of land for eighteen marks in Wilbourgham, of the
goods of Master Lawrence de Saint Nicholas." At a later date
we shall hear more about Master Lawrence de Saint Nicholas,
who was such a benefactor to the house. Eighteen marks,
or £12., seems a good price for six acres of land at that
date. Another charter, issued by Walter, the son of Philip, of
Little Wilbraham, seems to belong to the same date as the
preceding. This charter provides for the convent an annual
rent of twelve pence, arising from a messuage called Sparne,
abutting on the public street in the town of Little Wilbraham,
and lying between the land of Simon, the son of Osbert, and
the land of the canons of Anglesey: viz. sixpence to be received at the feast of Saint Michael and sixpence at Easter.

uit claim
f Mar-
aret le
Usser.   Following upon this are various undated documents connected with Anglesey. The first of these is a quit claim of
Margaret, widow of Hugh le Usser, of Bodekesham, of her
right in that piece of land of the fee of those persons which
Hugh, formerly her husband, gave to them for the celebration
of his obit, and of her rights in certain lands and fields in

---

[1] Brinkley Road.   [2] Now called Streetway.

odekesham and Wilbraham Parva, held by way of dower, or
ι exchange of the lands exchanged by her husband and by her
; one time for them. The obit here alluded to is the same
; the anniversary, or year's day, of burial. We find that
ugh, the son of Margaret, was in possession of certain lands in
ottisham in 1304, and seems to have been a member of a
mily of some importance in Bottisham.

Next comes the charter of Ralph Candos, of Fulbourn, who *Charter of*
anted sixpence rent in the town of Fulbourn, of that mes- *Ralph*
age which William Buche de Or (Goldenmouth) held of him *Candos.*
Fenstrete, to be rendered at the feast of Saint Michael.

Next comes the quit claim of Love, the daughter of John, *Quit claim*
e son of Leuric de Lada, of Bodekesham, who gave to the *of Love,*
daughter
nvent for eleven shillings sterling, which the brethren gave *of John,*
son of
er, all right and claim which she had, or could have, in that *Leuric de*
essuage which lay in the parish of Bodekesham, between the *Lada.*
essuage of Henry le Nephew and the messuage of Martin le
ore, and stretched towards the moor, and contained in breadth
ne perches and four feet, without any retention by her or by
y of hers. Here it is to be observed distinct reference is
ade to that tract of land known by name of the Moor, which
pellation is retained up to the present day.

We now come to a further purchase of land out of the goods *Charter of*
Master Lawrence de Saint Nicholas. What this purchase *Walter le*
New.
nsisted of is minutely described in the following charter of
alter le New, of little Wilbraham, viz. " of six acres of my
d in the fields of Little Wilbraham, with their appurten- .
ces, and the liberty of foldage, as much as belongs to so much
d ; to wit, in Dedcherlfield, that land which lies at the site
the mill near the land of Alan de Deresle, and abuts upon the
tivated land of Anglesey, being two acres. In Midlefield,
parcels of land lying near the lands of Alan de Deresle, and
tting upon the road which is called Strete, being three
ds. In the same field, two parcels of land, one at the head
he other, and one extends beyond Dullingham path to the
dland of Richard Aluard, and lie near the land of Alan de
resle, being three roods. In the same field, two parcels of
d, being half-an-acre, one of which extends beyond Dulling-

H. B. 13

ham path, and abuts upon the headland of Richard Aluard,
and the other is in the next furlong towards the East. In
Cambelfield, two acres, which abut upon the land of William
Talemasche at Skiggelhowe.   Moreover, I have given and
granted, and by this my charter have confirmed to the aforesaid brethren of Angleseye, half-a-mark of annual rent in the
town of Little Wilburham, with the homages of those paying
that rent and of their heirs, and with all things pertaining to
me or my heirs from those tenants; to wit, from Robert, the
son of Peter, the clerk, three shillings; from Walter, the
merchant of Cambridge, twelve pence; from Joaca and Ma-
billia, the daughters of Osbert, the burgess, twelve pence; from
Hugh, the son of Walter de Swapham, six pence; from William,
the son of Philip, sixpence; from Roger Curteis, sixpence;
from Eustace, the son of Roger, twopence. To have and to hold
to the aforesaid brethren, &c. (Endorsed) Charter of feofment
of Walter le Neve of six acres of land and half-a-mark of
annual rent, whereof from Robert, the son of Peter, three
shillings, and with homage, &c., as within.   Twenty marks of
the goods of Master Lawrence de Saint Nicholas."   The seal
appended to this document was of light-green wax, a portion
only remaining; when perfect it was round and 2½ inches in
diameter.   In the centre is a knight on horseback, imperfect;
of the legend only "Sigill. Walt'......." remains.

There is another charter of the same man which may be
referred to about the same date as the preceding; it says,—
"Know that I, &c., have given and granted, &c., five acres and a
half of my land in the fields of Wilburham with their appurtenances; to wit, one acre of my field which abuts upon the field
of Bodekesham, and a third part of the aforesaid field in length
and breadth, to wit, that part which is towards the east.   Also,
in the same field, a rood and a half which abut beyond the
highway near the land of Hilary the priest.   Also at Bregepath
half an acre.   Also a rood and a half which passes over beyond
Camegate.   Also half a rood which also passes over beyond the
same place.   Also one rood in Westfield between the land of
Clarice and the land of Osbert the son of Aldwin.   In Cambelfield half an acre which lies near Depegrave.   Also half an acre

which abuts upon the field of Wilburham between.........Also an acre and a half in the said field, near the land of Walter the son of Peter. Also three roods which lie near the land of William, the son of Robert, which abut upon the road of Hale, and one rood which abuts upon the croft of Alan the miller, and one in Dedcherlfield near Brodeway abutting upon the land of Walter the son of Peter, and one rood in Cambelfield between two roads of the breadth of fourteen feet near the land of Robert the son of Hervey, to have and to hold, &c. (Endorsed) The Charter of Walter Nevu." Hilary the priest is often mentioned in documents of the period relating to Anglesey. He was the son of Clarice mentioned above. These purchases were concluded about the year 1235 A.D., for we there find a fine or final concord was made during Trinity term between William Prior of Anglesey plaintiff, and Walter le Newu defendant, concerning fifty-five acres of land and eleven shillings and eight pence rent, with the appurtenances in Wilburgham. "Whereupon a plea of warranty of charter was summoned between them in the same court, to wit, that the aforesaid Walter has acknowledged the aforesaid land and rent with the appurtenances to be the right of the said prior, and of his church of Anglesey, as those which the same prior has of the gift of the aforesaid Walter. To have and to hold to the same prior and his successors and his church of Anglesey from the aforesaid Walter and his heirs in free and perpetual alms, doing therefore to the chief lords of that fee the service which belongs to the aforesaid land and rent for all service and exaction. And the same Walter and his heirs will warrant, &c. And the same prior has received the aforesaid Walter and his heirs into all the benefits and prayers which shall henceforth be performed in his church of Anglesey for ever. Cambridge."

But during the same Trinity term there was a suit made against the prior and convent in which they were easily beaten, and in which their claim was not probably very just, as the acknowledgment for the agreement was only one sparrowhawk. This suit was between Roger de Lade plaintiff, and William Prior of Anglesey defendant, of seventy acres of land and seven messuages with the appurtenances in Eltisley. And the prior

*Fine con-
cerning
land in
Eltisley.*
acknowledged the right of Roger de Lade. We have now
arrived at the year A.D. 1236, in which occur four very important documents relating to the benefactions of Master
Lawrence de Saint Nicholas.

*Master
Lawrence
de Saint
Nicholas.*
He appears to have been rector of Tyrrington near Lynn,
prebend of Tockerington in the diocese of York in 1190[1], and
chaplain and subdean to the Pope, but it does not seem clear
how his connection with the house of Anglesey arose. Possibly
he was a canon there. These documents throw so much light
on the early history of the monastery that they are quoted
in full:—

"To all the faithful in Christ to whom this present writing shall come. W. named Prior of Anglesey and the humble convent of the same place greeting in the Lord. Know
every one of you that we with one assent and will have consented in all things and for all things to the disposition and
provision of Master Lawrence de Saint Nicholas, subdean and
chaplain of the Lord the Pope, and a chief benefactor of our
house which he has made, touching as well the land bought
with his money, and the stock to be bought for the advantage
and profit of our house. And lest any contention or contradiction should arise in times to come respecting the said disposition and provision, the said Master Lawrence has disposed
and provided concerning the said lands and stock in this manner; namely, he has granted that all the profits arising, as well
from the lands of Mordun as of the lands bought and to be
bought with his money at Litlington, shall be for the support
of our house and the hospitality thereof for ever. Moreover,
he has granted that all the profits arising from eighty acres of
land lying in the greater town of Swapham, which were of the
fee of Eborard le Fraunceys, and which he received from us in
exchange for eighty acres of land lying in the fields of Bodekesham and Wilburham, and which he bought with his own
money, together with the issues and profits of six hundred of his
sheep, shall be for (the support of) the fabric of our church, and
for the construction of the chief cloister and of the chamber of
the prior until the full completion of the work. And that we

[1] Le Neve, *Fast. Eccl.* III. 271.

will ratify the said disposition and provision, and undoubtedly maintain the same firm and entire, we have in witness thereof to this present writing caused our seal to be affixed. Done at Barnwell on the fifteenth of the calends of August in the year of the Incarnation of the Lord 1236. These being witnesses, Sir William, subprior of Barnwell, Andrew a monk of Ely, Master Robert de Leycester, Master Walter de Tyrrington, Master Hamon de Mara, Master Richard de Kyrkeham, Master Alexander de Sancto Edmundo, Master Alexander de Ely and others. Moreover at the end let it be noted that the works aforesaid being completed and perfected, the aforesaid eighty acres of land and six hundred sheep ought to be again taken for the common benefit of our house with all honesty.

"Moreover, we H., by the grace of God, Bishop of Ely, commending and confirming the aforesaid disposition and provision in the Lord, any one who shall wish to nullify, impede, or disturb it, or shall subtract from, or diminish the fruits and profits arising from the lands and sheep before-named for the fabrics aforesaid, or cause anything to be subtracted or diminished therefrom, we solemnly restrict him with the chain of excommunication. And as to the other eighty acres of land, it shall be right that mention be made thereof when we have given our judgment. Nevertheless, we will, and firmly ordain, that it have the same effect in and for all things as regards the fruits and profits arising from those eighty acres which are above-named as given and granted in exchange for them. Done on the day, and in the place before-named, and in the presence. of the witnesses aforesaid."

Two seals of green wax are appended to this document, one is that of Hugh de Balsham, Bishop of Ely, much broken, the legend being "Sigillum Hugonis Dei Gra. Epi. Eliensis+." The other is the seal of the priory, being very nearly perfect. The device is the virgin and child on a bracket supported by angels; and the legend "angel' Anglesie sunt singna tip' q' Marie + [1]." Here then we find mention of the chief cloister and the chamber of the prior, which thus was commenced after the year 1236, and which now remains in an almost perfect state.

---

[1] Angeli Anglesie sunt signa tipique Marie.

The next document forms a sequel to the rising prosperity which the convent seemed now to enjoy. It is to prevent the contraction of loans and charging the establishment with debts, except under necessity as far as sixty marks. It runs as follows: "To all the faithful of Christ to whom this present writing shall come. W., Prior of the church of the Blessed Mary of Anglesey and the canons of the same place, greeting in the Lord everlasting. Whereas it is truly written that poverty well managed may be compared with riches, we wish it to be brought to the notice of every one of you that we wish to arrange and settle the poor condition of our house so regularly and moderately, God willing, that those things which we have may honestly suffice for us without any superfluity, and that it shall not be necessary elsewhere to seek the support of others by begging; and as we see many indeed come to great want because they had indiscreetly made themselves liable for greater debts than they could liquidate and pay, we, by the authority and with the assent of the venerable father and our Lord H., by the grace of God Bishop of Ely, and by the advice of discreet men, cause it to be for ever firmly observed under the penalty of excommunication, that no prior of our house shall henceforth be able to bind our house by receiving anything by way of loan, or by any other kind of bargain or contract. But if need shall require it, or necessity compel them, with the advice of all our brethren who might be in any way interested therein or be called thereto, he may be allowed to bind it with effect to the amount of sixty marks only, and not more in the whole or by parts. If, however, by chance it should happen that any inevitable or unexpected accident should occur on account of which it shall be thought proper to be bound for our necessity for the greater sum of the debt of the house, we deliberately provide that then the prior and canons of Anglesey may be permitted to have recourse, and shall recur to the counsel and aid of the Bishop of Ely for the time being while he is in England, and that they may freely and securely do whatsoever the said bishop may consider, with deliberation and counsel, is best to be arranged in such case of need.

"Now we also H., by the grace of God, Bishop of·Ely, will

and command the aforesaid disposition and provision, together with the decision to be settled and confirmed in the Lord, and that the same may be for ever considered among their rules most strictly, and that they be written out, so that any one by whom such loan may be contracted, who should be disposed to interfere with, or disturb the same, should know that he was under the bond of excommunication by the said decision and our own. In witness whereof to this writing there is put the seal of the said (bishop), together with the seal of the said prior and canons of Anglesey. Done in the year of the Incarnation of the Lord 1236, in the month of February. These being witnesses, Master John de Wlpet (Woolpit), Master William de Saint Edmund, Jerome de Caxtun, Philip de Pavili, William, the rector of the church of * * * * , Samson de Saint Edmund, and others." The seal of the bishop is gone. That of the Priory of Anglesey is much chipped.

Shortly after this Lawrence de Saint Nicholas died, and the prior and canons issued the following document in order to provide for his soul and the memory of his charity to the convent:—

"Whereas, according to the precepts of the Gospel we ought to love our enemies, to do good to those who hate us, and to pray for those who ill-use and persecute us, yet very much more are we bound and directed to love those who love us, and to pray for those who do us good, and have done so. Among whom, by a certain special prerogative of charity, we, the prior and canons of the Blessed Mary of Anglesey, and all our successors, are bound to pray with incessant devotion for the safety of the soul of Master Lawrence de Saint Nicholas, a chief benefactor of our house; and, as we ought to induce our successors to do this, and that it may never fall into oblivion on that account, we have caused these things to be written in our rules. In the first place therefore be it known, that, at his own expence and by his own care and diligence, almost the entire fabric of our church, with the cloister, refectory, dormitory, and prior's chamber, are completed. And besides that one hundred and nineteen acres of land which we have in the town of Mordun, and sixty-five acres which we have in the town of Litlington, and two acres and half-a-rood which we have in the town of

Fulbourn, and ninety-four acres which we have in the town of Wilburham and Queye, and thirty-one acres which we have in the town of Bodekesham, with all their appurtenances, and a rent of twenty-two shillings and sixpence, he caused to be bought with his own money, and by the inspiration of divine charity liberally and graciously conferred upon our house. And the sum of the said lands, to wit fifteen, twenty, and eleven acres, and half a rood, beside many other goods, we have also received from the same. But be it known, that of the land aforesaid eighty acres, to wit, forty which were bought of Walter le New, whose soul God preserve, and thirty-eight acres which were bought from Sir Walter, rector of the church of Little Wilburham, and three acres which were bought in the town of Bodekesham from Alice, of good-memory, daughter of Richard, son of Eustace, were, with our advice and assent, assigned by the said Master Lawrence, and specially deputed for the support of one canon of our house, who ought daily, for ever, to celebrate mass for the salvation of the soul of the said Master Lawrence. But if at any time by chance he shall not be able, his default shall be supplied by some one of his fellow-canons by the direction of the prior of our house for the time being until he shall be able, and when he shall decease some other canon of our house ought to be substituted for him within the same week in all things and for all things in the form aforesaid, and so henceforth for ever. And also with the authority of the venerable father and our Lord Hugh, Bishop of Ely, and he being present at Barnwell in full synod, we, and all our successors, bind ourselves to this for ever. And, at the last, be it known and noted that this writing ought to be diligently read once every month in our chapter." Thus then the goods of Master Lawrence de St Nicholas may be summed up as follows:—the profits of 600 sheep to go towards a building fund; 119 acres of land bought at Guilden and Steple Morden; 65 acres at Litlington; 2½ acres at Fulbourn; 94 acres at Wilbraham and Quy; 31 acres at Bottisham; 22 shillings and 6 pence rent in Bottisham; 81 acres of the aforesaid land lying in Wilbraham and Bottisham to go towards providing a canon to say daily mass for the soul of the benefactor, leaving therefore 230 acres for the common benefit of the house. Twice we have mentioned six acres of land bought for eighteen marks, that is £12. Therefore, if we were to take the same price throughout we should find that £622 were spent in lands alone, a large sum to be bestowed in benefactions at that time. There is one more document bearing on the money of Master Lawrence de St Nicholas. It is a quit claim *Quit claim* of Theodenus de Thostia, nephew of Master Lawrence de Saint *of Theode-* *nus de* Nicholas, for three marks, being a portion of the sum of ten *Thostia.* marks deposited in his name in the treasury of the Blessed Mary of Anglesey, by Master Lawrence de Saint Nicholas, under the security of his seal. The deed is dated at Anglesey in the year from the Incarnation of the Lord 1267, on the morrow of the Holy Agatha, the virgin and martyr, and concludes thus:— "And because I had not my own seal I have procured this to be confirmed by the seal of Sir Roman de Sclaccis. These being witnesses: Master Nicholas de Quicham, rector of the church of Quicham, Sir Luke the chaplain, Roman de Sclaccis, Nicholas de Berchinges, Reginald de Suberi, Thomas de La Lade and others[1]." This looks exceedingly as if these last five mentioned were canons of the house, and Sir Luke chaplain, to say mass for the soul of Master Lawrence de Saint Nicholas, but there is no collateral evidence to prove the point.

---

[1] Original in the Cotton Collection. All other documents, unless expressly mentioned, are in the new Record Office, Fetter Lane.

harter of illiam, he son of Iainer. THE prosperity and wealth of the convent now began to attain some proportions. After the benefactions just mentioned comes apparently, though there is no date to the document, the charter of William, the son of Mainer, confirming to the brethren the tenement with the appurtenances in Swaffham which Osbert his brother gave them in free alms, to wit, ten acres of land with the appurtenances which Alexander Milumes held of them, with Amice, sister of the benefactor, to be holden free and quit of all secular service and exaction. . William, the *rant of illiam he Cook,* cook, of Little Wilburham, granted and quit-claimed to Sir William de Fordham, Prior of Anglesey, and the convent of the same place, all right and claim in that manse, with one croft adjoining which was called Blaber's croft in the town of Wilburham, held of the said prior and convent: and William, son of *f Wil-am, son f Roger urteys.* Roger Curteys of Little Wilburham, chaplain, granted, remised, and quit-claimed to the same prior and the convent of Anglesey all right and claim in a messuage with the croft adjoining, which lay in Little Wilburham, between the land of Henry Schileman and the land formerly of Hugh, the son of Walter, abutting on the road which led to the church. Amongst the names of witnesses to this document occurs the name of Bartholomew the clerk, as well as Yvo the merchant, who figures in most of the documents of this period connected with Wilbraham, and is described as of that place, also John Wakelin or Walkelin of Couweye (= Quy), who seems to have been a person of much influence.

onfirma-on to llen de eche. At this time the prior and convent parted with some property in Ely. A charter was issued confirming to Elen de Beche for her homage and service all their messuage in Ely, which

Richard de Lada gave them, with one parcel of land opposite to and adjoining the same tenement, which lay between the land of Sarah, daughter of Cassandra, and the land of Amabilia daughter of Joachym, in Fig Street, with all the appurtenances to the same tenement belonging, whether more or less. To have and to hold from them and their successors to her and her heirs or to whoever she should please to give, bequeath, or assign the same, except to any other religious house than their own. Rendering annually to them and their successors eight shillings at two terms of the year, viz. Easter and Michaelmas. And if she were to make default of payment the prior and convent were to distrain on the said messuage within and without for chattels found in the said messuage and land aforesaid; but nevertheless the cattle or chattels were not to be removed from the town of Ely.

At the same date nearly as the above-mentioned document, *Pension to Sir Richard, rector* we find a Sir Richard, rector of the church of Meldeburne. *of Melbourn.* From his connection with Anglesey it is possible that he was the Richard de Lada who gave them lands in Ely. Anyhow, in consideration for the lands in Haslingfield and Barley, which were bought for the priory by the rector of Meldeburne or Melbourn, the convent agreed to allow an annual pension to be made to Sir Richard all the days of his life, viz. twenty marks to be paid at two terms of the year, to wit, at the Purification of the Blessed Mary (Feb. 2) and the feast of St John the Baptist (June 24), and after the death of the rector, Sir Richard, to support one secular chaplain to perform divine service for his soul and for the soul of Hugh Bishop of Ely, or the bishop for the time being, and for the souls of their benefactors, and of all faithful deceased for ever[1]. The allowance of this chaplain is thus minutely specified, and gives us some idea of the life of the convent at that period. They were to grant him a fit house and place, and every day he was to receive a white loaf, and "one other such as serving men eat," and a gallon and a half of the better ale, and two dishes with as much and such kind of soup as two monks receive in the refectory, and twenty

[1] Vide the document in Cole's MSS. Vol. xviii. fol. 139.

shillings sterling at two terms in the year, to wit, ten shillings
at Easter, and ten shillings at the feast of St Michael the archangel. His clerk was to receive daily one loaf such as serving
men eat, and half a gallon of the second kind of ale, and one
dish according to the custom of serving men. And the goods,
arising from the lands before mentioned, were to be applied to
the support of the sick monks in the infirmary, and to services
for the souls of the said Richard and Hugh, Bishop of Ely, and
all faithful deceased. The document which ratifies this trans-
action is dated at Anglesey, on the fourth of the calends of May,
the day of St Vitalis the martyr, in the seventeenth Lunar
cycle, and in the year from the Incarnation of the Lord 1251.
The first seal, says Cole, appended to the document is that of
the Priory of Anglesey in green wax. On the back is impressed
the seal of the prior. It is smaller than that of the house, and
represents our Lady standing and an angel with a scroll in his
hand with 'ave' on it, representing the salutation. Legend,
" Sigillum Willielmi prioris Anglesea." The other seal is that of
Hugh, Bishop of Ely, of pale brown wax, oval in shape, and
about three inches in diameter. In the centre is a figure of the
bishop in pontificalibus, with a mitre on his head, giving his
benediction with the right hand, and holding a crosier with his
left. Legend, " Hugo Dei Gracia Elyensis Episcopi." On the
back, and somewhat smaller in size, is the bishop's private seal,
having in the centre two figures standing beside the spire of a
church. These are probably St Edmund and St Etheldreda.
There is a half figure of God the Father at the top, and at the
bottom one of a bishop praying. Legend, " Me juvet Edmun-
dus Eldrede sine prece mundus."

harter of
ugh de
auden.
Up to this period the priory held the advowson of only one
benefice, namely, that of the parish in which their conventual
establishment was placed ; but by the following charter they
acquired that of Swaffham St Mary. And it is to be observed,
that of the two churches now standing in the same churchyard
of the parish called Swaffham Prior, the church now used is
dedicated to St Mary, and the ruined edifice dedicated to
St Cyriac. The parishes to which these churches belonged
were united by Act of Parliament in the year 1667, and within

the memory of this generation the church of St Cyriac was the one used for divine service, but on its falling into decay, it was partly pulled down, and the existing building added on to the tower of St Mary. The remains of the church of St Cyriac were then reserved as a mausoleum for the family of Allix, who reside at Swaffham House. The advowson of his church was given to the Bishop of Ely by Sir Philip de Burgh, lord of the manor of Borough Green[1]. But to return to the charter of Hugh de Crauden of the advowson of Swaffham St Mary. It runs as follows:—

"Know all both present and future that I Hugh de Crauden have given and granted, and by this my present charter have confirmed to God and the church of the Blessed Mary of Anglesey and the monks serving and who shall serve God there, in pure and perpetual alms for the safety of my soul and the souls of my ancestors, two acres of land with their appurtenances in the town and fields of Great Swafham together with the advowson of the church of the Blessed Mary in the same town, which said church is built upon one of the aforesaid two acres, the right of the patronage of which church belongs to my advowson, and which acre lies between the land which formerly belonged to William the son of Fulk, and the new highway which leads towards Burwelle, whereof one end abuts upon the wall of the aforesaid church, at the end of which acre the said church is built; and the other acre lies at Grisedale between my land and the land of the aforesaid monks of Anglesey in length and in breadth from the great ditch towards the north to my land on the south. To hold and to have the aforesaid acre of land with its appurtenances and with the advowson of the church aforesaid to them and to their successors freely quietly well and in peace, and to be possessed in pure and perpetual alms. So that neither I the aforesaid Hugh nor my heirs nor any one for or on account of us shall be able to claim or demand anything henceforth from the aforesaid lands with the appurtenances nor the advowson of the church aforesaid. And I the aforesaid Hugh and my heirs will warrant

---

[1] Vide Gough, *Sep. Mon.* I. ii. 220.

defend and acquit the aforesaid land with their appurtenances
and the advowson of the church aforesaid to the aforesaid canons
and their successors as is aforesaid against all men as well Jews
as Christians. And that this my gift and grant and confirmation of my present charter may remain ratified and established
for ever, I have put my seal to this writing, these being witnesses. Sir Gilbert Poche, Sir John des Eschalers, Sir John
de Ceelford the monk, Richard de Crauden, Hugh the son of
Hugh de Swafham, Hugh le Blund, Herbert de Haukeston,
Hugh de Himpigton, Yvo de Wilburham the merchant, Bartholomew the clerk of the same town, Roger de Habintune,
William de Hisleham, and others." In 1254 a final concord
accordingly was made between William, Prior of Anglesea
(that is I suppose William de Fordeham), plaintiff, by Hugh de
Tyrington, his canon (qu. the same as Hugh, afterwards prior ?)
who was put in his place to gain or to lose, and Hugh de
Craweden, defendant, of seven acres of land with the appurtenances in Great Swaffham and the advowson of the church
of the Blessed Mary in the same town. In the charter above
quoted we only see mentioned two acres of land, but as the
Prior of Anglesey had land adjacent at that time, it is possible
that 5 acres may have been of the gift of the same Hugh, and
this fine may include the two grants under one head. But
be that as it may, Hugh acknowledged the aforesaid land
and advowson to be right of the prior and his church as of
the gift of the aforesaid Hugh, to be held in free pure and
perpetual alms free and quit from all service and exaction for
ever. In 1258, four years afterwards, a document records the
collation of Hugh, Bishop of Ely, mentioning some arrangement as regards the vicar. It runs thus :—

"To all the sons of holy mother church by whom this present
writing shall be seen or heard. H. by the divine permission
the humble minister of the church of Ely, everlasting greeting
in the Lord. Regarding with the inmost eye of circumspection
and with pious affection of compassion how important it is that
the religious fighting for the eternal King should be under a
regular discipline of poverty, and should be supported therein
we condescend and wish it to become known to every one of you

by the tenor of these presents, that considering the poverty of the beloved sons in Christ the prior and monks of Anglesey in our diocese, and commending them for the honesty of their pious conversation as worthy of praises in the Lord, the church of the Blessed Mary of Swafham with all its appurtenances, the right of the patronage of which church is known in full right to belong to the said prior and monks, we, for the relief of the indigence of the same and for the support of the poor and of those resorting thereto for hospitality, with the assent and will of our chapter of Ely, being moved by the intuition of divine mercy, have granted and conferred and to their own proper and perpetual uses have converted the same, canonically instituting them as rectors in the same church, and have caused them to be inducted into corporal possession of the said church. Saving to us the collation of a vicar in the said church which we specially reserved to us and our successors in full right without the presentation and contradiction of the said prior and convent or of any other person and saving in all things the rights of our church of Ely. And we will that the same be taxed on profits to the value of several marks sterling by common estimation. And that this our grant may continue established for all times, we have caused this present writing to be corroborated by putting thereto our seal. These being witnesses. The Lord Walter our prior of Ely, Masters Roger de Leyrcester, and I. de Franesham, chaplains of the Lord the Pope, W. Engayne, Rector of the church of Lastowe[1], J. de Fyd, Clerk, Master William de Croylaunde, Henry Bateford and Nicholas Ware, Clerk, notary of this present writing, and many others. Given at Downam on the seventh of the calends of April, in the year of the Lord 1258, and in the second year of our pontificate." This collation was confirmed and ratified by the prior and chapter of Ely, at Ely, on the Ides of March, A.D. 1258, reserving to themselves in all things all right which they had in the church of St Cyriac, in the same town of Swaffham.

There arose, however, some dispute about the portion of the fruits of the advowson to be assigned to the vicar, and hence by

---

[1] Stowe, now Stow-cum-Quy.

the agreement of the Prior of Anglesey and Gilbert the perpetual vicar a taxation was to be made by Hugh de Stanford, commissary to the Bishop of Ely. The results of this are embodied in a document dated at Downham on the morrow of Saint George, in the year of our Lord 1260, and make the following provisions:—"Concerning the estimate of the expenses to be incurred about building the house for the vicar aforesaid by the Prior and Convent of Anglesey and the declaration of the profits of which the vicarage ought to consist. And, therefore, having deliberated beforehand—the vicarage is to be endowed with all the obventions of the altar, and tithe of hay, wool, milk and flax, and with other small tithes as well as the principal tithe of the curtilages, in lease with two acres from the priory of Ely for all (pensions?) assigned, and also with fifteen acres of land of the church and twelve acres of the land of the prior and convent assigned to the vicarage in (which?) the vicar is in possession. And also with sixteen shillings yearly which he shall receive in every year, to wit, of Ga...... and his heirs fourteen shillings for the tenement which he holds in the town aforesaid of the prior and convent of Anglesey; of Alice, the relict of Geoffrey Marshall, two shillings for the tenement which she holds in the town aforesaid of the aforesaid prior and convent. And the vicar for the time being in the same church shall have the portion of the vicar which by assessment is estimated as well worth seven marks at the common valuation. And by the distinct authority of my aforesaid lord, the said vicarage is to consist of the aforesaid, and the said vicar and his successors shall be contented with the aforesaid taxation and declaration; saving the tithes of all sheaves of any kind of corn and beans bound and heaped up according to the custom of August to the said prior and convent for ever. And the parties present, viz. the prior and convent, and the vicar for themselves, and their successors have expressly consented thereto, renouncing henceforth all exception and action and other things for the remedy of right by which this present ordinance might be impeded. And an addition is made to this ordinance and declaration by the consent of the parties that the vicar shall sustain all the ordinary charges of the church due and accustomed, to wit, in synodals and ornaments of the church and books, but the prior and convent shall sustain and repair the chancel.   Unusual and extraordinary burdens shall be sustained by each party in their due proportion.   And if the vicar for the time being shall sustain any damage for default of the warranty and defence and livery of the aforesaid twelve acres of the demesne of the said prior and convent, and of sixteen shillings annual rent in like manner from the demesne, the aforesaid prior and convent shall entirely restore it holding him free thereof.   And for the greater security the said prior and convent for themselves and their successors, and the vicar for himself and his successors have put their seals to this writing, together with the seal of (Hugh?) the bishop, and my seal.   Moreover, lest there should be any contention or cavil from henceforth concerning the house to be built for the use of the vicar, or even concerning the injury which the vicar has hitherto sustained for the non-building of his house, a tax of four marks shall be paid to the same vicar at two terms of the first year only.   But the old house with the loft, where, as arranged, the priest of the church was accustomed to inhabit, shall for ever remain for the use of the vicar, vicarage and cemetery."   Might that old house have been situated on the plot of ground at the corner of the churchyard now occupied by the school-house?

There seem, however, to have still continued some disputes till the time when Walter de Withersfield was prior, when a visitation was held by the Archbishop of Canterbury, through his deputies John de Bruyton, canon of the cathedral church of Wells, Master John de Ros, archdeacon of Salop, and William de Darby.   It was then stated that there were the parcels of tithes in the fields of Swaffham Prior, pertaining to the church of the Blessed Mary, there peacefully, quietly, and without any contradiction from the time when memory is not to the contrary.   First, the manor of the Prior and Convent of Ely with all its tenants free and copyhold.   Also, the manor called Shade-warfe, with all its tenants free and copyhold.   Also, the manor called Cotellys, with all its tenants free and copyhold. And so the advowson of S. Mary at Swaffham remained in undisturbed possession of the Priory of Anglesey up to the time of the dissolution, burdened with the above-mentioned provisions for a vicar to be maintained therein.

Mention has been previously made, in the charter of William, Prior of Anglesey, relating to the disposition of the goods of Master Lawrence de St Nicholas, of a certain Eborard le Fraunceys, who held the fee of eighty acres of land lying in the greater town of Swaffham, and who had received them in exchange for eighty acres lying in the fields of Bottisham and Wilbraham. In 1258 A.D., his son, Alan le Fraunceys, issues a charter appointing Richard le Fraunceys, his uncle, to be his attorney, to receive two marks of annual rent from the Prior and Convent of Anglesey, according to the tenor of the charter of Eborard his father, in which the said prior and convent were annually bound for the tenement which they held of him in Great Swaffham.

There is another charter, which, from the names of the witnesses, may be assigned to about the same period as the preceding. It is that of Martin Chamberlain of Wilburham, the son of Beatrice, who granted for the safety of her soul and those of her ancestors, and for a certain sum of money which they had given to her, all the lands and tenements which Hilary the chaplain of Wilburham and Stephen his brother formerly held. And all the lands and tenements which Beatrice, his mother, gave to a certain Walter, the son of William Burre of Wilburham, and which lands and tenements the same Walter gave to the aforesaid prior and convent. (This is undoubtedly the person styled Walter Bruere in the charter before mentioned of Walter, the son of Philip.) And all the lands and tenements which they had and held of his fee in the town and fields of Little Wilburham, &c. Rendering annually to her and her heirs six shillings and one penny; to wit, at the feast of St Michael three shillings, and at Easter three shillings, and one penny for all services, suits, customs, and secular demands. Saving to her and her heirs only two suits at her court in the town of Little Wilburham, to wit, at her first court after the feast of Saint Michael and at the first court after Easter, to which reasonable submission was to be made.

PEDIGREE OF CHAMBERLAIN.

Jordan, man of Alberic de Vere, = Beatrice, d. of Robert, s. of Ailric.
held adv. and man. of Little
Wilbraham in right of his wife.

Martin = Joane, died 1328.

Robert (or John,
vide Morant's *Essex*,
II. 535), of Radwinter,
co. Essex.

William = Milicent.

Catharine, = 1. Wm. Phelip,
coh. of And.   or Phippe, s. p.
de Bures.   = 2. Wm. de
                    Hemesi.

Elena, = John Oveine.
coh. of And.
de Bures.

Cecilia = Andrew de Bures,
d. s. p.   Steward of Eliz.
1351.   de Clare, in
            Bottisham.

Brion de
Hemesi.

We have now arrived at the year 1263 A.D., in which we *Fine.* ind mention of a new prior named Hugh. This is seen from a *Gerard de Bottisham* ine between Gerard de Bodekesham, plaintiff, and Hugh, prior *v. Hugh,* of Anglesey, deforciant, of forty shillings, which were in arrear *Prior of Anglesey.* io the same Gerard of an annual rent of eighteen marks which was owing to him. And the prior agreed for himself and his convent and his successors to pay the aforesaid Gerard eighteen marks during his lifetime. And in case of default, the aforesaid Ierard was to distrain the convent by their chattels found in the ands and tenements of the prior and convent in the town of Bodekesham. After the death of Gerard the annual payment vas to cease, and the prior was to be quit of all damages arising ιy reason of the afore-mentioned detention of rent for ever.

Somewhere about to this period is to be ascribed a docu- *Power of Attorney of the Prior of Christ Church, Canterbury.* ient which is very curious, as similar deeds have rarely een discovered. It is what is now called a power of ttorney, issued by N., Prior of Christ Church, Canterbury, a irge and influential monastery. This was possibly Nicholas andwich, who presided from 1244—1254. It runs thus[1]:—
N., Prior of Christ Church, Canterbury, to the discreet and ιligious men the Lord Prior of Anglesey and the holy convent f the same place, greeting in the Lord ever with sincere iarity. Be it known to your brotherhood that we have ppointed brethren Walter de Hatdfeld and Nicholas de Cam-

[1] Vide also *Notes and Queries*, Nov. 10, 1849.

14—2

bridge, monks of our church, the bearers of these presents, our procurators, to require and receive the book which is intituled: "Iohannes Crisostomus de laude Apostoli." In which volume are also contained "Hystoria vetus Britonum que 'Brutus' appellatur," and "Tractatus Roberti episcopi Herfordensis de compoto," which we formerly lent to Master Laurence de Saint Nicholas, then rector of the church of Tyrenton, and which after the decease of the said Master L. has remained with you and still continues. In witness whereof we have transmitted these our letters patent signed with our seal."

This may be the earliest instrument of this description yet known. By mention of the name of Nicholas de Cambridge it gives us a clue as to the origin of the book being left at Anglesey. This brother of the Priory of Christ Church was possibly a friend of Master Lawrence de St Nicholas, and by his instrumentation the book may have been lent to the rector of Tyrrington. This Master Lawrence has been frequently alluded to as the great benefactor of the house of Anglesey, and from the fact that the book remained in possession of the house after his death it is not improbable that he died within the precincts of the monastery. But be that as it may, this document proves the vigilance and care exercised to recover their property, and the liberality with which books were lent from one to another, while they were so rare and so eagerly sought after. Each book at that time contained often many different treatises, the subjects of which were entirely distinct, and which were so grouped together solely for purposes of preservation, while the coverings were so arranged as to admit of withdrawing or inserting some of these treatises at the pleasure of the owner. That the book in question was returned in all probability, is seen by reference to the catalogue[1] of the books of the monastery, made by Prior Henry Chichely in the early part of the 15th century, and referring to about 600 volumes; for there we find an entry of a volume commencing, "Iohannes Crisostomus de laude Apostoli" containing also the history of "Brut" and other works.

---

[1] Cotton MSS. Galba E. IV.

In 1261 some dispute arose about that portion of the estates *Plea.* of the priory situated in Litlington; amongst the pleas of *Prior of Anglesey,* jurats and assize in the 45th year of the reign of Henry the *v. Gunnora, wife* Third is the record of one in which "the Prior of Anglesey *of Walter* offered himself on the fourth day against Gunnora the wife of *de Leigthton.* Walter de Leigthton concerning a plea that the same Walter and Gunnora should keep to the same prior an agreement made between William formerly Prior of Anglesey, the predecessor of the aforesaid prior, and Hamon de Valoignes, the father of the aforesaid Gunnora, whose heir she is, concerning eighty acres and seven virgates and a half of land with the appurtenances in Litlington. And she did not come, &c. and made many defaults, so that it was commanded the sheriff that he should distrain her by all her lands, &c., and that he should have her body at this day. And the sheriff testifies that he had distrained her, &c., and therefore it was commanded the sheriff that he should distrain her by all her lands, &c., so that neither, &c., until, &c., and that of the issues, &c.; and that he have her body from Easter day in fifteen days before the Justices at Westminster. The same day was given to the aforesaid Walter by his attorney in the Bench." It also appears that this Gunnora was possessed of 40 shillings rent in Bottisham which were given to her by her father on marriage in 1257 A.D.[1]

No important event seems for some time now to take place in the convent. They were apparently very prosperous, and the prospects of adding to their wealth daily increasing in proportion as men left lands and money for the safety of their souls. A great many charters are found with nothing mentioned in them by which the date can be fixed with accuracy. It will therefore be sufficient to group them together and state the nature and conditions of the various benefactions with which the house was now endowed.

First then under the charter of Philip, son of Roger, the *Charter of* house became possessed of one acre of land in "Bradecroft," *Philip, son of Roger.* between the land of the monks of Wardune and the land of William Briton, as well as all right and demesne in the said

---

[1] Vide Add. MSS. 6041, fol. 92 b.

acre, saving that Margaret daughter of Richard Brun and her
heirs or assigns were to hold the said acre for ever in fee and
inheritance of the aforesaid house of Anglesey, by the service
of one penny by the year for all services and demands which
might arise upon the said land.

Richard Brun has been before mentioned; he gave certain
lands in Dullingham to the house.

Adam
Lode-
oc.

Another benefactor was Adam de Lodebroc, or Adam of the
Hall of Wilburham as he is styled. He demised to the priory
all the land he held of the Lady Alice Thalemasche in the field
of Wilburham, called the Hall, part of ten acres in lease there
which Alice Thalemasche let to him from the Feast of the
Purification of the Blessed Virgin, A.D. 1261, to the end of
thirty years next following, for twenty marks of silver which the
prior and convent gave into his hands. The charter then
curiously goes on to specify that, in default of warranty of the
said land to the prior and convent, the benefactor will bind
himself to pay ten pounds to the works at Westminster; and
for any damages or expenses which the prior and convent might
incur, the aforesaid Adam bound himself, for himself and his
heirs, under the lesser and greater sentence to be delivered by
any judge which the same prior and convent were to choose, to
be summoned by canonical right and judicially punished for
the refusal of the said damages and expenses.

Bartho-
mew, the
erk.

Bartholomew the clerk of Wilbraham is a name that has
hitherto often occurred incidentally in the charters of others,
as possessing land near that of the benefactor, or as one of the
witnesses—we now find him granting the homage of Katherine,
formerly the wife of Peter the clerk of Little Wilburham, and
the service of the annual rent of eighteen pence without any
deduction to be received of the aforesaid Katherine; to wit, at
the feast of St Michael nine pence, and at Easter nine pence,
which she was accustomed to pay him for the messuage with the
croft adjoining which lay between the messuage of the aforesaid
Katherine and the messuage of Wymer the chaplain, and for
one rood of land which Geoffrey the shepherd held of the same
in the same town, and whatsoever rights should accrue to him
from the aforesaid lands, to wit, in homages, reliefs, wards,

escheats, and any other foreign services, of the purchase of the Lady Matilda de Traly, for the pittance of the same monks on the day of the death and the anniversary of the aforesaid Lady Matilda de Traly; and while the said Matilda de Traly shall be alive, on the day of the anniversary of Sir William de Hobrige her father, to wit, on the tenth of the Ides of April, in free, pure and perpetual alms.

This instrument is endorsed :—The charter for the pittance of the canons—eighteen pence on the day of the anniversary of Lady Matilda Traly—now in the tenure of John le Lord.

The family of Traly resided at Quy, and seem to have been very influential. The successors of Lady Matilda were in regular possession of the manor up to the commencement of the 14th century.

Alice Talmasche of Wilbraham, the daughter of Humfrey of *Of Alice* Little Wilbraham, and the wife of Sir William Talmasche, knt., *Talmasche.* belonged also to an influential family. In her widowhood she granted and confirmed to the Prior and Convent of Anglesey, for the safety of her soul and for twenty shillings which they gave on their part, all that land which they had of her fee in the town and fields of Wilbraham Parva, to wit, all that land which Hillary the son of Claricia de Wilbraham formerly held, and all the land which Walter le Neve formerly held of her fee, and one messuage with a toft which Eustace the son of Roger formerly held, with all their appurtenances, liberties and easements, to wit, in meadows, feedings, and pastures, and in folds belonging to the aforesaid lands, to hold and to have of her and her heirs, &c ; rendering therefore annually to her and her heirs fourteen shillings and six pence at two terms of the year, namely, Michaelmas and Easter.

Many documents are to be found respecting the grants of Sir William Talemasche, but they are without much interest. The most important of them is a lease from Alice, daughter of Humphrey, to Hugh, Prior of Anglesey, of the manor of Little Wilbraham to farm for ten years. She however retained in her own hands "the close within the bridge in the baker's courtyard, with the great ditch, and free ingress and egress." The remainder with the mill from the pool up to the little ditch contained

53 acres, 3 manured and 12 of fold, together with 2 horses and
2 oxen. The convent were to keep in repair the houses of the
manor, viz. the chapel, a grange, an ox-stall, and a small house
and close. For the first three years they were quit of rent; for
the remaining seven, 100s. at Easter were to be paid.

f Robert
le Milden-
iall.

Robert de Mildehale (Mildenhall), son of Henry de Hali-
welle (Holywell near Huntingdon), granted for the safety of his
soul, and for twenty-three shillings sterling which the prior and
convent gave him as a fine, a rent of twenty-eight pence in the
town of Wilburham Regis, which he was accustomed to receive
annually of William Sabin and Ralph del Hylde; to wit, of
Ralph del Hylde twenty-one pence to be received at two terms,
viz. at Easter tenpence-halfpenny, and at the feast of St
Michael tenpence-halfpenny; and of William Sabin sevenpence
to be in like manner received at two terms, viz. at Easter
threepence-halfpenny, and at the feast of St Michael threepence-halfpenny; to wit, for that land which Hillary the priest
formerly held of his ancestors in the said town of Wilburham
Regis, to have and to hold, &c., rendering annually to him and
his heirs one halfpenny, to wit, at the feast of St Michael, for
all services, customs, and demands. This document has appended
to it an oval seal of dark green wax. In the centre is a cross
rayed or starred. Legend, " S'. Roberti de Haliwelle+."

f John
ve and
sabella.

Yvo the merchant, is a name frequently found in various
documents relating to Wilbraham. John Ive is probably his
son, who, with Isabella his wife, gave to the alderman of the
guild of the church of the Blessed Mary of Cambridge, and to
the brethren of the same guild, two shops in the street where
flesh is sold, &c. To have and to hold, &c., rendering therefore
annually for us and our heirs to the chief lords of the fees the
services thereof due and accustomed, to wit, to the Priory of
Anglesey, and the convent there, four shillings, and to the
king's custom, called "Hagable," eight pence, and to the celebration of the mass of the Blessed Virgin Mary four pence.
And to them and their heirs one rose at the feast of the Nativity
of Saint John the Baptist for all services and customs, and all
secular demands, &c.

There is another charter extant, probably of the same man

described as John the son of Yvo of Wilburham Parva. He granted an annual rent of three shillings and sevenpence-halfpenny which he was accustomed to receive of certain tenants, viz., of Andrew, the son of Roger, fifteen pence; of Roger, the son of the said Andrew, six pence; of Alan Aluard, seventeenpence-halfpenny; of Matilda, Agnes, and Margaret, the daughters and heirs of Robert de Chipenham, five pence; for the tenements which the said tenants held of him in the town and fields of Wilburham aforesaid, of the fee of the said prior and convent, with the reliefs, escheats, and all other appurtenances without any reserve.

Robert, the preacher, of Little Wilbraham, quitclaims to the *Of Robert,* convent at Anglesey all right in a certain annual rent of eight *the Preacher,* pence which he was accustomed to receive from a certain *of Little* messuage and croft in Little Wilburham, which said messuage *Wilbra-ham.* and croft Richard le Beste formerly held of John, son of Yvo at the green place near his messuage.

Isabella, daughter of this Robert and Isabella his wife, con- *Isabella,* firms the same grant by her charter couched in similar terms, *daughter of Robert,* but in which it is mentioned that the green place was near her *the* messuage formerly under the tenure of Walter de Cotesmor. *Preacher.* The same persons appear as witnesses in both documents.

Two charters extant of the family of Scaccario should, I *Of Geoffrey* think, belong to a somewhat earlier period than the preceding. *de Scacc-ario.* Geoffrey de Scaccario grants twenty shillings of annual rent in the towns of Great and Little Wilbraham; to wit, of Roesia the daughter of Roger Bissop, six shillings and six pence; and of Mabilia, who was the wife of Roger Louerd, two shillings; and of Catherine, who was the wife of Peter, of Little Wylburham, two shillings; and of Richard Galien three shillings; and of Alan le Shepherd, six pence; and of John, the son of Gerard, of Great Wylburham, eighteen pence; and of Richard Brien, of Little Wylburham, twelve pence; and of Hugh, the son of Walter de Swaffham, twelve pence; and of Andrew, the son of Roger, the son of Richard, eighteen pence; and of Simon, the son of Luke, of Great Wylburham, twelve pence; together with the homages of all the aforesaid tenants and their heirs, the wards, reliefs, escheats, and all other things which might chance in any manner, or at any time, to arise from the aforesaid tenants, and their heirs, and the tenements thereof without any reservation. To have and to hold, &c., rendering therefore annually for me and my heirs, to John de Fulney and his heirs, one pair of gloves, price one penny; for all services, customs, suits, aids, complaints, and all other kind of secular demands. Amongst the witnesses to this deed are Sir Martin the chamberlain, William Talamache, Robert Engayne, Hugh de Crauden, knights, Ivo de Wilburham, William Sabyn and others.

f Roger
e Scacc-
rio.

This rent had been previously granted to Geoffrey by his brother Roger, who also made a charter granting it to the convent. It is worded as the last-mentioned one of his brother, and attested by the same witnesses. From comparison with another document it appears that the right which John de Fulney had in this rent of twenty shillings was acquired by

f Sarra,
idow of
ohn de
ulney.

reason of his marriage with his wife Sarra, who received them in dower from her father. And so in 1272 A.D., when her husband was already dead, she gave up her right on behalf of himself and her heirs, and transferred it to the Prior and Convent of Anglesey. And the said prior and convent gave into her hands the sum of sixty shillings sterling.

CHAPTER V.

THORNHALL IN WICKEN.

N 1272, the same year as the last-mentioned document, we *Thornhall,* nd a lawsuit concerning some property which the priory had *in Wicken.* cquired in Wicken. But before adverting to this suit it is ecessary to look at the history of this property as given in hree charters which, though undated, are undoubtedly earlier han the year above-mentioned.

First then, it appears that Walter, the son of Richard, of *Charter of* ittle Iselham, granted to Torold de Burgo, brother of William, *Walter, son of* rior of Anglesey, for his homage and service, and for one *Richard,* undred shillings of silver, given to him as a fine, all the entire *of Little Iselham.* essuage, with its buildings and appurtenances, which Henry e Hupwere held of him in the town of Wykes (or Wicken), ear Spinney, where he dwelt, to wit, the moiety of Thornhale-roft in the aforesaid town, and without the same, with all its ppurtenances, to wit, in waters, meadows, grazings, and pas-ires, and in common, and with all other liberties to the afore-id tenement pertaining. To have and to hold to the aforesaid orold and his heirs for ever, to wit, begotten of Cecilia, the aughter of Henry de Hupwere, freely and quietly, well, and in eace. Rendering therefore annually to him and to his heirs hree shillings and nine pence at four terms, to wit, at the feast ' St John the Baptist, eleven pence and one farthing; at the ast of St Michael eleven pence and one farthing; at the feast ' St Andrew eleven pence and one farthing; and at Easter even pence and one farthing. Rendering also the moiety of he pound of cinnamon at Easter for all services, customs, and emands. "If moreover," the charter goes on to state, "the oresaid Cecilia shall happen to die without issue, then the oresaid Torold shall hold all the aforesaid tenement with the messuage and appurtenances, and all the liberties above-named, during his whole life. And I, Walter, will warrant," &c. Appended to this document is an oval seal of green wax, in the centre of which is a bird displayed, and containing the legend "S. Walterii fris............"

This charter contains many curious particulars. It is the only place where we learn the existence of Torold de Burgo and his brother William, Prior of Anglesey. The only William Prior of Anglesey about this time, is William de Fordham, who occurs in 1231, and seems to have continued to preside up to 1251 A.D. If there was another William, Prior of Anglesey, he must have immediately succeeded William de Fordham. John, vicar of Bodekesham, who was a witness to this charter, also occurs in 1251 A.D. at the earliest, and not much later. Cecilia within but a short time becomes the wife of Joseph de Rethe or de Regge, and therefore the date of this document cannot be much later than 1251. Now the Priory of Spinney in the parish of Wicken was founded by Sir Hugh de Malebisse, who married Beatrice, lady of the manor of Wykes (Wicken). The date of foundation is not known, but it was before the end of Henry the Third's reign. From the words, however, in the charter "prope spinetum ubi mansit," as applied to the residence of Henry de Hupwere (or Upware), it does not seem clear whether the meaning is, "near the spinney (or little wood) where he dwelt," or whether direct reference is made to the name of the religious house founded there, and consequently which is of prior date, the charter or the foundation of the religious house. But whether before or after, a priory was established for three canons of the order of St Austin. The manor together with the advowson of the priory passed into the hands of Mary Thornton, who became the wife of Sir Humfrey Bassingbourn. In spite of various benefactions, the house of Spinney went to decay in revenues and buildings, and eventually, in the year 1449, it was united to the cathedral monastery of Ely by Walter, Bishop of Norwich, the ordinary of the place.

Charter of Matilda de Somery. The next charter referring to Thornhall, but also undated, is that of Matilda de Somery, afterwards lady of the manor of sleham. This charter is in many parts illegible, but it states that she in her free widowhood grants all her part to her belonging by the death of William de .. .. (? Isleham) to Joseph and Cecilia, and their heirs and assigns, or to any one to whom they shall please to give, sell, or assign the same. To have and to hold, &c. Rendering, &c. the same sum and in the same way as stated in the previous charter. Appended to this document, which is marked "Anglesey," is a seal much broken, oval in form, and of white wax. In the centre is a bird. Joseph de Regge and Cecilia his wife accordingly granted the property to the house of Anglesey, and Matilda de Sumeri in her part issued a charter confirming it to them, and moreover quitclaiming them of the sum which she and her heirs were accustomed to receive "as contained in the charter to Joseph and Cecilia his wife." Possession seems to have been disputed and litigation ensued. A fine was therefore made between John, Prior of Anglesey, plaintiff, and Joseph de Bockisham and Cecilia his wife, defendants of this property, namely, one messuage and twenty acres of land with the appurtenances in Wykes, and Joseph and Cecilia acknowledged the right of the prior and church of Anglesey. Rendering therefore by the year one penny at Easter for all service, custom, and demand pertaining to the aforesaid Joseph and Cecilia and the heirs of the same Cecilia. And for this fine the prior gave ten marks of silver, which price seems to shew that the Priory of Anglesey were glad to get possession of the estate.

Five years after this fine, namely, in the year 1278 A.D., there occurs a document relating to a great dispute between the houses of Anglesey and Spinney. Feuds between religious houses were at this period exceedingly common, and we have previously observed how the house of Anglesey was at enmity with the Priory of Tunbridge, which had lands in the same parish as itself. Most of these disputes arose by reason of asserted rights to property, and as we have no mention of the cause of quarrel with the establishment at Spinney, we may fairly suppose that it referred to the tenement of Thornhall, in the immediate vicinity of the house.

Memoran-
dum of the
dispute be-
tween An-
glesey and
Spinney.

The following is a curious memorandum of the progress o
the quarrel:

"Be it remembered that whereas on the Saturday next afte
the feast of Saint Nicholas in the year of grace 1278; in th
church of the brothers minors near .... the proctor of th
religious men, the Prior and Convent of Anglesey on the Satur
day aforsaid by the appointment of the Lord Abbot of North
creych, had the place aforesaid appointed for proceeding ac
cording to the form of the defence before the said abbot, th
judge appointed by the lord the pope in the cause move(
between the said religious of Anglesey his masters on th
one part and the Prior and Convent of Spinney the mover
on the other part. And that the proctor sufficiently and law
fully appearing was prepared to do therein whatever right an(
justice demanded according to their tenor of the defence, bu
he did not find any mover in any way appear there nor any on
to declare to the judge, which it pertains to the office of th
mover to do by appearing on the day appointed and promotin
his business and not to the defendant; whereupon the sai(
proctor of the Prior and Convent of Anglesey complained tha
his masters were wearied with the troubles and expences ther
of and needlessly so by the Prior and Convent of Spinne
therefore the proctor of the said Prior and Convent of Anglese
publicly protested concerning the damages and expences whic
he claimed ought to be received from the said religious
Spinney before they should be again heard in the said cause
variance between them on account of their fault and negle
committed in this matter. In witness whereof the seal of t
Dean of Thingowe is appended to this present memorandu
Whether the Prior and Convent of Anglesey received anythi
for damages and expences already needlessly incurred, we
not know, but the cause seems to have continued to be und
dispute, and next year the following memorandum was made:
" It was thus concluded in the church of St Michael Cambrid
on Wednesday next after the feast of the Apostles Peter a
Paul in the year of the Lord one thousand two hundred a
seventy-nine, before the Dean of Christ's Church Cambrid
and Master Adam de London, rector of the church of Sut

delegate of the religious man the Prior of Huntingdon the judge appointed by the lord the pope, according to the form of his commission by the arrangement of the commissary in the cause referred by appeal to the apostolic see which had arisen between the religious men the Prior and Convent of Anglesey by John de Huntingdon, clerk, their procurator appearing on one part, and the Prior and Convent of Spinney by Master Hugh de Swafham, their procurator lawfully constituted, appearing on the other part; to wit, there being had a slight argument and the reasons being heard which were propounded by the party appealed against in opposition to the prayer of the party appealing, the judges by the authority of the said procuration and having consulted as to its sufficiency, have pronounced :—That whereas the party appealed against had propounded certain objections against the high judge contained in a certain schedule signed with the hand of the said judge, which being admitted and also arbitrators required for proving the same, and that being granted to them in the form of an oath;—at length by the consent of the party appealed against and deliberate advice being had in hopes of peace being concluded between the parties, the judges have appointed them a day for contesting in the cause of appeal, saving nevertheless to them the said objections in chief and direct judgment, to be then propounded and prosecuted with effect, and all other remedies required for any purpose if peace be not concluded, to wit: on Thursday next, the Feast of Saint Dionisius, in the same place as before, and each party is to do further therein what right shall require. These things were done in the presence of Masters Thomas de Wysebech, Hamond de Gatele, Geoffrey de Brunne, Sirs J. de Luvetot, William de Bedeford, chaplain, and others."

This is the last document extant that can be referred to this dispute, so that we do not gather for certain what was the result of the appeal, but it is most likely that the house of Anglesey gained the cause, as in Pope Nicholas' taxation in 1291 they are said to have 33s. 3½d. in Wykes. In 19 Edw. III. John de Bassingbourn, Lord of Badlingham (a hamlet of Chippenham) and Maud his wife made a lease of the frith fen

and other lands in Wicken, to the Prior of Anglesey; and in
20 Edw. III. a lease of the same was made between the same
parties for 7 years, rendering for the three first years a pound
of cummin and for the remaining four, 43s. and 4d. In
13 Edw. IV. John Wells the prior leased Thornhall to Robert
Byrde of Wicken, senior, for 20 years, at 20s., and in the
"ministers' accounts," after the dissolution, there occurs an
entry of 30s. of a farm of a tenement called Thornhall in
Wicken, with all its lands, meadows, grazings and pastures, &c.

Charter of Eustace, the son of Roger, of Little Wilbraham. The next grant of land made to the Priory of Anglesey
is that of Eustace, the son of Roger of Little Wilburham.
It consisted of a certain messuage with all the croft adjoining with its appurtenances in the town of Little Wilbraham,
lying between the croft of Alice Brienes and the croft which
was of William de Howes, abutting on Hale street. The
lords of the fee were to receive the accustomed service, viz.
eighteen pence a year, to wit, namely at Easter, nine pence,
and at the feast of St Michael nine pence. He also granted
at the same time a piece of land which he held of the Priory,
viz: of the fee of Walter le Newer, in the field of the said
Wilbraham, having in breadth seven perches, and in length
twenty-eight perches, measured at eighteen feet the perch[1]
lying between the land of William the son of Emma, and the
land of Simon the son of Stephen, the miller of Stowe, and
abutting at one end upon the croft which was Brien's and at
the other upon Dedcherlway. Also he granted one acre of land
of that fee, to wit, of the fee which Hillary the chaplain formerly held, that is to say, one half acre lying in Westfield near
the land of Matthew, son of Osbert, and abutting upon West
croft, and one other half acre lying in Dedcherlfield between
the land which formerly belonged to the said Hillary and the
land of the aforesaid Matthew. And moreover, one rood of
land lying in the field of Queye, between the land which
formerly belonged to Richard the son of Hubert, and between
the land of Richard the son of William, abutting upon Ded

---

[1] Here we have given the measurement of land in this part of England.
perch usually contained 16 feet. Vide Godwin, *Arch. Handbook*, p. 90. This
land was comprised in the grant made by Alice Talamasche.

cherlway at one end and at the other end upon the headland formerly of Brian Scut. Amongst the witnesses to the document confirming this grant, we find Sir Richard, parson of Wilbraham Regis, and this is the only indication we have of the existence of a separate church for that parish. Dedcherlfield, or Dead churl field, seems to mark the site of the Anglo-Saxon cemetery.

It would seem that about this time the priory had acquired some right to the advowson of the church of Saint Michael in Cambridge, which they afterwards lost, for by a fine made between John, Prior of Anglesey, and Thomas le Bedel[1] and Matilda his wife in 1274, in which suit the deforciants were represented by Robert the son of Robert de Maddingley, the aforesaid prior acknowledged the advowson to be the right of Matilda, and received accordingly the sum of twenty shillings sterling. *Fine. John, Prior of Anglesey, v. Thomas le Bedel and Matilda, his wife.*

During the next year there arose a more important suit out of a grant of one messuage and a hundred and twenty acres of land in Barley, the gift of Ralph the son of Ralph. By a fine however, concluded between John, the Prior of Anglesey, plaintiff, and Ralph the son of Ralph, deforciant, this property was acknowledged to be the right of the convent, free from all service and exaction, and the prior bound himself to receive Ralph and his heirs in all and singular the benefactions and orations which should henceforth be performed in his church for ever. But this apparently did not suffice to keep Ralph from seizing the land, for in 1278 he was attached to answer Henry, Prior of Anglesey, of a plea that he keep to him the fine made between John, predecessor of Henry, Prior of Anglesey, and himself. Whereupon a chirograph[2] was made between *Fine. John, Prior of Anglesey, v. Ralph, the son of Ralph.*

---

[1] Thomas le Bedel is probably the same personage as that called above Thomas, a servant of the University of Cambridge. The convent seems to have had some right to the advowson of St Michael, for a fine to that effect was concluded in 2 Edw. III.

[2] This is the first instance of the mention of a chirograph. It was a specification of the grant in the handwriting of the donor, an act suggested sometimes by the zeal of the donor, or more often, as here, by the caution of the monks. As but few of the higher classes even could write their own names at this period, chirographs were necessarily matters of rare occurrence. Vide Bentham's *Ely*, Suppl. p. 46, notes.

them, and whereas the aforesaid Ralph acknowledged the afore-said messuage and land to be the right of the prior and church of Anglesey, the same fine was levied between them in the aforesaid court, and the sheriff of Hertford distrained him to come twice in the year to the county of Hertford; to wit, once after the feast of Saint Michael, and once after Easter ; and to come twice in the year to the sheriff's turn, and for three shillings and three pence annual rent, due to the lord the king. And the aforesaid Ralph would not acquit the aforesaid prior as to all services and exactions, whereupon he said he was injured, and had damage to the value of £40, and Ralph came and defended the force and injury when, &c. And as to the sheriff's turn, he said, he is not bound to acquit the said prior thereof by the aforesaid fine, because he says that the sheriff's turn is a certain claim arising on account of any person residing in the hundred where the hundred court is held, and is not a service due by reason of any tenement ; moreover he said that by the statute of the lord the king Henry, father of the lord the now king, the afore-said prior nor any other-religious person is not bound to come to such turn unless his presence is specially required thereto[1]. Therefore as to that he was without day. And as to the aforesaid services, he acquitted the prior, and would make him satisfaction concerning the damages.

undred olls. The year 1279 A.D. marks an era in parochial histories, for in it were taken certain requisitions known as " Rotuli Hundred-orum" or " Hundred Rolls." These inquisitions were made shortly after the return of Edward the First to England, and had for their object to find out what were "the demesnes of the lord the king and the feudal fees, escheats, liberties, and all things pertaining to the fees and tenements of the lord the king as of all other persons whatever, and who hold the same

---

[1] The sheriff's turn or tourn was the great court leet of the county as the county court is the court baron; the sheriff took his turn or circuit about his shire twice a year, viz. after Easter and Michaelmas, and held a court in each respective hundred. Vide Tomlyn's *Law Dict.* sub voce. This land seems to. have been of the barony of Geoffrey de Scalers, vide Rot. Hund. i. 193, and was afterwards called the manor of Greenbury. Vide Clutterbuck, *Herts.* i. 381; Chauncy, *Hist. of Herts.*, p. 96; Salmon's *Hist. of Herts.;* p. 296.

in demesne as of demesne, in villenage as villeins, in servitude as serfs, by cottage tenure as cottagers, and afterwards by free tenure as free tenants, and in woods, parks, chaces, and warrens, in waters, in rivers, and in all liberties and fairs, markets and other tenures whatsoever and in any kind of manner, and of whom, whether of the mesne lords or of others, and for what fees and other tenures he used and ought to give scutage, and how much for the fee of any kind of honour, and who hold those fees, and how, and in what manner, and from what time." Thus an idea was to be gained of the condition of the king's property, and an insight obtained into the conduct of sheriffs and other officers who had taken advantage of the king's absence not only to defraud him and oppress the people, but to induce others to do the same. The rolls containing an account of these inquisitions are, consequently, most valuable indications of the extent of property owned as well by individuals as by corporate bodies, and some conception is afforded us of the amount held by the Priory of Anglesey, which, as will be seen, was not inconsiderable. Indeed from the year 1236 A.D., when the house was enriched by the generosity of Master Lawrence de Saint Nicholas, down to the end of the thirteenth century, the convent seems to have been more prosperous than at any subsequent point in its career. For the grants of lands and money to religious bodies, for the safety of the souls of the benefactors, had reached to such an extent as to become a gross abuse, and to endanger the good government of the country. Hence an act was passed to prohibit all benefactions of this kind, without special licence from the king; and so by these acts, called "the Mortmain Acts," when leave was given to bestow property upon religion, an inquisition, called "Inquisitio ad quod damnum," was held in order to inquire what, if any, damage would be done to the king and the country by such bestowal of land.

In the Hundred Rolls are mentioned as "jurors of the borough of Cambridge, Bartholomew the son of Michael, Nicholas Mort........, Robert Weymund, Henry Tuylet, Gerard de Wyvarn, William Seman, Richard Bateman senior, Geoffrey le Ferun, Richard Bateman junior, Robert de Maddingley,

Richard Goddring, John of Saint Edmund, Ralph de Thever-
sham, and Hugh de Brunne." Their verdict was as follows:—

Agnes, the daughter of Philip the tailor, holds one messuage
in the parish of Saint Peter, Cambridge, which descended to
her by right of inheritance by the death of the said Philip her
father, which said Philip held it of the scholars of Merton, and
renders therefore by the year, to the same scholars, 6 shillings,
and to the Prior of Anglesey, 2 shillings for the said messuage,
by what warrant the said prior receives the said rent they know
not.

Also the Prior and Convent of Anglesey hold one messuage
in the parish of Saint Michael, Cambridge, which said messuage
they have of the gift of Robert, son of Robert Huberd, and one
vacant place of land in the same parish, which they have of the
gift of the same Robert. And a certain granary, and a certain
other vacant place, which they have of the gift of the same
Robert, and one vacant place in the parish of Saint John, and
one messuage in the parish of Saint Peter without the gate of
Trumpington[1], and 8 acres of land in the fields of Barnwell,
and an annual rent of 5s. to be received of one messuage which
formerly belonged to Peter the son of Ivo, and 4s. annual rent
which they receive of Richard Bateman, and 6s. annual rent
which they receive of Berneus the butcher, which they have
of the gift of the said Robert the son of Robert Huberd, which
the same Robert had of ancient succession, by inheritance from
his ancestors; and they render for the said messuages, lands,
and rents, to the hospital of Saint John the Evangelist, 2d.
and to the bailiffs of Cambridge, who hold the said town at fee
farm of the lord the king at the custom called "Haggable," 11d.

Also the aforesaid prior and convent hold one shop in the
market of Cambridge, which they have of the gift of Hervey
the son of Seleda, in free, pure and perpetual alms.

Also they hold one messuage in the parish of Saint Peter,
without the gate of Trumpington, which they had of the gift of
Eustace the son of Ralph, which said messuage Stephen Ace
formerly held, in free, pure, and perpetual alms, by what
warrant the said prior holds the said messuage, they know not.

[1] Now St Mary the Less.

Also they hold the rent of 2s. of the gift of Simon, formerly chamberlain of E. Bishop of Ely, in pure and perpetual alms.

Also they hold an annual rent of 3s. of the gift of John de Ry, formerly rector of the chapel of Saint Edmund, to be received of a certain messuage without the gate of Trumpington in the parish of Saint Peter, which said messuage the said John de Ry had of the gift of Lawrence the son of Alan de Blakeham, which said Lawrence had the same of the gift of John, son of Arnold of Cambridge.

Sabina Huberd holds 9 acres of land at the turn of his town, of the Prior and Convent of Anglesey, and renders therefore by the year, to the said canons, 9s. for the land aforesaid in the parish of All Saints.

Also Hervey Pippe holds one messuage in the parish of Saint Peter without Trumpington gate, which he bought of the Prior and Convent of Anglesey, and the said prior and convent had it of the gift of Robert the son of Robert Huberd, which the same Robert had by right of inheritance by the death of Amice Godsel, his mother, and which the same Amice had by right of inheritance from her ancestors, and for which he renders by the year, to the same prior and convent, 3s.

The same Richard Bateman the younger holds three shops in the parish of Saint Michael at a fee farm, which he had of the gift of the Prior and Convent of Anglesey, and the said prior and convent had the same of the gift of Robert Hubert, and the said Robert had them by right of inheritance by the death of Cecilia Godso his friend, which same Cecilia had the same by ancient descent through her parents, and he renders therefore by the year to the aforesaid prior and convent 5s., and to the bailiffs of Cambridge who hold the said town at fee farm as is aforesaid at Haggable[1] one farthing.

The same Richard holds one messuage in fee in the parish of Saint Edward, which he had of the gift of the said Prior and Convent of Anglesey, which said prior and convent had the same of the gift of Robert Hubert, and the same Robert had it by inheritance after the death of Cecilia Godso, which same Cecilia had it of ancient succession from her ancestors, and renders

---

[1] Haga (Sax. Haegh) = house, gabellum = tax.

therefore by the year to the said prior and convent 6*d.*, also master Stephen Aseligfeld[1] the rector of the church of Saint Michael holds one messuage in the parish of Saint Michael, which same messuage Joan de Benewick gave to the same church in pure and perpetual alms, and the said Joan had the same of the gift of master Adam de Boudone, and the same master Adam bought it of Thomas Arinvene the upholder, and the said Thomas bought it of William de la Bruere the chaplain, and the said William had it by right of inheritance by the death of Thomas de la Bruere his father, which same Thomas had it by ancient purchase, and he renders therefore by the year to the said Sir William de la Bruere the chaplain 2*s.*, and to the prior and convent of Anglesey 12*d.*, by what warrant the said prior and convent receive the said rent they know not, and to the bailiffs of Cambridge who hold the said town to fee farm &c. for custom 2*d.* Also John, the son of William Waubert, holds one messuage in the parish of All Saints near the hospital of Saint John of Cambridge, which he had of the gift of John Torel his nephew, which messuage descended to the said John by inheritance after the death of Alan Torel his father, and the said Alan had it by descent from his ancestors, and renders therefore by year to Ralph the son of Felicia de Quoye 28*d.*, and to John Porthors and his heirs 12*d.*, and to master Robert Aunger 8*d.*, and to the Prior of Anglesey one penny.; by what warrant the said prior receives the same rent they know not.

The Prior of Anglesey holds in the town of Fulbourn of the gift of Matilda de Passelewe of the fee of the marshall in pure and perpetual alms half a virgate of land.

HUNDRED OF STANE.—*Encroachments, &c.*

Bodekesham. Martin de Lada holds one several meadow which used to be common, William the son of Richard holds one meadow which was common. The heirs of William the son of Martin hold one meadow in the same manner to the injury of

[1] Haslingfield.

the whole town ; the Prior of Anglesey appropriated to himself
two crofts which were common in open time and which contain
two acres.

The jury say that Sir Gilbert de Clare, Earl of Gloucester
and Hertford, holds Bodekesham entire in chief of the lord the
king of the honor of Walter Giffard, who was earl of Buckingham, which the countess Matilda, the mother of the said Gilbert,
now holds in dower for the term of her life. Also they say that
the same earl holds view of frankpledge in the aforesaid town
once in the year, and all things which pertain to view of frank-
pledge and whatever pertains to royalty, and held it from the
time from which memory exists not, but by what warrant we are
ignorant.

Also they say that the predecessors of the aforesaid earl
conferred the whole manor of Bodekam [1] with all the lands and
demesnes, and tenements in villenage and cottage, the meadows,
pastures, grazings, and mills, and liberty of bull and vert and
all other, the appurtenances and easements to two religious
houses, to wit, to the Prior and Convent of Anglesey the moiety
of all the aforesaid, and to the Prior and Convent of Thone-
bregge the other moiety, and to the aforesaid Prior and Convent
of Anglesey the advowson of the church of the Holy Trinity of
Bodekesham, which they now have and hold to their own proper use, and the manse where the said priory is established and
the conventual church is built, saving to them and their successors the free rents of the free tenants in the same town and
saving to the same suit of court, from three weeks to three
weeks, and saving to them the homages and reliefs of free
tenants and wards and escheats and all pleas.

The same Prior of Anglesey holds of the same earl 200 acres
of land in the same town of Bodekesham in pure and perpetual
alms of the gift of the ancestors of the said earl, nor do they do
any service.

The same prior holds one virgate of land of the said earl,
and renders by the year to the same 6d. and owes suit of court.

The same prior holds of the same earl half a virgate of land
in pure and perpetual alms, nor does he do any suit.

[1] Bottisham.

The same prior holds of the same earl certain meadows in
the aforesaid town, rendering therefore by the year 12d. to the
same earl, which were of Hugh Germain, and Hugh de Lada,
and which contain 12 acres and more as they think, but how
much they know not.

The same holds the moiety of one water-mill, and one wind-
mill of the same earl, in pure and perpetual alms, and for which
they do no service, and a fishery which is worth by the year 2s.

The same holds in villenage of the said earl six villeins,
each of whom holds 15 acres of land, and each of whom renders
by the year 42d., and each of whom does four days' works in
autumn, two with food and two without, and they also make
and carry eighteen cartloads of hay; to wit, from the feast of
Saint Michael to the birth of the Lord, they shall three times
plough and so forth, and each of them shall find one man to
mow the meadow once in the year, and to gather in the meadow,
and shall find one man or woman to gather the hay.

The Prior of Anglesey has five cottagers, each of whom does
one day's work, value one half-penny, on every Monday, except
in the weeks of Easter, the Nativity of the Lord, and Pentecost.

Free tenants of the Prior of Anglesey in Botekesham :—

Alan the fisherman holds one messuage of the Prior of
Anglesey, of the fee of the earl by service of 12d.

The wife of Martin Albard[1] holds one messuage of the same
prior by service of 3d. of the same fee.

Martin at the moor holds one messuage of the same prior
by service of 4d. of the same fee.

Peter Wymere holds one messuage of the same prior by
service of 2s. of the fee of the same earl.

Margaret de Attleburwe[2] holds one messuage of the same
by service of 18d. of the fee of the earl.

Richard the cuwerer holds one messuage of the same by
service of 18d. of the same fee.

[1] Probably the same person described elsewhere as Martin Aluard.
[2] Attleborough.

Richard Engayne holds one messuage of the same by service of 18*d*. of the fee of the earl.

Nicholas the son of Luke holds one messuage of the same prior, and renders by the year 18*d*. of the earl's fee.

Thomas of the chamber holds one messuage of the same by the service of 18*d*. of the fee of the earl.

John Pychard holds one messuage of the same by service of 4*d*. by the year of the same fee.

Henry the son of Otto holds one messuage of the same by the service of 12*d*. of the fee of the earl.

Also Richard Engayne holds one messuage of the same by service of 6½*d*. of the fee of the earl.

Alice de Attleburwe holds one messuage of the same by service of 3*d*. of the fee of the earl.

The heir of Thomas le Lef holds 4 acres of land of the same by the service of 3*s*. of the same fee.

Geoffrey at the cross holds one croft and one acre of land of the same by service of 12*d*. of the same fee.

Ivo the son of Martin Gerard holds 3 acres of land of the same by service of 18*d*. of the same fee.

The heir of Nicholas Thone holds one messuage and 2 acres of land of the same by service of 23*d*. of the same fee.

John the son of Wymer holds one messuage and 4 acres of land of the same by service of 8*s*. of the same fee.

The heir of Fulk le Mason holds one acre of land of the same by service of 2*s*. 4*d*. of the same fee.

Geoffrey Pychard holds 3 rods of land of the same by service of 8*d*. of the same fee.

Geoffrey the marshall holds 3½ acres of land of the same by service of 18*d*. of the same fee.

Richard Strongeray holds one messuage and half an acre of and and renders by the year 18*d*. of the fee of the earl.

Peter Pycot holds 5 acres of land of the same by service of 18*d*. of the fee of the earl.

Isabella le Hert holds one half acre of land of the same by service of 12*d*. of the same fee.

Henry le King holds one messuage of the same by service of 8*d*. of the fee of the earl.

Thomas the mason holds one messuage of the same by service of 3s. of the fee of the earl.

The heir of Andrew Carpenter holds one messuage of the same by service of 4s. 6d. of the fee of the earl.

Richard the son of Elen holds one messuage and one croft of the same by service of 12d. of the same fee.

The wife of Walter Pycot holds one messuage and a croft of the same by service of 18d. of the same fee.

Richard the son of Joseph holds 4 acres of land and two messuages of the same by service of 4s. 4d. of the same fee.

John the son of Albin holds three rods of land of the same by service of 18d. per annum of the same fee.

Henry Doget holds one half acre of land of the same by service of 6d. of the same fee.

Ralph the son of Stephen holds one messuage and one acre and a half of land of the same by service of 22d. of the same fee.

Ralph the son of Alice holds one messuage and one rod of land of the same by service of 6d. of the same fee.

William Robercot and Joan his wife hold one acre of land of the same by service of eighteen pence of the same fee.

Sir Elias de Bekingham holds one acre of land of the same by service of 2s. of the same fee.

Thomas the chaplain holds one messuage of the same prior by service of 18d. of the same fee.

Simon Alward and his wife hold one messuage of the same by service of 28d. of the same earl.

William the bailiff of Swafham holds one messuage of the same by service of 12d. of the same fee.

The heir of Thomas de Teversham holds one messuage of the same by service of 12d. of the same fee.

Ralph the tailor holds one messuage and one croft of the same by service of 2s. of the same fee.

Hugh Atgrave and his wife hold one rood and a half of the same by service of 8d. of the same fee.

Stephen le Gleys holds one small messuage of the same by service of 18d. of the same fee.

Richard beyond the road holds one messuage of the same by service of 8d. of the fee of the earl.

Hugh Atlane holds one messuage and a croft of the same by ervice of 2*s.* of the same fee.

Robert the chaplain holds one messuage of the same by ser- ice of 13*d.* of the fee of the earl.

Roger Hauck holds one messuage of the same by service of 2*d.* of the same fee.

Andrew Griance holds one messuage of the same by service f 3*d.* of the same fee.

Little Wilbraham. Also the Prior of Anglesey holds four ustomaries, and each of them holds 15 acres of the aforesaid e by servile works, the names of whom are Richard Machen, Valter Goding, John Atgrene, and Henry Elys, to wit, from the east of Saint Michael to the feast of Saint Peter ad vincula n every week each of them shall find two animals for the lough on Monday, and they shall sow, and in autumn they hall reap for four weeks, and they shall do fourscore works nd average and pay 2½*d.* for fee farm, and at the feast of Saint Iichael each of them shall give a goose, and at the Nativity ach shall give two hens.

The same prior holds 15 acres of land of the aforesaid fee in ure and perpetual alms.

The Prior of Anglesey holds 40 acres of land of Edmund the on of Walter by service of 13*s.* 6*d.*

Andrew the son of Roger holds 22½ acres of the Earl of xford by service of 7*s.*

The same holds of the Prior of Anglesey 4 acres by service f 2*s.* 6*d.*

Adam the son of Roger holds 15 acres of land of the Prior f Anglesey by service of 6*s.*

John the son of Yvo holds a part of land of the Prior of nglesey by service of 15*s.* 7*d.*

Alan Leman holds 2 acres of land of the Prior of Anglesey y service of 6*d.*

The Lady Milicent the chamberlain holds half a knight's e in name of dower of the Earl of Oxford by suit of court and ard of the castle of Hechingham[1], and by scutage when it hall happen, and has four customary tenants and each of them

---

[1] Hedingham, co. Essex.

holds 15 acres of land by servile works, whose names are John
Heved, Walter at the Millway, Adam Emmis and William Hild-
smith, these four do as the men of the Prior of Anglesey in all
things; and there are two quarterars, Robert Bisset and Thomas
Galien, who do the half in all things as the aforesaid tenants of
the fee of the Lady Milicent; three crofters, Henry Biddele,
Henry Cook, and the tenant of the lands of Letherwine, each of
whom does the same works as the quarterars, except ploughing
and average; but each of them gives at the Nativity of the
Lord two hens, and the heirs of Sir Jordan the chamberlain have
the advowson of the church.

William the son of Simon holds of the Prior of Anglesey 5
acres by service of 18d.

Henry Skileman holds one acre and a half of the Prior of
Anglesey by service of 2s. 6d.

John Bissop holds three acres of land of the Prior of Anglesey by the service of 3s.

The same John holds of the Prior of Anglesey one rood and
a half of land by service of 12d.

William Curteys holds 3½ acres of land of the Prior of
Anglesey by service of 13d.

Richard the miller holds one messuage of the Prior of
Anglesey by service of 2s. 6d.

Oliver Porter holds one rood and a half of land of the Prior
of Anglesey.

Robert the preacher holds one rood of the Prior of Anglesey
by service of 12d.

Walter Geoffrey holds 3½ roods of the Prior of Anglesey by
service of 4d.

John the monk holds one rood of land in exchange from the
Prior of Anglesey by service of one halfpenny.

Walkelin de Coweye holds 4 acres of land of Edmund the
son of Walter and of Lady Milicent and of the Prior of Anglesey
particularly, wherefore he pays to the Lady Milicent six capons,
to Edmund the son of Walter two capons, and to the Prior of
Anglesey four capons.

The Prior of Anglesey holds in Little Wilbraham 40 acres
of Edmund the son of Walter by service of 13s. 6d.

The same prior holds 30 acres of Lady Milicent by service of 6s. 1d.

Walter Wymer holds 3½ acres with one messuage of the Prior of Anglesey by service of 14d.

John Sabin holds one messuage with half an acre of the Prior of Anglesey by service of 8d.

William the cooper holds half an acre and one messuage of the same prior by service of 8d.

The same Edmund the son of Geoffrey holds of the Prior of Anglesey 20 acres by service of 6s.

Robert the chamberlain holds 9 acres of the Prior of Anglesey by service of 6s. 6d.

William Maysey holds three rods of the Prior of Anglesey and one messuage by service of 12d.

Also Thomas de Borewell holds one messuage and one acre of the same prior by service of 12d.

John the son of Thomas holds one messuage of the Prior of Anglesey and also 4 acres by service of 6d.

Edmund the son of Walter holds 40 acres by parcels of the Prior of Anglesey, and of Adam the son of Roger, and of John son of Ivo, and of John Capper, and Andrew son of Roger, by service of 4s. 3d.

The same Edmund holds two tenants, and each of them holds 7½ acres, the works of each of which are the same as half customar's of the Prior of Anglesey.

Stowe and Coye. The jury say that the Prior of Anglesey holds of William Enganye 12 acres, the services of which they do not know.

Encroachments, &c. They say that the Prior of Anglesey made encroachment upon the common of Stowe and Coye and inclosed it with a ditch to the extent of 4 acres in the time of King Henry, father of the present lord the King Edward.

The same prior stopped up his pool of water to the injury of Stowe and Coye.

Sales, &c. They say that Robert Enganye sold 12 acres to the Prior of Anglesey, as is aforesaid.

Cottagers. John Hubert holds 10 acres of land of the Prior of Anglesey by the service of 7s. 6d., and the prior holds them

of the Earl of Oxford, and the Earl of the King. Also let it
be inquired if any religious men have entered into, and the
fees, &c.

They say that the abbot of Saint Mary York, &c., free
tenants of the same abbot.

The Prior of Anglesey holds one meadow of half an acre
for 7*d.*

Villeins of the same Manor.

The Prior of Anglesey holds in Hasting[1] 5 acres of Elias de
Haswelle doing by the year to the Lord Robert de Typetot,
2*s.* 4½*d.*

The same prior holds one hide, which contains one hundred
and twenty acres, in the same town, by purchase from Elias de
Haswelle, which hide Elias held of Richard Pelham, paying 2*s.*
by the year, and he was accustomed to come to the sheriff's
turn, but this is now withdrawn because they are religious, and
he was accustomed to do suit to the county, and this is withdrawn; they know not by what warrant.

Thus we get an aggregate idea of the property held by the
convent at this period, and indeed it was not inconsiderable.
The bulk of it lay in the parishes of Bottisham, Wilbraham,
Swaffham Prior, Haslingfield, Barley in the county of Hertford, and the town of Cambridge.

[1] ? Haslingfield.

CHAPTER VI.

CROSS ERECTED IN MEMORY OF WALTER, VICAR OF TYRRINGTON.

FOUR years after the date of these inquisitions, viz., in 1288, *Cross erected in memory of Walter, Vicar of Tyrrington.* we find that Hugh, Bishop of Ely, granted a release of twenty days' penance "to all those, in whatever diocese, who should care to have this indulgence ratified, and who, contrite in heart, truly penitent, and trusting in their prayers, should piously and devoutly come to the conventual church of the Blessed Mary of Anglesey, for the purpose of praying and hearing divine service, or should pass by a certain cross, near Anglesey, erected for the soul of Walter, formerly vicar of Tyrrington, and who should say with a devout mind a holy prayer and the salutation of the Blessed Virgin for the soul of the said Walter, resting in the church aforesaid, and also for the souls of all faithful deceased."

It does not appear what connection Walter, the vicar of Tyrrington, had with the house of Anglesey, nor where the cross stood that was erected to his memory. In the will of Thomas Gaytts, of Bottisham, dated October the twentieth, 1531, and proved on the twenty-seventh of January in the year following, there is a bequest of 6s. 8d. "to the making of the cross at the Green Hill," but it does not seem to refer to a former one erected to the memory of Walter, late vicar of Tyrrington, but rather to the making of the cross, such as formerly stood on most village greens.

Subsequent to the year in which the above-mentioned document is dated, is another of an uncertain period, but probably ranging from 1288 to 1304. It contains a list, though partial, of the possessions of the monastery in the town of Cambridge, and on the back of it are some monkish verses very difficult to decipher and translate. The property, however, mentioned is *List of posses- sions in Cam- bridge.*

seen by the following transcript: "The Prior and Convent of Anglesey hold one shop in the market of Cambridge of the gift of Hervey, the son of Se(man?), in free, pure and perpetual alms; also, they hold one messuage of the gift of Ichath (? Ralph), the son of Ralph, which said messuage Stephen Athe formerly held, and it lies at ....gate, in free, pure and perpetual alms; also, they hold a rent of two shillings of the gift of Simon, the chamberlain, formerly belonging to E. Bishop of Ely, in free and perpetual alms.

"Also, they hold an annual rent of three shillings of the gift of John de Ry, formerly rector of the chapel of Saint Edmund, to be received of a certain messuage without the gate of Trumpington, in the parish of Saint Peter; which said messuage the said John de Ry had of the gift of Laurence, the son of Alan de ..abenham, which said Laurence had it of the gift of John the son of Arnold de Cambridge.

"Also, they hold one messuage which is called the Stone House, in the parish of Saint Michael, of the gift of Robert the son of (Hubert?), formerly Robert Hubert's, and one place in the same parish, towards the water, which was formerly the leather-house of Thomas Tuylet, and another place in the same parish, towards Alexhye, and a third place at Cholleshyze which formerly belonged to Absalom Cholle, and one messuage towards the chapel of Saint Edmund.........of land lying in parcels in the fields of W..........an annual rent of five shillings from one messuage, which formerly belonged to Peter, the son of Symon, of the gift of the aforesaid Robert, which messuage the aforesaid Robert had of old from his predecessors by right of inheritance, and renders by the year............of Cambridge who hold the same town to fee farm of the lord the king, to the custom called Haggable, eleven pence, and to the hospital of Saint John two pence, and an annual rent of four shillings and sixpence of Richard Bateman[1]."

[1] John P. of Anglesey conceded to Sir Simon de Bertone, vicar of the church of St John the Baptist, Cambridge, the place called "Cholleshethe," formerly belonging to Absalom, son of Absalom Cholle, in the parish of St John, measuring in length from east to west 60 perches, 8 feet; and in breadth on the south side 24 feet, together with the cart road by the water side, rendering to him a pound of cinnamon at the feast of the Assumption of the B. V. M.

Of these possessions the Stone House continued in the hands of the convent up to the time of the dissolution; for it is accounted for in the minister's accounts of 27—28 Hen. VIII., and is called by the same name. From its being mentioned by the side of the leather-house of Thomas Tuylet, it would seem to have been a house where stone was kept for building purposes, and possibly cut, and may have been also used for storing foreign stone, which was brought up the river to it. Alexhye, and Cholleshyze also, seem to have been wharves, though these names do not afterwards occur. But though the prosperity of the convent is shewn by this partial list of its possessions, the inner life of its members is indicated by the elegiac verses found on the back of this document. They are of sufficient interest to be quoted entire as far as they can be made out :—

Scevola tu comodis[1] apud omnes nullus apud te;
Alterius siccas pocula nemo tuum.
Aut tu [pasce alios] an desine velle vocari;
Dedecuit sem[per] sumere nilque dare.
Precessit didimus sequitur qui non didimavit,
Anglicus judicus quintus uterque Deo[2].
Papa Bonefacius nec sit idem benedictus
A re nomen habe benefac, benedic, benedicte,
Aut hoc perverte[3] malefac, maledic, maledicte.
Flecte parens Christi natum piiorqu[e parent]em
Audi clamantem fili [precibus]que rogantem
Quod quia jus[titium est.] Do veniam...[4]
Qui serit a tergo satis est improvidus ergo:
Laude Romanum qui serit ante manum.
Purpurea cum bisso[5] dignum te fecit abisse;
Et penis gravibus splendidus ille cibus.
Et qui de pleno nil es largitus egeno,
Qua tua lingua perit pena perhennis erit.

" Thou, Scevola, eatest at all men's table, no one at thine. Thou drainest the cups of another, no one thine. Either on thy part feed others, or wish no

---

[1] " Comedis," it should be. I have inserted words to fill up the sense where the true reading is doubtful.

[2] It is impossible to make anything of this line as it stands. " Angens judicis questus uterque Deo" makes sense, but it is not the original.

[3] " Perverte" is right, and contains a false quantity. It should be " perverse."

[4] The original here is " et f'ri." which is impossible to bring into scansion. I propose " Do veniam et gratiam."

[5] Does not scan; but probably correct.

H. B.   16

more to be invited. It is a disgraceful thing always to take and to give nothing. Thy predecessor's name was Thomas; after him comes one who hesitated not: [Harsh in his judgments; either reproved by God.] The present Pope's name is Boniface, but he is not thus blessed. Take thy name from the fact, do good, bless, blessed one; or, on the other hand, do evil, curse, cursed one. Bend, O parent of Christ, thy Son; and thou more dutiful listen to the call of thy parent and her prayers, with which she entreats thee, for thus it is right. I give pardon (also to thy brother). He who sows behind him is therefore sufficiently improvident. Praise the Roman who sows before his hand. Purple and fine linen has made thee worthy of an abyss; and that food teems with heavy penalties. And because of full means thou hast bestowed nothing on the needy, where thy tongue perishes shall be everlasting torment."

These satirical lines are evidently addressed to a person styled Scævola (left-handed), who was a constant guest, but who could not be prevailed upon to play the part of host. The mention of Pope Boniface's name seems to fix the date somewhere between the years of 1294 A. D. and 1303 A. D., during the pontificate, that is, of Boniface the Eighth. Boniface the Ninth reigned from 1389 to 1404, which period does not seem to accord with the date of this document. Line 5 contains evidently a play on the name of Thomas, who was called Didimus, from the fact of his doubting. But who the Thomas alluded to does not seem clear, as there is no one of the name of Thomas to be found in the list of priors, canons, or vicars of Bottisham at this period. The latter part is evidently alluding to the parable of Dives and Lazarus. But though we cannot with any certainty fix on the person against whom these lines are directed, we find that much scandal and noise concerning the reputation of the convent was occasioned by the conduct of *Thomas de* Thomas de Luton, a servant of the house, whose conduct may *Luton.* have been alluded to in the line beginning "Precessit Didimus." The Bishop of Ely took serious notice of these rumours at a visitation held about this time, and subsequently addressed the following letter to the convent:—"W., by the Divine mercy Bishop of Ely, to his beloved sons in Christ, the prior and convent of Anglesey, greeting, grace and blessing. When we were lately exercising the office of visitation in your monastery, we understood, by the deposition of certain persons, that Thomas de Luton, your servant, was defamed, as living in a state of incontinence with Joan de Wendedytton within the precinct o your monastery, by reason of which rumour, and for avoiding scandal, we directed him to be provided with a habitation without your monastery. And the same Thomas then absenting himself, though not from contumacy, and afterwards appearing, and firmly asserting that he was entirely free from the said crime, prayed earnestly to be admitted to his purgation. Now we have thought proper to assent to such his just petition, as no one opposed him therein. And the aforesaid Thomas personally appeared on the day and in the place which our official had appointed him in that matter, and canonically purged himself before us concerning the said excess. We therefore, in the name of God, restore the same Thomas to his character and former estate fully as to all things by these presents. Enjoining you, by virtue of obedience, that you esteem him within your monastery as you did before our visitation, so that, for the future, we hear no noise or clamour about it, nor that you occasion him any disturbance or injury on account thereof. Given at Doddington on the eighth of the Ides of August in the year of the Lord 1296, and in the sixth year of our pontificate." After this date we hear no more about Thomas de Luton, and we may suppose that the scandal subsided.

Before this in 1289 the priory had become involved in some dispute about the will of Symon vicar of Bottisham, the advowson of which lay in their gift. The cause eventually came into the court of the archdeaconry of Ely, and was heard before P. de Dereby, the judge appointed to try all causes. It does not appear what the actual point at issue was, but when the case came on for judgment, it was stated that common friends had intervened, and an amicable arrangement had been made, viz. that the prior and convent agreed to pay to the executors or their proctor the sum of ten shillings of silver by way of concluding the dispute. One of these executors it is stated was Hugh, called Atlane, of Botekysham, who was a man of some property, as his name often occurs in documents relating to the sale or interchange of lands. *Will of Sir Symon, formerly perpetual vicar of Botekysham.*

Grants of land to the priory now became rarer and more sparing, but there are two of uncertain date, which, if not belonging to this period, may be now mentioned. The first is *Charter of Thomas de Burgo.*

that of Thomas de Burgo, who from other sources we learn was lord of the manor of Swaffham, which was called after his name, and is now called Burgh Hall. The charter states that he gave all the land which Ralph Eir held of him in the town of Swaffham, to wit, five acres of land with a messuage and appurtenances, rendering therefore to him and his heirs two shillings, that is to say, at Easter twelve pence, and at the feast of Saint Michael twelve pence, for all services, secular customs, and demands, except foreign service, to wit, as much as belongs to such a tenement of that fee. The other charter is that of William de Kaen, lord of Carenchiis, who granted to the prior and convent all the land which they held in the town of South Morden[1] of his fee of the gift of Walter de Stanford, rendering annually to him the sum of two shillings and nine pence at the four terms of the year for all things services and secular demands. But the last document connected with the house of Anglesey at the close of the thirteenth century is the roll of the taxation of the goods, rents, and profits of religious persons in the archdeaconries of divers counties in the kingdom of England, made in the year of our Lord 1291. This is what is commonly called Pope Nicholas' taxation, by which all the taxes of the king as well as the Pope were regulated until the survey made in the 26th year of the reign of Henry the Eighth.

Under the heading,

"Taxation of the churches in the diocese of Ely made by authority of the Bishops of Winchester and Lincoln," we find—

"Taxation of the temporal goods of the city and diocese of Ely.

"Goods of the Priory of Anglesey.

		£	s.	d.
"In Anglesey	sum	24	7	8
In Wilberham Parnel[2]	„	7	12	4
In Wilberham Regis	„		6	0
In Steeple Mordon	„	4	10	0
In Litlington	„	3	6	8

Charter of William de Kaen.

Pope Nicholas' taxation.

---

[1] Probably Steeple Morden.   [2] Parva.

		£.	s.	d.
In Fulburn . . . sum		3	14	0
In Haselyngfeud . . . „		2	17	6
In Swapham Prior . . „		4	4	0
In Swapham Bolebek . .			6	0
In Cambridge . . . „		2	17	11
In Stowe . . . . „		2	0	0
In Gildenmordon . . .			10	0
In Queye . . . . „		2	0	5
In Dullingham . . .			5	0
In Wilburham Magna . . „			6	1
Sum total		59	3	7

Deanery of Fordham.

In Wyken	1	13	3½

Deanery of Braughing, co. Herts.

In Berle	4	13	4
In Stanndon		6	0
Sum	4	19	4

In Deanery of Samphorde.

In Berdefeud Magna . . .	2	0

In Deanery of Clare.

In Thurlowe Parva	13	0

Of Spirituals, in the Deanery of Camps.

The Church of Bodekesham . .	26	13	4
Vicar of the same	5	0	0
Portion of the Prior of Longa Villa in the same	4	13	4
The Church of St Mary at Swafham .	9	6	8
So that the temporals of the Priory amounted to	66	11	2½
And the spirituals to . . .	36	0	0 „

Agreement with Sir Geoffrey, Rector of Wendlyng-ton.

One of the most important connexions of religious houses with the outside world was that of hospitality; accordingly agreements seem often to have been made respecting allowances of food, and more particularly bread and ale. This beverage was always famous at conventual establishments, and in our own day the ale of our Universities, which grew out of the monastic property, still justly preserves its notoriety. For a long time after the dissolution one of the principal questions asked of incumbents of churches was, Do they maintain hospitality? and the village clergyman is still expected to contribute largely towards the assistance of the poor amongst his congregation. Often however it became necessary in monasteries to get rid of their duties of hospitality by the payment of a proportionate sum of money. So Robert de Estre took from the Prior of Anglesey twenty-five shillings because he was unwilling to entertain him[1]; and in like manner in the year 1300 an agreement was made between Roger de Weston, who had succeeded to the priorate of Anglesey, and Sir Geoffrey, rector of the church of Wendlyngton, regarding a certain exhibition of bread and ale which the said Sir Geoffrey was accustomed to receive, and ought to receive, as in the charter of the said prior and convent was more fully contained. The agreement states that "the said Sir Geoffrey has demised to the aforesaid prior and convent the said exhibition of bread and ale from the said eighth of the ides of May till the same term in the next year fully completed for three marks and a half of silver (£2. 6s. 8d.), which the same religious will pay to the aforesaid Sir Geoffrey at Anglesey, or to the bearer of these letters, at the terms within written, to wit, at the feast of the Nativity of Saint John the Baptist in the year aforesaid one mark, at the feast of Saint Michael next following one mark, at the feast of the Nativity of our Lord next following one mark, and at the feast of Easter next following half a mark, under the penalty of forty pence of silver to be paid to the lord archdeacon of Ely for every term of such payment which shall not be kept. In witness whereof the seal of the chapter of the said prior and convent and the

---

[1] Rot. Hund. Vol. i. p. 53. He was sheriff for Cambs: 55 and 56 Hen. III. and 1 and 2 Edw. I. Vide Fuller's *Worthies*, ed. 1840, Vol. i. p. 248.

seal of the said Sir Geoffrey are alternately appended to these presents made in the form of a chirograph. Given at Anglesey on the day and year aforesaid."

On the back of this document is a very interesting record of *List of* certain books delivered to the monks on the .... day of *Books.* .... in the seventh year of the reign of King Edward (i.e. Edw. II. 1314). At this period books were exceedingly scarce and therefore valuable, and they were probably doled out to the canons of the house for the purpose of study and devotion as well as safe custody. We have before seen what care was taken that the book lent to the former vicar of Tyrington should be returned to the safe keeping of the monastery to which it belonged. The following is the list of works and the names of those to whose keeping they were confided :—

With the lord prior (Roger de Weston). "The parables of Solomon, a psalter with——."

With Sir John de Bodekesham (late prior). "The epistles of Paul......Certain notes upon the psalter and a book of the miracles of the Blessed Mary with the miracles of Saints."

With the subprior. "The book of the life of St Thomas the martyr."

With E. de Ely. "The fourth book of sentences with sermons...... The book of Reymund. The book of vices and virtues and a pastoral."

With R. Pichard. "The book of Alquin; the book of John de Tyringtone with Cato and others."

With Henry Muchet. "The book of the life of Saint Mary Magdalene, and remedies."

With Walter de Gilwilden (elected prior in 1338). "The book of S...... bound in cloth; a hymnary glossed with constitutions. Belet[1] bound and a life of saints."

With Richard de Queye. "Homilies of Gregory upon the evangelists, bound in black leather." Among the common books : "Decrees, Decretals, the first part of the morals of Job, a book of abuses, a book of justice remaining with Master Adam de Wilburham."

With Walter de Wyth (Withersfield). "The book of Innocent upon the Sacraments, with Belet and an introduction in one volume."

Also with the subprior. "A Psalter glossed which was in the custody of Master Henry de Melreth. Also another psalter glossed, in pawn with Isabella Siccadona."

[1] Probably the works of John Belethus, published in Migne's *Patrologie*, Vol. CCII.

These books appear to have been of the same character as those usually to be found in monastic libraries. They were almost all books of devotion or lives of martyrs and saints.

The "liber Alquin" was probably the work of the famous Albinus or Alcuinus, whose writings are still preserved. This author was a native of York, and an ecclesiastic of the same city. He was sent on an embassy to Charlemagne, and afterwards became Abbot of St Martin of Tours, where he was buried. He died on the 19th of May, 804 A. D.

From this list we gather also a complete list of the canons of the house, including Sir John de Bodekesham, who had been prior, but who had resigned the office. Thus the full number exclusive of the prior was eight, while Master Adam de Wilbraham was probably not ordained, but only an inmate, or perhaps a servant of the house. The mention of the psalters as being in pledge with Isabella Siccadona is a clear indication of the condition of the convent which was then beginning to decline in favour rather than increase in prosperity.

spute
th Hugh
Usser.

Mention has been made already of the dispute in 1300 A. D.; between the two religious houses of Anglesey and Tonbridge. In the same year the former house also had a quarrel with a landholder in Bottisham named Hugh le Usser, the son of Margaret, the wife of Hugh le Usser, who had been before a benefactor to the house. The following is the account of the pleadings in assize[1]: "The assize comes to acknowledge whether Roger, Prior of Anglesey, brother John de Bodekesham, brother William de Angleseye, Richard the blessed, William de Weston, Peter de Fulburn, Hugh Aluard, John de Cotemor, William, the son of Gilbert le Ken, William Danbe, Henry the son of Walter of the fen, John de Gaysle, the younger, and Alan the Palmer, unjustly, &c., disseised Hugh, the usher of Bodekesham, of his common of pasture in Bodekesham which belongs to his free tenement in the same town since the first, &c. And whereupon he complains that they disseised him of the common, &c., of commoning with all kinds of cattle for the whole year in nine acres

---

[1] Plac. 27 Edw. I. m. 18.

and a half of pasture, and in two acres of land in open time, &c.
And the prior comes by Simon de Stowe, his bailiff, and answers
for himself and all the others as a tenant. And as to the aforesaid pasture he says that the tenement is not pasture but arable
land, and he says that he did no injury or disseisin because he
says that he found his church seised thereof, &c. And if it is
committed, he says that the aforesaid Hugh ought not to common there with his cattle except in open time and not during
the whole year. And as to the aforesaid two acres of land he
says that the tenement is the several meadow of the same prior
and not arable land, and that he found his church aforesaid
seised thereof, &c. And if it is committed, he says that the
aforesaid Hugh was never in seisin of the commoning there, and
if this he puts himself upon the assize. And Hugh does the
like. Therefore let an assize be taken. Afterwards the aforesaid Hugh as to the aforesaid two acres of land does not pursue,
&c., therefore the aforesaid prior is without day, therefore, &c.
The jury say upon their oath that the aforesaid Hugh was in
seisin of the commoning in the aforesaid pasture of nine acres
and a half as is complained until the aforesaid prior, brother
John de Bodekesham, brother William, John de Cotemor,
Gilbert le Ken, and William, unjustly, &c., disseised him. And
therefore it is adjudged that the aforesaid Hugh shall recover
his seisin thereof against them by view of the acknowledgers—
and the prior and others are in mercy. And in like manner the
aforesaid Hugh is in mercy for his false claim against the others,
&c.—Damages 12 pence."

The first licence to receive land under the Mortmain acts *Grant of John de Grey.*
was given to the Convent of Anglesey in the year 1316 A. D.
Letters patent were then issued by King Edward the Second,
giving leave to John de Grey to assign to the prior and convent
one acre and a half of land with the appurtenances in Lammas
in Anglesey, contiguous to the area of the convent, on the condition of their paying to the chief lords of the fee the services
due and accustomed: and by a singular mistake in the letters
patent the brethren are styled Friars Minors. The name of
Lammas has quite disappeared, nor is it known where the plot
of ground was situated. . . . .

*onfirma-
ion of the
lection of
Valter de
Vithers-
ield,
*rior.

During this same year a change took place in the government of the monastery. Roger de Weston, the late prior, was
probably dead, and was succeeded by Walter de Withersfield,
who was already one of the canons of the establishment. The
installation of the priors was an office reserved to the archdeaconry of Ely, and so we find the following document ratifying
the election; "Be it known to all by these presents that we,
the official of the lord Archdeacon of Ely, have received the
mandate of the venerable father the lord John, by the grace of
God (Bishop), elect of Ely, and canonically confirmed in these
words. John, by the divine permission, elect and confirmed
(Bishop) of Ely, to the Archdeacon of Ely or his official, greeting
in the Lord the Saviour. Whereas the late election of brother
Walter de Wytheresfield, canon of the church of Anglesey, in
our diocese, as prior of the same monastery, has been canonically
celebrated and by our authority legally confirmed, to the same
prior so confirmed we have committed and granted the administration of the spiritualities thereof, and also of the temporalities as much as we can, and now do grant the same by these
presents. We command you by your duty of obedience so far
as that you install the said person so confirmed according to the
right form and custom of our aforesaid church, and that you
perform the things which pertain to that act with effect in our
name and authority, always saving the rights and customs of our
church aforesaid in all things. To do all and singular which
things we commit to you our office with the power of canonical
coercion. Given at Wrtie (?) on the fourteenth of the calends
of October, in the year of the Lord one thousand three hundred
and sixteen. Therefore by the authority of this mandate we
have installed the aforesaid brother, Walter de Wytheresfield,
as prior of the conventual church of Anglesey aforesaid, according to the form of the right and custom of the aforesaid church
of Ely, and we have completed those things which pertain to
that act with the effect, force, and authority, above noted, the
right of the church of Ely and the customs thereof in all things
being always saved. In witness whereof the seal of the con-
sistory of the aforesaid lord Archdeacon of Ely is applied to
these presents. Given at Anglesey on the fifth of the nones o

October in the aforesaid year of the Lord." We must not forget that the patronage of the priory lay in the hands of the family of Clare, and accordingly the right of presentation would have at this date devolved upon Elizabeth, the daughter of Gilbert the Red, and formerly wife of John de Burgh, who died three years before. Later on in the history of the monastery we find a more complete record of the proceedings that took place on the election to this office when it was entrusted to the canons themselves.

The patrons of the convent seem to have exercised great *Ivor le* power. Amongst other things they had the right of granting *lardiner.* certain pensions out of the revenues of the establishment. During the minority of Gilbert, Earl of Clare, who was slain at the battle of Bannockburn, the honor of Clare came under the control of Ralph Monthermer, who had married Joan de Acres, widow of Gilbert the Red, much to the king's displeasure. There is a very curious document which shews that this Ralph granted a pension of twenty-eight shillings sterling to be received annually by a certain Ivor the lardiner of Cardiff, under the condition that it should be taken away if the prior and convent were charged with any other person during his lifetime by the said Ralph and Joan. Accordingly by this deed, dated at Bodekysham on the Saturday next before the feast of the apostles Philip and James, in the eleventh year of the reign of King Edward the son of King Edward, Ivor renounces his claim as Gilbert de Clare, the son of Joan, the Countess of Gloucester and Hertford, had granted it to a certain Edward de Iseby. It does not appear what connexion either of these pensioners had with the priory, or what was the reason of the stipend having been granted.

CHAPTER VII.

PAYMENT OF A TENTH.

Payment of a tenth. IN the year 1318 A. D. Pope John the twenty-second granted the King of England for the relief of his debts a tenth for one year. Richard de Hertfordingbury, a canon of Waltham Holy Cross, was appointed sub-collector for the Archdeaconry of London and Middlesex by the Bishops of Winchester and Exeter: and so acting as deputy of the principal collectors, he received four shillings and eleven pence halfpenny farthing for the first moiety of the tenth of the Prior of Anglesey for his temporal goods in the aforesaid Archdeaconry of Middlesex. This sum would be for those temporalities situated in the county of Hert-

Accounts. fordshire. But while, from various taxations, we get some idea of the revenues of the monastery, we can glean some light on its expenditure from the accounts which are extant of various offices in the 1st year of the reign of Edward the Third. This "compotus," or yearly expenditure, includes many curious items, and gives an insight into the domestic life of the inmates of the convent. They may be classed under seven different heads :—

I. That of the sacrist, Walter de Yelvedon, extending from Michaelmas to Michaelmas, 1 and 2 Edw. III.

II. That of the guardians of the work of the church, John de Wygenhale and Richard de Bodekysham, from Easter to Easter, 2 and 3 Edw. III.

III. That of the almoner, John de Wygenhale, from Michaelmas to Michaelmas, 1 and 2 Edw. III.

IV. That of the gardener, William de Wilbraham, from 1326 to Jan. 1327, and from Michaelmas to Michaelmas, 1 and 2 Edw. III.

V. That of the mill, held by Richard Robertot, temp. Edw. II., and of two other mills.

VI. That of the grange, under Richard de Bodekysham, rom Michaelmas to Michaelmas, 1 and 2 Edw. III.

VII. That of the rectory of Bodekesham, under Richard de Temesford, serving there from Michaelmas to Michaelmas, l and 2 Edw. III.

The sacrist accounts for 4s. 8½d. received from rents of as_size in Bottisham; for one pound of wax received from John Creke[1] for a tenement in Westley belonging to the high altar; for the yearly offerings which amounted that year to 15s., no inconsiderable sum for that period; and for wine made and sold to the value of 1s., proving that the convent had a vineyard. A ploughshare sells for 1s. 8d.; 3 stone 4 lbs. of wool sell for 14s. 6d.; wheat sells at 4s. the quarter, and malt at the same price; a colt 3 years old sold for 12s.; a draught-horse at 9s.; a heifer at 7s. 6d.; four ewes at 5s. 6d., and a wether for 1s. 6d. Amongst the expenses are the following items, shewing the yearly consumption of various articles; e. g. 50 lbs. of wax per year, 26s.; 26 lbs. of cotton-wicked candles, 3s. 7d.; 3 lbs. of wax, 6d.; 22 gallons of wine, bought per annum, for the celebration of the mass, 8s. 3d.; 3 joists, 3 lamps, and one glass jar, 8d.; two men sowing one acre and one rood by hand, 3s.; 2 ells of sandall, and the pay of the tailor for making two apparels[2] of the prior's cloth, 7d.; 8 horse-shoes and one piece of iron, 6½d.; winter keep of 18 bullocks out of the town, 3s. 6d.; 3 acres ½ a rod reaping and tying, 2s. 8d.; thrash-ing 3½ quarters of wheat, 7½d.; 8½ quarters of barley, 8½d.

The receipts were £7. 6s. 10¼d., and the expenses £6. 14s., so that a balance remained in hand of 12s. 10¼d.

The stock that he had remaining was as follows :—

2 draught-horses, 1 cart-colt, 43 sheep, 16 ewes, 4 lambs, 2 hogs, 2 feres[3], 13 skins, and 11 lbs. of wax left over, 50 lbs. bought, 1 lb. rent of tenement in Westley, and 7 lbs. of arrear; used in church last year 48 lbs.; remaining 21 lbs.

In the account under heading II. there are no items of in-

---

1 This would be the Sir John de Creke whose brass is in Westley church, and is engraved in Lysons' *Cambridgeshire*, and other works.
2 Small ornaments on the upper part of the amice.
3 A Fere is a small sheep which has not had a lamb.

terest, except 20s. received from the vicar of Waterbeach for the farm at Swaffham, for Michaelmas term, in the 2nd year of the lease.

Total receipts £7. 12s. 10d.; paid £4. 3s.; balance in hand £3. 9s. 10d.

In the almoner's account (No. III.), we find that the rents from Litlington and Mordon, for one year, came to £1. 4s. Amongst the items of expenditure for the poor occurs:—

	s.	d.
Paid for one coat and 2 hoods......	4	7
4 pair of boots	2	0
Distribution of bread	1	4
Maunday money	3	4

Total receipts £3. 0. 10d.; expenses £4. 10s.; therefore £1. 9s. 2d. still due from this account[1].

In the gardener's account we find mention of the various things grown for the use of the convent, such as onions, pot-herbs, pears, apples, vetches, 24 gallons of which were for mustard, madder, teasles sold to the fuller, nettles, hemp and flax, garlic and linseed.

Total receipts £1. 1s. 6¾d.; expenditure 6s. 6¾d.; so he owed 15s., which he paid over to the account, and went away clear.

In the account of William de Wilbraham, gardener: receipts, 13s. 8d.; expenses, 10s. 1¼d.; balance in hand, 3s. 6¾d.

The account of the mills is of little interest. The rent of one of them seems to have been as much as £3. 6s. 8d.; receipts, £3. 13s. 8d.; expenses, £2. 19s. 2d.

Under the account of the grange, we find 5 quarters 2 bushels of wheat, quoted as the produce of Wicken, shewing that at that time the tenement of Thornhall was still in the hands of the convent. There is also an account of white peas used in making soup for the use of the monastery.

Total receipts, £4. 14s. 5d., also 5d.; expenses, £4. 14s. 0½d.; so he owes 9½d.

---

[1] Each office seems to have had apportioned to it a certain quantity of land to farm.

Of the Rectory of Bottisham, total receipts, £5. 0s. 9¾d. ; xpenditure, £5. 3s. 2½d. ; so was overspent 2s. 4¾d.[1]

The wealth of the convent had visibly declined owing to *Grant of* 1e scarcity of benefactors, by reason of the Mortmain acts, and *Eliz. de* *Burg*[h] 'om other causes, when it found a new patron in Eliz. de *Lady* 'urgh, Lady Clare. She was the daughter and heiress of *Clare.* 'ilbert de Clare, surnamed the Red, and his wife Jean D'Acres, 'ho was daughter to Edw. I., and must not be confounded with 'aat Eliz. de Clare who was her granddaughter, and became 1e wife of Lionel, Duke of Clarence. The first intimation of 'er intention of further endowing the house of Anglesey is 'iven us in the Patent Roll of the 4th year of the reign of 'Idw. III.[2], in which a letter, dated January 15th, 1331, grants a 'cence to Elizabeth de Burgh, Lady Clare, who is also styled 'ousin of the king, that she might grant to the Prior and 'onvent of Anglesey twenty pounds of rent with the appurte- 'ances in Lakenheath in the county of Suffolk, upon the con- 'ition that the prior and convent should find certain chaplains 'o celebrate divine service every day for ever, in the church of 'nglesey, for the souls of the king's progenitors, and for the 'holesome estate of the same Elizabeth, as long as she should 've, and for her soul when she should depart the light, and for 1e souls of all faithful deceased.

These letters patent were next year followed by others[3], 'ated on the eighteenth day of July, making further provision 'j regards this rent. Licence had previously been given to the 'rior of Ely to receive from Elizabeth de Burgh her manor of 'akenheath with the appurtenances, and one messuage, and 'venty-four acres of land with the appurtenances, on condition '[' their paying to Elizabeth de Burgh and her heirs an annual

[1] There occur in these accounts various words whose meaning is obscure. *raghet* appears to have been a mixture of barley and oats, and was malted; *hak* is the grain left after gleaning; *impes* is a term used, meaning grass or 'sturage; a *seam* of iron (Lat. summa)=a load; a *treis* of coal? what mea- 're; *midstys?* what; and *tactand* seems to denote some sort of oaten cake 'ven to the poor. In Norfolk in the present day a tough piece of meat is said to 've a good deal of "tack" in it.

[2] Part II. m. 13.

[3] Pat. Roll. 5 Edw. III. Part II. membrane 27. Vide also *Liber niger* ': Wigmore, Harl. MSS. No. 1240, fol. 94, and Add. MSS. No. 6041, fol. 83.

rent of twenty pounds. These letters now provide that leave should be granted to Elizabeth de Burgh to assign this twenty pounds rent charged upon the said manor, messuage, and land, to the Prior and Convent of Anglesey. After this licence had been so granted, a final concord was made in the November of the same year, between the Prior of Anglesey, plaintiff, and Elizabeth de Burgh, deforciant, and the aforesaid Elizabeth acknowledgeth the right of the Prior of Anglesey; and the prior on his part promised to receive the said Elizabeth and her heirs into all and singular the benefactions and orations which should henceforth be done in his church aforesaid. And this agreement was made by the command of the lord the king.

In the next year, viz. 1333 A.D., an indenture[1] was made specifying, "that whereas, &c., &c., as in the letters of the same lord the king aforesaid is contained. We therefore, the said Prior and Convent of Anglesey, being seised of the aforesaid rent by the licence of the same lord the king, and by the gift and assignment of the same Elizabeth in form aforesaid, grant for us and our successors to be bound to find in our house aforesaid two competent secular chaplains by us the Prior and Convent of Anglesey, to be chosen to perform divine service every day at the altar of the Holy Cross in our church of Anglesey for ever, for the wholesome estate of the same Elizabeth as long as she shall live and for her soul when she shall have departed this life, as well as for the souls of her ancestors and heirs and those of all faithful deceased. And also we the said Prior and Convent of Anglesey grant for us and our successors that we will find for the aforesaid chaplains fit residence within the close of our priory, and to find them sufficient and proper food at our table, and to allow to each of them the aforesaid rent of twenty pounds twenty shillings of silver for their robes and other necessaries at the feast of Saint Michael and Easter by equal portions annually, or if it shall seem to be more convenient to us we grant for us and for our successors that we

[1] Vide Dugdale, *Monasticon*, Vol. VI. p. 259. Vide also another copy of the same document, *Aug. Office*, K. 72, appended to which is the seal of Roger Damory, of green wax, nearly perfect, containing the shields of Damory, Clare, Burgh, and Verdon.

will annually render to the aforesaid chaplains for the time being twelve marks of the aforesaid rent to be for ever received from the hands of us and of our successors at two terms of the year by equal portions annually, to wit, at the feasts of Saint Michael and Easter, unless we can agree for the smaller sums with the aforesaid sufficient chaplains for the performance of the aforesaid chantry for ever. And if it shall happen that the said chaplains or either of them should be sick so that such divine service could not be celebrated, we bind us and our successors to execute the aforesaid chantries by our own religious men of our house aforesaid until he or they shall recover health, or if it should happen that the aforesaid chaplains or either of them should die or be sick so that he cannot be present and we cannot produce the said secular chaplains before the feast of Saint Michael then next following, we bind us and our successors to execute the aforesaid chantries or chantry by our brethren in form aforesaid at the feast of Saint Michael then next following, by which time we bind us that we will provide such secular chaplain or chaplains for such default when it shall happen. And if it shall happen that we or our successors should make default in the support of the said chaplains, or that for three weeks or a month the aforesaid chantry should cease contrary to the form aforesaid, then we bind us and our successors and permit us to be bound to the aforesaid Elizabeth her heirs or assigns in twenty pounds annually to be yearly received by equal portions at the aforesaid two terms of the year, to wit, Easter and Michaelmas, from all our lands and tenements in Bodekisham which are of the fee of the same Elizabeth, and that the aforesaid Elizabeth and her heirs or assigns may distrain in all our lands and tenements aforesaid for the said rent so in arrear in form aforesaid. And we the aforesaid Elizabeth will and grant for us and our heirs that the residue of the whole rent of said twenty pounds shall remain for ever to the office of the kitchen of the said house in augmentation of the dishes of the said prior and convent and to the aforesaid prior and convent and their successors for the execution and support of the other charges and necessaries of the house by equal portions according to the disposition of the prior and convent for the time being. And we the said Elizabeth De Burgh grant for us and our heirs that if the aforesaid manor, messuage, and land, wherefrom the rent of the said twenty pounds comes, or a part of the same manor, messuage, and land should be recovered against the Prior and convent of Ely or their successors by us or our heirs or any other persons by default of us or of our heirs by reason of a prior right or action, so that the aforesaid Prior of Anglesey or his successors be not able to have or obtain the aforesaid rent or part of the same rent by the hands of the said Prior of Ely or his successors, then the same Prior and convent of Anglesey shall be quit as regards a rated proportion of the rent so annulled touching the aforesaid chantry, and a portion of the aforesaid twenty pounds in which the said Prior and convent of Anglesey are bound to us and our heirs as is aforesaid from the tenements which they hold of us in Bodekisham. In witness whereof to this indenture, as well the said Elizabeth as the aforesaid Prior and convent of Anglesey have alternately put their seals. These being witnesses. Sir Henry de Ferers[1], Sir John de Cambridge[2], Sir Alexander de Walesham, Sir John de Wantone, Sir Thomas de Chedworth[3], Robert de Fenkeriche and others. Given at Anglesey on Saturday next after the feast of Saint Matthew the apostle in the sixth year of the reign of King Edward the Third since the conquest."

The terms of this indenture are sufficiently precise, and hence we see that these secular chaplains, or "poor Sir Johns," as they were called, were thought able to live upon 6 marks, =£4 per annum[4]. There is no other mention made of the altar of the Holy Cross within the chapel of the priory. It was probably one of the minor altars, as the church was dedicated to Saint Mary.

About the same time, or rather three days earlier, the same lady Elizabeth de Burgh executed another document granting

---

[1] Held the manor of Frating, in Essex, and died in 1343. Vide Morant's Essex, I. 449.

[2] One of the King's Justices.

[3] As will subsequently appear, a benefactor of the house of Anglesey.

[4] Vide further Bishop Fleetwood, Chronicon Preciosum, Ed. 1707, p. 142. Ed. 1745, p. 116.

to the canons the right of choosing their own prior when that office should fall vacant, in order to shew clearly her right to the patronage of the convent. This instrument is dated on September the 22nd, 1333. But Elizabeth was desirous of further benefiting the condition of the house by another grant. With this view she obtained licence of the king[1] to give and assign fourteen pounds rent, with the appurtenances, in Bottisham, Swaffham Bulbeck, and Horningsey, in the county of Cambridge, and view of frank-pledge of her men and tenants in the said town of Bottisham, as well as the advowson of the church of Donmawe (Dunmow), in the county of Essex. In 1337 further letters patent[2] were issued, specifying that leave had been granted in former letters to the said Elizabeth de Burgh to assign the said advowson of Dunmow to the prior and convent. "And now," it is stated, "on behalf of the aforesaid Elizabeth we have been prayed, that whereas the priory aforesaid is of her patronage, we would be pleased, for the security of the sub-prior and convent of the place aforesaid, and their successors, to grant that we or our heirs, by reason of the said advowson of the church aforesaid, by the same Elizabeth, so to be given and assigned, although it be holden of us in chief, would never in any way exact or demand in future anything touching the advowson of the priory aforesaid, or the custody of the temporalities of the same in the time of the vacancy of the same priory." And this request the king granted, saving always to him and his heirs his right as regards the custody of the same priory, if they should have any right to the same from any other cause. And this actually happened, for Edward the Fourth became heir to the estates of the family of Mortimer, Earl of March, into whose hands the advowson of the priory subsequently passed. But though these letters patent were issued by the crown, it does not appear that the advowson of the church of Dunmow ever fully passed under the control of the monastery of Anglesey, nor did they ever present in the time of a vacancy.

In the year 1336 letters patent were issued, granting leave

[1] Pat. Roll. 7 Edw. III., Part II. mem. 15.
[2] Ib. 10 Edw. III., Part I. mem. 27.

to Elizabeth de Burgh to give and assign to the prior and
convent three messuages, three tofts, one mill, fifty-seven acres
of land, three acres of meadow, and thirty-four shillings rent,
with the appurtenances, in Great Walsingham and Little Walsingham, held of the king in chief, to have and to hold to them
and their successors, to find two secular chaplains to celebrate
divine service every day in the chapel of the Blessed Mary the
Virgin, newly built by the same Elizabeth within the priory
aforesaid, according to the ordinance in that behalf made for
ever[1]. So that it appears, that besides these benefactions above
stated, the same lady had built for the monastery a chapel
dedicated to the Blessed Virgin Mary, probably adjoining to
their chapel, already erected by the munificence of Master
Laurence de Saint Nicholas.   But the prior and convent of
Anglesey did not long retain possession of these messuages and
lands in Walsingham[2].   An inquisition, "ad quod damnum,"
was ordered to be taken in the thirtieth year of Edward the
Third's reign, by Guy Seintcler, the escheator for the county
of Norfolk, to enquire if any and what damage would accrue
to the king if the prior and convent of Anglesey should give
and assign the aforesaid messuages, &c., to the prior and convent of Walsingham, rendering to the same prior and convent
of Anglesey and their successors twelve marks by the year for
ever. The inquisition was held at Walsingham on the 9th of
July, 1356, A.D., before the following jury :—Bartholomew de
Wythone, Roger Galoun, Robert de Inlond, Henry Pouwer,
Thomas Warner, Robert Galoun the younger, John at Mill,
Robert de Hildegrave, Edward Elwyne, Thomas Jacob, John
de Bedingham, and John Hessel.   Upon the result of the
inquisition being that the jurors declared that the aforesaid
proposed grant would not damage the king's interests, letter
patent were issued, giving licence for one mark to be paid into
the hanaper office to the prior and convent of Anglesey, to
grant and assign the said messuages and lands to the prior and
convent of Walsingham, rendering, therefore, to the aforesaid
prior and convent of Anglesey and their successors, the sur

[1] Pat. Roll. 9 Edw. III., Part i. mem. 27.
[2] In the county of Norfolk.

of twelve marks by the year for ever.   And in the same way
licence was given to the prior and convent of Walsingham to
receive the same.   These letters were issued on the twenty-
fourth day of July, 1356, A.D.[1]   The rent arising out of these
lands seems to have been paid to the convent up to the time
of the dissolution; but when the "valor ecclesiasticus" was
taken in the reign of Henry the Eighth, the rent from the
manor of Walsingham Collinghams amounted by the year to
£3. 13s. 4d.

In the year 1355 the following indenture was made between
Elizabeth de Burgh and the prior and convent of Anglesey,
relative to the two secular chaplains appointed to say mass for
her soul.   It witnesseth "that whereas the aforesaid prior and
convent are charged perpetually to find two chaplains to perform divine service in their church of Anglesey for the said
lady Elizabeth and her ancestors, for a certain rent, therefore
to them by the said Elizabeth perpetually given, to be received of the prior and convent of Ely from certain lands and
tenements in Lakenheath, in the county of Cambridge, which
the said prior and convent of Ely hold of the gift of the said
lady Elizabeth for ever.   And whereas, by the recent request
of the said lady Elizabeth, the aforesaid prior and convent of
Anglesey by their deed have granted to Master Robert de
Spalding an annual pension of one hundred shillings, to be
received from year to year, at the feasts of Saint Michael the
Archangel and Easter, by equal portions for the term of his
life; the said Elizabeth wills and grants for herself and for her
heirs, that the said prior and convent of Anglesey shall be discharged from the finding of one chaplain during the time that
they shall continue charged towards the said Master Robert in
respect of the said pension of one hundred shillings in form
aforesaid.   And to make full satisfaction for the said pension of
one hundred shillings, the said lady Elizabeth wills and grants,
for herself and for her heirs, to the said prior and convent of
Anglesey, eight shillings and one penny of rent by the year,
which she has been accustomed to receive by the hands of

----

[1] Pat. Roll. 30 Edw. III., Part II. mem. 10.

Agnes Geffrey, her tenant, in the town of Bodekesham. And that the said prior and convent of Anglesey may have and hold their lands, discharged of eleven shillings and eleven pence of rent by the year, which they hold of the said lady Elizabeth in the town of Bodekesham, for the time that they shall continue charged to the said Master Robert in respect of the pension of one hundred shillings above named, in the form aforesaid. Saving, in every way, to the said lady Elizabeth and her heirs, all other services due by the said prior and convent of Anglesey and Agnes Geffrey, her tenant, for the lands and tenements which they hold of the said lady Elizabeth, in the town of Bodekesham. In witness whereof to these indentures, the aforesaid lady Elizabeth of the one part, and the prior and convent of Anglesey of the other part, have interchangeably put their seals. Given at Berdfield on the twenty-fourth day of April, in the twenty-ninth year of the reign of King Edward the Third since the conquest[1]."

On account of the subsequent poverty of the house, the prior and convent became unable to support these two chaplains, and in 1475, by letters patent, they were absolved from finding these chaplains, upon the condition, that two of the canons of the house should celebrate mass for the king and queen, and for the souls of William Alyngton and Joan his wife[2].

Elizabeth de Burgh, Lady Clare, whose benefactions have just been enumerated, likewise shewed some further favour to the house of Anglesey; for in her will, dated 1355, and proved Dec. 3rd, 1360, she bequeaths "to the house of Anglesey ten marks, and the vestment of red cloth of gold of taffata, with three crests of silver surmounting the shoulders[3]:" and Edmund Mortimer, Earl of March, her descendant, in his will dated Jan. 22, 1381—2, bequeathed forty marks to the convent[4].

[1] Dugdale, *Monasticon*, Vol. VI.
[2] Pat. Roll. 15 Edw. IV., Part I. mem. 20.
[3] Royal Wills, No. 32.
[4] Ib., No. 110.

CHAPTER VIII.

GRANT OF WILLIAM DE GOSFIELD.

ʀ is not recorded who were the first chaplains appointed under *Grant of* ɪe benefaction of Elizabeth de Burgh; but we find the names *William de Gosfield.* ' William de Arderne and Seman de Wytheresfield, chaplains, ɪcluded in the list of benefactors at this period; and hence, as ɪere was no other chantry founded for secular priests, they ʃay have been preferred to perform masses for Lady de Clare. ɪut in the inquisition "ad quod damnum" which preceded ɪeir grants, there is included one also from William de Gos- ɪld[1], whose charter bears the date of 1327 A.D., and therefore ɪserves prior mention. William de Gosfield, then, by this ɪed, released and quitclaimed the convent of two marks of ɪnual rent due to him for certain lands held in the town of ɪvaffham Prior. For this grant the prior and convent con- ɪled what was called a corrody, the nature of which is mi- ɪtely specified. It was of no uncommon occurrence at this ɪne for pensions of meat and drink to be assigned in con- ɪleration of grants of lands. Something of a similar character ɪ have already seen in the case of Ralph de Monthermer and ɪɔr le Lardiner of Cardiff. The difference between a corrody ɪd a pension appears to be this. In the case of a corrody, an ɪowance of meat, drink, and sometimes clothing, was made to ɪfounder, or benefactor, towards the sustentation of such an ɪɔ amongst his servants as he thought fit to bestow it upon: ɪt a pension implied a sum of money, or an allowance of food, ɪɪen to one of the benefactor's chaplains for his better main- tɪance until such time as he may be provided with a benefice[2].

---

[1] He was Custos of the House or Hospital of St John, at Cambridge, now Sʾohn's College, which office he resigned in 1332 A.D. Vide Baker's *Hist. of S.John's*, Ed. Mayor, I. 52.

[2] Vide Tomlyn's *Law Dictionary*, sub voc.

In the present case the prior and convent of Anglesey declare unanimously that they will give to one poor man, who shall be chosen by the prior on behalf of the aforesaid William, every day throughout the year for ever a good repast of meat and drink, a decent cloth being placed before him, before the door of the refectory, or in the chamber of the prior before the prior, or elsewhere, in the presence of men, within the priory of the church aforesaid.

Grants of William de rderne nd Seman e Withers- eld. Twelve years after the date of this charter an inquisition "ad quod damnum" was ordered to be held by William Trussel the escheator on this side Trent relative to a proposed grant from William de Arderne, chaplain, and Seman de Wytheresfield, chaplain, of three messuages, thirty and a half acres of land, with the appurtenances in Wilbraham and Queye, and at the same time relative to the grant of William de Gosfield of twenty-six shillings and eightpence annual rent in Swaffham Prior. We have had before an instance of an inquisition of this kind in the case of the grants of Elizabeth de Burgh. The usual questions were ordered to be put, that is to say, whether it would be and what damage or prejudice to the king or others, of whom were the lands holden, by what service, of how much annual value were they, who were the mesne lords, what lands and tenements remain to the benefactors, and how and of whom holden, and whether there remain sufficient to perform all necessary services to the king and country. This inquisition, then, was held at Bottisham, before the above-mentioned escheator, on the first day of February, in the twelfth year of the reign of King Edward the Third, before the following jurors: John the son of Roger, Alan Athelward, Richard Shaleman, John Geffrey, John Picott, Ivo Gerard, Richard Pychard, Roger de Barle, John Schapman, John the son of Margaret, John Osbern, and Thomas of the Stronde. They declare, "that it is not to the damage or prejudice of the lord the king or of any other person that the lord the king should grant to William de Arderne, chaplain, and Seman de Wytheresfield (who was probably some connection of the prior), chaplain, that they might give and assign to the prior and convent the said messuages and lands in Bodekesham, Wilbraham, and Queye, and to William de Gosfield that he might give to the same twenty-six shillings and eightpence rent with the appurtenances in Swafham Prior. To have and to hold to the same prior and convent and their successors for ever in part satisfaction of twenty pounds of land and rent with the appurtenances by the year according to the true value of the same which the lord the king by his letters patent granted to the aforesaid prior and convent to be acquired as well of their own fee as of any other excepting lands and tenements which may be holden of him in chief. And they say that twenty-four acres of the land aforesaid and two messuages with the appurtenances in Bodekesham Wilburham and Queye are holden of the aforesaid prior in socage by fealty and by service of seven shillings and twopence to be paid therefrom to the same prior annually, and they are worth by the year in all issues according to the true value of the same beyond the aforesaid rent resolute twelve shillings and sixpence. And they say that one messuage and five acres of the land aforesaid are holden of the lady de Clare by fealty and by service of two shillings and sixpence to be paid therefrom annually, and they are worth by the year beyond the aforesaid rent resolute thereof three shillings and twopence. And they say that one acre and a half of land with the appurtenances in Bodekesham and Wilburham are holden of Walter de Trayly by service of three pence to be paid therefrom to the same Walter annually, and they are worth by the year beyond the aforesaid rent resolute thereof sixpence. And they say that the aforesaid twenty-six shillings and eightpence rent with the appurtenances in Swafham Prior is holden of the aforesaid prior by service of four shillings and sixpence to be paid therefrom to the said prior annually and the aforesaid rent is worth by the year beyond the rent resolute thereof twenty-two shillings and twopence. And they say that the aforesaid Prior of Anglesey, Walter de Trayly, and the lady Clare are the mesne lords &c. concerning the messuages &c. aforesaid. And they say that there remain to the same William de Arderne and Seman beyond the gift and assignment aforesaid one hundred and two acres of land with the appurtenances in Bodekesham and Wilburgham, and they are holden of the lady Clare by the service of one-fourth part of a knight's fee. And they are worth by the year in all issues four pounds. And they say that there remain to the same William de Gosfield beyond the gift and assignment aforesaid two carucates of land with the appurtenances in Swafham Prior and they are holden of the Bishop of Ely by knight's service. And they are worth by the year in all issues ten pounds. And they say that the lands and tenements remaining to the same William de Arderne, Seman, and William de Gosfield beyond the gift and assignment aforesaid are sufficient for the due performance &c. And they say that the same William de Gosfield and the heirs of the same William de Arderne and Seman may be placed in assizes jurates and all other acknowledgments whatsoever as the same William de Gosfield and the ancestors of the same William de Arderne and Seman have been accustomed to be placed in before the donation and assignment aforesaid. So that the country shall not be burdened &c. In witness whereof the aforesaid jurors &c. Given on the day and year and in the place aforesaid." Accordingly letters patent were issued witnessed by the king at Westminster on the sixth day of February 1338 A.D., authorising the afore-mentioned grants[1].

But in 1344 A.D. a further grant was made by the same William de Arderne, chaplain, and Seman de Wytheresfield, chaplain. Another inquisition "ad quod damnum" was held at Bottisham before Warin de Bassingbourn the escheator for the counties of Cambridge and Huntingdon, on the tenth of May, by the oath of Richard Skelman, John Rous, William Walkelyn, William de Laonden, Hugh Brown, John Sturmy, John Lord, Thomas Seman, John James, John Chapman, John the son of Roger the younger, and Geoffrey Rycher. The following are the answers to the questions, which were those usually put. "They say that it would not be to the prejudice &c. to assign &c. three messuages, one toft, fifty acres of land, with the liberty of a fold, and ten shillings rent, with the appurtenances in Bodekesham, Stowe, Quye, Fulburn, and Little Wilbraham. To have and to hold, &c. in part satisfaction of

---

[1] Pat. Roll. 12 Edw. III., Part I. mem. 29.

venty pounds of land or rent with the appurtenances by the
ear according to the true value of the same which the lord
he king by his letters patent granted to the same prior and
onvent, &c. And they say that one messuage and twenty
even acres of the land aforesaid with the appurtenances in
odekesham are holden of Elizabeth de Burgh, lady de Clare,
y the service of two shillings and four pence by the year and
uit to the court of the said lady in Bodekesham from three
eeks in three weeks. And they say that another messuage
ad twelve acres of land and ten shillings rent with the appur-
nances in Bodekesham and Queye are holden of the aforesaid
rior of Anglesey by the service of eight shillings to be annually
aid to the same prior therefrom. And that the toft aforesaid
ith the appurtenances in the same town of Bodekesham is
olden of Nicholas Thone by the service of eightpence by the
ear. And they say that three acres of the land aforesaid with
he appurtenances in Stowe and Queye are holden of the abbot
Ramsey by the service of one rose by the year. And they
y that five acres of the land aforesaid with the liberty of a
ld with the appurtenances in Little Wilbraham are holden of
illiam Chamberlayne by the service of fourpence by the year.
nd that one messuage and three acres of the land aforesaid
ith the appurtenances in Fulburn are holden of John de Shar-
lowe by the service of five shillings by the year. And they
y that the aforesaid messuages toft and land with the appur-
nances are worth by the year in all issues according to the
ue value of the same besides rents resolute and the services
oresaid twenty-four shillings and not more, because twelve
res of the land aforesaid lie fresh near the moor of Bodesham and Wilbraham. And they say that Elizabeth de Burgh
dy de Clare, the Prior of Anglesey, Nicholas Thone, the abbot
Ramsey, William Chamberlayne and John de Shardelowe are
e mesne lords, &c. And they say that there remain to the
me William and Seman besides the gift and assignment afore-
id two messuages and eighty acres of land with the appur-
nances in the towns of Bodekesham and Queye which are
lden of the Earl of Oxford and lady de Clare and Walter
ayly by knight's service. And they are worth by the year

beyond reprises......(?) shillings. And they say that the same tenements so remaining to the same William and Seman are sufficient for the customs, &c. In witness whereof, &c. Given on the day and year and in the place aforesaid." The letters patent authorising this grant are dated at Westminster on the ninth of June in the eighteenth year of the reign of King Edward the Third[1].

In the next year the prior and convent seem to have made further acquisitions of land from William de Arderne and Seman de Withersfield. For the Court Rolls of that year state that they paid the sum of 13s. 4d. for the right of entry into the lands of these clerks, viz. in all the lands and tenements which late belonged to Master Henry de Thrippelawe, and in one messuage and 2½ acres of land formerly belonging to John Mitchell, and in one messuage in three roods of land formerly belonging to Gilbert le Bocchere, chaplain, and in one cottage formerly belonging to Geoffrey Alezsa, and in one cottage formerly belonging to John Tone, and in 16 acres of land and 4s. rent acquired by the said William and Seman of divers tenements in Bottisham, and in 2 acres of land lying in Angerhale of the fee of the lady in Bottisham[2].

Lease of lands in Fulbourn to Robert Freborn.

Some evidence of the condition and value of the lands of the monastery may be gathered from various leases entered into at this period of its history. One such document is here cited as an instance of the way in which lands were then held: " On Saturday, the feast of the holy Margaret the virgin, in the fifth year of the reign of King Edward the Third (that is, July 13, 1331) since the conquest, it was thus agreed between Walter, the prior of Anglesey, and the convent of the same place on the one part, and Robert Freborn of Fulburn on the other ; to wit, that the aforesaid prior and convent have

---

[1] Pat. Roll. 18 Edw. III., Part i. mem. 9.

[2] It seems possible that during this year Elizabeth de Burgh was a guest at the monastery, and contributed something to their welfare. For in the accounts of Wm. Henry, bailiff of the estate at Whaddon, there occurs the following item: " Paid to the countess of Clare at Anglesey on the 8th day of March (19—20 Edw. III.), to her steward for her necessities, £33. 3s." Mention is also made of messengers going from Whaddon to Campesey, so that the site of our monastery must be the Anglesey to which allusion is made.

granted and demised, and to farm delivered, to the said Robert all the land which they have in the town and fields of Fulburn, with liberty of foldage and the meadows grazings and pastures, in any manner belonging to the said land, and with all its appurtenances. To have and to hold to the aforesaid Robert, and his executors or assigns, from the day of the making of these presents to the feast of the Blessed Michael next following, and from the said feast of the Blessed Michael to the end of eleven years next following, and fully to be complete. Rendering, therefore, annually to the said prior and convent and their successors, forty-six shillings and eight pence of silver, in the conventual church at Anglesey at two terms of the year; viz. on the feast of the Purification of the Blessed Mary the virgin, next following the day of the making of these presents, twenty-three shillings and four pence, and on the feast of the nativity of Saint John the Baptist next following, twenty-three shillings and four pence, and so from year to year, and term to term, during the term aforesaid. Doing also for the aforesaid prior and convent and their successors, to the chief lords of those fees during the term aforesaid, the services thereof due and of right accustomed. And he shall pay all prises, and royal tallages, and contributions, and all other burdens in the meantime arising therefrom, without any diminution of the said farm of forty-six shillings and eight pence. And the old upon the said land he shall maintain in every year according to the season, and the said land he shall plough, manure, lay-fallow, and re-plough as the season and the condition of the land shall require. And if it shall happen that the aforesaid Robert, his executors and assigns, shall make default for a fortnight after any of the terms appointed for the payment of the said farm, or shall contravene or neglect any of the conditions above expressed in the aforesaid agreement, the said Robert grants for himself, his executors or assigns, that the aforesaid prior and convent may enter into and retain for ever the aforesaid land with the whole of the crops being thereon, and with all the other goods and chattels found upon the said land by their own authority, without any contradiction of the said Robert or of any other person. Moreover, the aforesaid

prior and convent and their successors will warrant the aforesaid land, with the liberty of foldage, and with the meadows,
grazings, pastures, and all their appurtenances, to the aforesaid
Robert and his executors and assigns to the end of the term
aforesaid, in form aforesaid.   In witness whereof to one part of
this writing indented, remaining in the custody of the said
Robert, the said prior and convent have put the common seal
of their chapter.   And the said Robert has put his seal to the
other part, remaining with the said prior and convent.   These
being witnesses : Richard Robertot, John de Geddynges, Nicholas Tone, Thomas Ranglion, Ivo Gerard and others.   Given at
Anglesey on the day and year above written."

ase of   Another lease of a similar character, though undated, be-
enney." longs clearly to this period, as it is in the priorate of Walter de
Wytherisfield.   According to this document, the place called
"Henney," with the appurtenances in Cambridge, "lying in
length and breadth to the bank which extends from the great
bridge of the town aforesaid to the little bridge of the same
town," was demised to John de Cambridge and Joan his wife,
and Thomas and John, sons of the same John and Joan.   Rendering, therefore, for their lives annually at Easter one clove
gilliflower, and after their deaths the said Thomas and Joan
his sister, shall pay at the same feast sixpence, and after their
deaths it to revert to the house[1].   That portion of the town
of Cambridge called "Henny," as marked in the old maps,
included the block of houses situated in Silver Street and Mill
Lane, but from this account it would seem to have extended
much further down the river, if not up to the hospital of Saint
John, now Saint John's College.   The tenement of the priory of
Anglesey, called "the stone-house," was here situated, as well
as "the leather-house," and a place towards Alexhye and another at Cholleshyze, mentioned in the partial list of the possessions of the monastery in Cambridge, which has been already
quoted.

rant to   Prior Walter de Witheresfield was now dead, and was suc-
. Cha-   ceeded by Walter de Yelvedon, sacrist and canon of the house.
um of
rinkley.

[1] From transcript in Cole's MSS.

we have already seen from the licence of Elizabeth de
rgh, he was elected not by the family of De-Clare, who were
) patrons of the house, but by his fellow monks. The poverty
the house was increasing, but it is possible that it received
ne addition to its revenues about this period, recorded perhaps
a document which has long since ceased to exist, as we find
rant of a habitation within the ambit of the priory, made to
. Chanium of Brinkley, and M. his wife, by W., prior of
glesey and the convent of the same place. This house is
scribed as " that which formerly belonged to W. le Neve "
ho, it will be remembered, was so much connected with the
nvent by reason of the land which he held in Wilbraham),
vith its ambit, to wit, as it is bounded by the water on the
e side, and on the other side by a certain hedge near the
use of our carpenter." This grant was to endure for the
es of both, and they and their servants were to have the
ht of free ingress and egress, of going and returning from the
resaid house by the gates of the monastery.

Walter de Yelvedon had held office as prior for but a little *Lease to*
re than a year when, in the name of the convent, he made *John Fifere.*
ease to John Fifere of Bottisham, who was to succeed John
Schortmede as tenant of 5 acres of arable land lying in
dcherlfield in Wilbraham Magna. The term of this lease
s to be twelve years, and the rent was fixed at 11s. guarded
the usual provisos.

But in 1341 A.D. the convent received a grant from John *Grant of*
deffray of Dullingham of one penny annual rent due to him *John Madeffray.*
n John de Dullingham son and heir of Peter de Dullingham
certain lands and tenements in the town of Dullingham.
) same John de Dullingham was also named as the attorney
he aforesaid John Madeffray for the payment of one pound
vax to be paid annually. And this form of bequest was not
ommon; for we have already mentioned that on behalf of a
ement held in Westley John de Creke was also bound to
. a pound of wax for the use of the high altar in the con-
tual church.

Four years after this another charter was framed whereby *Of John de*
n de Sutton the younger of Great Wilbraham bound him- *Sutton the younger.*

self to deliver to the prior and convent a certain part of his messuage, called the Valettes in Wilbraham aforesaid, with a part of the curtilage adjoining, to wit, that which Thomas Gofornont inhabited near the tenement of Richard the Palmer, for which part the aforesaid Thomas was accustomed to render two shillings and sixpence by the year; and one rood of land lying in the middle field near the land of John Reÿgnald on the one side and the land of John de Engayne on the other side abutting on the land of John Tonild. Also he granted eighteenpence of annual rent to be yearly received at the feast of Saint Michael, to wit, of John de Sutton the elder twelvepence, and of William at the gate of the church sixpence, they being his tenants in the town aforesaid; together with ninepence from himself and certain of his tenements in the town aforesaid to be yearly received on the feast of the nativity of Saint John the Baptist. To have and to hold the aforesaid part of a messuage, &c. &c. from the feast of Saint Michael next to come after the date of the making of these presents to the end of thirty-two years next following fully to be complete, in recompence of four shillings and ninepence to the same due yearly by him and his heirs, to wit, for rent of assize by the year, three shillings and one penny, and twentypence of the farm of a certain croft, called the Valettes croft, with a certain parcel of a messuage which John Mayners a tenant of the aforesaid prior and convent inhabited in the town aforesaid near his dwelling, which croft with the parcel of the messuage aforesaid containing six perches in length and two perches in breadth he took from the same prior and convent for the annual farm aforesaid at the term aforesaid. He also bound himself to repair, when necessary, the house situated upon the aforesaid part of a messuage. This indenture is dated at Wilbraham on the Sunday next after the feast of Saint Mary Magdalen in the eighteenth year of the reign of King Edward the Third from the Conquest.

xemplifi-
ation of
axation.
    Probably the prior and convent were involved in some litigation about this time, for in 1341 A.D. by the Patent Rolls[1] it appears that at the request of the prior, Walter de Yvilden,

---

[1] Pat. Roll. 15 Edw. III., Part III. mem. 8.

an examination of the roll of the taxation of the temporalities of the house was made by royal order by the Treasurer and Barons of the Exchequer. The account of this exemplification mentions only the goods of the convent in the Diocese of Ely, and those in Wyken in the Archdeaconry of Fordham, and tallies minutely with Pope Nicholas' taxation in 1291. No mention is however made of their possessions in Barley or adjacent spots in the county of Hertfordshire. Perhaps, however, this inquiry was made for the purpose of collecting a ninth which was granted to the king in 1341 in addition to two whole tenths levied upon the goods of the clergy. The following account of Bottisham is taken from the Inquisition ordered in that year. "Hundred of Stane. Bottisham. Taxed at £36. 7s. 8d. Item. He answers concerning £16 of the aforesaid ninth of garbage, wool, and lambs delivered by Nicholas Tone, Richard Robetot, John Jemes, John the son of Margaret, and other men of the same parish, whence 48 shillings are of the portion of the Prior of Angleseye and 48 shillings of the portion of the Prior of Tunbrigg, the church of which, together with the vicarage of the same, and the portion of the Prior of Longa Villa and the portion of the Prior of Bernwell is taxed at £36. 6s. 8d. And so the same ninth does not attain to the tax by £20. 6s. 8d., nor does the value of the church in all the issues of the same attain to the tax by 21s. 8d., by reason that four-fifteenths of the land have lain fresh on account of the impotence of the tenants, and even the fortieth part of the crops have perished in the same year, to the diminution of the value of the aforesaid ninth of 24s. 8d.; and so the ninth aforesaid is worth in the same year as is above mentioned, and no more. So it is reckoned by the oath of Richard Robetot, Nicholas Tone, Richard Pichard, John de Stowe, John Kynessone, John the son of Margaret, William Marshal, Richard Porter, John de Aston, John Piket, John Geffrey, and John Gilberd before the aforesaid jury of assessors." By the same inquisition, it was found that the prior and convent paid for their temporalities in Quy with the prior of Barnwell 2s., in Wilbraham Parva with the prior of Hatfield 9s. 3d., in Swaffham Prior 12s., in Barley 8s. 4d., and in Litlington 10s. This taxation was based upon the inquisition made in 1291 A.D., and the report of it clearly shews what the condition of the country was, owing to the wars which were being carried on against France.

But though grants and benefactions were now few and far between, the convent became enriched in 1346 A.D., owing to the liberality of a priest named Thomas de Cheddeworth. This benefactor was probably intimately connected with Elizabeth de Burgh, as his name occurs as a witness to one of the documents relating to the benefactions of that lady, and one of his own charters is dated at Clare. He seems to have been a person of considerable property, for Alice de Hurst surviving William de Hurst her husband, during her widowhood, by her deed dated Monday, June 6, 10 Edw. II., did grant to Thomas de Cheddeworth, clerk, and Robert de Cheddeworth his brother and their heirs, all the manor of Caldecote near Ashwell, in the county of Hertfordshire, with the advowson of the church, &c. Thomas de Cheddeworth, clerk, by a deed dated Nov. 21st, 14 Edw. II., granted this manor and advowson to Adam de Newnham, perpetual vicar of Newnham. Adam de Newnham sold it to Hugh, abbot of the church of Saint Albans, by a deed issued in 14 Edw. II.; and to confirm the title, Sir Thomas de Cheddeworth, in consideration of £100 sterling, did discharge the abbot against the right of Alice de Hurst, her sons and daughters, by a deed, dated at Saint Albans on the Tuesday after the feast of Saint Luke, in the next year[1]. He became possessed of the manor of Frating in Essex in the following way: Alice de Frating, the only daughter and heiress of John de Frating, who died in 1308, brought the manor of Frating to her husband, Robert de Cheddeworth. This estate was settled by a fine in 1320 and 1321, being described as 200 acres of arable land, 4 of meadow, and 12 of wood, with the appurtenances in Great Bentleigh, &c. Under Henry de Ferrar or Ferrers, who died in 1343, Thomas de Cheddeworth clerk, held this manor as one knight's fee, the estate being then worth £10 a year[2]. Little further is known of the life of this man; but in 1345 A.D., an Inquisition was ordered to be taken

---

[1] Vide Chauncy, *Hist. of Herts.* p. 99.
[2] Vide Morant's *Hist. of Essex*, Vol. I. p. 449.

"ad quod damnum," to see if permission might be granted to him to give and assign to the prior and convent of Anglesey one messuage, one hundred and eighty acres of land, two acres of meadow, ten acres of pasture, six acres of wood, and fifteen shillings rent, with the appurtenances in Braughing, in the county of Hertford. Accordingly, an inquisition was taken at Barkway, in the county of Hertford, before the escheator, John de Coggeshale, on the 29th of September, in the twentieth year of the reign of King Edward the Third since the conquest over England, and in the seventh of his reign over France, by virtue of a certain writ to this inquisition, attached by the oath of Thomas Morice, John Gladesey, John de Bradenach, Alan de Reede, Maurice Caproun, Walter de Thorp, John de Grenebury, Nicholas Nethwyk,.....Spyre, Peter de Berkynge, Robert Cosyn, and Ralph at Water, jurors. And they said that it would not be to the damage or prejudice of the lord the king, or of any others, if it should please the lord the king to grant to Thomas de Cheddeworth, clerk, that he might give and assign to the Prior and Convent of Anglesey one messuage, &c., &c. in Braughyng : To have and to hold to them, and their successors for ever, in part satisfaction of twenty pounds of land and rent with the appurtenances, as the writ attached to this inquisition alleged. And they said that the messuage, land, &c. and rent aforesaid, with the appurtenances, were holden of Robert de Rokele, by the service of one penny by the year for all service, and they were worth by the year in all issues four pounds. Also they said, that the aforesaid Thomas had sufficient lands and tenements at Fratyng, in the county of Essex, beyond the gift and assignment aforesaid, for the due performance of the customs, &c. Also they said, that the aforesaid land and tenements remaining beyond the gift and assignment aforesaid, were holden of the heir of Henry de Ferrers, and were worth by the year in all issues ten pounds. This document is endorsed : "By the Chancellor. Because they have letters of licence for acquiring twenty pounds of land and rent by the year[1]." Accordingly, on the eighth day of November, 1346 A.D., letters patent were issued giving leave to the prior and con-

---

[1] Inq. ad quod damnum, 19 Edw. III. No. 31.

18—2

vent to acquire the same land[1]. Probably between 1348 and 1349 A.D., for the document is undated, a chantry was founded in honour of Sir Thomas de Cheddeworth, as appears by the following confirmation of the same :—

"To all the sons of the holy mother church, William de Pecham, rector of the church of Kingeswood, in the diocese of Canterbury, to the reverend father in Christ and Lord, the lord Thomas, by the grace of God, acting vicar general in spiritualities of the lord Bishop of Ely, now in remote parts, greeting, in the author of salvation. Know that we have inspected the letters of our beloved in Christ, the prior and convent of the monastery of Anglesey, in the diocese of Ely, of the tenor which follows. To all the sons of holy mother church to whom this present writing shall come, brother Walter, by the divine permission, prior of the monastery of the Blessed Mary of Anglesey, in the diocese of Ely, and the convent of the same place, greeting, in the Lord everlasting. Whereas, Sir Thomas de Cheddeworth graciously offered to us and our monastery, out of his pious devotion, all his lands and tenements with the appurtenances in Braghinge, in the county of Hertford, in the dioces of London. We willing, as we are induced thereto by reason of humanity, to make what recompence we are able to the sam Sir Thomas for the safety of his soul, on account of such bene fits to us granted, with one will and consent grant for us an our successors, that we will find and support for ever, at ou expense, two competent secular priests, celebrating divine ser vice every day in our monastery aforesaid, for the soul of th same Sir Thomas when he shall be deceased, as well as for th souls of John and Agnes, his father and mother, and of Rober his brother, and for the souls of his ancestors and benefactor and of all faithful deceased. So that the said priests shall b enjoined that they every day in the week shall say the office o the dead, to wit, 'Requiem eternam' and 'Placebo,' with al other things which belong to such office, and that in the begin ning of each mass the same priests shall speak and pray with high voice for the soul of Sir Thomas de Cheddeworth. More over, we will and grant that on the eve of the anniversary o

[1] Pat. Roll. 20 Edw. III. part III. membrane 17.

the said Sir Thomas in every year a solemn service shall be
performed, and on the day of the anniversary itself, when and
as often as it shall happen, except it be on a Sunday or feast-
day, and then on the next week-day following, a mass shall be
fully celebrated at the high altar in the choir, for the soul of
the same Sir Thomas, by our prior for the time being, or his
locum tenens. And that the same chantry, with the aforesaid
service and charge be inviolably continued for ever, we submit
us and our church and our successors freely in that behalf to
the compulsion of the lord Bishop of Ely for the time being,
that he by himself, or his official, or commissary, in all their
visitations in our monastery, or without if need be, they shall
diligently enquire whether the aforesaid chantry, with the
aforesaid service and charge, be duly celebrated or not. And
that the same father the bishop, or his official, or commissary,
shall compel us the said prior and convent, and our successors,
to complete the aforesaid chantry with the statute by any sentence of suspension, excommunication, or interdict whatsoever,
when need shall be in that behalf. And if it shall happen to
be in doubt whether the aforesaid chantry, with the charge and
service aforesaid, shall be sustained or not, before that at the
procurement of the heirs, or next of kin, or other friends of the
said Sir Thomas, or of the ordinaries, or of any other persons
whatever, any act of compulsion, or complaint, or process be
made against the aforesaid prior and convent or their successors in any court whatsoever, for ascertaining the truth thereof,
an oath shall be administered to the prior, subprior, and chanter
of our church for the time being in that behalf. In which
oath, if the aforesaid prior, subprior, or chanter make default,
or are in any way contumacious in taking the same, we will
and grant for us and our successors, that immediately the said
lord the bishop for the time being, or his official, or commissary,
may coerce and compel us and our successors for the defects so
apparent, according to the exigency of the case, and the contents and effect of the aforesaid obligation. Moreover, we will
and grant, that on the day of the anniversary of the aforesaid
Thomas, the same ordinance and grant be read and published
every year in our chapter, before our convent and the executors

of the will of the said Sir Thomas, his next of kin and friends,
and before any other honest persons who may have any interest
in that matter, for the information of the living and the memory of the dead; which same letters, and all the things
contained in the same as far as pertains to us, we confirm by
the ordinary authority of the said reverend father, and hold
the same equally ratified and accepted with all and singular
their said contents. In witness of all which things we have
caused these our letters confirmatory to be corroborated by
the seal of the said reverend father, which we use by his
command in this matter. Given." (Date wanting, but it is
between the years of 1348 and 1349[1].) This ordinance did not
long remain binding, for another instrument was effected
whereby the convent was released from finding one chaplain,
in the year 1351 A.D. It details clearly the then condition of
the house, and is worded as follows :

"To all to whom this present indented writing shall come,
Thomas de Cheddeworth, clerk, greeting in the Lord. Whereas
the religious men, the prior and convent of the Blessed Mary of
Anglesey, in the county of Cambridge, by their writing signed
with their common seal, are bound and obliged to find at their
own proper expense two competent secular priests to celebrate
divine service for ever in the church of Anglesey, aforesaid, for
my soul, and for the souls of my father and my mother, and
those of my ancestors, and for all souls for whom I am bound to
do good or to pray, on account of which I had given and granted
to the same religious men, the prior and convent and their
successors for ever, all the lands and tenements, rents, and
services, with the appurtenances, which I had in the town of
Braghyng, in the county of Hertford. I, moreover, afterwards
carefully considering the great and ruinous miseries which have
occurred, on account of the vast mortality of men in these days,
to wit, that lands lie uncultivated in many and innumerable
places, not a few tenements daily and suddenly decay and are
pulled down, rents and services cannot be levied, nor the advantage thereof generally had can be received, but a much
smaller profit is obliged to be taken than usual. I being

---

[1] From transcript in Baker's MSS.

unwilling that the aforesaid religious men, the prior and convent of Anglesey aforesaid, nor their successors, shall be henceforth charged with the true value of the said lands and tenements, rents and services, with the appurtenances, by the aforesaid chantry of two priests, know ye that I have granted, and by these presents have remised to the aforesaid religious men, the prior and convent of Anglesey aforesaid, and their successors for ever, the charge and support of one of the said two priests. So that from henceforth they be not bound to find but one fit secular priest to perform divine service for ever, as is aforesaid, at their own costs. So that the said priest for the time being shall receive in every year for his salary from the aforesaid prior and convent and their successors, five marks of silver at the four terms of the year, to wit, at the feasts of the Nativity of the Lord, Easter, the Nativity of Saint John the Baptist, and Saint Michael the Archangel, by equal portions, unless they are able to agree with the same priest in any other proper manner at his pleasure. In witness whereof, to one part of this Indenture remaining with the religious men, the aforesaid prior and convent of Anglesey aforesaid, I have put my seal; and to the other part remaining with me, the aforesaid religious men, the prior and convent of Anglesey aforesaid, have put their common seal. Given at Clare on the tenth day of the month of May, in the year of our Lord one thousand three hundred and fifty one[1]." So that, whereas the chaplains appointed under the benefactions of Elizabeth de Burgh were thought able to live upon six marks yearly, this chaplain was to exist upon five marks only, a clear indication of the poverty to which the house was reduced.

Following close upon the benefactions of Sir Thomas de *Grant of* Cheddeworth is a small one of John Byssop of Little Wilbra- *John* ham. By his charter he remises, releases, and for ever for *Byssop.* himself and his heirs, quitclaims to Walter de Yeveldene, prior of Anglisseye, and the convent of the same place, all the right and claim which he had, or in any way might have, in one half-acre of land which Robert Wymer held of the fee of the said

---

[1] From transcript in Baker's MSS. Vol. XL. Vide also Cole MSS. Vol. XXIII. from Bishop Lisle's Register, fol. 36 *b.*

prior, which half-acre of land lay in the Westfield of Wilburgham aforesaid, at the head of the croft of John Byssop, and it
was a headland; and in one acre of land which John de Hotone
held in the same field, of the same fee, and one head of which
abutted upon the Millway; and in the rents, homages, reliefs,
escheats, and wards, to the aforesaid lands and tenements in
any way belonging.   This charter is dated at Bodkisham, on
the Tuesday next after the feast of the Purification of the
Blessed Mary, in the twenty-second year of the reign of King
Edward the Third from the conquest[1].

[1] In 1348 Emma, abbess of Waterbeach, bound herself and the convent to
pay to the prior and convent of Anglesey 3s. annual rent for a tenement which
she held of them in "la petite curie" of Cambridge, formerly belonging to
Bartholomew Peryn.   Vide *Aug. Office Records.*

CHAPTER IX.

ELECTION OF A PRIOR.

IT was probably a year before his death when Walter de *Election* Yeveldene, Prior of Anglesey, was summoned to attend a *of Prior* *Richard de* chapter at St Paul's, by a mandate from the Bishop of Ely, *Wrattinge.* dated at Downham on the 2nd of April, 1351 A.D.; for in the next year brother Richard de Wratting was elected to become the head of the convent. An account of the confirmation of his election is given in Bishop Lisle's register. It runs thus;—"Brother Thomas, Bishop, &c., to his beloved son the perpetual vicar of Bodkesham, greeting, grace, and blessing. The constituted procurators of our beloved sons, the subprior and convent of the conventual church of Anglesey, have in our presence presented, under their procuratorial authority, brother Richard de Wrottyng, a canon of the said church, as elected to the place of prior, humbly supplicating that we would regard the said elect, as well as the business of the said election, as it pertains to us to further the same. Willing therefore to observe the canonical statutes, as well touching the procurators as the elect, we have assigned Monday next, before the feast of Saint Margaret the virgin, in the church of Over, before us or our commissary to introduce the business aforesaid, all who are required being called together. Therefore on your devotion we command you as much as we can, that as well the co-elect in that behalf, as the opposers if any such there be, should appear by name or generally, in the church of Anglesey where the election is said to be made, and that by peremptory call and summons all those who wish to oppose, should be required to appear in the church of Over before us or our commissary. Given at Somersham, on the fourth day of July, 1352, and in the seventh year of our consecration. Brother Thomas, Bishop,

&c., to his beloved master Richard Noreys, canon of Exeter, our chancellor. This was for the chancellor to confirm the election. Dated 15 July, 1352, at Somersham. Upon the certificate of the vicar that no co-elected or opposer appeared, and on proclamation at Over where the same happened, the said chancellor finding that everything was canonical, on the 17th of July at Over, confirmed the election, and gave him the care of the spiritualities and temporalities of the convent; which was ratified by the bishop the same day at Somersham, namely the 17th of July, 1352, and the same day gave him a mandate to the official of the archdeacon of Ely for his instalment, with an order for the canons and other persons of the convent to obey the said brother Richard de Wrottyng, prior of Anglesey, as their lawful prior[1]."

ant of illiam crne of asling-ld.

During the same year we have an intimation of the liberality of William Sterne, of Haslingfield, towards the monastery. For an inquisition, "ad quod damnum," was ordered to be taken relative to the proposed grant by William Sterne, of six messuages, one sheepfold, and thirty-two acres of land with the appurtenances in Barnwell, Cambridge, Bottisham, Quy, Stow, Great Wilbraham, Little Wilbraham, and Swaffham Prior; and also respecting a proposed grant of twelve acres of land, with the appurtenances in Bottisham, Cambridge, and Hinton, which Juliana, the daughter of Simon Bernard, held for her life, of the inheritance of the aforesaid William Sterne, and which, after the death of the aforesaid Juliana, was to revert to the aforesaid William and their heirs, after the death of the same Juliana, that they might remain to the aforesaid prior and convent: To hold together with the aforesaid messuages &c., in part satisfaction of twenty pounds of land and rent with the appurtenances by the year, according to the true value of the same. Accordingly an inquisition was taken at Cambridge, before Thomas de Grey, the escheator for the county of Cambridge, on the Wednesday next after the feast of the Decollation of Saint John the Baptist, in the twenty-sixth year of the reign of king Edward the Third since the

---

[1] From transcript in Cole's MSS. Vol. XXIII.

onquest, by the oath of Richard de Arderne, Henry de Mid-
elton, John Wyth, Roger de Refham, William Chapman,
imon Sherman of Cambridge, Simon Littlebode, John Wymer,
ohn Hoton, Richard Skyleman, Robert Bette, and William
[uberd, jurors. They declared that it would not be to the
amage or prejudice of the lord the king, or of others, if the
foresaid grant should be licenced to be made; that one mes_
uage and five acres of land, of the messuages and land afore_
id in Bottisham, were holden of Elizabeth de Burgh, lady de
lare, by the service of eight shillings by the year, to be
early paid to the same Elizabeth; and three messuages, and
urteen acres of land, in the towns of Quy and Bottisham, were
olden of the prior of Anglesey by the service of three shillings
y the year, to be annually paid to the same prior; and five roods
land of the land aforesaid in the town of Quy were holden
William Huberd, by the service of one penny by the year,
be annually paid to the same William; and three roods of
e land aforesaid in Bottisham, were holden of Edmund de
aus, by the service of two pennies by the year, to be annually
id to the said Edmund; and the aforesaid sheepfold in Swaff-
m Prior, was holden by John de Briggeham, by the service
one halfpenny by the year, to be annually paid to the same
hn; and two messuages and twelve acres of land with their
ppurtenances, of the messuages and lands aforesaid in Cam-
idge and Barnwell, were holden of the prior of Barnwell
d of the prior of Sempringham, by the service of nine
illings by the year, to be annually paid to the same priors
r all services; and twelve acres of land, of the land aforesaid,
the towns of Cambridge, Barnwell, and Hinton, which
liana the daughter of Simon Bernard held for her life, were
lden of Seman de Witheresfield, by the service of four
illings by the year, to be annually paid to the same Seman
r all services. And they said that the aforesaid six mes-
ages &c., were worth by the year in all issues, according
the true value of the same, beyond reprises and rents reso-
e, twenty shillings. And they said that the aforesaid twelve
res of land, with the appurtenances, in the towns of Barn-
ll, Cambridge, and Hinton, when the reversion of the same

should accrue after the death of Juliana, the daughter of Simo.
Bernard, were then worth by the year, beyond the rent
resolute, six shillings and eightpence. And they said tha
there remained to the said William Sterne of Haslingfield, i
the county of Cambridge, besides the gifts and assignmen
aforesaid, one messuage and four score acres of arable land, i
the town of Haslingfield, which were holden of Sir Rober
Scales, by knight's service, and which were worth by the yea
in all issues, according to the true value of the same, fou
pounds ten shillings. And they said that the aforesaid mes
suage &c., were sufficient for the due performance of th
customs &c. In witness whereof the aforesaid jurors &c.[1] Th
family of William Sterne removed from Haslingfield, and set
tled at Quy, where they possessed no inconsiderable property
From a branch of this family sprung Roger Sterne, archbisho
of York, and grandfather of Lawrence Sterne, the celebrate
author of *Tristram Shandy*. But this by the way. Lettei
patent were issued by the king on the 23rd of January, in th
26th year of his reign, authorising William Sterne to assig
the above-mentioned lands to the prior and convent of An
glesey, and the prior and convent to receive the same[2]. An
so, in the next year, William Sterne, by an indenture betwee
him and Richard de Wratting the prior, and the convent o
Anglesey, granted the said lands and messuages to the mona
tery. In his charter these messuages are more minutel
specified:—"one messuage and shops adjoining, and their ap
purtenances in Barnwell, which formerly belonged to Simo
Bernard, near the tenement of the late Richard Tonnot, an
one messuage with shops, built in the high street of Cambridg
late of the aforesaid Simon, and formerly of Henry de Hyr
dreskle, near the tenement of Henry de Tangmere, extendin
in breadth from the tenement of the aforesaid Henry d
Tangmere, which was formerly that of John Someri, to th
tenement formerly that of Robert de Toft, taverner, and i
length abutting at one end upon the high street, and the othe
end upon the tenement formerly of John Arnold, John Byntr

---

[1] Inq. "ad quod damnum," 26 Edw. III. No. 48.
[2] Pat. Roll. 26 Edw. III. part III. mem. 1.

nd Robert atte Corner on the last part towards the market.....
nd we, the said prior and convent of Anglesey, have given and
onfirmed all our lands and tenements in Haslingfield and
Hardeleston, with the meadows, grazings, pastures, with the
homages, rents, and services of all our tenants there, with
all other things in any way pertaining to them, to the aforesaid
William, by our present charter indented.'

But before this time the prior and convent of Anglesey *Pleas rela-*
seem to have been involved in legal proceedings connected *tive to pos-*
with their property in Barley. In the register of the abbey *Barley.*
of Chatteris is preserved a record of two pleas in the 28th and
29th year of the reign of Edward the Third before the barons
of the exchequer. Unfortunately, the MS. is so mutilated,
that it is impossible to reproduce the entire account, but the
substance may be gathered from the remaining portion of the
writing[1]. The nuns of Chatteris, who were presided over by
an abbess, were established before the Norman Conquest, and
had great possessions; and in the town of Barley, up to the
time of their dissolution, held the manor of Mincingbury, while
the convent of Anglesey held that of Greenbury of the barony
of the family of Scales[2]. In the first of these pleas it is stated
that the prior and convent of Anglesey paid as a ninth the
sum of eight shillings and fourpence, for their temporalities in
Barley, and by Pope Nicholas' taxation, which was then valid,
was reckoned at four pounds twelve shillings and fourpence,
while that of the abbey of Chatteris was reckoned at ten
pounds two shillings and tenpence, and it was found that these
temporalities were annexed to their respective houses. But
in the second of these pleas there is little more than an
exemplification of the roll of taxation, by which it appears
that the priory of Anglesey was obliged to pay the sums
already mentioned as a ninth, as well as forty-two shillings
in Shepreth, sixteen shillings in Barrington, and fifty shillings
and a penny-halfpenny in Foxton.

It will be remembered that, in consideration of the grant *Charter of*
Robert
Sterne.

---

[1] Vide Brit. Mus. Cott. MSS. Julius A. 1, fol. 176 b.
[2] Clutterbuck, *Hist. of Herts.* I. 381; Chauncy, *Do.* p. 96; Salmon, *Do.*
296.

of William Sterne, of Haslingfield, the prior and convent had parted with certain lands in that town. In 1361 A.D. Robert Sterne had come in possession of these estates, and granted an annual rent of ten shillings out of them to Richard de Arderne, William de Horwood, Sir John Reson, rector of the church of Saint Benedict, Cambridge, and Sir Richard, rector of the church of Sanford. The right to this rent these parties disposed of in consideration of one messuage in the parish of Saint Benedict, Cambridge, on the condition that Robert Sterne or his heirs should make no further claim thereto. The document, embodying these provisions, is dated at Cambridge, on the Sunday next after the feast of Saint Michael the archangel, in the thirty-fifth year of the reign of King Edward the Third since the conquest, and bears the seal of William Sterne[1].

ease to he Master nd Scholrs of orp. Ch. oll.

Part of the property of the convent in Cambridge is described in a lease to Master Thomas de Elbeslee, the elder, master of the house of Corpus Christi and the Blessed Mary, of Cambridge, of one messuage with its appurtenances lying in the Mill Street, at Cambridge, between the little lane of Henney, and a certain house of the master and scholars of the house of Saint Michael, and abutting at one end upon the ditch of the lord the king, and at the other end upon the highway of Hennell, rendering yearly three shillings of silver at two terms of the year, namely, the feasts of Easter and Michaelmas[2]. The highway of Hennell, as marked in old maps of Cambridge, occupied the same ground as what is now called King's Parade, and from this to the river was designated by the name of Henney.

ine beween P. of . and ichard tte Halle Little tokton.

During the next year, that is to say, 1363 A.D., a fine was concluded between the prior and convent of Anglesey, and Richard Atte Halle, of Little Stokton, and Alice his wife, deforciants of a corrody and land. We have before seen the nature of the corrodies with which the house was charged. But in this case the grant was a large one, as it consisted of seven white loaves, four loaves entirely of wheat, seven gallons

---

[1] From transcript in Cole's MSS.   [2] Ibid.

of ale, seven dishes of meat, fish and eggs, and four candles every week, and of two thousand turves for fuel, to be received every year from the priory, and of a certain place of land containing in length three perches and a half, and in breadth three perches, to be had in the same priory. Probably the prior was very zealous to get rid of this burden upon the house, then reduced to a state of poverty, for he gave the large sum of one hundred marks of silver to be released from this obligation.

Two years after this, we find some account of a lease of property in Barnwell to Alan Redhed, and Margaret his wife. By an indenture made between the contracting parties this land is described as "nine acres and a half lying in the fields of Barnwell, whereof one acre and a half lie in the hall between the land of the prior of Barnwell and the land of the prior of Sempringham, and abut upon Trumpeton-ford, and half an acre lies between the land of Barnwell and the land of Simon Bernard, and abuts upon Horspath, and half an acre of land lies between that of the prior of Barnwell on both sides, and abuts upon Horspath, and one acre of land lies between the land of the prior of Barnwell and that of the nuns of Saint Rhadegund, and abuts upon Hyntonwey, and half an acre which Hugh Smyth sold lies between the land of the white monks and that of the prior of Barnwell, and abuts upon the road aforesaid, and one acre and a half of land lies between the land of the prior of Barnwell on both sides, and abuts upon the same road not far from the clay-pits, and half an acre lies between the land of Thomas Joachim and the land formerly of Thomas of the Chamber, and abuts upon the land of Juliana Bernard, and half an acre of land lies between the land of the prior of Barnwell on both sides, and abuts upon Horspath, and half an acre lies between the land of the white monks and that of the nuns aforesaid, and abuts upon the land of the prior of Barnwell, and half an acre lies in the same furlong between the land of the prior of Barnwell and the land of the chapel of Steresbrog[1], and three roods lie between the land of the said prior and the land of the said chapel, and abut upon the bank,

Lease to Alan Redhed and Margaret.

---

[1] Sturbridge Chapel.

and one acre and one rood lie between the land of the prior of Barnwell and the land of the said chapel, and abut upon the bank. To have and to hold, &c., for the term of the lives of the said Alan and Margaret, and of either of them. Rendering therefore to the aforesaid prior and convent and their successors yearly, at the feast of St Peter 'ad vincula,' thirteen shillings and fourpence sterling."

ease to hn mond.

In 1368 A.D., the prior and convent entered into a lease with John Simond, of Little Wilbraham, and Margaret his wife, and Edmund their son. This was concerning " a certain messuage with a house built thereon called the Hall-house[1]; except a dove-house in the garden of the said messuage retained to the same prior and convent and their attorneys with free ingress and egress to and from the same. Reserving also to the same prior and convent, or their attorneys and tenants, free residence with ingress and egress into the house, and the messuage aforesaid, whensoever and as often as it shall please them to come there to hold their courts without the contradiction of any one. Also they have granted and to farm demised to the aforesaid John and Margaret, and Edmund their son, for their whole lives and that of the longer liver of them and their executors, for one whole year next after the death of the said John and Margaret, and of Edmund their son, sixty-three acres of arable land, with the liberty of a fold in the crofts and fields of the aforesaid town as they lie by parcels in the fields aforesaid. Rendering annually to the same prior and convent and their successors for the whole time aforesaid, forty-one shillings and twopence of silver, on the feast of Saint Peter 'ad vincula.' And they shall render to the chief lords for the aforesaid prior and convent and their successors due service, to wit, the rent of twenty-one shillings of silver, without any diminution of the farm aforesaid." And they were to keep the premises in full repair, and in case of arrear or non-payment of rent, the prior and convent were to distrain.

isitation.

Five years after this, in 1373 A.D., we have a record of a visitation which took place on the Wednesday next after the

---

[1] Formerly tenanted by Adam de Lodebroc.

east of Saint Peter "ad vincula." The account states that whereas we William de Quye the prior of the said priory ave examined each of the brethren, and found that none of hem seemed to require correction, we dismiss the said priory nd convent, and each of the brethren and canons of the said riory from this visitation by our decree[1]." A complete list *Subsidy* f the canons of the house is gathered from the subsidy roll *Roll.* f the second year of the reign of Richard the Second, from which it appears that

Brother William de Quye, prior, taxed under £100, paid	20s.
Brother William Bodekesham, subprior and canon	20d.
John de Bodekesham, canon thereof	20d.
William de Lode, canon thereof.....................	20d.
Richard Wollepyt, canon thereof	20d.
William Tiryngton, canon thereof.	20d.
John de Cambridge, canon thereof	20d.
Sum	30s.

We hear but little of the affairs of the convent till the year *Lease to* 385, when it appears that they made a lease of their property *John and* 1 Barley to John and Avise Teye and their issue. The docu- *Teye.* ient recording this is much mutilated, but we gather that ie convent demised "all the messuage with buildings and fteen acres of land with their appurtenances lately held by Villiam Sabyn in the town of Berlee, together with fifteen cres and three roods of demesne lands in............Westfield ı Adburghdane near the land of the Priory of Royston, one cre and three roods in one piece as above, two acres near the nd of John Clede .... near a .... by accident ' water, and one acre and a half in Churchfield at Meldebourns ear the land of Thomas le Hore and in Stonyden abutting oon the .... street, two acres and a half near the land rmerly of Reginald de Teye, and one acre at Stoyle near the nd formerly of Nicholas Burnel knight, and one acre in ourtebournedene · near the land......... the land formerly of

---

[1] From transcript in Baker's MSS. Vol. xxv.

John Bunt, and one acre at Elrinestub near the land formerly of
Nicholas de Wilton, and one acre and three roods in one piece
at Chalkedown near the land formerly of John Bunt, and one
acre and three roods on Lynelhib near the land now of Thomas
le Hore, and one acre and a half at Waterdene near the land of
William Undirwod .... their appurtenances. Rendering
therefore annually fifteen shillings of silver at the four terms of
the year, viz. at the feasts of Saint Andrew, the Purification of
the Blessed Mary, the Invention of the Holy Cross, and Saint
Margaret the virgin, by equal portions with reliefs of his heirs
aforesaid when they shall happen after the death of the said
John and Avise." And they were to bear the talliages of the
king and other burdens arising from those lands, and they were
to keep the premises in good repair and to inhabit the messuage,
and convey their goods there, and cultivate the land properly in
all things. Nor were they to demise the said messuage or land
to any one without the licence of the prior and convent, and
they were to do suit of court there annually; and in case of
non-performance of the articles described, the prior and convent
were to enter into the said messuage and land, and retain the
same, with goods and chattels found thereon. This document
is dated at Anglesey, on the Tuesday next before the feast of
Corpus Christi, in the eighth year of the reign of King Richard
the Second from the Conquest.

*ease to
obert
asselewe.*
· Some years after this, by an indenture dated at Bottisham
on the 4th of July, 1391 A.D., prior Wm. Quy on behalf of the
convent granted a lease to Robert Passelewe of Bottisham of
eleven acres of arable land situated in the parish above-mentioned. Of these six acres and a half of wheat lay in the northfield in two divisions on the west side of Howemere, the heads
of which abutted on the land of the same prior and convent
towards the south, and half an acre next the land of the same
Robert on the west abutting upon Craney. One rood lay next
the land of the same Robert on the south, with its head abutting upon Saxbridgemore. In the Stonefield, three roods of
wheat next the land of the aforesaid Robert on the east, with
their heads abutting upon the field of Quy: half an acre there
at Rystinghill next the land of the aforesaid Robert on the

west, the head of which abutted on the field of Little Wilbraham: three roods of wheat on the west of Godlowesmere next
the land of the aforesaid Robert, the heads abutting on the land
of the prior of Tunbridge towards the south: one half of a rood
and a half at the weir next the land of the aforesaid Robert on
the east, the head abutting upon the weir: one acre between
two half acres of the said Robert, the heads abutting on Woodway: one rood and a half near the land of the said Robert,
abutting upon Woodway: one acre lying towards Ryner, of
which two selions lie between the land of the aforesaid Robert,
and one selion on the east of the said Robert, the head abutting
upon Woodway. Also in Whitefield, two roods lying in length
next Chalpitway, one rood of the aforesaid Robert lying between the aforesaid roods, and the heads abutting toward the
south on the land of the aforesaid prior and convent: also one
rood lying beyond Newmarket-way next the land of the aforesaid Robert, the heads abutting upon Sourmore: half an acre
lying beyond the aforesaid way between the land of the aforesaid Robert, the head abutting upon the said more: six selions
lying in Shottlondes, containing three roods, one selion of the
said Robert lying between the said selions, and the heads abutting upon Sourmore: three-quarters of a rood at the Follies
between the land of the aforesaid Robert, the heads abutting
towards the west on the land of the aforesaid Robert: one rood
at Foxholes next the land of the aforesaid Robert on the east,
the head abutting on the Follies: one rood at Woodway, between two roods of the aforesaid Robert, abutting on the said
way: one rood towards the heath next the land of the said
Robert on the west, the head abutting on the said way: another
rood towards the heath next the land of the said Robert on the
east, the head abutting upon the said way: another rood towards the heath next the land of the said Robert on the east,
the head abutting on the said way. This lease was to continue
for twenty years at a yearly rent of 13s. 4d. to be paid at the
convent at Anglesey.

Although the circumstances of the house of Anglesey were
daily growing more reduced, the convent still retained its
importance amongst the other religious foundations in the diocese

of Ely; for in 1408 the prior John Huy was appointed to collect a tenth from the clergy on behalf of Thomas of Lancaster, son of King Henry IV., who had been nominated to the post of Lieutenant of Ireland. From him it seems were received twenty pounds, from the Bishop of Ely one hundred pounds, and from the laity of the county of Cambridge ninety-five pounds for that purpose[1].

But he was also called upon to decide in a case which had arisen respecting the house of S. Michael in Cambridge. This John Illeigh, alias Horwode, was perhaps some connection of William Horwode whose name occurs as a witness to the grant of William Sterne and others, and who therefore resided in Cambridge or the vicinity. But anyhow John Illeigh founded by certain annual rents a provision for two scholars and a chaplain to say mass for his soul in the house of Saint Michael in Cambridge, but as a chaplain had not been appointed, and as it was found that there was not sufficient money to maintain one, the master and scholars petitioned the pope, Boniface the Ninth, that the rents might be henceforth devoted to the use of two scholars only under this foundation, and that they might be released from finding a chaplain. They alleged that in consequence of the hardness of the times the rents set apart for this foundation had much decreased in value, nor was there sufficient probability of future increase to guarantee in years to come the fulfilment of the obligation which John Illeigh had imposed upon them; so that the pope writes to the Prior of Anglesey on the 12 Calends of December, in the fourteenth year of his pontificate, viz. 1403 A.D., commanding the prior to use his discretion in granting or not the prayer of the house of Saint Michael. Accordingly on the 12th of July, 1408 A.D., in the 2nd year of Pope Gregory the Twelfth, he writes a letter, stating that having holden an inquisition, and finding that the allegations were true, he formally releases the house from furnishing the chaplain aforesaid, upon the condition of their making special commemoration of the aforesaid John Illeigh, rector of Icklingham[2], in their daily mass. Amongst the names of the

---

[1] Cotton MSS. Titus B. xi. fol. 9 b in Nicholas, *Proc. of Priv. Co.* Vol. i. p. 313.　　　　　　　　[2] In Suffolk.

tnesses to this document, occurs the name of Nicholas
.ynard, perpetual vicar of Bottisham[1].

A break of forty years now occurs in the history of our *Grant to*)nastery, during which no intelligence of its deeds or condition *the King* 1 be found. Henry the Fifth, the valiant prince, had succeeded *and Agnes* *Jacob.*
the throne of his father, to be followed by the unlucky
.ncastrian, Henry the Sixth. To him in 1448 the convent
.nted a portion of their "Henney" property, namely, "a
:tain vacant place of land lying between a certain mill of the
.ster and scholars of the house or college of Corpus Christi
d the Blessed Mary on the south side, and another vacant
.ce of our land on the north side, and which abuts at the east
d upon our land and at the west end upon the king's highway,
d contains in breadth at the west end twelve feet of assize
d a half, and in breadth at the east end ten feet of assize,
d contains in length from east to west sixteen feet of assize[2]."
.ese two vacant "places" of land the king, by letters patent
.ued in the following year, granted to a certain Agnes Jacob
.n free, pure and perpetual alms[3]."

In the same year, 1449 A.D., the convocation of the diocese *Particu.* Canterbury met in the church of Saint Paul's, London, on *lars of a* 2 fourteenth day of November, and continued sitting till the *tenth.*
.renteenth of July next following. The prelates and clergy
.ere assembled then granted for the defence of the Church and
.gdom a tenth, consisting of two shillings in the pound. The
.lowing particulars are handed down to us relative to the
.lection of this tenth from the house of Anglesey. "Nor do
.y render account of such tenth of the spiritual goods of the
.or and convent of Anglesey within the diocese aforesaid
.y), to wit, from the church of Bodekesham, in the deanery of
.mpes, which is taxed at 40 marks, from the church of the
.ssed Mary of Swafham there which is taxed at £9. 6s. 8d., or
.ortion in the church of Harleston in the deanery of Barton,
.ich is taxed at 40s. by the year, because the goods and
.sessions of the same prior and convent are by accident and

---

[1] From a deed preserved in Trinity College, Cambridge.
[2] From transcript in Cole's MSS.
[3] Roll. Pat. 27 Hen. IV. part 1, mem. 1.

misfortune and poverty so much reduced and diminished as is
contained in the letters of certificate of the same Bishop.   Nor
do they render account of such tenth of the temporal goods of
the same prior and convent within the diocese aforesaid, which
said temporalities are taxed at £59. 3s. 7d. by the year as is
contained in the said roll of the taxation of temporalities for the
cause aforesaid noted in the next preceding particular (by
accident very much impoverished and diminished.)"

ardon.   In 1450 the prior and convent seem to have favoured in
some way the insurrection of Jack Cade, for in 32 Hen. VI. a
full pardon sealed with the great seal was delivered to John
Danyell and the convent, freeing them from the sentence passed
against them three years before, providing only that they were
not implicated in the murder of Adam bishop of Chichester,
which took place at Portsmouth, and Wm. bp. of Salisbury at
Eddington.

lection of   Until the year 1461 A.D. we have no further notice of the
ohn   affairs of the priory.   In that year however, John Daniel, the
ellys,   late prior, resigned, and the house was called upon to elect a
rior.   priest to fill the office.   The process of the election given in
Bishop Gray's register, 1457—1461, is of sufficient interest to be
given entire :—

"William, &c. to Master Richard Hanecok, our official, greeting.   We commit to you power to admit the resignation of
brother John Daniel prior of the house of the canons of Anglesey.   Given at Nounham (Downham ?) on the 8th day of
January, 1461, and in the eighth year of our consecration.

"Cecilia, mother of the most Christian Prince Edward, by
the grace of God King of England, &c., Duchess of York, to the
venerable and religious men the subprior and convent of
Anglesey, in our patronage, greeting.   On your behalf it has
been prayed us, that whereas your church is vacant by the
resignation of the prior, we would be pleased to grant to you
licence thereto directing you as much as we can that such a one
shall be elected by you as shall be devoted to God, faithful to you,
and able, proper and circumspect in the affairs of the said church.
Given at London, on the tenth day of January, in the first year
of the reign of our very dear son, King Edward the Fourth.

"To the reverend bishop, &c. your humble and devout sons, the subprior and convent of the order of Saint Augustine of Anglesey, obedience, &c. To your reverend fatherhood we make known that our conventual church being lately vacant by the resignation of brother John Danyell, the late prior, into your sacred hands and admitted by Master Richard Hanecok in our chapter house in our said priory, and there first notified on the twelfth day of January, 1461, and on the same day at ten o'clock in the forenoon, the subprior Thomas Cambrygge, a canon and president, and all the canons and brethren being in the chapter-house, they fixed on the same day for the election of a new prior, having said the mass of the Holy Ghost, and rang the bell for a chapter and meeting there again, about eleven o'clock, viz. Thomas Cambrygge, subprior, John Danyell, late prior, John Wellys, steward of the house and sacrist, William Mylys, priest, John Wrottyng and Lawrence Rede, deacons. The subprior, at the gates of the church and the door of the chapter-house, caused proclamation to be made for all to come who had voices in the election, and none appearing, he precluded all further proceedings that way: and there called these secular persons for their advice, viz. Master Richard Hanecok as a lawyer, Master Thomas Bury and Master Robert Bredon as notaries, and Master William Spencer and Master Robert Knyght priests, and M.A.'s, of York diocese as witnesses. Then the hymn *Veni, Creator Spiritus* was sung, and the general constitution *Quia propter* explained in English, and Master Richard Hanecok by their order read the admonitions and protestations against any excommunicated to have any doings in the election. Then the seculars retired from the chapter-house, but the notaries and witnesses were recalled. And the said persons beginning to consider by what means they should best proceed in the form of election, and it being discovered as by the inspiration of the Holy Ghost, without any other instigation, but unanimously, amicably, and by common consent, that without any contradiction, difficulty and delay, it would greatly please all the canons, John Wellys alone excepted, if they might elect the same brother and our fellow canon to be prior of the same priory, he being a religious, provident, discreet, and honest man, approved in the religion aforesaid for many years, remarkable and especially commended for his virtues, being thirty years of age and upwards, born in lawful wedlock and lawfully constituted in the priestly office, expressly professed in the said priory, very circumspect both in spiritual and temporal things, knowing and being well able to protect and defend the rights of the priory, against whom indeed nothing could be known to be objected, and so they the said canons suddenly and as if inspired only with one consent and will, and moved by one spirit, elected him as prior with one voice, each of them saying—the said John alone excepted—I will and elect the same John to be prior; and although those who are under the operation of the holy spirit of God are not under the law and cannot be bound by the narrow forms of right, yet of our abundant grace and for the fuller expression of our will, I Thomas Cambryge the subprior, by the command of the said convent, the said John alone excepted, choose the said John to be prior, which election they all agreed to, upon which a *Te Deum* was chanted, and Master Richard Hanecok declared the election to the clergy and the people—upon this they begged his assent to his election. Nevertheless the said elect, often excusing himself, and alleging his insufficiency, prayed delay till the second hour after the noon of the same day. When that hour had arrived the subprior went to the elect in a certain high chamber and required him instantly to give his assent to the said election, and at length after very many excuses, being unwilling as he asserted further to resist the divine will, he was overcome by our entreaties, and being in due time again asked to consent to the said election, he affirmed the same and consented thereto. And therefore we beseech your fatherhood that as the confirmation of the election and of the elect pertains to you, that you would be pleased to confirm it to him. These things were given and done in the year 1461, in the fourth year of the pontificate of Pope Pius the Second, and I, Robert Bredon, notary public, &c. was present.

"Be it remembered that the resignation was read by brother John Danyell in the chapter house on the twelfth of January, about the eighth hour in the presence of Master Richard Hanecok, L.D., official of Ely, and commissary for the admission of such resignation, there being present Thomas Bury and Robert Bredon, notaries, Thomas Lokton, John Ansty and William Alyngton, esquires. Which being done, the subprior and the chapter proceeded to the election of the future prior. Commission from the bishop to master Richard Hanecok, to confirm the election of brother John Wellys, prior of Anglesey. Given at Downham, 14th January, 1461, and in the eighth year of our consecration. On the 24th of January this election was confirmed in the conventual church of Anglesey, by master Richard Hanecok. The prior then swore canonical obedience to the bishop. And consequently master John Parmenter the official of the lord archdeacon of Ely installed the aforesaid brother John Wellys, so elected and confirmed, on the same day on which he was confirmed, in the accustomed stall of the prior, and with all his rights and appurtenances[1]."

Prior John Danyell upon his resignation received a pension from the convent, the terms of which are shadowed forth in the following document: "This bill made the morrow next after the feast of Corpus Christi in the year of King Edward Fourth the second, witnesseth, that Sir John Wellys, prior of Anglesey, with the consent and the agreement of the convent of the same place, and Sir John Danyell late prior of the same place, have voluntarily agreed and condescended that the said Sir John Danyell shall have for his pension and for all his other messuage · as it is specified afterward; that is to say, six marks in money yearly to be payed at two terms of the year that is to say, forty shillings at Michaelmas next following, and forty shillings at Easter next after, and forty shillings at Michaelmas next after that, and so forth yearly during his life at the terms afore rehearsed. Also the said late prior shall have within the same priory a chamber with a chimney next paradise garden with a chamber and a soler[2] above in the end of the same, with the sedge-house annexed thereto, and a garden with a pond in the same garden, which chamber is on the north side over the church against the end of the chapter-house going . . . . by the thorn, during

---

[1] From transcript in Cole's MSS.
[2] soler = a small room.

his life, and the reparation of the same chamber and the garden to be made and done at the cost of the house of Anglesey aforesaid. Also the said late prior shall have yearly and daily during his life into his chamber, when he is sick or diseased, in meat and drink two canons' rights[1], and when he is in good health to sit at the prior's mess, and yearly to have half a hundred fagots and a dozen tallow candles. Also the said late prior shall have a man attending upon him yearly found at the cost of the said house, that is to say, meat and drink and a yeoman's gown, the which man shall be at the election of the said late prior. Also the said late prior shall have weekly for his living to his chamber two gallons of the convent ale and three cast of bread; and the prior that now is and the house to bear all the charge and the cost that shall pertain to the engrossing these matters aforesaid. And the said late prior to sing when he is disposed in the chapel of Saint Edmund. Made at Anglesey the eighteenth day of June the year of our Lord M.CCCC.LXII.

> William Gray, Ely.
> Prior John Wellys.
> Prior John Danyell."

[1] *i.e.* a double allowance.

CHAPTER X.

GRANT OF JOHN HADDOLF.

FOR more than a hundred years we find no mention of a *Grant of* grant to the house. But in the year 1469, that is eight years *John Haddolf.* after the election of the new prior, the prior and convent entered into a lease of certain land in Stow-cum-Quy, or Stow-Queye, as it was then called, belonging to a certain John Haddolf, senior, husbandman. This is described as "five roods of arable land with all the appurtenances lying together in the field of Stowe Quye, called the Tunfield, near the land of John Ansty, esquire, on the one side, and the land of John Rook on the other side, and the north end abuts upon the stubly meadow." This lease was for the term of seventy-eight years, rendering annually to John Haddolf, his heirs or assigns, or to his certain attorney one gilliflower at the feast of Saint Peter 'ad vincula.' The indenture is dated on the twenty-second day of January, but on the twentieth day of February next following another document was drawn up, according to which the said John Haddolf released, remised, and entirely for him and his heirs for ever quit-claimed, to the prior and convent all right, estate, title, claim, &c. to the aforesaid land. And so the land remained in the hands of the monastery.

Very scanty, however, at this period are the documents *Lease of* which should exist to tell us something of the history of the *land in Westley to* establishment. Indeed we hear of nothing till the year *Robert* 1491 A.D., when the prior and convent on the twentieth day of *Ranewe.* September made an indenture with Robert Ranewe, of Westley, demising to farm to the aforesaid Robert Ranewe one messuage with a croft and certain lands adjoining thereto, near the land of the Prior of Bynham[1], and between the land late of

---

[1] In Norfolk. A cell to St Alban's Abbey, founded by Peter de Valoricis before 1093 A.D. It belonged to the Benedictine order.

Simon de Sextun, &c. This lease was for the term of eighty years, rendering to the prior and convent or their successors two shillings at the feasts of the Purification of the Blessed Mary and the Nativity of Saint John the Baptist, by equal portions[1].

John Wellys held the priorate for twenty-eight years[2]; during his incumbency Thomas Morton was appointed to fill the episcopal throne of Ely, the same bishop who took a leading part in the attempts to drain the fens, and gave his name to a cut called "Morton's leam." Great festivities were held at Ely at the installation of this prelate, at which were present the abbots of Thorney, Bury and Ramsey, and the priors of Ely, Barnwell and Anglesey. These were invited to the dinner held after the ceremony and were all present. From the account given by Bentham in his *History of Ely*[3], this dinner was on a most sumptuous scale, and the dishes such as would be calculated to satisfy the palate of the greatest epicure. All kinds of fish, flesh and fowl were to be had that the fen-country could produce, while between the courses appropriate verses were sung by the minstrels in readiness.

ohn
evering-
on, Prior.

homas
urwell,
rior.

After John Wellys, came John Leverington, in 1489 A.D.; but he did not fill the office for long; for in 14 Hen. VII., he was succeeded by Thomas Burwell. Of these two priors we have little or no account beyond the mention of their names. Thomas Burwell, however, made a lease of certain messuages and orchards in Cambridge to Wm. Gayton, prior of the house and church of St Edmund in Cambridge of the order of Sempringham canons. But after the incumbency of Thomas Burwell, the election of a new prior fell to the Bishop of Ely[4], and

eorge
olland,
rior.

George Holland, then Prior of Stoneleigh, in Huntingdonshire, was chosen to fill the office in 1508 A.D. His incumbency

[1] From a document transcribed in Cole's MSS. Vol. xviii.

[2] Among the Min. accounts (*Misc.* Vol. iv. $\frac{29}{41}$), are the rolls of the courts held by this prior at Wilbraham in the years 2—11, Ed. IV. They contain, however, no items of special interest.

[3] p. 179, Ap. p. 36.

[4] Vide Cole MSS. Vol. iv. p. 11 b. Possibly Cole is in error here, for John Leverington became Prior of Barnwell, according to Dugdale, on Feb. 14, 1489. Vide *Mon. Angl.* Vol. vi. p. 84.

lasted seven years, and after his resignation he was awarded a
pension, as appears from the following document:—

"In the name of God. Amen. We having heard, seen,
and understood the causes before us, Thomas Pellys, Doctor of
Laws, Commissary of the Lord Bishop of Ely, specially deputed,
rightly and lawfully urged in the cause within written touching
a certain annual pension assigned by us by the ordinary authority of the said reverend father of the fruits and possessions of
the monastery of the Blessed Mary and Saint Nicholas of
Anglesey, to Sir George Holland, late prior there, the discreet
man Edward Haynes, a notary public, appearing before us and
exhibiting his procuration for the said George in the presence
of the honest man Master Robert Chapman, a notary public,
procurator of the prior and convent, prayed a certain pension
to be assigned to him and on his behalf, to wit, to Sir George
Holland, of the goods of the monastery aforesaid."

Upon which the commissary proceeds to determine that,
having thoroughly examined the case, he found Sir George was
regularly professed in the order of Saint Augustine, and had been
canonically elected Prior of Anglesey, which office he had resigned into the sacred hands of James, Bishop of Ely, and had by
his proctor intreated the then Bishop of Ely, Nicholas, to be
pleased to assign a proper pension from the rents of the monastery.

"We therefore, Thomas Pellis, commissary, &c. having considered the quality, condition, estate and position, as well as the
labours, anxieties, and cares of the said Sir George, which he bore
and sustained for the benefit of the said monastery during the
time of his incumbency thereof; and lest the said Sir George, to
the discredit of the clergy, should be defrauded of, and not possess the necessaries of life, contrary to the dignity and position
of the degree of priest, we ordain and assign in the place and
by the authority of the said reverent father, a certain annual
pension of ten marks annually to be paid to the same Sir
George, with the consent of the Prior and Convent of Anglesey,
for the support of the same Sir George during his natural life.
To be paid to the same Sir George, in the church of the Holy
Trinity at Cambridge, at the four usual terms of the year, &c.
We admonish also the said prior and convent, that they and

their successors shall within the space of fifteen days immediately following the aforesaid feasts pay the said quarterly
payments, or that the said Sir George might enter possession
and pay himself, &c.[1]."

*John
Barton,
Prior.*
Upon the resignation of George Holland, John Barton was
elected prior, but he only continued to hold office for a very
short time; for within a short time Queen Catherine writes to
the sub-prior and house, commanding them not to elect a prior
in the room of John Barton resigned, without her orders[2]. He
was succeeded by William Seggewicke, a canon of Barnwell,
who was ordained acolyte in 1488 A.D., sub-deacon in 1490 A.D.[3],
and became vicar of Waterbeach in 1509 A.D.[4]. The process of
his election is given us in Bishop West's register, and was as
follows :—

"On the fifteenth day of February, 1515, in the fourth indiction, in the third year of the pontificate of the most serene
lord the Pope Leo the Tenth, before the lord bishop sitting in
judgment in the church of Wilburton in a certain business of
the confirmation of the election made in the conventual church
of the canons regular of Anglesey of Sir William Seggewyke a
canon regular of Barnwell, elected as prior or pastor of Anglesey, there appeared the venerable men Sir William Swyfte
subprior of Anglesey and master Thomas Falke bachelor of
laws, procurators of the religious men the president and chapter
of Anglesey, &c. The tenor of whose procuration is as follows:

"Be it known to all men that we Sir Richard Hoore president of the monastery of the Blessed Mary and Saint Nicholas
of Anglesey and the convent of the same place, Sir William
Swyfte subprior and Master Thomas Falke our procurators
&c. Given in our chapter-house the 12th February 1515.
Which procuration being read and admitted by the lord, there
appeared before the lord John Bewyster called the summoner
of the diocese of Ely by virtue of a citatory mandate to him
directed. The tenor of which mandate is as follows:—

---

[1] From transcript in Cole's MSS. *Bishop West's Register.*
[2] Vide *Calendar of State Papers*, Domestic series.
[3] Cooper, *Ath. Cant.* Vol. I. p. 51.
[4] Clay's *Waterbeach*, p. 59.

"Nicholas, Bishop &c. to John Brewster and John Langham, learned men, greeting, &c. on behalf of the religious men, &c. We therefore charge and command you as much as we can that any opposers whom you may find and all other persons by a public edict of citation to be publicly propounded at the doors of the convent church where the said election should be celebrated, so that if any one should wish to elect any in opposition to the person chosen or to oppose the form of election, they should be cited to appear before us in the church of Wilburton on the 15th day of February before noon, &c. Given at Somersham on the 28th of January 1515, and in the first year of our consecration. And because we have not our seal at hand, therefore we have ordered it to be made good by appending the seal of our Commissary.

"Then John Brewister certified that he had executed the mandate, and no one appeared to oppose anything concerning the election. Upon which Master Thomas Falke, the procurator for the convent, exhibited the decree of the election, the tenor of which follows :—

"To the reverend lord the bishop &c., William Swyfte subprior and the convent &c., obedience &c. To your reverend atherhood we bring information that our conventual church being lately vacant by the free surrender of Sir John Barton the last prior into the sacred hands of the reverend William, Archbishop of Canterbury, to whom all ecclesiastical jurisdiction belongs when the see of Ely is vacant, and to us was committed the care of electing a new prior by the most excellent lady the Lady Catherine Queen of England and France and Lady of Ireland, the foundress of the same convent, we William Swifte subprior, Sirs Richard Hoore, Roger Sporle the steward, Robert Dullingham the sacrist, Simon Hullocke the kitchener, John Boner, Thomas Hancock, Christopher Hobly, and William Netton, canons regular of the said monastery of the order of Saint Augustine, expressly professed therein in sacred things, and being of age, and lawfully constituted in the priestly office on the sixteenth day of December, 1515, in the fourth indiction the third year of the most blessed lord pope Leo the Tenth assembled in our chapter-house, and have arranged concerning

the settlement of the day on which the election should be
made. Thence to the seventeenth of December by the subprior, with the consent of all assembled in the place aforesaid.
Saturday, to wit, the twenty-second of December at ten o'clock
was assigned for the election of the prior. The subprior also
appointed Sir Richard Hoore, canon of Anglesey, to cite Sir
Thomas Hawkyn, John Byrd, and William Proose, canons of
Anglesey, who were absent. And consequently the subprior,
by the consent of all, Sir Richard Hoore alone excepted, caused
all the canons by our same brother, Sir Richard Hoore, to be
cited in the stalls of the choir, and also at the door of the chapter-house, to be present with us on the said day and place.
On which day, the twenty-second of December, a mass of the
Holy Ghost being first solemnly celebrated at the high altar,
we the canons, forming the convent and meeting at the striking of the bell in the chapter-house, the grace of the Holy
Ghost was invoked by singing the hymn "Veni, Creator Spiritus." Then the cause of the chapter was declared at our
request by the venerable man, Master Thomas Pellys, doctor of
laws, commissary, and usual official of the Lord Bishop, whom
all the canons received, as our director and adviser, to direct
and advise us touching anything to be done in such election,
and Masters Robert Chapman and Thomas Falke, notaries public, to testify and reduce into writing all things done and had
by us, as well as Masters John Ireland, bachelor of sacred theology, William Rede, bachelor of laws, and Thomas Stacy, notary
public, were chosen to witness and bear evidence to the truth
of those things which should happen to be done in their presence touching the said matter.

"Then Sir Richard Hoore exhibited the citatory mandate
which he had executed, and could not find the said three
absent canons anywhere in the convent, wherefore he had at
the usual places publicly cited them to appear on the day
of election. Immediately after this all the present canons in
the chapter-house, when the absentees were again cited, and
not appearing, they were declared ' contumaces.'

"Then Dr Pellys read the licence of election from Queen
Catherine, dated 'at my lord's manor of Greenwich the twen-

tieth day of November, in the seventh year of the reign of my
Lord Henry the Eighth. Then the subprior read the moni-
tions against any suspended or excommunicate persons inter-
fering in the election, advising all such to get absolved, that
the election might not be delayed. Then, there remaining
none in chapter-house but the canons and the aforesaid seculars, Dr Pellys read to the electors the constitution 'Quia
propter.'

"After the reading of which, and no one immediately intervening with any proposal, communication, or interval for the
election of any person, or touching the manner and form of
such election, Sir William Swyfte the subprior nominated the
religious man Sir William Segewyke, a canon of the order of
Saint Augustine, and expressly professed of our profession, in
the monastery of Saint Giles of Barnwell, as a liberal, provident and discreet man, born in lawful wedlock, of full age,
and duly constituted of the order of priests, favourably commended as to life, manners and knowledge, circumspect in
spiritual and in temporal things, knowing and determining to
defend and protect the rights of our monastery—as prior of
our said monastery of Anglesey—and chose and approved him
hereto. Which being so done by him, immediately we the
other canons, not one of us objecting, but suddenly and at the
same time rising from our seats in the said chapter-house, and
no proposal, or act, or fact, intervening for the election of any
person as our prior, but without any interval, and as is verily
believed, inspired by the grace of the Holy Ghost, peacefully elected the same Sir William Seggewyke as our prior,
with one will, one determination, and one voice. And consequently, we committed to our subprior our authority, that he,
both in the name of himself and of us, should publicly choose
the same Sir William Seggewyke before us, as his and our
choice, &c.

"The election being made, we the canons chanting the
canticle, 'Te Deum Laudamus,' in a solemn manner, and proceeding from the said chapter-house, and finding our said
elected in the cloister of our conventual church, and bringing
him to the greater altar of the same church, and at length

H. B. 20

such canticle and prayer being ended, and the suffrages taken
touching the said elected by the subprior chanting, immediately, master Thomas Pellys publicly declared, in the vulgar
tongue, the said elected person to the clergy and people, assembled in the said church by the sound of bells. Then in
the chapter-house they appointed Sir Richard Hoore to be
their procurator, to intimate the election to the elect.

"On the same day, about the third hour after noon, the
same procurator went to Sir William Seggewyke, our elect, in
a certain high chamber, on the north side of our church, and
asked him whether he would consent to the election they had
made of him, which request being made, the said elect declared
to our procurator that he wished to deliberate what he should
do touching so great and arduous a matter. Afterwards, at
about the fourth hour, the procurator again went to him,
earnestly and frequently asking him to consent to the election;
at length the elect consented to such election, at about the
fourth hour, being unwilling to resist the divine will, &c.

"All which things we intimate to your reverend fatherhood,
humbly supplicating you to approve and confirm this our
decree of our election, and the said election itself, and the
person of our said elected by your ordinary and pontifical
authority, and that you will be graciously pleased to bless the
said elect, and impose the hands of blessing upon him... These
things were given and done as above. Given as to the sealing
thereof, on the 18th of January, 1515.

"And I, Robert Chapman, of the diocese of Ely, public
notary, by the apostolic authority &c., was present &c. And I,
Thomas Falke, bachelor of laws, of the diocese of Norwich,
public notary, by apostolic authority &c., was present &c.

"Which same decree being exhibited and read by the command of the bishop, master Falke, the procurator aforesaid,
demanded that any one who wished to object to the aforesaid
election, should be first publicly summoned before the lord,
and then at the doors of the church aforesaid, which was
granted, at whose petition the lord publicly caused all cited
persons to appear, by John Langham his apparitor general,
and none appearing, the bishop declared them contumacious.

"Then the said proctor exhibited from the convent of Anglesey a summary petition, or article, reciting the whole proceedings to the bishop, desiring him to ratify and confirm them, which being read to the bishop and admitted, the said procurator desired a certain space, which being granted, he exhibited the instruments, letters, and other acts relating to this business, and first, the letters of licence from Queen Catherine, sealed with her great seal, and the instrument of resignation by brother John Barton, with the decree of the election.

"Then follows the licence of election as before. In the name of God. Amen. By this present public instrument, let it be known to all men, that in the year 1515, in the third indiction, and in the third year of the pontificate of the lord the Pope Leo the tenth, on the last day of August but one, at the first hour after noon, before the venerable man Master William Fayrhayr, doctor of laws, spiritual vicar of the reverend Lord William, Archbishop of Canterbury, primate of all England, and legate of the apostolic see, to whom all spiritual jurisdiction, which would belong to the see of Ely when occupied, now belongs, the said see being vacant, in the church of Saint Michael, Cambridge, and in the presence of my notary and witnesses, the venerable man John Barton, Prior of Anglesey, with bended knees, and his hands joined in the hands of the aforesaid Master William Fayrhayr, made his resignation, and resigned his said priory, &c., there being present, Master John Eccleston, professor of sacred theology, Master Richard Henrison, &c. And I Geoffrey Wharton, clerk of the diocese of Carlisle, notary public, by apostolic authority, &c., was present. After this, the proctor or the convent begged the bishop to ratify and confirm the whole business; which the bishop did by a sentence of confirmation that all the proceedings were canonical and right; upon which Sir William Seggewyke, the prior elect and confirmed, swore canonical obedience to the bishop.

"Which being so done, the same reverend father received the foresaid elect and confirmed with the kiss of peace, and directed him to be inducted and installed into the real possession of the said monastery, by his archdeacon, or official, by his decree and letters which he directed to his archdeacon or official, to this effect: "Nicholas, bishop, &c., to our beloved son in Christ, our Archdeacon of Ely, or his official, holy greeting and bless- ing. Whereas we have been informed, touching the election made in the conventual church of Anglesey, of Sir William Seggewyke, late canon in the priory of Barnwell, as Prior of Anglesey, &c., we commit and direct to you that as much as you can, you induct and install the said person so elected, and by us confirmed and blessed in the possession, &c. Given at Somersham, &c. Therefore these things being so done, the lord solemnly impressed the gift of benediction upon the afore- said prior, so elected, and confirmed, and really blessed him[1]."

After this notice, given in Bishop West's register, we hear no more of Prior William Seggewyke. But a prior named William Reche held a court at Little Wilbraham on the 28th of March, 1576. It is exceedingly improbable that William Seggewyke resigned within three months of his appointment; for we should most likely have had some evidence of so un- usual an occurrence; and so we must, I think, conclude that he is the same person called subsequently by the name of William Reche, taking his name from his native place in the hamlet of Swaffham Prior. But at the same time, there is not enough direct evidence to confirm this, and the letters P. W. R. on the existing stone door-cases, give us no idea whatever of another name by which Prior William Reche was called[2]. But William Reche, who was mentioned as prior in 1525 A. D., must have had many anxieties in his administration of the affairs of the monastery. For monastic institutions were on the wane, and rumours of dissolutions had doubtless gone forth. Bottisham must have been one of the earliest parishes in which the change that was soon to take place must have been talked of freely. For the monastery of Tunbridge, which had large possessions in Bottisham, was dissolved in January, 1525 A. D., and an inquisition had been held, in order to shew exactly of what its property consisted. Tunbridge priory was dissolved

---

[1] From transcript in Cole's MSS.
[2] Since the above was written I find, from the records of the nunnery of Swaffham Bulbeck, that the family of Seggewicke of Reach was much connected with the latter monastery.

with seventeen others, because its circumstances were reduced, and Wolsey by that means could lay his hand upon it : but its annual revenue attained to a greater sum than that of Anglesey ; and it seems strange that the latter monastery escaped the same fate. This might have been owing to the exertion of Queen Catherine, its patron and foundress, in its favour.

While thus men's minds must have been fully occupied in considering the future of the ecclesiastical affairs of the country, it is natural to look for some indication, in the history of the parish, of the esteem in which the house of Anglesey was held. In this however, we are disappointed ; and we can find nothing which bears on the opinion then entertained of the internal condition of the house, of its hospitality, its morality, or of its connection with the outside world. There is but one exception to this, viz. the evidence afforded us by the bequests to the convent, contained in contemporaneous wills of the parishioners. These however are few : from 1515 A. D., down to the time of the dissolution, there are but seven, and the sums bestowed in proportion to the legacies are small. Two of these bequests are however worthy of remark. Simon Shereman in his will, made in 1527, bequeaths to the Prior of Anglesey, *to help to hallow the churchyard,* 6s. 8d. But it does not specify what churchyard, whether at Bottisham parish church, or at Anglesey, for Anglesey too had its cemetery. Probably however it was the former, for the monastery held the rectorial tithes of the parish church, and this may have been some addition then made to the burial ground already in use. In the same year, John Wright gives legacies to the Prior, to Sir Boner, and to every canon of the house, so that we may infer that Sir Boner held rank next after the prior, and therefore was subprior, though this fact is not mentioned elsewhere. In 1584, John Boner, Bonar, or Bonyard, as his name is written, had succeeded to the priorate, when he received a mandate from Bishop Goodrick, dated the 15th of September in that year, giving notice of his design of visiting the monastery on the 26th of September. The certificate of the execution of the mandate from the prior, is dated on the 20th of September, and contains a list of the canons of the house. These were :—

Sir John Boner, prior.

Sir Robert Dullyngham, subprior.

Sir William Swyfte,
Sir Richard Hore,
Sir Simon Hullock, } priests.
Sir John Halyday,
Sir WilliamNorth,

John Thorne, } noviciates professed[1].
John Bunt,

This is the latest list we possess of the brethren in the convent, and it is probable they continued to inhabit the building until the time of the surrender.

Valor Ecclesiasticus. The next year was marked by the " valor ecclesiasticus," an inquisition, in order to discover, for the purpose of taxation, the value of all and singular the castles, demesnes, manors, lands and tenements, rectories, vicarages, chantries, free chapels, and all other possessions as well spiritual as temporal, to any spiritual or other kind of persons belonging, having any spiritual promotions. In this document is to be found the following items respecting the Priory of Anglesey :—

"Diocese of Ely.

County of Cambridge.

Deanery of Campes.

Bottisham, rectory appropriated to the priory of Anglesey.

The priory of Anglesey, and the temporalities and spiritualities by the year are worth £124. 19s.

Deanery of Walsingham, in the archdeaconry of Norwich, in the diocese of Norwich.

Priory or monastery of Walsingham.

Richard Vowell, prior there.

Rent resolute, out of the manor of Walsingham.

Colynghams by the year, to wit, to the Prior of Anglesey, in the county of Cambridge, 73s. 4d.

Abbey of Nutley. Annual pension from the priory of Anglesey, £4. 13s. 4d.

Newenton Longville, co. Oxon, pension from the priory of Anglesey, proceeding from the church of Bottisham, 100s."

[1] From transcript of Bishop Goodrick's register in Cole's MSS.

During these latter years we have some record of various Courts held at Wilbraham. courts held at Little Wilbraham, by the prior of the house and others. These were as follows :—

"The first court of Master Richard Bryndholme, Bachelor of Laws, first chaplain of the perpetual chantry in the church or chapel of the Blessed Michael, of Great Ricote, in the county of Oxford there established, holden on the 16th day of May, in the twentieth year of the reign of King Edward the Fourth.

"The jury presented that the Prior of Anglesey and Richard Foster owed a suit of court.

"Court of the prior and convent of Anglesey, holden on Tuesday next after the feast of the Apostles Simon and Jude, in the twenty-first year of the reign of King Edward the Fourth. John Anstey, esquire, steward.

"At the court held for the said prior and convent 16 Edw. IV., it was presented that John Hancok atte Crosse had alienated fourteen acres of land to different persons, among whom Thomas Bradle, Rector of Wilbraham, was one: and 19 Edw. IV., Mr Robert Morton being steward. On the 19th of June to that court comes Thomas Bradle, the rector of the parish church there, and did fealty to the lord for four acres of land lying in parcels in a certain field called Westfield. And on Tuesday before the feast of Corpus Christi, 21 Edw. IV., the jury say upon their oath that Thomas Draper, of London, holding the lands of the late rector there owes suit of court, &c. And on Tuesday after the feast of Saint Faith the Virgin, 22 Edw. IV., to this court comes the aforesaid Thomas Cole, and does to the lord fealty for three acres and a half of land, formerly John Reman's, and afterwards Thomas Bradley's, clerk, &c.

"Court of Sir Thomas Burwell, Prior of Anglesey, and of the convent of the same place, holden there on the fourth day of the month of June, in the fourteenth year of the reign of King Henry the Seventh.

"The same prior held a court also on the 9th of October, 16 Hen. VII.

"Court of Sir George Hollande, Prior of Anglesey, and the convent of the same place, holden there on Friday next after the feast of Saint Thomas the Apostle, in the twenty-fourth year of the reign of King Henry the Seventh.

"Sir Gilbert Talbot, Knt. was commanded to be here at the next court to do fealty to the lord for the lands late Thomas Sewall's, namely, for sixty-two acres which he holds of the lord, and renders by the year 10s. 4d., and suit of court[1].

"Court of the prior and convent of Anglesey holden there on Monday the twenty-fifth day of June, in the seventh year of the reign of King Henry the Eighth.

"The jury say upon their oath that Sir Gilbert Talbot, Thomas Taylour, John Hancock, Thomas Sewall of Wilbraham, the tenants of the lands of William, and William Oliver are suitors to the court and owe suit, &c.

"On this day Sir Richard Hoore, Sir William Swifte, and Sir William Letton, monks of the priory aforesaid, took full and quiet possession and seisin of one tenement late in the tenure of William Hankok, &c.

"The first court of William Reche, Prior of Anglesey, holden there on the twenty-eighth day of the month of March, in the seventh year of the reign of King Henry the Eighth.

"The said Prior William Reche held another court on the eighteenth of September, in the ninth year of King Henry the Eighth, when the jury found that Sir Gilbert Talbot Knt., who held of the lord divers lands and tenements, died since the last court, and it is not known yet who is his next heir.

"John Wood, gentleman, steward.

"At another court held by the same Prior William Reche, on the 22nd of September, 16 Hen. VIII., the jury say upon their oath that Sir Gilbert Talbot, Knt., and the guardian of the light of the Holy Sepulchre, gave to the lord for a fine this day for releasing their suit of court, each of them as marked over their head.

"The same Prior William Reche held a court on the 28th of September, 17 Hen. VIII.

---

[1] Vide Claus. de anno 44 Edw. III. mem. 2, and inq. post mortem, 22 Ric. II. Vol. III. p. 16, where he is stated to have of the priory of Anglesey 100s. rent as parcel of the possessions of the manor of Newenton.

"At the court of John Hind, one of the King's serjeants-at-law, there holden on the eighth day of December in the thirty-second year of the reign of King Henry the Eighth, it appeared by the homage that Thomas Ward who held one cottage of the Lord of the Manor, &c.

"At the first court of the Lady Ursula Hynde, widow, there holden 16 June, 5 Edw. VI. &c.[1]"

[1] From transcript in Cole's MSS.

CHAPTER XI.

DISSOLUTION.

THERE is no account still extant of any formal surrender of the monastery into the hands of the king; but it must have taken place somewhere between the 30th of January, 1535 A. D., the year of the "valor," and the 4th of February, 1536, for this latter is the date of the act for the annexation to the crown of certain dissolved monasteries, of which Anglesey was one. It is not probable that any violence was offered, for the priory of Tunbridge had surrendered, and we do not find amongst the parishioners much evidence of attachment to the conventual establishment of Anglesey; for in the last list of canons we find but one name of a Bottisham family, that of John Bunt, and he was but a noviciate.

It is natural to enquire, what was the fate of those who were called upon to surrender house and home. On the twentieth day of October, in the sixth year of the reign of King Edward the Sixth, letters patent were issued to ....., Knight, Philip Paris, Esquire, and Thomas Rudstone, and George Eden, gentlemen, directing them to enquire what persons were receiving pensions from religious property that had been confiscated. And in a book containing the names of such persons we find:— "Anglesey, late priory—To John Boner, late prior there, by year £20." His name also appears in the certificate of the said commissioners. The name of Boner, Bonyard, or Banyard, is still found in the parish of Horningsey. But some of the canons of the house seem to have been appointed to the incumbency of parish churches in the vicinity. John Boner, the late prior, was presented in July 1538 by Sir Ed. North to the rectory of Brinkley[1], while Simon Hullocke, who was the son of

---

[1] Vide Baker MSS., Harl. MSS. No. 2043, fol. 57. He was alive in 1553 A.D. Vide Baker MSS. Vol. xxviii. fol. 150, and Webb MSS. fol. 124.

John Hullocke, of Quy, became parish-priest at Swaffham Prior, St Mary, the advowson of which belonged to the monastery[1]. This office he held in 1548 A. D., but probably died soon after. Robert Dullingham probably continued to reside in the parish of Bottisham, for his name occurs as a witness to the will of John Manning in 1540 A. D., and he had a legacy of 20d. from John Hasyll, of Swaffham Bulbeck, in 1543. As he was admitted "ad primam tonsuram" in 1499 or 1500 A. D., he was probably of a ripe age when he died[2]. William Swyfte, too, must have been old at the dissolution, as he was ordained deacon in 1491-2, and did not probably long survive. His name does not occur again. His contemporary was Richard Hore, who is never again heard of, nor were John Halyday, nor William North. John Thorne and John Bunt, who were only noviciates, may have forsaken the habit of religion. The latter *Family of* belonged to a family very numerous in the parish, the names *Bunt.* of many members of which appear in contemporaneous wills, and subsequently in the parish registers[3]. So many John Bunts are to be found, that it is difficult to speak with certainty of the death of the noviciate. One John Bunt died in 1569, of whom nothing further is known. The will of another was proved in 1547 A. D. He was probably brother of Thomas Bunt, who in 1552 A. D. was appointed with others to have the custody of the plate of Bottisham church. A John Bunt married and had one son and four daughters, and another John Bunt, who died in 1605-6, had by Ellen his wife seven sons and three daughters; but as there is no account of the years between the last of the wills in which the name occurs and the first year of the parish registers, it is impossible to form an accurate notion of the pedigree of this family.

The minister's account for the year 27-28 Henry VIII., *Property* gives us the best idea of the property of the monastery after *of the Mo-* the dissolution. It will therefore be stated entire:— *nastery at the Dissolution.*

---

[1] Vide Wills, from Ely registers, Cole's MSS. Vol. LX.

[2] Among the pensions given in 1 Mary, a Rob. Dullingham received 25s. for the free chapel at Shelford Magna.

[3] Thomas Bunte de Botisham occurs in a list of gentry, A. D. 1433. Vide Fuller's *Worthies*, ed. 1840, Vol. I. p. 245.

"*The manor of Anglesey with the site of the late priory there*. The account of William Burnell, bailiff there for the time aforesaid.

Farm of the site of the late priory there, with the demesne land to the same pertaining]. The same renders account of £31. 11s. 11¾d. of the farm of the site of the late monastery there, with 400½ acres of land, and 1 rood of arable land, 180 acres of sterile land, 30 acres of meadow, 12 acres of underwood, and 3 acres called Ox Acre, late in the cultivation and occupation of the prior and convent aforesaid, with the late priory so appraised and rented by the tenants there[1], and let to farm to Sir John Hynde, serjeant-at-law, paying therefore at the two terms of the year equally by the year.

Sum £31. 11s. 11¾d., examined.

Bottisham. And of £18. 14s. 7d. of the rents and farms there by the year, as appears by the rental of the parcels thereof made, and shewn and examined upon this account.

Sum £18. 14s. 7d., examined.

Longmeadow. And of £8. 12s. 6d. of the rents and farms there by the year, as appears by the said rental.

Sum £8. 12s. 6d., examined.

Lodestreet. And of 56s. 8½d. of the rents and farms there by the year, as by the said rental more fully appears.

Sum 56s. 8½d., examined.

Little Wilbraham. And of £10. 7s. 4d. of the rents and farms there by the year, as appears by the rental aforesaid.

Sum £10. 7s. 4d., examined,

Great Wilbraham. And of 7s. of rents at will there by the year, as by the same rental.

Sum 7s., examined.

Stowquye. And of 65s. of the rents and farms there by the year, as by the said rental fully appears.

Sum 65s., examined.

---

[1] These are stated afterwards to have been: Henry Barnard, Thomas Wren, John Monsey, William Webbe, Robert Bridekyrke, John Wood, Bartholomew Bangold or Bangolfe, and Thomas Tomsonne. Robert Bridekyrke was parish priest, and the names of the rest with their descendants occur repeatedly in the parish registers.

Barnwell. And of £4 of the rents and farms there by the year, as by the rental aforesaid more fully appears.

Sum £4, examined.

Hynton. And of 2*s.* of free rent there by the year, as appears by the same rental.

Sum 2*s.*, examined.

Little Thurlowe. And of 2*s.* 3½*d.* of rents at will there by the year, as in the rental aforesaid fully appears.

Sum 2*s.* 3½*d.*, examined.

Swaffham Bulbeck. And of 4*s.* of the rents of customaries there by the year, as appears by the rental aforesaid as above.

Sum 4*s.*, examined.

Swaffham Prior. And of 14*s.* of the rents and farms there by the year, as appears by the rental aforesaid shewn and examined. Sum 14*s.*, examined.

Wykes[1]. And of 30*s.* of the farm of a tenement called Thornhall there, with all the lands, meadows, grazings, and pastures, with all and singular their appurtenances, as Robert Fletcher lately occupied the same, and now by Sir Leonard Messynger and his assigns, by indenture dated 10th day of October, in the 27th year of the reign of King Henry the Eighth, for the term of forty years, to be paid at the feasts of the Annunciation of the Blessed Virgin Mary and Saint Michael the Archangel equally[2]. And the aforesaid Leonard and his assigns shall well and sufficiently repair the said tenements, with all the houses built thereon, and shall sustain and maintain the same in all things, at their proper costs and expenses, during the term aforesaid, and the same, sufficiently repaired, shall give up at the end of their term. And, moreover, the aforesaid Leonard and his assigns will annually pay, or cause to be paid, to the lord of Wykes aforesaid, for a certain rent issuing out of the land aforesaid, 8*s.* 4*d.*, as in the indentures aforesaid is more fully contained—this year being the first of his term.

Sum 30*s.*, examined.

---

[1] Now called Wicken.

[2] This lease appears to have been made by the crown, and therefore the dissolution must have taken place before October, 1535 A. D.

Fulborne. And of 40s. for the farm of all the lands and meadows of the said late priory, with the appurtenances, called Anglesey lands, lying in Fulborne aforesaid, with all and singular their appurtenances, by Sir Nicholas Woodd and his assigns, by indenture dated the 24th day of January, in the thirteenth year of the reign of King Henry the Eighth, for the term of forty years, to be paid at the terms of the Purification of the Blessed Virgin Mary and Saint Peter ad vincula by equal portions, as in the indentures aforesaid is more fully contained—this year being the 16th of his term. And of 6d. from the same Nicholas for the free rent of a close called [1] in Fulborne aforesaid, paid at the feast of Saint Michael the Archangel only, as in the indenture aforesaid fully appears. Sum 40s. 6d., examined.

Dullingham. And of 5s. for rent at will there by the year, as by the said rental fully appears.

Sum 5s., examined.

Westley. And of 2s. for rent at will there by the year, as appears by the rental aforesaid.

Sum 2s., examined.

Cokhamsted. And of £9. 13s. 11d. for rents and farms there by the year, as appears in parcels in the rental aforesaid.

Sum £9. 13s. 11d.

Litlington. And of 44s. for rents and farms there by the year, as fully appears by the rental aforesaid.

Sum 44s., examined.

Steple Mordon and Gylden Mordon. And of 66s. 8d. for rents and farms there by the year, as appears by the rental aforesaid.

Sum 66s. 8d., examined.

Cambridge. And of 31s. 8d. for rents and farms there by the year, as appears by the rental aforesaid. And of 46s. 8d. for the farm of the rent of one tenement there, called the Stonehouse, with all the houses built upon the same, demised to Robert Lane, baker, and his assigns, by indenture dated the eighteenth day of February, in the 28th year of the reign o King Henry the Eighth, for the term of 20 years, to be paid at

---

[1] Blank in orig.

the terms of Saint Michael the Archangel and the Annunciation
of the Blessed Virgin Mary equally, all repairs being at the
costs and charges of the said prior and convent during the term
aforesaid, as in the indenture aforesaid is more fully contained,
this year being the first of his term.

Sum 78s. 4d., examined.

Rectory of Swaffham Prior. And of £16 for the farm of
the rectory and mansion there called Anglesey House, with the
tithes of grain, as well as the lands, meadows, pastures and
fishery, with the folding and all other tithes and commodities
to the said rectory pertaining or belonging demised to Thomas
Rawlyns and his assigns, by Indenture dated the 18th day of
February, in the 26th year of the reign of King Henry the
Eighth, for the term of 33 years, to be paid at the terms of the
Purification of the Blessed Virgin Mary and Saint Peter 'ad
vincula' equally. And the aforesaid prior and convent will
repair all the houses and edifices sufficiently in all things in the
first year of the term of the tenancy aforesaid, as well as erect a
new barn, and the same being once sufficiently repaired as
aforesaid, the said farmer and his assigns shall repair the same
from time to time, and the same sufficiently repaired in all
things shall give up at the end of their term, as in the
Indenture aforesaid is more fully contained, this year being the
first year of the term. Sum £16.

The Rectory of Bottisham. And of £26. 16s. 4d. for the
farm of the rectory there by the year, with the glebe land and ·
tithes of grain and hay, as well as all houses and other appurtenances whatsoever to the said rectory pertaining or belonging,
demised to George Carleton and his assigns by indenture under
the seal of the Court of Augmentation, dated the   [1] day of
                  [1] in the   [1] year of the reign of King Henry the
Eighth, for the term of 26 years, to be paid at the terms of
Saint Michael the Archangel and the Annunciation of the
Blessed Virgin Mary equally, all repairs, except timber, tiles
and slates, being at the costs and charges of the said farmer and
his assigns during the term aforesaid. And the aforesaid lord
the king and his successors will bear all charges, as well ordinary

[1] Blank in orig.

as extraordinary, towards any persons whatever during the term
aforesaid, and will exonerate the said farmer thereof, as in the
indenture aforesaid is more fully contained, this year being the
[1] of his term.

Sum £26. 16s. 4d. examined.

Pensions of the Priory of Ely. And of £20 from the prior
and convent there for a certain annual pension issuing out of
the monastery aforesaid by the year granted to the Prior and
Convent of Anglesey aforesaid, from the time when the memory
of man does not exist, as in divers accounts of the said late Priory
of Anglesey aforesaid is fully contained. Sum £20.

Walsingham. And of 73s. 4d. received of the Prior and
Convent of Walsingham aforesaid for a like annual pension
granted of old to the said Prior and Convent of Anglesey
aforesaid, as fully appears as well by the rental as by divers
accounts of preceding years.

Sum 73s. 4d. examined.

Sale of wood. For any profit arising from the price of
wood or underwood there sold this year he does not answer,
because no such wood or underwood was there sold during the
time of this account, by the oath of the accountant.

Sum nothing.

Perquisites of Court. Nor does he answer for any profits
arising from perquisites of courts holden there this year, because
no courts were holden there for the time of this account.

Sum nothing.

Sum total of the receipts, £170. 7s. 5¾d.

Rent resolute. Of which the same accounts in rent resolute
to the Lady the Queen for lands in Bottisham at 21s. 10d. by
the year, to wit, for this year 11s. 2d.; and paid to Thomas
Clyfford for a tenement called Sentry-house, by the year 4s., and
paid to the lord Vaux for lands there, by the year, 2s. 11d., and
paid to the Duke of Richmond for tenements there, by the year,
12d., and paid to the Sheriff of Cambridge for suit of the
county, by the year, 3s. 4d., and paid to the same sheriff for his
turn, by the year, 2s., and paid to the chantry of Ricott in the
county of Oxford, for lands in Little Wilbraham, to wit, at 17s.,

---

[1] Blank in orig.

by the year, for this year 8s. 6d., and paid in aid to the sheriff for lands there by the year 12d., and paid to the Earl of Wiltshire for lands in Fulborne, by the year 21d., and paid to the Prior of Barnwell for lands there at 11s. by the year, to wit, for this year 5s. 6d., and paid to the Master and Fellows of Gundevile Hall for lands there by the year 20d., and paid to Thomas Manote, Esquire, for lands there by the year 10d., and paid to the Master of the Hospital of Stavey for lands in Hynton, by the year 12d., and paid to Edmund Mordaunt for lands in Swaffham Bulbek by the year 2s., and paid to the Prior of Saint John of Jerusalem in England for lands in Great Wilbraham by the year 20d.

Sum 29s. 5d., examined.

Fees and annuities with other things. And in the fee of John Hynde, steward of all the demesnes, manors, lands and tenements late pertaining to the dissolved priory of Anglesey aforesaid, by the year 26s. 8d., and in the annuity of John Pamplyn, by the letters patent late of John Fordeham, formerly prior there, and the convent of the same place thereof made to the said John, the date of which is the last day but one of November, in the 24th year of the reign of King Henry the Eighth. To have and enjoy the annuity aforesaid during the natural life of the same John, and to take and receive the said annuity or annual rent of 20s. annually at the feasts of Easter and Saint Michael the Archangel by equal portions to be paid, as in the said letters patent is more fully contained, to wit, in the allowance of such annuity for the said term of Saint Michael the Archangel occurring within the time of this account, 10s.; and in the fee of the said accountant, being bailiff there on account of his exercising and occupying such office at 53s. 4d. by the year, to wit, in the allowance of such fee for the term of Saint Michael the Archangel, happening within the time of this account, 26s. 8d.; and in the wages of the clerk of the auditor writing this account, as the clerks of the auditor of the lord the King of his duchy of Lancaster used to be allowed, to wit, in such allowance according to the form and effect of a certain act in the Parliament, holden at Westminster on prorogation to the 4th day of February, in the 27th year of the reign aforesaid, for the establishment of the court of the augmentation of the revenues of the crown of the same lord the King concerning the said rewards, profits and commodities of the auditor of the said lord the King of his court aforesaid among other things lately established and provided, 2s., and in the expenses of the steward holding courts there this year (   )[1].

Sum 65s. 4d.

Annuities. And in annuities paid to the warden and fellows of Winchester College, Oxford, for a certain annual pension granted to the same warden and fellows, and their successors for ever, as by the rental and other accounts of preceding years it fully appears, to be paid at the feast of Saint Michael the Archangel, 100s.

And to the abbot and convent of Notley in the county of Bucks, for a similar annual pension, to the same abbot and convent, as by the rental fully appears, £4. 13s. 4d.

And paid the vicar of Swafham Prior, the Blessed Mary, for a like annual pension, granted to the same and his successors of old from the said rectory, at £4. 9s. 4d. by the year, as by the rental fully appears, to be annually paid at the feasts of Easter and St Michael the Archangel, to wit, of the moiety of such pension for the said term of Saint Michael the Archangel, to the time of this account, 44s. 8d.

And paid to the Bishop of Ely for his visitation, one year with another, 22s. 2¾d., not paid this year.

Sum £11. 18s.

Delivery of money. And in money by the said accountant delivered to William Leigh, esquire, receiver of the lord the king, for the augmentation of the revenues of the crown, of the same lord the king, in the county of Cambridge, for the issues of his office, due at the feast of Saint Michael the Archangel, for the said 28th year of the king aforesaid, as appears by a bill thereof, signed with the hand of the same receiver, delivered on this account, and remaining among the memoranda of this year, £41. 7s. 8¼d.

And to the same receiver, by the hands of John Hynd, farmer of the site of the late priory aforesaid, and the demesne lands of the same, of the issues of the same, due at the feast

---

[1] Blank in orig.

aforesaid by acknowledgment of the said receiver, before the auditor without a bill, £15. 15s. 11¾d.

And to the same receiver, by the hands of George Carleton, farmer of the rectory of Bottisham, for the issues of the same, at the same feast by the acknowledgment of the same receiver, before the auditor without a bill, £26. 16s. 4d.

Sum £84. 0s. 0¼d. Sum of all the allowances and liveries aforesaid, £100. 12s. 9¾d.

And he owes £69. 14s. 8½d. half a farthing. Of which there are allowed to him 10s. for the moiety of 20s., being the rent of a certain meadow, called as is above, charged in the rental, because it is granted to John Pamplyn for the term of his life, without rendering anything therefrom, as in the letters patent above specified fully appears. And he is exonerated as to £67. 13s. 8¾d., because John Fordham, formerly prior of the house or dissolved monastery of Anglesey aforesaid, occupied the site of the late priory aforesaid, as well as the demesne lands of the same priory up to the time of the dissolution of the same, and the profits of the same, to the value of £15. 15s. 11¾d. and half a farthing, he had and received to the use and for the expenses of the house there, and also £51. 17s. 8¼d. in money he received from the tenants and farmers aforesaid, to the same use by his acknowledgment before the auditor, and he owes 31s. 0½d. Whereof in divers rents in arrear this year, 31s. 0½d.

Nothing touching the same accountant concerning his arrears this year, because he withdraws quit[1].

Comparing this statement with the account given in the "valor," it will be found that they correspond all but 3d. But we see no mention made of any chantries, or secular or other chaplains paid to serve them, so that we must suppose that they had fallen into disuse, owing to the poverty of the house and other causes. Under the heading of Cokhamsted is included the property of the house in Barley.

---

[1] It would appear therefore that John Fordham and John Bonar were one and the same person, called at one time by his own surname, at another by his native place, and this must have been the case with William Seggewyke or William Reche.

And so the monastery of Anglesey became the property of the king, to bestow upon whom he thought proper. The lands shortly after this became divided. The manor in Little Wilbraham fell into the hands of Mr Thomas Wale, a citizen of London, who, in 1625, gave it to the corporation of the city of Coventry in trust for charitable uses[1].

. The manor of Greenbury likewise continued for some time in the hands of the crown, till Edward VI. bestowed it upon Sir Robert Chester, knt., and his heirs for ever[2]. The rectory of Bottisham was granted to King's Hall, now Trinity College, by the king, Henry VIII., in the 32nd year of his reign[3]. That of St Mary at Swaffham Prior, which became the property of the see of Ely, was amalgamated with that of St Cyriac, by act of parliament, in 1667 A.D., and the bishop and dean and chapter of Ely present alternately.

---

[1] Vide Lyson's *Cambs.* p. 284. By indenture dated 10 Oct. 26 Hen. VIII., a messuage in Little Wilbraham, called Hallehouse, together with 80 acres of arable land with liberty of 3 folds, was let by the monastery for the term of 40 years to John Roger and John Hullocke, at a rent of 53s. 4d. On the 26 Oct. 1566 this tenement was let by the crown to Robert Payne; the fine being rated at 4 years' rent amounted to £10. 13s. 4d. The tenement of Thornhall in Wicken on the 7th of May, 1574, was let to John Cotton, the fine paid amounting to £6.

[2] Clutterbuck, *Hist. of Herts*, Vol. I. p. 34; Chauncy, *Hist. of Herts*, p. 96.

[3] Letters Patent, 8 April, 32 Hen. VIII. part 7; Baker MSS. Vol. xxviii. p. 161; Webb MSS. fol. 126.

ANGLESEY PRIORY.

1854

VIEW FROM NORTH EAST.

1854

SOUTH PORCH.

(To face Page 325)

CHAPTER XII.

GRANT TO JOHN HYNDE.

THE site of the dissolved convent remained in the hands of the crown for but a short time. John Hynde, who was the steward of the lands and so well knew their value, obtained a grant of them from the king in the thirtieth year of his reign, and the document, dated Feb. 4, is preserved amongst the "originalia" rolls. Portions of it give an idea of what was then left of the monastic buildings. It is thus recorded:—

  "Know that we in consideration of the good faithful and gratuitous service by our beloved counsellor John Hynde one of our serjeants at law to us aforetime done and to be done, and also for six hundred and forty-nine pounds eighteen shillings and four pence of our lawful money of England paid to our use into the hands of the Treasurer of the augmentation of the revenues of our crown for the time being, of our special favour certain knowledge and mere motion have given and granted and by these presents do give and grant to the same John. Hynde all the house and site of the late monastery or priory of Anglesey in our county of Cambridge, suppressed and dissolved by the authority of Parliament together with the church bell-tower and cemetery of the same late monastery or priory as well as all our messuages houses...barns, stables, granges, dove-cotes, mills, walls, gardens, orchards, waters, pools, fishponds, land, foundation, and soil, as well within as without and next and near to the site sept circuit ambit and precinct of the afore-said priory or monastery. And also all our demesnes or manors of Anglesey, Bottesham, Stourey otherwise called Stokquy, Longmeadow and Lodestreet with their appurtenances...to the said late monastery or priory belonging and pertaining. Also all and singular messuages, tofts, mills, gardens, cottages, lands,

Grant to John Hynde.

tenements, meadows, grazings, pastures, moors, marshes, furze
and heath, woods, underwoods, rents, reversions, services, farms,
fee-farms, annuities, and rents, and farms of tenants, and customs
of our farmers, villains with their belongings, knights' fees,
wards, marriages, escheats, reliefs, heriots, courts leet, views of
frankpledge, and all things which to view of frankpledge pertain or belong or ought to or might pertain or belong, assize and
assay of bread, and all estrays, goods and chattels, waived waters,
weirs, fishponds, warrens, commons, fisheries, turbaries, foldages,
and liberties, fold courses of sheep and all other our rights possessions and hereditaments whatsoever &c., as fully and entirely &c., as John Bonar, otherwise Bonyard, late prior of the
said monastery, or any one of his predecessors &c., had held &c.,
which came or ought to have come into our hands by reason
and occasion of a certain act, for the dissolving of certain monasteries &c., begun in our Parliament at London, on the third day
of November, in the twenty-first year of our reign, and thence
adjourned to Westminster, and by divers prorogations continued
to and on the fourth day of February in the twenty-seventh
year of our reign, and then holden there among other things
settled and provided &c., excepting nevertheless always and to
us and to our heirs for ever reserved all and all manner of
rectories, and vicarages, and advowsons of rectories and vicarages
whatsoever. Which same site, manors, &c., given and granted
are of the clear annual value of sixty-four pounds, and not more.
To have hold, enjoy, &c., to the aforesaid John Hynde his heirs
and assigns for ever. To hold of us our heirs and successors in
chief by knight's service, to wit, by the tenth part of one knight's
fee. Rendering moreover thence annually to us our heirs and
successors six pounds and eight shillings in the name of a tenth
&c., to be paid at the feast of Saint Michael the Archangel, &c.
And moreover of our richer grace we will, and grant that we
our heirs and successors will from time to time and for ever exonerate, acquit, and hold harmless, the same John Hynde his
heirs and assigns against any persons touching a certain annual
pension of one hundred shillings issuing on behalf of the pre-
misses and annually to be paid to the master or warden and
fellows and scholars of the college of Winchester, established in

the university of Oxford and their successors, and of four pounds thirteen shillings and four pence in like manner annually issuing on behalf of the premises, and to be paid to the abbot of the monastery of Nottley in the county of Bucks, and their successors, and of four pounds ten shillings and four pence annually issuing and to be paid on behalf of the premises to the vicar of the parish church of Swafham Prior in our said county of Cambridge...also we will and by these presents we grant to the aforesaid John Hynde, that he may have these our Letters Patent duly made and sealed under our great seal of England, without in any way rendering paying or making any fine or fee great or small to us in our hanaper or elsewhere to our use. Because express mention &c. In witness whereof &c. witness the king at Westminster, on the fourth day of February."

Thus the first lay possessor of the site of the late monastery was John Hynde. From whence he sprung is not clear, but his rise was a rapid one, and he seems to have been specially under the king's favour. His position as a lawyer, and his previous connection with the county of Cambridge, made him no doubt an exceedingly useful man in assisting to carry out so delicate a task as the dissolution of monasteries, and the inauguration of a new system. As early as November 5th, 1515 A.D., he was created a Justice of the Peace for the Isle of Ely, and shortly afterwards he was justice of gaol delivery for the castle of Wisbeach, and at Ely Barton. Four years after this he was lecturer at Grays Inn, and in 1527 held the office of double lecturer there; but in the 23rd year of Henry the Eighth's reign he became serjeant-at-law, and on Nov. 4th, 1546, was created Chief Justice of the king's bench, and was afterwards made knight. But little is known of his wife. She was the daughter of John Curson, of Buckhall, in Norfolk, and was probably buried at Maddingley, in which parish John Hynde held a fine estate. At her death she left three sons and three daughters, of whom Thomas is perhaps the same as the person styled Thomas Hynde of Maddingley, gent., while Oliver held an estate at Toft in 1578 A.D. The three daughters, Sibilla, Catharine, and Mary, were married, and the first two had issue. But Sir Francis Hynde, knt., as elder brother succeeded to the

Family of Hynde.

estate at Maddingley, and was a person of great possessions, for besides holding Maddingley and the manor of Anglesey with the site of the monastery in the parish of Bottisham, he held many other manors, besides messuages and parcels of land &c., including the advowsons of Wilbraham Parva, Toft, Eversden and the manor of Histon-Ethelred and rectory of Histon of the king, by the 20th part of a knight's fee[1]. He served the office of High Sheriff for Cambs. and Hunts. in the years 1561, 1570 and 1589 A.D., and was knight of the shire in 1558 —9, 1572, and 1588 A.D., in which last Parliament he is styled a knight. His uncle Thomas became a priest, and held the rectory of Eversden Parva in 1537, Shelford Parva, which he resigned in 1539, and Girton and Cottenham in 1543. Sir Francis died on March 31st, 1595, and his funeral obsequies were celebrated with great splendour, a full account of which is given by Cole. His wife Jane, the daughter of Sir Edmond Verney, knt. of Penley in the county of Hertford, bore him five children, three sons and two daughters. The eldest, Sir William Hynde though twice married, died without issue, and the estates came to his brother, Sir Edward, who had issue by his third marriage; but his grandson had but one daughter Jane, who married Sir John Cotton, of Landwade, and thus the estates at Maddingley passed into the hands of the Cotton family. The manor and house of Anglesey was sold after the death of Sir Francis Hynde, and then came into the hands of the family of Folkes or Fowkes. There is no direct evidence that any of the Hynde family ever resided at Anglesey. It probably was left to go to ruin, and thus give time for the people to reconcile themselves to the now

---

[1] In Archbishop Laud's "Annual Account of his Province to the king" for the year 1639, we find an account of the destruction of this church:

"It was likewise presented to the Bishop, that about forty years ago, one Sir *Francis Hinde* did pull down the church of *St Ethelred*, in *Histon*, to which there then appertained a vicarage presentative, and forced the parishioners to thrust themselves upon another small church in the said town, to the great wrong of the parishioners thereof. And that the lead, timber, stones, bells, and all other materials, were sold away by him, or employed to the building of his house at *Madingley*. And that, now it is called in question, the people (not being able of themselves to reedify the church) can get no redress against the descendant from the said Sir *Francis*, because the heir was a child, and in wardship to your majesty."

ARMS: A. on a chev. gu. 3 lozenges O. int. 3 goats' heads erased az. collared and attired O. on a chief sa. a lion pass. guard. erm.
CREST: A demi-eagle az. guttée de larmes beaked O. collared A. and charged on the heart with an escallop O.

John Hynde, buried at St Dunstan's in = Ursula d, of John Curson, of Buckhall, co. of Norfolk.
the West, London, Oct. 18, 1550.

Sir Francis, knt., = Jane, d. of
died at Madding-| Sir Edward
ley, Mar. 21, 1595,| Verney, knt.,
æt. 65, bur. Ap. 6,| of Penley,
at that place.| Herts.

Oliver.   Thomas.   Sibilla = Sir John Cutts, of Childerley, and had issue.

Catharine = Geoffrey Colville, of Newton, Isle of Ely. — issue.

Mary = Clement Chicheley, of Wimpole.

Sir William, = (1) Elizabeth, d. of Thomas, Lord Wentworth. D. s. p.
died 1606.
(2) Eliz. d. of W. Lawrence of St Ives, relict of John Hd, of Dry Drayton. D. s. p.

Sir Edward = (1) Alice, d. of John Billet, of London. D. s. p.
= (2) Unknown, D.s.p.

(3) Unknown, John. D. s. p.

Jane = (1) Wm. West, of Bucks.
= (2) John of Newenham, Beds.
= (3) Sir Edward Radcliffe, knt., bro. and h. to Thos. Radcliffe, afterwards Earl of Sussex. D. s. p.

Ursula = John Machell, of Hackney.

William.   Judith.

John.   Francis.   Robert.   Edward.

Anthony = * * * *
Edward = * * * *

Jane, died = Sir John Cotton,
1672, Oct. 3,| of Landwade.
aged 62 yrs.| issue.

accomplished dissolution.   But in the parish register an entry
of marriage is to be found of Richard Kirk, of Shelford in
the county of Hampshire, gent., to Sibell Hinde, on the 6th of
July, 1565.   Still this Sibell Hinde cannot be shewn to be one
of the descendants of the serjeant, for his daughter Sibilla married Sir John Cutts of Childerley[1].

amily of
'okes.

It was just after the site and manor of Anglesey had passed
from the hands of the Hynde family when it was visited by
that famous antiquary, Sir Henry Spelman.   The result of this
visit is described by Stevens in his *Monasticon Anglicanum,*
who calls it the "Anonimus Abby in Cambridgeshire."   He
says :—"Not knowing the name of this place, I can say no more
concerning it, than what I find in Sir Henry Spelman's *History*
of Sacrilege, p. 281, which is this; 'Travelling through Cambridgeshire, and passing through a town there, called Anglacy,
I saw certain ruinous walls, which seemed to have been some
monastery; hereupon I asked one of the town if it had not
been an abby: He answered me, yes; I demanded of him whose
it was; he said, Mr Foulkes.   I asked him, further, how long
he had had it?   He said, his father, a Londoner, bought it;
then I desired to know of him what children he had?   The
man answered me, none; saying, further, that he had a son,
who, displeasing him as he was grafting, he threw his grafting
knife at his son, and therewith killed him[2].'"   It is almost impossible to make out much concerning this family of Fokes, or
to confirm or refute this story of the death of the son.   For at
this time in Bottisham there appear from the registers to have
been two, if not three, distinct families of this name, which is
spelt Foulkes, Fowkes, and Fokes, almost indiscriminately.
The burial register of St Dunstan in the West has the following entry :—"1600, Sept. 12. buried John Fowks, gent., out
of Mr Gunter's house."   As Serjeant Hynde was also buried
here, and as this John Fowks appears to have only resided at
Mr Gunter's at the time of his death, it may seem probable
that he was the purchaser of the estate from Wm. Hynde for

[1] For some account of this family vide Cole MSS. Vol. XL. p. 347 et seq.
[2] Stevens, *Mon. Angl.* ed. 1722, Vol. I. p. 506.

his son. But John Fokes, gent., possibly his son, resided at Anglesey in 1608; for, on the 15th of December of that year, he was married in the parish church to Susanna the widow of Thomas Webbe, whose connection with Bottisham has been already described. Her death took place in June, 1621 A.D., while he was buried Dec. 25th, 1617 A.D. There is an entry in the register of the burial of John Fowkes, Jan. 6th, 1626—7, who may have been a son; and John Folkes, buried May 16th, 1633 A.D., also possibly one of this family, but no entry can be made to corroborate the story of the mishap with the grafting knife[1]. In 1619 a fine was concluded between Susanna Fokes, widow, and Humphrey Lowe, gent., whereby for the sum of £120 he became possessed of the priory estate, consisting of one messuage, one dovecote, two gardens, 90 acres of land, 10 acres of pasture, and one acre of wood. But in the year 1627 A.D. the property again changed hands, for it was bought by Thomas Hobson the celebrated Cambridge carrier, who also *Hobson.* leased the neighbouring nunnery of Denney, in the parish of Waterbeach. Two years afterwards Hobson conveyed it to Thomas Parker, who, by marriage with his daughter Elizabeth, *Parker.* became his son-in-law. It is this conveyance which is alluded to in Hobson's will, dated December 27, 1630, and containing codicils of Dec. 31, and Jan. 1, 1631, in which he states that he had provided for his daughter Elizabeth and Lady Clarke in his life-time, and leaves them therefore £6. 13s. 4d. as a fatherly remembrance[2].

This Thomas Parker, who was the son of John Parker of Little Norton, by Jane, daughter of James Bate of Jordenthorpe in Norton, his second wife, came originally from Lees Norton, in the county of Derbyshire, and settled here. He probably constructed the present manor-house, as the style of architecture accords with that date, and pulled down the chapel,

---

[1] An inquisition, held 19 May, 1639, states that John Fowkes, gentleman, held a messuage with a croft, 2 acres, 3 roods of arable land, 2 closes, and 106 acres of land in Bottisham at the time of his death. Cole MSS. Vol. xxxvii. fol. 91 b. But this John Fowkes does not appear to have ever been in possession of the estate at Anglesey.

[2] Harl. MSS. No. 4115, fol. 74; Peck, *Hist. Coll.* p. 47.

which would by that time have been in ruins. By his wife he
had three sons and three daughters born at Bottisham, whose
names are cut on various pieces of stone to be found about the
house, and at his death he was succeeded by his son Thomas[1].
After him came Alexander Parker, who seems to have been one
of the same family, though whose son is uncertain. Anyhow,
this last by his wife Elizabeth had four children, viz. Elizabeth,
born in 1703 A.D., and buried the same year, Isabella, born in
1705 A.D., Alexander, born in 1707 A.D., and Elizabeth, born in
1713 A.D. His daughter Patty was silly; and Mr Parker, according to local tradition, used to enter his house by means of
a peculiar whistle, which he always had with him. One day,
when he was absent in London, a man came to the house, and
imitating his whistle, contrived to gain admittance to the
building. Once inside he opened the door to his confederates,
and they proceeded to strip the house of all the plate. The
servants were at length alarmed, but one was soon completely
stunned by a blow. The remainder were then tied by the
arms and legs, and the plate, of which there was a good deal,

John Parker of Little Norton, = (2) Jane, d. of James Bate of Jordenthorpe.
    Derbyshire.

Thomas Parker, = c. 1627, Elizabeth, d. of
of Lees Norton, | Thomas Hobson of
co. Derby; | Cambridge,
bap. Mar. 31, 1609, | alive in 1667.
d. ant. 1655.

Thomas, bap.	Elizabeth,	Dorothy,	William,	Simon,	Elinor,
Dec. 9, 1627;	bap. June 20,	bap. May 10,	bap. July 18,	bap. Nov. 4,	bap. Oct.
bur. Mar. 26,	1628.	1631.	1632.	1633.	1634.
1683–4.					

Alexander = Elizabeth * * *
    | alive in 1720.

Elizabeth,	Isabella,	Alexander[2],	Elizabeth,
born Sept. 1,	born Jan. 18,	bap. June 3, 1707.	bap. July 10, 171
bap. Sept. 3, 1703,	bap. Feb. 8, 1705-6.		
bur. Sept. 27, 1703.			

[1] In a roll of the levies during the civil war, much mutilated, may be read the foll
entry :—1 Dec. 1645. Thomas Parker, late of Anglesey Abbey, in the county of Camb
receiver of the moneys given for the free benevolence for Ireland.

[2] Vide *Gent. Mag.* Vol. XVII. p. 199. "Died Ap. 3, 1747, Alex. Parker, attorney-
and deputy-clerk of the errors in the exchequer chamber." ? the same.

was handed out; and when Patty's property was being handed out, she cried, "Turn again, turn again, here's my siller a'coming." The robbers escaped with their booty, and were never captured by the police, who were soon set on their track.

In 1667 A.D. Elizabeth Parker, widow, concluded a fine for the manor of Anglesey, but the records for that year are lost. In 1678 A.D. a fine was made between Thomas Parker and Geo. Downing, knt. for lands in Bottisham, and in 1708 A.D. between the wife of Alex. Parker and Wm. Stephenson for the same. In 1716 the wife of Alex. Parker concluded a fine for the manor of Anglesey with Dionysius Lisle, gent., and in 1720 with the mayor and corporation of London for lands in Bottisham.

In the year 1736 A.D., according to Messrs. Lysons, the last of the Parker family sold the manor of Anglesey to Sir George Downing, the founder of Downing College. As this sale was effected after the date of his will, whereby he bequeathed all his estates for the purpose of endowing the college which bears his name, the fee of the manor became vested in Sir Jacob Downing, his heir-at-law, whose widow's nephew, Jacob John Whittington, Esq., sold it in 1793 to the Rev. George Jenyns. At his death it became the property of George Jenyns, Esq. But Mr Parker, when he sold the manor, reserved the site of the priory, and it was not sold till the year 1739 A.D. It then became the property of Sam. Shepheard, Esq., M.P., and descended to his granddaughters. They sold it to Elizabeth the widow of Soame Jenyns, Esq., and by her it was bequeathed to the Rev. G. Jenyns, at whose death it was purchased of the executors by the Rev. John Hailstone, and is now held by his widow.

APPENDIX IV.

Terrier of lands held by the Priory of Anglesey in the time of Prior John Danyell.

Bottisham. Thomas Melman tenet tenementum inter rectoriam et tenementum vocatum Spensers cum crofta duarum acrarum adjacente. Item tene xij acras in iij campis unde in *Northfeld* iij rodas super Brodyng juxta terram Simonis Elys nuper Gransdens; " dimidiam acram apud Mellehyl juxta terram Willielmi Vaus, abbuttantem super terram prioris de Tunbridge in tenurâ vicarii et Bilney;" iij rodas ultra howeymere juxta terram prioris de Tunbridge in tenura Willielmi Gerveis, abbuttantes super foreram nuper sacristani; j rodam et dimidiam juxta terram prioris de Tunbridge, abbuttantes super foreram prædicti prioris; j rodam juxta terram vicarii, abbuttat super vi rodas prioris de Anglesey in tenura Thomæ Rande; j rodam et dimidiam lanciantem ultra Anglesey Wey usque Mitylwey inter terram Willielmi Vaus ex utraque parte. *Whytefeld.* iij rodas in Vineyere juxta terram S. Elys nuper Gransdens abbuttantes super foreram ii bendissh; "j rodam et dimidiam apud Angerhale croft juxta terram John Taylor, quoddam pykking abbuttantem super terram quondam Normans;" dimidiam acram apud Onervales juxta terram Thomæ Bunte, abbuttantem super Onervale; j acram in le botome of the felt juxta terram in bendish, abbuttantem super brodin havyd; dimidiam acram apud Schortland juxta terram Willielmi Alyngton, abbuttantem super foreram Willielmi Alington; j rodam et dimidiam inter terram Edmundi Preston et quondam Johannis Thurston, abbuttantes super foreram Willielmi Alington; j rodam et dimidiam prope Swafhamfeld inter Tunbridge and Alingtons, abbuttantes super Tunbridge in tenura T. Moris; dimidiam rodam et quarteram unius rodæ inter Tunbridge et sacristani et abbuttant super foreram in bendissh. *Stonyfeld.* j rodam et dimidiam super Woodwey ultra Camwey juxta terram Willielmi Alington, abbuttantes super foreram prioris de Tun bridge; iij acras ad finem ville inter terram prioris de Tunbridge in tenura Johannis Dransuere, abbuttantes super Woodwey; j rodam et dimidiam apud le Wyche inter semitam ducentem ad Wilbraham et terram Willielmi Norman, abbuttantes super portwey; iij rodas in media quarentena inter caput de Wilbraham et portwey juxta terram Willielmi Norman abbuttantes super terram prioris de Anglesey vocatam 'le wend;' j rodam et dimidiam super campum de Wilbra-ham juxta terram Johannis Sorel nuper Dransuerd; j rodam in rodisdaleden inter duas rodas prioris de Anglesey, terra prioris de Tunbridge ex utraque parte, abbuttantem super j rodam in tenura J. Sikman; dimidiam acram super Woodwey inter terram Johannis Mytilwey et terram Willielmi Alington in tenura Johannis Gaudyn; ij rodas apud blakehams inter terram prioris de Anglesey ex utraque parte abbuttantes super viam ducentem usque Wilbraham. *Lytilfeld.* Dimidiam acram inter terram prioris de Anglesey et terram prioris le Tunbridge, abbuttantem super vinerium; j rodam inter terram prioris de Tunbridge et terram Ricardi Forster abbuttantem super vij acras prioris de Anglesey vocatas Alwynpece; j rodam pasturæ in le Were juxta priorem de Tunbridge abbuttantem super le dam.

Summa. xiiij acras, iij rodas per xiiij*.

Ricardus Forster tenet Hertwelhylpece, continentem iiij acras et dimidiam et v acras in vj peces, nuper in tenura Johannis Passelewe; item v acras in ij peces et semitam usque Sent yves lane per medium: in *Stonyfeld* ix acras vocatas Axinodumpece[1]: In *Whytefeld* fox-hole-pece continentem iij acras et dimidiam; item dimidiam acram juxta terram Johannis White de Swafham. (*In another hand.*) [1] ? Ox *meadow piece.*

Summa. xxvij acras et dimidiam per xxvij*. vj*.

Ad hanc eandem curiam venit John Beneryche et cepit de domino priore una cum magistro Alexandro Prior tenementum nostrum in Langemeda juxta tenementum Johannis Howson cum croftam adjacentem et......jacet per foreram cum suis pertinentibus tenendum sibi et Johannæ uxori ad terminum quinque annorum proximo......per quod datum ut patet in capite hujus rotuli absque vera, reparacione, et sectâ curiæ solvendum annuatim nostro ad duos anni terminos videlicet pasche et Michaelis per equales porciones. Item Johannes cepit per acram quam......Robertus Athil nuper tenuit ad terminum ix annorum per x*. per annum. Ricardus Mar-hal et Johannes Vaas sen*. ceperunt xiij acras in iij campis, videlicet, acras in *Northfeld* semel aratis......Anglesey juxta fossatam et lices prope introhitum et in fine ejusdem abbuttat super ferthynghyl.

In *Whytefeld* v acras vocatas Lokhy pece super Woodwey, et in
Stonyfeld vij acras apud legorys.   Tenendum ad terminum xx annorum, solvendum annuatim xvij˙.

Summa xvij˙.

~~Robertus Lakke tenet in *lytylfeld* iij acras in lytylfeld prope l
cote le acra vj˙. cum j acra.~~

~~Summa ix˙. per......~~

~~Johannes Bangolfe tenet tenementum et croftam nuper in tenur
Thome Stonham.......vj acras iij rodas de ley vocatas grendenhede.~~

~~Summa x˙. et l˙.   Summa iij^u.~~

Terrarium prioris et conventus de Anglesey in campis de Berne
well et Cantabrigia.

Barnwell
and Cam-
bridge.
In primis in cley anglys one rood and the secunde furlong butt
ing agens the eldern wey betwixt the white canons and sometym
Adam de infirmarer.   In bradinerefeld ij selions containing j acr
betwene the prior of Bernewell and the nonnys; j roda in the sam
field at old Mylle way on the east side and over Whertdole sometym
John Cornertard and the land sometyme Thomas of Cambridge
dimidia acra in the same felde at hyntonwey northware in the furlon
lyand south and north an the est half betwene the prior de Berne
well and sometyme S. Repham; dimidia acra abovyn est bradinere
balk betwene the nonnys and the prior of bernewell; j roda e
dimidia at mamaunt's-balk up on hyntonwey betwene the balk an
the prior of bernewell; j roda at fyrmes-croft betwene the prior c
bernewell and the nonnes; j roda at roserchekker betwene the prio
of bernwell and sometyme John Maryz; j roda there ny betwene th
land sometyme Will. Rider on bothe sydes, acra et dimidia there n
of the whych most oft is an hedlonde, by it Cotton's, sometym
P. Caile; j acra at Gaysles-hedlande which is clepyd 'the kings acre
by the prior of Bernewell; dimidia acra in the same furlonge b
a rood and a half of the prior of bernewell; dimidia acra there n
by the ferst of the long furlonge and butting on the estest land c
mertymer's dole, horspath betwixt; ij acres, half acres, in the strecch
in the furlong that lyith most south and north, abutting north, an
beginnyth fast by the dich betwene the nonnes and the prior c
bernewell agens noket's acre; dimidia acra at south bradiners dol
betwene the prior of bernewell of both syds; j roda in mortymer
dole next the balk betwene the prior of bernewell on both syds
dimidia acra in the third furlong of bradinerfeld betwene the pric
of bernewell and sometyme Thomas de Cambridge; dimidia acra i

the same furlong benethin bradiners as one turnyth in bradinere on the lyft hande to bernewell-ward betwene the nonnes and sometyme William Harwod; j acra in mylk furlong betwene the white canons sometyme......Thrippelowe; j roda in fesant croft betwene the prior of bernewell and the amry lond of the same prior; j acra betwene the same awmry londe and rode of the prior; j acra at est bradiner-balk in the furlong that lyeth est and west a lytil beside the vj acre dole of bernewell betwene sometyme Adam de infirmarer and some-tyme B. Peryn; j roda et dimidia at fesant croft the beginning of mylk furlong betwene sometyme Hugonis Smyth and vj selions of huntindon lande; dimidia selio that conteyneth iij acres wod harde of mylk furlong beside v selions of the prior of bernewell next the dich; dimidia acra in Chenydole furlong a lytyl beside seynt Gylys and betwene the nonnes and sometyme Alice Stebbyng; ij acrae the last of the same furlong by the fen; iij rode in est enhale in the fur-long at Walnut doles ende agen the Re betwene the prior of berne-well and sometyme Hugonis Smyth; j acra in the same furlong betwene sterbrege lod and the prior of bernewell; dimidia acra at the iij furlongs ende betwene Sterbrege and bernewell on the north syde of the wey betwene the nonnes and the white canons; dimidia acra there neer by betwene the prior of bernewell on bothe sids; dimidia acra vel alias j roda et dimidia in the Myddilfeld in the myddel and secunde betwene Hadstokwey and Hynton, the last of the same furlong by the prior of bernewell; one acre in the furlong agen hynton wey betwene the prior of bernewell and sometyme Thomas of Cambridge; j acra in longedole furlong betwene the prior of bernewell on bothe sydes; dimidia acra in Richard-dole betwene the prior of bernewell and the nonnes; one acre in the forthfeld, the furlong that lyth north and south at trumpiton forth betwene some-tyme B. peryn and the prior of bernewell; ij acræ et dimidia ther by betwene sometyme peter berningham and the white chanons; j acra in·hynton felde in the tenure of philip grower et dimidia acra.

Summa. xxiiij acræ et dimidia alias iij rodæ.

Summa firme ejus, le acræ xvj^d, xxxviij^s.

Willielmus Ryzes tenet peciam de throkkyng continentem xij *Bottisha* acras per xvj^s. viij^d.

Johannes Vaas tenementum vocatum hayt vij rodas et dimidiam pitanciarum cum pertinentibus cum prato de Throkkyng et molendi-num sine dato per annum xxiij^s. iiij^d.

Luke v acras compostas et duas tunc aratas ex opposito molen-dini xxv^s.

H. B.   22

Thomas Melman ij acras.............................xˢ.

Johannes Benerych.................................xxiiijˢ. vjᵈ.

Idem ij acras et dimidiam super le wey nuper Swafham wey cum jacente iiijˢ. vjᵈ.

Reginald Flynte j rodam et dimidiam in Whitess juxta terram quondam Roberti Mason, peciam vocatam Whitepece.

Alan Carter tenementum cum crofta, iij rodis adjacentibus per vjˢ. le acre.

John Godale iiij acras in Whitefeld super le were aratas per vijˢ. iiijᵈ. et iij acras de pecia prioris juxta Johannem Canynham per iijˢ. Summa. xˢ. iiijᵈ.

R. Brandon j acram ejusdem peciæ per xijᵈ.

Johannes Dransuerd j croftam iij rodarum nuper in tenurâ Galfridi Atcliff pro anno priore per xijᵈ.

Ricardus Forster tenet in Northfeld hertwelhylpece continentem iiij acras et dimidiam et peciam molendini continentem v acras et dimidiam semel aratas et v acras in secunda quarentena de Mytylwey et jacent juxta semitam ententam a molendino usque Cantebrigiam compostatas cum falda et semel aratas, v acras in ij peciis qualibet in fine alterius et semitam vocatam sentyves path lanciantem ultra finem ejus. *Stonyfelde* oxmedupece, ix acras semel aratas. *Whyte-*
(Sic in ori- *feld*, foxholepece iij acras j rodam et dimidiam semel aratas—qui
ginal.) ~~tenet dimidiam acram et dimidiam rodam in Chalcroft juxta alteram dimidiam eidem Ricardo ex una parte et terram in tenura Johannis Whyte de Swapham ex altera parte, et iiij acras in Whites feu jacentes juxta le Were et abuttantes super le Were et extendit usque Whitwell.~~

Summa xxxij acræ j roda et dimidia. Summa per xxxijˢ.

R. Marham; *Northfeld.* vij acras vocatas Sondipece in tercia quarentena de Mytylwey ex parte occidentali juxta semitam ducentem usque Quye. In *Stonyfelde* vij acras vocatas xx akyrbrede. In *Whitefeld* viij acras in ij peciis abbuttantes super woodwey et forthwey. Item in eodem campo j acram et dimidiam juxta terram Ricardi forster abbuttantes super Streteway. Item iij rodas super woodwey juxta terram nuper Johannis Magot quæ quidem iij rodæ nuper fuerunt in tenura Willielmi Ryzes.

Summa. acræ xxiiij per xxiiijˢ. et solvet pro isto anno pro composta xijˢ. Summa totalis xxxvjˢ.

Sic in ori- ~~Stephanus Gyn tenet dimidiam acram et dimidiam rodam in
inal.) frenshys croft per vijˢ. ob. hoc anno præterito.~~

Willielmus Rede junior tenet xxvij acras in iij campis, videlicet ix acras in *Northfeld* in ij peciis ex apposito molendini. In *Stonyfeld* vj acras de ocæcocæpece et iij acras vocatas Whitepece in Balshams. lade sed non foreram ejusdem. In *Whitefeld* ocæcocæpece, ix acras semel aratas. Tenendum ad terminum xij annorum reddendo annua-tim xxvijˢ.

Summa. xxvijˢ. et pro arura vijˢ. vjᵈ.

Thomas Bunte tenet xx acras ed dimidiam, vij in *Northfeld* ix acras et j rodam in superiore pecia, xviij acras juxta priors croft ij vices aratas. In *Stonyfeld* vij acras j rodam de......inter vj acras ejusdem peciæ in tenura Willielmi Rede et iij rodas prioris de Anglesey, ~~in tenura Johannis Bangolf ex altera parte,~~ in tenura (Sic in ori-dicti Thomæ. In *Whitefeld* le blackbrede, iiij acras et dimidiam et ginal.) j rodam jacentem juxta dictam peciam solvendum annuatim xxˢ. vjᵈ. ad duos anni terminos videlicet Purificationem Beatæ Mariæ et Nati-vitatem Sancti Johannis Baptistæ per equales porciones.

Summa. xxˢ. vjᵈ. et ixᵈ.

Ad hanc curiam dominus concessit Thome Mannyng et Margaretæ *Thomas* uxori suæ unum tenementum cum gardino adjacente juxta rectoriam *Mannyng.* et duas acras terræ cum j acra jacente in *Stonyfeld* super woodwey et aliam acram in *Whytefeld.* Tenendum sibi et Margaretæ uxori suæ ad totum terminum vitæ utriusque eorum et prædicti Thomas et Margaret prædictum tenementum sustentabunt et reparabunt sump-tibus et expensis suis propriis per totum tempus supra dictum excepto quod dominus inveniet eis interum stramen et haustum solvendum domino annuatim vjˢ. viijᵈ. ad quatuor anni terminos videlicet ad terminos Natalem, Pascham, Nativitatem Sancti Johannis Baptistæ et Sancti Michaelis per equales porciones et admissus est tenens[1].

---

[1] There is also a terrier of lands in the fields of Fulbourn and......covering about ⅓ of a membrane, but the writing is so faint as to be nearly illegible. The same is the case with the roll containing the rental of the priory in Great and Little Wilbraham. In the former parish the sum total is 7s. 6d. In the latter, the sum of the rents is £1. 11s. 10½d., of the farms £3. 17s. 2d.

.

APPENDIX V.

From the register of Walter Gray, Archbishop of York, we are
enabled to glean a few further particulars respecting Master Lawrence
de Saint Nicholas. It would seem that the prebend of York, which
he afterwards held, was in the time of his predecessor of no certain
value, but to it was devoted a share in the common revenues of the
church, varying more or less according to the prosperity of the season.
But, on account of the small number of canons who kept residence,
Archbp. Gray and his chapter, in the time of Dean Roger, framed a
statute enacting that only those who resided should have a share in
the division of the revenues. By this statute the holder of the prebend held by Master Lawrence de Saint Nicholas was to have whether
he resided or not a yearly payment of six marks: and as this sum
was less than that allotted to other prebendaries, the archbishop
further gave Master Lawrence the church of Tockerington, in the
county of Northumberland. The confirmation of Richard, Bp. of
Durham, is dated 5 June, 1223, and specifies the resignation of
Nicholas de Aubeny, the last rector. Master Lawrence, who was presumably a foreigner, does not seem to have resided, and hereupon the
Dean and Chapter of York refused to pay him the six marks on the
ground that he was otherwise provided for. Accordingly the pope,
Honorius III., gives his permission to Master Lawrence to hold the
church of Tockerington in addition to his prebend and his other benefices; and shortly after he writes to the archbishop, prohibiting him
and his chapter from depriving the prebend of his rights, and commanding them as they wish for his favour to shew charity towards
his chaplain. And so he enjoins them to pay him regularly the six
marks, whether he resides or not, and if he resides to grant him his
share in the division of the common revenues. To the Dean and
Chapter he writes in the same terms, as well as to the bishop of Lincoln, saying that if, after the departure of Master Lawrence de St.
Nicholas from England, any of his rents or property is withheld, he
will force the withholders to pay the loss. Vide Add. MSS. 15,352,
359. 15,353, 334, 356. Reg. Album III. 856, quoted by Raine in
his edition of Archbp. Gray's Register for the Surtees' Soc. 1872, pp.
148, 154, 155.

INDEX NOMINUM.

H. B.

INDEX LOCORUM.

INDEX OF PEDIGREES.

DIRECTIONS TO THE BINDER.

Cambridge:

PRINTED BY C. J. CLAY, M.A.
AT THE UNIVERSITY PRESS.

Lightning Source UK Ltd.
Milton Keynes UK
UKHW02f0848060818
326815UK00009BA/785/P